C J Lambert

Jung Institute

Gemeindestr. 27

U. Dayton

BOLLINGEN SERIES XX

THE COLLECTED WORKS

OF

C. G. JUNG

VOLUME 16

EDITORS

SIR HERBERT READ

MICHAEL FORDHAM, M.D., M.R.C.P.

GERHARD ADLER, PH.D.

THE PRACTICE

OF

PSYCHOTHERAPY

**ESSAYS ON THE PSYCHOLOGY OF THE TRANSFERENCE
AND OTHER SUBJECTS**

C. G. JUNG

TRANSLATED BY R. F. C. HULL

14 ILLUSTRATIONS

BOLLINGEN SERIES XX

PANTHEON BOOKS

THIS EDITION IS BEING PUBLISHED IN THE
UNITED STATES OF AMERICA FOR THE BOL-
LINGEN FOUNDATION BY PANTHEON BOOKS
INC., AND IN ENGLAND BY ROUTLEDGE &
KEGAN PAUL, LTD. IN THE AMERICAN EDI-
TION, ALL THE VOLUMES COMPRISING THE
COLLECTED WORKS CONSTITUTE NUMBER XX
IN THE BOLLINGEN SERIES. THE PRESENT
VOLUME IS NUMBER 16 OF THE COLLECTED
WORKS, AND IS THE THIRD TO APPEAR.

LIBRARY OF CONGRESS CATALOG CARD NUMBER: 52-8757
MANUFACTURED IN THE U. S. A. BY H. WOLFF
NEW YORK, N. Y.

EDITORIAL NOTE

This volume contains, in addition to "Psychology of the Transference," published as a separate volume in Switzerland, all Professor Jung's various papers on psychotherapy. Only two works of importance have not previously appeared in English: "Principles of Practical Psychotherapy" and "Psychology of the Transference." The first contains a new formulation of the analytical relationship; this formulation Jung calls the dialectical procedure. The second gives the only authoritative statement from his pen of the way in which the individuation process expresses itself in the transference.

It was felt that since many will read this volume who may have not an adequate classical scholarship at their command, a translation of the Latin quotations from little known alchemical texts, in the final paper, would be of assistance in promoting a deeper understanding of the material. A bibliography giving details of the extensive literature has been added; in it a number of English and American editions of foreign books will be found, though the translations in these volumes have not necessarily been used in the text. All bibliographical references are printed in boldface type.

The sources of the translations are given in the table of contents, and further bibliographical details will be found at the opening of each paper. The Latin and Greek passages were originally translated by Dr. A. Wasserstein and were later somewhat revised by Dr. Marie-Louise von Franz, whose expert knowledge of alchemical Latin has been invaluable.

TRANSLATOR'S NOTE

Certain of the essays in this volume were previously translated and published in *Contributions to Analytical Psychology* (London and New York, 1928), *Modern Man in Search of a Soul* (London and New York, 1933), and *Essays on Contemporary Events* (London, 1947). I wish to thank Mrs. Cary F. Baynes and Miss Mary Briner for permission to make full use of those texts in preparing the present revised versions. My particular thanks are due to Miss Barbara Hannah for placing at my disposal her draft translation of the opening chapters of "Psychology of the Transference."

It may be noted that two papers, "Some Aspects of Modern Psychotherapy" and "The Therapeutic Value of Abreaction," were written by Professor Jung in English, and are published here only with certain editorial modifications.

TABLE OF CONTENTS

PART ONE

GENERAL PROBLEMS OF PSYCHOTHERAPY

PART TWO

SPECIFIC PROBLEMS OF
PSYCHOTHERAPY

CONTENTS

LIST OF ILLUSTRATIONS

Figures 1–10 are full pages, with woodcuts, reproduced from the *Rosarium philosophorum, secunda pars alchemiae de lapide philosophico* (Frankfort, 1550). The sections which they pertain to are indicated in brackets.

Figures 11–13 are full pages reproduced from the textless picture book *Mutus liber, in quo tamen tota philosophia hermetica . . . depingitur* (La Rochelle, 1677). They are described on page 320, note 1.

I

GENERAL PROBLEMS
OF
PSYCHOTHERAPY

I

I

PRINCIPLES OF
PRACTICAL PSYCHOTHERAPY[1]

1   Psychotherapy is a domain of the healing art which has developed and acquired a certain independence only within the last fifty years. Views in this field have changed and become differentiated in a great variety of ways, and the mass of experience accumulated has given rise to all sorts of different interpretations. The reason for this lies in the fact that psychotherapy is not the simple, straightforward method people at first believed it to be, but, as has gradually become clear, a kind of dialectical process, a dialogue or discussion between two persons. Dialectic was originally the art of conversation among the ancient philosophers, but very early became the term for the process of creating new syntheses. A person is a psychic system which, when it affects another person, enters into reciprocal reaction with another psychic system. This, perhaps the most modern, formulation of the psychotherapeutic relation between physician and patient is clearly very far removed from the original view that psychotherapy was a method which anybody could apply in stereotyped fashion in order to reach the desired result. It was not the needs of speculation which prompted this unsuspected and, I might well say, unwelcome widening of the horizon, but the hard facts of reality. In the first place, it was probably the fact that one had to admit the possibility of different interpretations of the observed material. Hence there grew up various schools with diametrically opposed views. I would remind you of the Liébeault-Bernheim French method of suggestion therapy, *rééducation de la volonté;* Babinski's "persuasion"; Dubois' "rational psychic orthopedics"; Freud's psychoanalysis, with its emphasis on sexuality and the unconscious;

1 [Delivered as a lecture to the Zurich Medical Society in 1935. Published as "Grundsätzliches zur praktischen Psychotherapie," *Zentralblatt für Psychotherapie,* VIII (1935): 2, 66–82.—EDITORS.]

3

Adler's educational method, with its emphasis on power-drives and conscious fictions; Schultz's autogenic training—to name only the better known methods. Each of them rests on special psychological assumptions and produces special psychological results; comparison between them is difficult and often well-nigh impossible. Consequently it was quite natural that the champions of any one point of view should, in order to simplify matters, treat the opinions of the others as erroneous. Objective appraisal of the facts shows, however, that each of these methods and theories is justified up to a point, since each can boast not only of certain successes but of psychological data that largely prove its particular assumption. Thus we are faced in psychotherapy with a situation comparable with that in modern physics where, for instance, there are two contradictory theories of light. And just as physics does not find this contradiction unbridgeable, so the existence of many possible standpoints in psychology should not give grounds for assuming that the contradictions are irreconcilable and the various views merely subjective and therefore incommensurable. Contradictions in a department of science merely indicate that its subject displays characteristics which at present can be grasped only by means of antinomies—witness the wave theory and the corpuscular theory of light. Now the psyche is infinitely more complicated than light; hence a great number of antinomies is required to describe the nature of the psyche satisfactorily. One of the fundamental antinomies is the statement that *psyche depends on body and body depends on psyche*. There are clear proofs for both sides of this antinomy, so that an objective judgment cannot give more weight to thesis or to antithesis. The existence of valid contradictions shows that the object of investigation presents the inquiring mind with exceptional difficulties, as a result of which only relatively valid statements can be made, at least for the time being. That is to say, the statement is valid only in so far as it indicates what kind of psychic system we are investigating. Hence we arrive at the dialectical formulation which tells us precisely that psychic influence is the reciprocal reaction of two psychic systems. Since the individuality of the psychic system is infinitely variable, there must be an infinite variety of relatively valid statements. But if individuality were absolute in its particularity, if one individual were totally different from every other individual, then psychology would be impossible as a science, for it would consist in an insoluble chaos of subjective opinions. Individuality, however, is only relative, the complement of human conformity or likeness; and therefore it is possible to make statements of general validity, i.e., scientific statements. These statements relate only to those parts of the psychic system which do in fact conform, i.e., are amenable to comparison and statistically measurable; they do not relate to that part of the system which is individual and unique. The second fundamental antinomy in psychology therefore runs: *the individual signifies nothing in comparison with the universal, and the universal signifies nothing in comparison with the individual.* There are, as we all know, no universal elephants, only individual elephants. But if a generality, a constant plurality, of elephants did not exist, a single individual elephant would be exceedingly improbable.

2 These logical reflections may appear somewhat remote from our theme. But in so far as they are the outcome of previous psychological experience, they yield practical conclusions of no little importance. When, as a psychotherapist, I set myself up as a medical authority over my patient and on that account claim to know something about his individuality, or to be able to make valid statements about it, I am only demonstrating my lack of criticism, for I am in no position to judge the whole of the personality before me. I cannot say anything valid about him except in so far as he approximates to the "universal man." But since all life is to be found only in individual form, and I myself can assert of another individuality only what I find in my own, I am in constant danger either of doing violence to the other person or of succumbing to his influence. If I wish to treat another individual psychologically at all, I must for better or worse give up all pretensions to superior knowledge, all authority and desire to influence. I must perforce adopt a dialectical procedure consisting in a comparison of our mutual findings. But this becomes possible only if I give the other person a chance to play his hand to the full, unhampered by my assumptions. In this way his system is geared to mine and acts upon it; my reaction is the only thing with which I as an individual can legitimately confront my patient.

3   These considerations of principle produce in the psychotherapist a very definite attitude which, in all cases of *individual* treatment, seems to me to be absolutely necessary because it alone is scientifically responsible. Any deviation from
this attitude amounts to therapy by suggestion, the kind of therapy whose main principle is: "The individual signifies nothing
in comparison with the universal." Suggestion therapy includes
all methods that arrogate to themselves, and apply, a knowledge
or an interpretation of other individualities. Equally it includes
all strictly technical methods, because these invariably assume
that all individuals are alike. To the extent that the insignifi-
cance of the individual is a truth, suggestive methods, technical
procedures, and theorems in any shape or form are entirely
capable of success and guarantee results with the universal man
—as for instance, Christian Science, mental healing, faith cures,
remedial training, medical and religious techniques, and countless other isms. Even political movements can, not without
justice, claim to be psychotherapy in the grand manner. The
outbreak of war cured many a compulsion neurosis, and from
time immemorial certain miraculous localities have caused neurotic states to disappear; similarly, popular movements both
large and small can exert a curative influence on the individual.

4   This fact finds the simplest and most nearly perfect expression in the primitive idea of "mana." Mana is a universal medi-
cinal or healing power which renders men, animals, and plants
fruitful and endows chieftain and medicine-man with magical
strength. Mana, as Lehmann has shown, is identified with anything "extraordinarily potent," or simply with anything impressive. On the primitive level anything impressive is therefore "medicine." Since it is notorious that a hundred intelligent
heads massed together make one big fathead, virtues and en-
dowments are essentially the hallmarks of the individual and
not of the universal man. The masses always incline to herd
psychology, hence they are easily stampeded; and to mob psychology, hence their witless brutality and hysterical emotionalism.
The universal man has the characteristics of a savage and must
therefore be treated with technical methods. It is in fact bad
practice to treat collective man with anything other than "technically correct" methods, i.e., those collectively recognized and
believed to be effective. In this sense the old hypnotism or the

6

still older animal magnetism achieved, in principle, just as much as a technically irreproachable modern analysis, or for that matter the amulets of the primitive medicine-man. It all depends on the method the therapist happens to believe in. His belief is what does the trick. If he really believes, then he will do his utmost for the sufferer with seriousness and perseverance, and this freely given effort and devotion will have a curative effect—up to the level of collective man's mentality. But the limits are fixed by the "individual-universal" antinomy.

5   This antinomy constitutes a psychological as well as a philosophical criterion, since there are countless people who are not only collective in all essentials but are fired by a quite peculiar ambition to be nothing but collective. This accords with all the current trends in education which like to regard individuality and lawlessness as synonymous. On this plane anything individual is rated inferior and is repressed. In the corresponding neuroses individual contents and tendencies appear as psychological poisons. There is also, as we know, an overestimation of individuality based on the rule that "the universal signifies nothing in comparison with the individual." Thus, from the psychological (not the clinical) point of view, we can divide the psychoneuroses into two main groups: the one comprising collective people with underdeveloped individuality, the other individualists with atrophied collective adaptation. The therapeutic attitude differs accordingly, for it is abundantly clear that a neurotic individualist can only be cured by recognizing the collective man in himself—hence the need for collective adaptation. It is therefore right to bring him down to the level of collective truth. On the other hand, psychotherapists are familiar with the collectively adapted person who has everything and does everything that could reasonably be required as a guarantee of health, but yet is ill. It would be a bad mistake, which is nevertheless very often committed, to normalize such a person and try to bring him down to the collective level. In certain cases all possibility of individual development is thereby destroyed.

6   Since individuality, as we stressed in our introductory argument, is absolutely unique, unpredictable, and uninterpretable, in these cases the therapist must abandon all his preconcep-

tions and techniques and confine himself to a purely dialectical procedure, adopting the attitude that shuns all methods.

7   You will have noticed that I began by presenting the dialectical procedure as the latest phase of psychotherapeutic development. I must now correct myself and put this procedure in the right perspective: it is not so much an elaboration of previous theories and practices as a complete abandonment of them in favour of the most unbiased attitude possible. In other words, the therapist is no longer the agent of treatment but a fellow participant in a process of individual development.

8   I would not like it to be supposed that these discoveries dropped straight into our laps. They too have their history. Although I was the first to demand that the analyst should himself be analysed, we are largely indebted to Freud for the invaluable discovery that analysts too have their complexes and consequently one or two blind spots which act as so many prejudices. The psychotherapist gained this insight in cases where it was no longer possible for him to interpret or to guide the patient from on high or *ex cathedra,* regardless of his own personality, but was forced to admit that his personal idiosyncrasies or special attitude hindered the patient's recovery. When one possesses no very clear idea about something, because one is unwilling to admit it to oneself, one tries to hide it from the patient as well, obviously to his very great disadvantage. The demand that the analyst must be analysed culminates in the idea of a dialectical procedure, where the therapist enters into relationship with another psychic system both as questioner and answerer. No longer is he the superior wise man, judge, and counsellor; he is a fellow participant who finds himself involved in the dialectical process just as deeply as the so-called patient.

9   The dialectical procedure has another source, too, and that is the *multiple significance of symbolic contents.* Silberer distinguishes between the psychoanalytic and the anagogic interpretation, while I distinguish between the analytical-reductive and the synthetic-hermeneutic interpretation. I will explain what I mean by instancing the so-called infantile fixation on the parental imago, one of the richest sources of symbolic contents. The analytical-reductive view asserts that interest ("libido") streams back regressively to infantile reminiscences and

there "fixates"—if indeed it has ever freed itself from them. The synthetic or anagogic view, on the contrary, asserts that certain parts of the personality which are capable of development are in an infantile state, as though still in the womb. Both interpretations can be shown to be correct. We might almost say that they amount virtually to the same thing. But it makes an enormous difference in practice whether we interpret something regressively or progressively. It is no easy matter to decide aright in a given case. Generally we feel rather uncertain on this point. The discovery that there are essential contents of an indubitably equivocal nature has thrown suspicion on the airy application of theories and techniques, and thus helped to range the dialectical procedure alongside the subtler or cruder suggestion methods.

10   The depth-dimension which Freud has added to the problems of psychotherapy must logically lead sooner or later to the conclusion that any final understanding between doctor and patient is bound to include the personality of the doctor. The old hypnotists and Bernheim with his suggestion therapy were well enough aware that the healing effect depended firstly on the "rapport"—in Freud's terminology, "transference"—and secondly on the persuasive and penetrative powers of the doctor's personality. In the doctor-patient relationship, as we have said, two psychic systems interact, and therefore any deeper insight into the psychotherapeutic process will infallibly reach the conclusion that in the last analysis, since individuality is a fact not to be ignored, the relationship must be dialectical.

11   It is now perfectly clear that this realization involves a very considerable shift of standpoint compared with the older forms of psychotherapy. In order to avoid misunderstandings, let me say at once that this shift is certainly not meant to condemn the existing methods as incorrect, superfluous, or obsolete. The more deeply we penetrate the nature of the psyche, the more the conviction grows upon us that the diversity, the multidimensionality of human nature requires the greatest variety of standpoints and methods in order to satisfy the variety of psychic dispositions. It is therefore pointless to subject a simple soul who lacks nothing but a dose of common sense to a complicated analysis of his impulses, much less expose him to the bewildering subtleties of psychological dialectic. It is equally

9

obvious that with complex and highly intelligent people we shall get nowhere by employing well-intentioned advice, suggestions, and other efforts to convert them to some kind of system. In such cases the best thing the doctor can do is lay aside his whole apparatus of methods and theories and trust to luck that his personality will be steadfast enough to act as a signpost for the patient. At the same time he must give serious consideration to the possibility that in intelligence, sensibility, range and depth the patient's personality is superior to his own. But in all circumstances the prime rule of dialectical procedure is that the individuality of the sufferer has the same value, the same right to exist, as that of the doctor, and consequently that every development in the patient is to be regarded as valid, unless of course it corrects itself of its own accord. Inasmuch as a man is merely collective, he can be changed by suggestion to the point of becoming—or seeming to become—different from what he was before. But inasmuch as he is an individual he can only become what he is and always was. To the extent that "cure" means turning a sick man into a healthy one, cure is change. Wherever this is possible, where it does not demand too great a sacrifice of personality, we should change the sick man therapeutically. But when a patient realizes that cure through change would mean too great a sacrifice, then the doctor can, indeed he should, give up any wish to change or cure. He must either refuse to treat the patient or risk the dialectical procedure. This is of more frequent occurrence than one might think. In my own practice I always have a fair number of highly cultivated and intelligent people of marked individuality who, on ethical grounds, would vehemently resist any serious attempt to change them. In all such cases the doctor must leave the individual way to healing open, and then the cure will bring about no alteration of personality but will be the process we call "individuation," in which the patient becomes what he really is. If the worst comes to the worst, he will even put up with his neurosis, once he has understood the meaning of his illness. More than one patient has admitted to me that he has learned to accept his neurotic symptoms with gratitude, because, like a barometer, they invariably told him when and where he was straying from his individual path, and also whether he had let important things remain unconscious.

12   Although the new, highly differentiated methods allow us
an unsuspected glimpse into the endless complications of psychic relationships and have gone a long way to putting them on
a theoretical basis, they nevertheless confine themselves to the
analytical-reductive standpoint, so that the possibilities of individual development are obscured by being reduced to some general principle, such as sexuality. This is the prime reason why
the phenomenology of individuation is at present almost virgin
territory. Hence in what follows I must enter into some detail,
for I can only give you an idea of individuation by trying to
indicate the workings of the unconscious as revealed in the observed material itself. For, in the process of individual development, it is above all the unconscious that is thrust into the fore-
front of our interest. The deeper reason for this may lie in the
fact that the conscious attitude of the neurotic is unnaturally
one-sided and must be balanced by complementary or compensatory contents deriving from the unconscious. The unconscious
has a special significance in this case as a corrective to the one-
sidedness of the conscious mind; hence the need to observe the
points of view and impulses produced in dreams, because these
must take the place once occupied by collective controls, such
as the conventional outlook, habit, prejudices of an intellectual or moral nature. The road the individual follows is defined
by his knowledge of the laws that are peculiar to himself; otherwise he will get lost in the arbitrary opinions of the conscious
mind and break away from the mother-earth of individual instinct.

13   So far as our present knowledge extends, it would seem that
the vital urge which expresses itself in the structure and individual form of the living organism produces in the unconscious
a process, or is itself such a process, which on becoming partially
conscious depicts itself as a fugue-like sequence of images. Persons with natural introspective ability are capable of perceiving
fragments of this autonomous or self-activating sequence without too much difficulty, generally in the form of visual fantasies,
although they often fall into the error of thinking that they
have *created* these fantasies, whereas in reality the fantasies have
merely occurred to them. Their spontaneous nature can no
longer be denied, however, when, as often happens, some fan-
tasy-fragment becomes an obsession, like a tune you cannot get

11

out of your head, or a phobia, or a "symbolic tic." Closer to the unconscious sequence of images are the dreams which, if examined over a long series, reveal the continuity of the unconscious pictorial flood with surprising clearness. The continuity is shown in the repetition of motifs. These may deal with people, animals, objects, or situations. Thus the continuity of the picture sequence finds expression in the recurrence of some such motif over a long series of dreams.

14   In a dream series extending over a period of two months, one of my patients had the water-motif in twenty-six dreams. In the first dream it appeared as the surf pounding the beach, then in the second as a view of the glassy sea. In the third dream the dreamer was on the seashore watching the rain fall on the water. In the fourth there was an indirect allusion to a voyage, for he was journeying to a distant country. In the fifth he was travelling to America; in the sixth, water was poured into a basin; in the seventh he was gazing over a vast expanse of sea at dawn; in the eighth he was aboard ship. In the ninth he travelled to a far-off savage land. In the tenth he was again aboard ship. In the eleventh he went down a river. In the twelfth he walked beside a brook. In the thirteenth he was on a steamer. In the fourteenth he heard a voice calling, "This is the way to the sea, we must get to the sea!" In the fifteenth he was on a ship going to America. In the sixteenth, again on a ship. In the seventeenth he drove to the ship in an automobile. In the eighteenth he made astronomical calculations on a ship. In the nineteenth he went down the Rhine. In the twentieth he was on an island, and again in the twenty-first. In the twenty-second he navigated a river with his mother. In the twenty-third he stood on the seashore. In the twenty-fourth he looked for sunken treasure. In the twenty-fifth his father was telling him about the land where the water comes from. And finally in the twenty-sixth he went down a small river that debouched into a larger one.

15   This example illustrates the continuity of the unconscious theme and also shows how the motifs can be evaluated statistically. Through numerous comparisons one can find out to what the water-motif is really pointing, and the interpretation of motifs follows from a number of similar dream-series. Thus the sea always signifies a collecting-place where all psychic life

originates, i.e., the collective unconscious. Water in motion means something like the stream of life or the energy-potential. The ideas underlying all the motifs are visual representations of an archetypal character, symbolic primordial images which have served to build up and differentiate the human mind. These primordial images are difficult to define; one might even call them hazy. Cramping intellectual formulae rob them of their natural amplitude. They are not scientific concepts which must necessarily be clear and unequivocal; they are universal perceptions of the primitive mind, and they never denote any particular content but are significant for their wealth of associations. Lévy-Bruhl calls them "collective representations," and Hubert and Mauss call them *a priori* categories of the imagination.

16   In a longer series of dreams the motifs frequently change places. Thus, after the last of the above dreams, the water-motif gradually retreated to make way for a new motif, the "unknown woman." In general, dreams about women refer to women whom the dreamer knows. But now and then there are dreams in which a female figure appears who cannot be shown to be an acquaintance and whom the dream itself distinctly characterizes as unknown. This motif has an interesting phenomenology which I should like to illustrate from a dream series extending over a period of three months. In this series the motif occurred no less than fifty-one times. At the outset it appeared as a throng of vague female forms, then it assumed the vague form of a woman sitting on a step. She then appeared veiled, and when she took off the veil her face shone like the sun. Then she was a naked figure standing on a globe, seen from behind. After that she dissolved once more into a throng of dancing nymphs, then into a bevy of syphilitic prostitutes. A little later the unknown appeared on a ball, and the dreamer gave her some money. Then she was a syphilitic again. From now on the unknown becomes associated with the so-called "dual motif," a frequent occurrence in dreams. In this series a savage woman, a Malay perhaps, is doubled. She has to be taken captive, but she is also the naked blonde who stood on the globe, or else a young girl with a red cap, a nursemaid, or an old woman. She is very dangerous, a member of a robber-band and not quite human, something like an abstract idea. She

is a guide, who takes the dreamer up a high mountain. But she is also like a bird, perhaps a marabou or pelican. She is a man-catcher. Generally she is fair-haired, a hairdresser's daughter, but has a dark Indian sister. As a fair-haired guide she informs the dreamer that part of his sister's soul belongs to her. She writes him a love-letter, but is another man's wife. She neither speaks nor is spoken to. Now she has black hair, now white. She has peculiar fantasies, unknown to the dreamer. She may be his father's unknown wife, but is not his mother. She travels with him in an airplane, which crashes. She is a voice that changes into a woman. She tells him that she is a piece of broken pottery, meaning presumably that she is a part-soul. She has a brother who is prisoner in Moscow. As the dark figure she is a servant-girl, stupid, and she has to be watched. Often she appears doubled, as two women who go mountain-climbing with him. On one occasion the fair-haired guide comes to him in a vision. She brings him bread, is full of religious ideas, knows the way he should go, meets him in church, acts as his spiritual guide. She seems to pop out of a dark chest and can change herself from a dog into a woman. Once she appears as an ape. The dreamer draws her portrait in a dream, but what comes out on the paper is an abstract symbolic ideogram containing the trinity, another frequent motif.

17   The unknown woman, therefore, has an exceedingly contradictory character and cannot be related to any normal woman. She represents some fabulous being, a kind of fairy; and indeed fairies have the most varied characters. There are wicked fairies and good fairies; they too can change themselves into animals, they can become invisible, they are of uncertain age, now young, now old, elfin in nature, with part-souls, alluring, dangerous, and possessed of superior knowledge. We shall hardly be wrong in assuming that this motif is identical with the parallel ideas to be found in mythology, where we come across this elfin creature in a variety of forms—nymph, oread, sylph, undine, nixie, hamadryad, succubus, lamia, vampire, witch, and what not. Indeed the whole world of myth and fable is an outgrowth of unconscious fantasy just like the dream. Frequently this motif replaces the water-motif. Just as water denotes the unconscious in general, so the figure of the unknown woman is a personification of the unconscious, which I have

called the "anima." This figure only occurs in men, and she emerges clearly only when the unconscious starts to reveal its problematical nature. In man the unconscious has feminine features, in woman masculine; hence in man the personification of the unconscious is a feminine creature of the type we have just described.

18   I cannot, within the compass of a lecture, describe all the motifs that crop up in the process of individuation—when, that is to say, the material is no longer reduced to generalities applicable only to the collective man. There are numerous motifs, and we meet them everywhere in mythology. Hence we can only say that the psychic development of the individual produces something that looks very like the archaic world of fable, and that the individual path looks like a regression to man's prehistory, and that consequently it seems as if something very untoward were happening which the therapist ought to arrest. We can in fact observe similar things in psychotic illnesses, especially in the paranoid forms of schizophrenia, which often swarm with mythological images. The fear instantly arises that we are dealing with some misdevelopment leading to a world of chaotic or morbid fantasy. A development of this kind may be dangerous with a person whose social personality has not found its feet; moreover any psychotherapeutic intervention may occasionally run into a latent psychosis and bring it to full flower. For this reason to dabble in psychotherapy is to play with fire, against which amateurs should be stringently cautioned. It is particularly dangerous when the mythological layer of the psyche is uncovered, for these contents have a fearful fascination for the patient—which explains the tremendous influence mythological ideas have had on mankind.

19   Now, it would seem that the recuperative process mobilizes these powers for its own ends. Mythological ideas with their extraordinary symbolism evidently reach far into the human psyche and touch the historical foundations where reason, will, and good intentions never penetrate; for these ideas are born of the same depths and speak a language which strikes an answering chord in the inner man, although our reason may not understand it. Hence, the process that at first sight looks like an alarming regression is rather a *reculer pour mieux sauter,*

15

an amassing and integration of powers that will develop into a new order.

20   A neurosis at this level is an entirely spiritual form of suffering which cannot be tackled with ordinary rational methods. For this reason there are not a few psychotherapists who, when all else fails, have recourse to one of the established religions or creeds. I am far from wishing to ridicule these efforts. On the contrary, I must emphasize that they are based on an extremely sound instinct, for our religions contain the still living remains of a mythological age. Even a political creed may occasionally revert to mythology, as is proved very clearly by the swastika, the German Christians, and the German Faith Movement. Not only Christianity with its symbols of salvation, but all religions, including the primitive with their magical rituals, are forms of psychotherapy which treat and heal the suffering of the soul, and the suffering of the body caused by the soul. How much in modern medicine is still suggestion therapy is not for me to say. To put it mildly, "consideration of the psychological factor" in practical therapeutics is by no means a bad thing. The history of medicine is exceedingly revealing in this respect.

21   Therefore, when certain doctors resort to the mythological ideas of some religion or other, they are doing something historically justified. But they can only do this with patients for whom the mythological remains are still alive. For these patients some kind of rational therapy is indicated until such time as mythological ideas become a necessity. In treating devout Catholics, I always refer them to the Church's confessional and its means of grace. It is more difficult in the case of Protestants, who must do without confession and absolution. The more modern type of Protestantism has, however, the safety-valve of the Oxford Group movement, which prescribes lay confession as a substitute, and group experience instead of absolution. A number of my patients have joined this movement with my entire approval, just as others have become Catholics, or at least better Catholics than they were before. In all these cases I refrain from applying the dialectical procedure, since there is no point in promoting individual development beyond the needs of the patient. If he can find the meaning of his life and the cure for his disquiet and disunity within the framework of an existing credo—including a political credo—that should

16

be enough for the doctor. After all, the doctor's main concern is the sick, not the cured.

22   There are, however, very many patients who have either no religious convictions at all or highly unorthodox ones. Such persons are, on principle, not open to any conviction. All rational therapy leaves them stuck where they were, although on the face of it their illness is quite curable. In these circumstances nothing is left but the dialectical development of the mythological material which is alive in the sick man himself, regardless of history and tradition. It is here that we come across those mythological dreams whose characteristic sequence of images presents the doctor with an entirely new and unexpected task. He then needs the sort of knowledge for which his professional studies have not equipped him in the least. For the human psyche is neither a psychiatric nor a physiological problem; it is not a biological problem at all but—precisely—a psychological one. It is a field on its own with its own peculiar laws. Its nature cannot be deduced from the principles of other sciences without doing violence to the idiosyncrasy of the psyche. It cannot be identified with the brain, or the hormones, or any known instinct; for better or worse it must be accepted as a phenomenon unique in kind. The phenomenology of the psyche contains more than the measurable facts of the natural sciences: it embraces the problem of mind, the father of all science. The psychotherapist becomes acutely aware of this when he is driven to penetrate below the level of accepted opinion. It is often objected that people have practised psychotherapy before now and did not find it necessary to go into all these complications. I readily admit that Hippocrates, Galen, and Paracelsus were excellent doctors, but I do not believe that modern medicine should on that account give up serum therapy and radiology. It is no doubt difficult, particularly for the layman, to understand the complicated problems of psychotherapy; but if he will just consider for a moment why certain situations in life or certain experiences are pathogenic, he will discover that human opinion often plays a decisive part. Certain things accordingly seem dangerous, or impossible, or harmful, simply because there are opinions that cause them to appear in that light. For instance, many people regard wealth as the supreme happiness and poverty as man's greatest curse, al-

17

though in actual fact riches never brought supreme happiness to anybody, nor is poverty a reason for melancholia. But we have these opinions, and these opinions are rooted in certain mental preconceptions—in the *Zeitgeist,* or in certain religious or anti-religious views. These last play an important part in moral conflicts. As soon as the analysis of a patient's psychic situation impinges on the area of his mental preconceptions, we have already entered the realm of general ideas. The fact that dozens of normal people never criticize their mental preconceptions— obviously not, since they are unconscious of them—does not prove that these preconceptions are valid for all men, or indeed unconscious for all men, any more than it proves that they may not become the source of the severest moral conflict. Quite the contrary: in our age of revolutionary change, inherited prejudices of a general nature on the one hand and spiritual and moral disorientation on the other are very often the deeper-lying causes of far-reaching disturbances in psychic equilibrium. To these patients the doctor has absolutely nothing to offer but the possibility of individual development. And for their sake the specialist is compelled to extend his knowledge over the field of the humane sciences, if he is to do justice to the symbolism of psychic contents.

23   I would make myself guilty of a sin of omission if I were to foster the impression that specialized therapy needed nothing but a wide knowledge. Quite as important is the moral differentiation of the doctor's personality. Surgery and obstetrics have long been aware that it is not enough simply to wash the patient—the doctor himself must have clean hands. A neurotic psychotherapist will invariably treat his own neurosis in the patient. A therapy independent of the doctor's personality is just conceivable in the sphere of rational techniques, but it is quite inconceivable in a dialectical procedure where the doctor must emerge from his anonymity and give an account of himself, just as he expects his patient to do. I do not know which is the more difficult: to accumulate a wide knowledge or to renounce one's professional authority and anonymity. At all events the latter necessity involves a moral strain that makes the profession of psychotherapist not exactly an enviable one. Among laymen one frequently meets with the prejudice that psychotherapy is the easiest thing in the world and consists in

the art of putting something over on people or wheedling money out of them. But actually it is a tricky and not undangerous calling. Just as all doctors are exposed to infections and other occupational hazards, so the psychotherapist runs the risk of psychic infections which are no less menacing. On the one hand he is often in danger of getting entangled in the neuroses of his patients; on the other hand if he tries too hard to guard against their influence, he robs himself of his therapeutic efficacy. Between this Scylla and this Charybdis lies the peril, but also the healing power.

24   Modern psychotherapy is built up of many layers, corresponding to the diversities of the patients requiring treatment. The simplest cases are those who just want sound common sense and good advice. With luck they can be disposed of in a single consultation. This is certainly not to say that cases which look simple are always as simple as they look; one is apt to make disagreeable discoveries. Then there are patients for whom a thorough confession or "abreaction" is enough. The severer neuroses usually require a reductive analysis of their symptoms and states. And here one should not apply this or that method indiscriminately but, according to the nature of the case, should conduct the analysis more along the lines of Freud or more along those of Adler. St. Augustine distinguishes two cardinal sins: concupiscence and conceit (*superbia*). The first corresponds to Freud's pleasure principle, the second to Adler's power-drive, the desire to be on top. There are in fact two categories of people with different needs. Those whose main characteristic is infantile pleasure-seeking generally have the satisfaction of incompatible desires and instincts more at heart than the social role they could play, hence they are often well-to-do or even successful people who have arrived socially. But those who want to be "on top" are mostly people who are either the under-dogs in reality or fancy that they are not playing the role that is properly due to them. Hence they often have difficulty in adapting themselves socially and try to cover up their inferiority with power fictions. One can of course explain all neuroses in Freudian or Adlerian terms, but in practice it is better to examine the case carefully beforehand. In the case of educated people the decision is not difficult: I advise them to read a bit of Freud and a bit of Adler. As a rule they soon

find out which of the two suits them best. So long as one is moving in the sphere of genuine neurosis one cannot dispense with the views of either Freud or Adler.

25 But when the thing becomes monotonous and you begin to get repetitions, and your unbiased judgment tells you that a standstill has been reached, or when mythological or "archetypal" contents appear, then is the time to give up the analytical-reductive method and to treat the symbols anagogically or synthetically, which is equivalent to the dialectical procedure and the way of individuation.

26 All methods of influence, including the analytical, require that the patient be seen as often as possible. I content myself with a maximum of four consultations a week. With the beginning of synthetic treatment it is of advantage to spread out the consultations. I then generally reduce them to one or two hours a week, for the patient must learn to go his own way. This consists in his trying to understand his dreams himself, so that the contents of the unconscious may be progressively articulated with the conscious mind; for the cause of neurosis is the discrepancy between the conscious attitude and the trend of the unconscious. This dissociation is bridged by the assimilation of unconscious contents. Hence the interval between consultations does not go unused. In this way one saves oneself and the patient a good deal of time, which is so much money to him; and at the same time he learns to stand on his own feet instead of clinging to the doctor.

27 The work done by the patient through the progressive assimilation of unconscious contents leads ultimately to the integration of his personality and hence to the removal of the neurotic dissociation. To describe the details of this development would far exceed the limits of a lecture. I must therefore rest content with having given you at least a general survey of the principles of practical psychotherapy.

II

WHAT IS PSYCHOTHERAPY? [1]

28   It is not so very long ago that fresh air, application of cold water, and "psychotherapy" were all recommended in the same breath by well-meaning doctors in cases mysteriously complicated by psychic symptoms. On closer examination "psychotherapy" meant a sort of robust, benevolently paternal advice which sought to persuade the patient, after the manner of Dubois, that the symptom was "only psychic" and therefore a morbid fancy.

29   It is not to be denied that advice may occasionally do some good, but advice is about as characteristic of modern psychotherapy as bandaging of modern surgery—that is to say, personal and authoritarian influence is an important factor in healing, but not by any means the only one, and in no sense does it constitute the essence of psychotherapy. Whereas formerly it seemed to be everybody's province, today psychotherapy has become a science and uses the scientific method. With our deepened understanding of the nature of neuroses and the psychic complications of bodily ills, the nature of the treatment, too, has undergone considerable change and differentiation. The earlier suggestion theory, according to which symptoms had to be suppressed by counteraction, was superseded by the psychoanalytical viewpoint of Freud, who realized that the cause of the illness was not removed with the suppression of the symptom and that the symptom was far more a kind of signpost pointing, directly or indirectly, to the cause. This novel attitude—which has been generally accepted for the last thirty years or so—completely revolutionized therapy because, in contradiction to suggestion therapy, it required that the causes be brought to consciousness.

[1] [First published as "Was ist die Psychotherapie?," *Schweizerische Aerztezeitung für Standesfragen*, XVI: 26 (June, 1935), 335–39.—EDITORS.]

30   Suggestion therapy (hypnosis, etc.) was not lightly abandoned—it was abandoned only because its results were so unsatisfactory. It was fairly easy and practical to apply, and allowed skilled practitioners to treat a large number of patients at the same time, and this at least seemed to offer the hopeful beginnings of a lucrative method. Yet the actual cures were exceedingly sparse and so unstable that even the delightful possibility of simultaneous mass treatment could no longer save it. But for that, both the practitioner and the health insurance officer would have had every interest in retaining this method. It perished, however, of its own insufficiency.

31   Freud's demand that the causes be made conscious has become the leitmotiv or basic postulate of all the more recent forms of psychotherapy. Psychopathological research during the last fifty years has proved beyond all possibility of doubt that the most important aetiological processes in neurosis are essentially unconscious; while practical experience has shown that the making conscious of aetiological facts or processes is a curative factor of far greater practical importance than suggestion. Accordingly in the course of the last twenty-five or thirty years there has occurred over the whole field of psychotherapy a swing away from direct suggestion in favour of all forms of therapy whose common standpoint is the raising to consciousness of the causes that make for illness.

32   As already indicated, the change of treatment went hand in hand with a profounder and more highly differentiated theory of neurotic disturbance. So long as treatment was restricted to suggestion, it could content itself with the merest skeleton of a theory. People thought it sufficient to regard neurotic symptoms as the "fancies" of an overwrought imagination, and from this view the therapy followed easily enough, the object of which was simply to suppress those products of imagination—the "imaginary" symptoms. But what people thought they could nonchalantly write off as "imaginary" is only one manifestation of a morbid state that is positively protean in its symptomatology. No sooner is one symptom suppressed than another is there. The core of the disturbance had not been reached.

33   Under the influence of Breuer and Freud the so-called "trauma" theory of neuroses held the field for a long time. Doctors tried to make the patient conscious of the original

22

traumatic elements with the aid of the "cathartic method." But even this comparatively simple method and its theory demanded an attitude of doctor to patient very different from the suggestion method, which could be practised by anyone with the necessary determination. The cathartic method required careful individual scrutiny of the case in question and a patient attitude that searched for possible traumata. For only through the most meticulous observation and examination of the material could the traumatic elements be so constellated as to result in abreaction of the original affective situations from which the neurosis arose. Hence a lucrative group treatment became exceedingly difficult, if not impossible. Although the performance expected of the doctor was qualitatively higher than in the case of suggestion, the theory was so elementary that there was always the possibility of a rather mechanical routine, for in principle there was nothing to prevent the doctor from putting several patients at once into the relaxed condition in which the traumatic memories could be abreacted.

34   As a result of this more exhaustive treatment of the individual case it could no longer be disguised that the trauma theory was a hasty generalization. Growing experience made it clear to every conscientious investigator of neurotic symptoms that specifically sexual traumata and other shocks may indeed account for some forms of neurosis, but not by any means for all. Freud himself soon stepped beyond the trauma theory and came out with his theory of "repression." This theory is much more complicated, and the treatment became differentiated accordingly. It was realized that mere abreaction cannot possibly lead to the goal, since the majority of neuroses are not traumatic at all. The theory of repression took far more account of the fact that typical neuroses are, properly speaking, developmental disturbances. Freud put it that the disturbance was due to the repression of infantile sexual impulses and tendencies which were thereby made unconscious. The task of the theory was to track down these tendencies in the patient. But since by definition they are unconscious, their existence could only be proved by a thorough examination of the patient's anamnesis as well as his actual fantasies.

35   In general the infantile impulses appear mainly in dreams, and that is why Freud now turned to a serious study of the

dream. This was the decisive step that made modern psychotherapy a method of individual treatment. It is quite out of the question to apply psychoanalysis to several patients at once. It is anything but a mechanical routine.

36   Now whether this form of treatment calls itself "individual psychology" with Adler or "psychoanalysis" with Freud and Stekel, the fact remains that modern psychotherapy of whatever kind, so far as it claims to be medically conscientious and scientifically reliable, can no longer be mass-produced but is obliged to give undivided and generous attention to the individual. The procedure is necessarily very detailed and lengthy. True, attempts are often made to shorten the length of treatment as much as possible, but one could hardly say that the results have been very encouraging. The point is that most neuroses are misdevelopments that have been built up over many years, and these cannot be remedied by a short and intensive process. Time is therefore an irreplaceable factor in healing.

37   Neuroses are still—very unjustly—counted as mild illnesses, mainly because their nature is not tangible and of the body. People do not "die" of a neurosis—as if every bodily illness had a fatal outcome! But it is entirely forgotten that, unlike bodily illnesses, neuroses may be extremely deleterious in their psychic and social consequences, often worse than psychoses, which generally lead to the social isolation of the sufferer and thus render him innocuous. An anchylosed knee, an amputated foot, a long-drawn-out phthisis, are in every respect preferable to a severe neurosis. When the neurosis is regarded not merely from the clinical but from the psychological and social standpoint, one comes to the conclusion that it really is a severe illness, particularly in view of its effects on the patient's environment and way of life. The clinical standpoint by itself is not and cannot be fair to the nature of a neurosis, because a neurosis is more a psychosocial phenomenon than an illness in the strict sense. It forces us to extend the term "illness" beyond the idea of an individual body whose functions are disturbed, and to look upon the neurotic person as a sick system of social relationships. When one has corrected one's views in this way, one will no longer find it astonishing that a proper therapy of neuroses is an elaborate and complicated matter.

38   Unfortunately, the medical faculties have bothered far too little with the fact that the number of neuroses (and above all the frequency of psychic complications in organic diseases) is very great and thus concerns the general practitioner in unusually high degree, even though he may not realize it. Nevertheless his studies give him no preparation whatever in this most important respect; indeed, very often he never has a chance to find out anything about this subject, so vital in practice.

39   Although the beginnings of modern psychotherapy rest in the main on the services of Freud, we should be very wrong if we—as so often happens—identified psychological treatment with Freudian "psychoanalysis" pure and simple. This error is certainly fostered by Freud himself and his adherents, who, in most sectarian fashion, regard their sexual theory and their methodology as the sole means of grace. Adler's "individual psychology" is a contribution not to be underestimated, and represents a widening of the psychological horizon. There is much that is right and true in the theory and method of psychoanalysis; nevertheless it restricts its truth essentially to the sexual frame of reference and is blind to everything that is not subordinate to it. Adler has proved that not a few neuroses can be more successfully explained in quite another way.

40   These newer developments of theory have as their therapeutic aim not only the raising to consciousness of pathogenic contents and tendencies, but their reduction to original "simple" instincts, which is supposed to restore the patient to his natural, unwarped state. Such an aim is no less praiseworthy than it is logical and promising in practice. The wholesome results are, when one considers the enormous difficulties in treating the neuroses, most encouraging, if not so ideal that we need wish for nothing better.

41   Reduction to instinct is itself a somewhat questionable matter, since man has always been at war with his instincts—that is to say, they are in a state of perpetual strife; hence the danger arises that the reduction to instinct will only replace the original neurotic conflict by another. (To give but one example: Freud replaces the neurosis by the so-called "transference neurosis.") In order to avoid this danger, psychoanalysis tries to devalue the infantile desires through analytical insight, whereas

individual psychology tries to replace them by collectivizing the individual on the basis of the herd instinct. Freud represents the scientific rationalism of the nineteenth century, Adler the socio-political trends of the twentieth.

42   Against these views, which clearly rest on time-bound assumptions, I have stressed the need for more extensive individualization of the method of treatment and for an irrationalization of its aims—especially the latter, which would ensure the greatest possible freedom from prejudice. In dealing with psychological developments, the doctor should, as a matter of principle, let nature rule and himself do his utmost to avoid influencing the patient in the direction of his own philosophical, social, and political bent. Even if all citizens are equal before the law, they are very unequal as individuals, and therefore each can find happiness only in his own way. This is not to preach "individualism," but only the necessary pre-condition for responsible action: namely that a man should know himself and his own peculiarities and have the courage to stand by them. Only when a man lives in his own way is he responsible and capable of action—otherwise he is just a hanger-on or follower-on with no proper personality.

43   I mention these far-reaching problems of modern psychotherapy not, indeed, to give an elaborate account of them but simply to show the reader the sort of problems which the practitioner comes up against when his avowed aim is to guide the neurotic misdevelopment back to its natural course. Consider a man who is largely unconscious of his own psychology: in order to educate him to the point where he can consciously take the right road for *him* and at the same time clearly recognize his own social responsibilities, a detailed and lengthy procedure is needed. If Freud, by his observation of dreams—which are so very important therapeutically—has already done much to complicate the method, it is rendered even more exacting, rather than simplified, by further individualization, which logically sets greater store by the patient's individual material. But to the extent that his particular personality is thereby brought into play, his collaboration can be enlisted all the more. The psychoanalyst thinks he must see his patient for an hour a day for months on end; I manage in difficult cases with three or four sittings a week. As a rule I content myself with two, and

once the patient has got going, he is reduced to one. In the interim he has to work at himself, but under my control. I provide him with the necessary psychological knowledge to free himself from my medical authority as speedily as possible. In addition, I break off the treatment every ten weeks or so, in order to throw him back on his normal milieu. In this way he is not alienated from his world—for he really suffers from his tendency to live at another's expense. In such a procedure time can take effect as a healing factor, without the patient's having to pay for the doctor's time. With proper direction most people become capable after a while of making their contribution—however modest at first—to the common work. In my experience the absolute period of cure is not shortened by too many sittings. It lasts a fair time in all cases requiring thorough treatment. Consequently, in the case of the patient with small means, if the sittings are spaced out and the intervals filled in with the patient's own work, the treatment becomes financially more endurable than when undertaken daily in the hope of (problematical) suggestive effects.

44   In all clear cases of neurosis a certain re-education and regeneration of personality are essential, for we are dealing with a misdevelopment that generally goes far back into the individual's childhood. Accordingly the modern method must also take account of the philosophical and pedagogical views of the humane sciences, for which reason a purely medical education is proving increasingly inadequate. Such an activity should in all cases presuppose a thorough knowledge of psychiatry. But for adequate treatment of dreams a plentiful admixture of symbolical knowledge is needed, which can only be acquired by a study of primitive psychology, comparative mythology, and religion.

45   Much to the astonishment of the psychotherapist, the object of his labours has not grown simpler with deepened knowledge and experience, but has visibly increased in scope and complexity; and in the clouds of the future the lineaments of a new practical psychology have already begun to take shape, which will embrace the insights of the doctor as well as of the educator and all those whose concern is the human soul. Till then, psychotherapy will assuredly remain the business of the doctor, and it is to be hoped that the medical faculties

will not long continue to turn a deaf ear to this plea addressed to the doctor by the sick. The educated public knows of the existence of psychotherapy, and the intelligent doctor knows, from his own practice, the great importance of psychological influence. Hence in Switzerland there is already a fine body of doctors who stand up for the rights of psychotherapy and practise it with self-sacrificing devotion, despite the fact that their work is often made bitter for them by ridicule, misinterpretation, and criticism, as inept as it is malevolent.

III

SOME ASPECTS OF
MODERN PSYCHOTHERAPY [1]

46 Modern psychotherapy finds itself in rather an awkward position at a public-health congress. It can boast of no international agreements, nor can it provide the legislator or the minister of public hygiene with suitable or workable advice. It must assume the somewhat humble role of personal charity work versus the big organizations and institutions of public welfare, and this despite the fact that neuroses are alarmingly common and occupy no small place among the host of evils that assail the health of civilized nations.

47 Psychotherapy and modern psychology are as yet individual experiments with little or no general applicability. They rest upon the initiative of individual doctors, who are not supported even by the universities. Nevertheless the problems of modern psychology have aroused a widespread interest out of all proportion to the exceedingly restricted official sympathy.

48 I must confess that I myself did not find it at all easy to bow my head to Freud's innovations. I was a young doctor then, busying myself with experimental psychopathology and mainly interested in the disturbances of mental reactions to be observed in the so-called association experiments. Only a few of Freud's works had then been published. But I could not help seeing that my conclusions undoubtedly tended to confirm the facts indicated by Freud, namely the facts of repression, substitution, and "symbolization." Nor could I honestly deny the very real importance of sexuality in the aetiology and indeed in the actual structure of neuroses.

49 Medical psychology is still pioneer work, but it looks as if the medical profession were beginning to see a psychic side

[1] [Written in English. Read at the Congress of the Society of Public Health, Zurich, in 1929. First published in *Journal of State Medicine* (London), XXXVIII: 6 (June, 1930), 348–54.—EDITORS.]

to many things which have hitherto been considered from the physiological side only, not to mention the neuroses, whose psychic nature is no longer seriously contested. Medical psychology seems, therefore, to be coming into its own. But where, we may ask, can the medical student learn it? It is important for the doctor to know something about the psychology of his patients, and about the psychology of nervous, mental, and physical diseases. Quite a lot is known about these things among specialists, though the universities do not encourage such studies. I can understand their attitude. If I were responsible for a university department, I should certainly feel rather hesitant about teaching medical psychology.

50   In the first place, there is no denying the fact that Freud's theories have come up against certain rooted prejudices. It was to no purpose that he modified the worst aspects of his theories in later years. In the public eye he is branded by his first statements. They are one-sided and exaggerated; moreover they are backed by a philosophy that is falling more and more out of favour with the public: a thoroughly materialistic point of view which has been generally abandoned since the turn of the century. Freud's exclusive standpoint not only offends too many ideals but also misinterprets the natural facts of the human psyche. It is certain that human nature has its dark side, but the layman as well as the reasonable scientist is quite convinced that it also has its good and positive side, which is just as real. Common sense does not tolerate the Freudian tendency to derive everything from sexuality and other moral incompatibilities. Such a view is too destructive.

51   The extraordinary importance which Freud attaches to the unconscious meets with scant approval, although it is an interesting point with a certain validity. But one should not stress it too much, otherwise one robs the conscious mind of its practical significance and eventually arrives at a completely mechanistic view of things. This goes against our instincts, which have made the conscious mind the *arbiter mundi*. It is nevertheless true that the conscious mind has been overvalued by the rationalists. Hence it was a healthy sign to give the unconscious its due share of value. But this should not exceed the value accorded to consciousness.

52   A further reason for hesitation is the absence of a real medical psychology, though there may be a psychology for doctors.
Psychology is not for professionals only, nor is it peculiar to
certain diseases. It is something broadly human, with professional and pathological variations. Nor, again, is it merely instinctual or biological. If it were, it could very well be just a
chapter in a text-book of biology. It has an immensely important social and cultural aspect without which we could not
imagine a human psyche at all. It is therefore quite impossible
to speak of a general or normal psychology as the mere expression of a clash between instinct and moral law, or other incon-
veniences of that kind. Since the beginning of history man has
been the maker of his own laws; and even if, as Freud seems
to think, they were the invention of our malevolent forefathers,
it is odd how the rest of humanity has conformed to them and
given them silent assent.

53   Even Freud, who tried to restrict what he called psychoanalysis to the medical sphere (with occasional, somewhat in-
appropriate excursions into other spheres), even he was forced
to discuss fundamental principles that go far beyond purely
medical considerations. The most cursory professional treatment of an intelligent patient is bound to lead to basic issues,
because a neurosis or any other mental conflict depends much
more on the personal attitude of the patient than on his infantile history. No matter what the influences are that disturbed
his youth, he still has to put up with them and he does so by
means of a certain attitude. The attitude is all-important.
Freud emphasizes the aetiology of the case, and assumes that
once the causes are brought into consciousness the neurosis will
be cured. But mere consciousness of the causes does not help
any more than detailed knowledge of the causes of war helps
to raise the value of the French franc. The task of psychotherapy is to correct the conscious attitude and not to go chas-
ing after infantile memories. Naturally you cannot do the one
without paying attention to the other, but the main emphasis
should be upon the attitude of the patient. There are extremely
practical reasons for this, because there is scarcely a neurotic
who does not love to dwell upon the evils of the past and to
wallow in self-commiserating memories. Very often his neurosis

consists precisely in his hanging back and constantly excusing himself on account of the past.

54   As you know, I am critical of Freud in this particular respect, but my criticism would not go so far as to deny the extraordinary power of the retrospective tendency. On the contrary, I consider it to be of the greatest importance, so important that I would not call any treatment thorough that did not take it into account. Freud in his analysis follows this regressive tendency to the end and thus arrives at the findings you all know. These findings are only *apparent* facts; in the main they are interpretations. He has a special method of interpreting psychic material, and it is partly because the material has a sexual aspect and partly because he interprets it in a special way that he arrives at his typical conclusions. Take for instance his treatment of dreams. He believes that the dream is a façade. He says you can turn it inside out, that this or that factor is eliminated by a censor, and so forth.

55   I hold that interpretation is the crux of the whole matter. One can just as well assume that the dream is not a façade, that there is no censor, and that the unconscious appears in dreams in the naïvest and most genuine way. The dream is as genuine as the albumen in urine, and this is anything but a façade. If you take the dream like this, you naturally come to very different conclusions. And the same thing happens with the patient's regressive tendency. I have suggested that it is not just a relapse into infantilism, but a genuine attempt to get at something necessary. There is, to be sure, no lack of infantile perversions. But are we so certain that what appears to be, and is interpreted as, an incestuous craving is really only that? When we try, conscientiously and without theoretical bias, to find out what the patient is really seeking in his father or mother, we certainly do not, as a rule, find incest, but rather a genuine horror of it. We find that he is seeking something entirely different, something that Freud only appreciates negatively: the universal feeling of childhood innocence, the sense of security, of protection, of reciprocated love, of trust, of faith—a thing that has many names.

56   Is this goal of the regressive tendency entirely without justification? Or is it not rather the very thing the patient urgently needs in order to build up his conscious attitude?

57   I believe that incest and the other perverted sexual aspects are, in most cases, no more than by-products, and that the essential contents of the regressive tendency are really those which I have just mentioned. I have no objection to a patient's going back to that kind of childhood, nor do I mind his indulging in such memories.

58   I am not blind to the fact that the patient must sink or swim, and that he may possibly go under as the result of infantile indulgence; but I call him back to these valuable memories with conscious intent. I appeal to his sense of values deliberately, because I have to make the man well and therefore I must use all available means to achieve the therapeutic aim.

59   The regressive tendency only means that the patient is seeking *himself* in his childhood memories, sometimes for better, sometimes for worse. His development was one-sided; it left important items of character and personality behind, and thus it ended in failure. That is why he has to go back. In my volume *Psychological Types* (84), I tried to establish the general lines along which these one-sided developments move. There are two main attitudes which differ fundamentally, namely introversion and extraversion. Both are perfectly good ways of living, so long as they co-operate reasonably well. It is only a dominating one-sidedness that leads to disaster. Within this very general framework there are more subtle distinctions based upon whatever function is preferred by the individual. Thus somebody with a good brain will develop a powerful intellect at the expense of his feelings. Or again, the facts perceived by the realist will obliterate the beautiful visions of the intuitive. All such people will look back to childhood when they come to the end of their particular tether, or they will hanker for some state when they were still in touch with the lost world, or their dreams will reproduce enchanting memories of a past that has sunk into oblivion.

60   By adopting a more idealistic philosophy, one can interpret things differently and produce a perfectly decent and respectable psychology which is just as true, relatively speaking, as the sordid underside. I do not see why one should not interpret the facts in a decent and positive way when one can easily afford to do so. For many people this is much better and more encouraging than to reduce everything to primitive constitu-

ents with nasty names. But here too we must not be one-sided, because certain patients are all the better for being told some drastic but cleansing truth.

61   Freud's original idea of the unconscious was that it was a sort of receptacle or storehouse for repressed material, infantile wishes, and the like. But the unconscious is far more than that: it is the basis and precondition of all consciousness. It represents the unconscious functioning of the psyche in general. It is psychic life before, during, and after consciousness. And inasmuch as the newborn child is presented with a ready-made, highly developed brain which owes its differentiation to the accretions of untold centuries of ancestral life, the unconscious psyche must consist of inherited instincts, functions, and forms that are peculiar to the ancestral psyche. This collective heritage is by no means made up of inherited ideas, but rather of the possibilities of such ideas—in other words, of *a priori* categories of possible functioning. Such an inheritance could be called instinct, using the word in its original sense. But it is not quite so simple. On the contrary, it is a most intricate web of what I have called archetypal conditions. This implies the probability that a man will behave much as his ancestors behaved, right back to Methuselah. Thus the unconscious is seen as the collective predisposition to extreme conservatism, a guarantee, almost, that nothing new will ever happen.

62   If this statement were unreservedly true, there would be none of that creative fantasy which is responsible for radical changes and innovations. Therefore our statement must be in part erroneous, since creative fantasy exists and is not simply the prerogative of the unconscious psyche. Generally speaking, it is an intrusion from the realm of the unconscious, a sort of lucky hunch, different in kind from the slow reasoning of the conscious mind. Thus the unconscious is seen as a creative factor, even as a bold innovator, and yet it is at the same time the stronghold of ancestral conservatism. A paradox, I admit, but it cannot be helped. It is no more paradoxical than man himself and that cannot be helped either.

63   There are sound philosophical reasons why our arguments should end in paradox and why a paradoxical statement is the better witness to truth than a one-sided, so-called "positive"

statement. But this is not the place to embark on a lengthy logical discourse.

64   Now if you will bear in mind what we have just said about the significance of the unconscious, and if you will recall our discussion of the regressive tendency, you will discover a further and cogent reason why the patient should have such a tendency, and why he is quite justified in having it. To be retrospective and introspective is a pathological mistake only when it stops short at futilities like incest and other squalid fantasies, or at feelings of inferiority. Retrospection and introspection should be carried much further, because then the patient will not only discover the true reason for his childhood longings, but, going beyond himself into the sphere of the collective psyche, he will enter first into the treasure-house of collective ideas and then into creativity. In this way he will discover his identity with the whole of humanity, as it ever was, is, and ever shall be. He will add to his modest personal possessions which have proved themselves insufficient. Such acquisitions will strengthen his attitude, and this is the very reason why collective ideas have always been so important.

65   It looks as if Freud had got stuck in his own pessimism, clinging as he does to his thoroughly negative and personal conception of the unconscious. You get nowhere if you assume that the vital basis of man is nothing but a very personal and therefore very private *affaire scandaleuse*. This is utterly hopeless, and true only to the extent that a Strindberg drama is true. But pierce the veil of that sickly illusion, and you step out of your narrow, stuffy personal corner into the wide realm of the collective psyche, into the healthy and natural matrix of the human mind, into the very soul of humanity. That is the true foundation on which we can build a new and more workable attitude.

IV

THE AIMS OF PSYCHOTHERAPY [1]

66   It is generally agreed today that neuroses are functional psychic disturbances and are therefore to be cured preferably by psychological treatment. But when we come to the question of the structure of the neuroses and the principles of therapy, all agreement ends, and we have to acknowledge that we have as yet no fully satisfactory conception of the nature of the neuroses or of the principles of treatment. While it is true that two currents or schools of thought have gained a special hearing, they by no means exhaust the number of divergent opinions that actually exist. There are also numerous non-partisans who, amid the general conflict of opinion, have their own special views. If, therefore, we wanted to paint a comprehensive picture of this diversity, we should have to mix upon our palette all the hues and shadings of the rainbow. I would gladly paint such a picture if it lay within my power, for I have always felt the need for a conspectus of the many viewpoints. I have never succeeded in the long run in not giving divergent opinions their due. Such opinions could never arise, much less secure a following, if they did not correspond to some special disposition, some special character, some fundamental psychological fact that is more or less universal. Were we to exclude one such opinion as simply wrong and worthless, we should be rejecting this particular disposition or this particular fact as a misinterpretation—in other words, we should be doing violence to our own empirical material. The wide approval which greeted Freud's explanation of neurosis in terms of sexual causation and his view that the happenings in the psyche turn essentially upon infantile pleasure and its satisfaction should be instruc-

1 [Delivered as a lecture at a congress of the German Society for Psychotherapy, 1929. Published as "Ziele der Psychotherapie" in *Seelenprobleme der Gegenwart* (Zurich, 1931), pp. 87–114. Previously trans. by C. F. Baynes and W. S. Dell in *Modern Man in Search of a Soul* (London and New York, 1933).—EDITORS.]

tive to the psychologist. It shows him that this manner of thinking and feeling coincides with a fairly widespread trend or
spiritual current which, independently of Freud's theory, has
made itself felt in other places, in other circumstances, in other
minds, and in other forms. I should call it a manifestation of
the collective psyche. Let me remind you here of the works of
Havelock Ellis and Auguste Forel and the contributors to
Anthropophyteia; [2] then of the changed attitude to sex in Anglo-
Saxon countries during the post-Victorian period, and the broad
discussion of sexual matters in literature, which had already
started with the French realists. Freud is one of the exponents
of a contemporary psychological fact which has a special history
of its own; but for obvious reasons we cannot go into that here.

67   The acclaim which Adler, like Freud, has met with on both
sides of the Atlantic points similarly to the undeniable fact that,
for a great many people, the need for self-assertion arising from
a sense of inferiority is a plausible basis of explanation. Nor
can it be disputed that this view accounts for psychic actualities which are not given their due in the Freudian system. I
need hardly mention in detail the collective psychological forces
and social factors that favour the Adlerian view and make it
their theoretical exponent. These matters are sufficiently obvious.

68   It would be an unpardonable error to overlook the element
of truth in both the Freudian and the Adlerian viewpoints, but
it would be no less unpardonable to take either of them as the
sole truth. Both truths correspond to psychic realities. There
are in fact some cases which by and large can best be described
and explained by the one theory, and some by the other.

69   I can accuse neither of these two investigators of any fundamental error; on the contrary, I endeavour to apply both hypotheses as far as possible because I fully recognize their relative rightness. It would certainly never have occurred to me to
depart from Freud's path had I not stumbled upon facts which
forced me into modifications. And the same is true of my relation to the Adlerian viewpoint.

70   After what has been said it seems hardly necessary to add
that I hold the truth of my own deviationist views to be equally
relative, and feel myself so very much the mere exponent of
another disposition that I could almost say with Coleridge: "I

2 [Published at Leipzig, 1904–13.—EDITORS.]

believe in the one and only saving Church, of which at present I am the only member." [3]

71   It is in applied psychology, if anywhere, that we must be modest today and bear with an apparent plurality of contradictory opinions; for we are still far from having anything like a thorough knowledge of the human psyche, that most challenging field of scientific inquiry. At present we have merely more or less plausible opinions that cannot be squared with one another.

72   If, therefore, I undertake to say something about my views I hope I shall not be misunderstood. I am not advertising a novel truth, still less am I announcing a final gospel. I can only speak of attempts to throw light on psychic facts that are obscure to me, or of efforts to overcome therapeutic difficulties.

73   And it is just with this last point that I should like to begin, for here lies the most pressing need for modifications. As is well known, one can get along for quite a time with an inadequate theory, but not with inadequate therapeutic methods. In my psychotherapeutic practice of nearly thirty years I have met with a fair number of failures which made a far deeper impression on me than my successes. Anybody can have successes in psychotherapy, starting with the primitive medicine-man and faith-healer. The psychotherapist learns little or nothing from his successes, for they chiefly confirm him in his mistakes. But failures are priceless experiences because they not only open the way to a better truth but force us to modify our views and methods.

74   I certainly recognize how much my work has been furthered first by Freud and then by Adler, and in practice I try to acknowledge this debt by making use of their views, whenever possible, in the treatment of my patients. Nevertheless I must insist that I have experienced failures which, I felt, might have been avoided had I considered the facts that subsequently forced me to modify their views.

75   To describe all the situations I came up against is almost impossible, so I must content myself with singling out a few typical cases. It was with older patients that I had the greatest difficulties, that is, with persons over forty. In handling younger

3 [It has not been possible to trace this quotation and to find the original wording.—EDITORS.]

38

people I generally get along with the familiar viewpoints of Freud and Adler, for these tend to bring the patient to a certain level of adaptation and normality. Both views are eminently applicable to the young, apparently without leaving any disturbing after-effects. In my experience this is not so often the case with older people. It seems to me that the basic facts of the psyche undergo a very marked alteration in the course of life, so much so that we could almost speak of a psychology of life's morning and a psychology of its afternoon. As a rule, the life of a young person is characterized by a general expansion and a striving towards concrete ends; and his neurosis seems mainly to rest on his hesitation or shrinking back from this necessity. But the life of an older person is characterized by a contraction of forces, by the affirmation of what has been achieved, and by the curtailment of further growth. His neurosis comes mainly from his clinging to a youthful attitude which is now out of season. Just as the young neurotic is afraid of life, so the older one shrinks back from death. What was a normal goal for the young man becomes a neurotic hindrance to the old—just as, through his hesitation to face the world, the young neurotic's originally normal dependence on his parents grows into an incest-relationship that is inimical to life. It is natural that neurosis, resistance, repression, transference, "guiding fictions," and so forth should have one meaning in the young person and quite another in the old, despite apparent similarities. The aims of therapy should undoubtedly be modified to meet this fact. Hence the age of the patient seems to me a most important *indicium*.

76   But there are various *indicia* also within the youthful phase of life. Thus, in my estimation, it is a technical blunder to apply the Freudian viewpoint to a patient with the Adlerian type of psychology, that is, an unsuccessful person with an infantile need to assert himself. Conversely, it would be a gross misunderstanding to force the Adlerian viewpoint on a successful man with a pronounced pleasure-principle psychology. When in a quandary the resistances of the patient may be valuable signposts. I am inclined to take deep-seated resistances seriously at first, paradoxical as this may sound, for I am convinced that the doctor does not necessarily know better than the patient's own psychic constitution, of which the patient himself may be

quite unconscious. This modesty on the part of the doctor is altogether becoming in view of the fact that there is not only no generally valid psychology today but rather an untold variety of temperaments and of more or less individual psyches that refuse to fit into any scheme.

77   You know that in this matter of temperament I postulate two different basic attitudes in accordance with the typical differences already suspected by many students of human nature—namely, the extraverted and the introverted attitudes. These attitudes, too, I take to be important *indicia*, and likewise the predominance of one particular psychic function over the others.[4]

78   The extraordinary diversity of individual life necessitates constant modifications of theory which are often applied quite unconsciously by the doctor himself, although in principle they may not accord at all with his theoretical creed.

79   While we are on this question of temperament I should not omit to mention that there are some people whose attitude is essentially spiritual and others whose attitude is essentially materialistic. It must not be imagined that such an attitude is acquired accidentally or springs from mere misunderstanding. Very often they are ingrained passions which no criticism and no persuasion can stamp out; there are even cases where an apparently outspoken materialism has its source in a denial of religious temperament. Cases of the reverse type are more easily credited today, although they are not more frequent than the others. This too is an *indicium* which in my opinion ought not to be overlooked.

80   When we use the word *indicium* it might appear to mean, as is usual in medical parlance, that this or that treatment is indicated. Perhaps this should be the case, but psychotherapy has at present reached no such degree of certainty—for which reason our *indicia* are unfortunately not much more than warnings against one-sidedness.

81   The human psyche is a thing of enormous ambiguity. In every single case we have to ask ourselves whether an attitude or a so-called *habitus* is authentic, or whether it may not be just a compensation for its opposite. I must confess that I have so often been deceived in this matter that in any concrete case

4 [Viz., thinking, feeling, sensation, and intuition.—EDITORS.]

I am at pains to avoid all theoretical presuppositions about the structure of the neurosis and about what the patient can and ought to do. As far as possible I let pure experience decide the therapeutic aims. This may perhaps seem strange, because it is commonly supposed that the therapist has an aim. But in psychotherapy it seems to me positively advisable for the doctor not to have too fixed an aim. He can hardly know better than the nature and will to live of the patient. The great decisions in human life usually have far more to do with the instincts and other mysterious unconscious factors than with conscious will and well-meaning reasonableness. The shoe that fits one person pinches another; there is no universal recipe for living. Each of us carries his own life-form within him—an irrational form which no other can outbid.

82 All this naturally does not prevent us from doing our utmost to make the patient normal and reasonable. If the therapeutic results are satisfactory, we can probably let it go at that. If not, then for better or worse the therapist must be guided by the patient's own irrationalities. Here we must follow nature as a guide, and what the doctor then does is less a question of treatment than of developing the creative possibilities latent in the patient himself.

83 What I have to say begins where the treatment leaves off and this development sets in. Thus my contribution to psychotherapy confines itself to those cases where rational treatment does not yield satisfactory results. The clinical material at my disposal is of a peculiar composition: new cases are decidedly in the minority. Most of them already have some form of psychotherapeutic treatment behind them, with partial or negative results. About a third of my cases are not suffering from any clinically definable neurosis, but from the senselessness and aimlessness of their lives. I should not object if this were called the general neurosis of our age. Fully two thirds of my patients are in the second half of life.

84 This peculiar material sets up a special resistance to rational methods of treatment, probably because most of my patients are socially well-adapted individuals, often of outstanding ability, to whom normalization means nothing. As for so-called normal people, there I really am in a fix, for I have no ready-made philosophy of life to hand out to them. In the majority

of my cases the resources of the conscious mind are exhausted
(or, in ordinary English, they are "stuck"). It is chiefly this
fact that forces me to look for hidden possibilities. For I do not
know what to say to the patient when he asks me, "What do
you advise? What shall I do?" I don't know either. I only know
one thing: when my conscious mind no longer sees any possible road ahead and consequently gets stuck, my unconscious
psyche will react to the unbearable standstill.

85   This "getting stuck" is a psychic occurrence so often repeated during the course of human history that it has become
the theme of many myths and fairytales. We are told of the
Open sesame! to the locked door, or of some helpful animal
who finds the hidden way. In other words, getting stuck is a
typical event which, in the course of time, has evoked typical
reactions and compensations. We may therefore expect with
some probability that something similar will appear in the reactions of the unconscious, as, for example, in dreams.

86   In such cases, then, my attention is directed more particularly to dreams. This is not because I am tied to the notion
that dreams must always be called to the rescue, or because I
possess a mysterious dream-theory which tells me how everything must shape itself; but quite simply from perplexity. I
do not know where else to go for help, and so I try to find it
in dreams. These at least present us with images pointing to
something or other, and that is better than nothing. I have no
theory about dreams, I do not know how dreams arise. And I
am not at all sure that my way of handling dreams even deserves the name of a "method." I share all your prejudices
against dream-interpretation as the quintessence of uncertainty
and arbitrariness. On the other hand, I know that if we medi-
tate on a dream sufficiently long and thoroughly, if we carry
it around with us and turn it over and over, something almost
always comes of it. This something is not of course a scientific
result to be boasted about or rationalized; but it is an important
practical hint which shows the patient what the unconscious is
aiming at. Indeed, it ought not to matter to me whether the result of my musings on the dream is scientifically verifiable or
tenable, otherwise I am pursuing an ulterior—and therefore
autoerotic—aim. I must content myself wholly with the fact that
the result means something to the patient and sets his life in

motion again. I may allow myself only one criterion for the
result of my labours: Does it work? As for my scientific hobby—
my desire to know *why* it works—this I must reserve for my
spare time.

87   Infinitely varied are the contents of the initial dreams, that
is, the dreams that come at the outset of the treatment. In many
cases they point directly to the past and recall things lost and
forgotten. For very often the standstill and disorientation arise
when life has become one-sided, and this may, in psychological
terms, cause a sudden loss of libido. All our previous activities
become uninteresting, even senseless, and our aims suddenly
no longer worth striving for. What in one person is merely a
passing mood may in another become a chronic condition. In
these cases it often happens that other possibilities for developing
the personality lie buried somewhere or other in the past, unknown to anybody, not even to the patient. But the dream may
reveal the clue.

88   In other cases the dream points to present facts, for example marriage or social position, which the conscious mind has
never accepted as sources of problems or conflicts.

89   Both possibilities come within the sphere of the rational, and
I daresay I would have no difficulty in making such initial
dreams seem plausible. The real difficulty begins when the
dreams do not point to anything tangible, and this they do
often enough, especially when they hold anticipations of the future. I do not mean that such dreams are necessarily prophetic,
merely that they feel the way, they "reconnoitre." These dreams
contain inklings of possibilities and for that reason can never
be made plausible to an outsider. Sometimes they are not plausible even to me, and then I usually say to the patient, "I don't
believe it, but follow up the clue." As I have said, the sole criterion is the stimulating effect, but it is by no means necessary
for me to understand why such an effect takes place.

90   This is particularly true of dreams that contain something
like an "unconscious metaphysics," by which I mean mythological analogies that are sometimes incredibly strange and
baffling.

91   Now, you will certainly protest: How on earth can I know
that the dreams contain anything like an unconscious metaphysics? And here I must confess that I do not really know. I

know far too little about dreams for that. I see only the effect on the patient, of which I would like to give you a little example.

92   In a long initial dream of one of my "normal" patients, the illness of his sister's child played an important part. She was a little girl of two.

93   Some time before, this sister had in fact lost a boy through illness, but otherwise none of her children was ill. The occurrence of the sick child in the dream at first proved baffling to the dreamer, probably because it failed to fit the facts. Since there was no direct and intimate connection between the dreamer and his sister, he could feel in this image little that was personal to him. Then he suddenly remembered that two years earlier he had taken up the study of occultism, in the course of which he also discovered psychology. So the child evidently represented his interest in the psyche—an idea I should never have arrived at of my own accord. Seen purely theoretically, this dream image can mean anything or nothing. For that matter, does a thing or a fact ever mean anything in itself? The only certainty is that it is always man who interprets, who assigns meaning. And that is the gist of the matter for psychology. It impressed the dreamer as a novel and interesting idea that the study of occultism might have something sickly about it. Somehow the thought struck home. And this is the decisive point: the interpretation works, however we may elect to account for its working. For the dreamer the thought was an implied criticism, and through it a certain change of attitude was brought about. By such slight changes, which one could never think up rationally, things are set in motion and the dead point is overcome, at least in principle.

94   From this example I could say figuratively that the dream meant that there was something sickly about the dreamer's occult studies, and in this sense—since the dream brought him to such an idea—I can also speak of "unconscious metaphysics."

95   But I go still further: Not only do I give the patient an opportunity to find associations to his dreams, I give myself the same opportunity. Further, I present him with my ideas and opinions. If, in so doing, I open the door to "suggestion," I see no occasion for regret; for it is well known that we are susceptible only to those suggestions with which we are already se-

44

cretly in accord. No harm is done if now and then one goes astray in this riddle-reading: sooner or later the psyche will reject the mistake, much as the organism rejects a foreign body. I do not need to prove that my interpretation of the dream is right (a pretty hopeless undertaking anyway), but must simply try to discover, with the patient, what *acts* for him—I am almost tempted to say, what is actual.

96   For this reason it is particularly important for me to know as much as possible about primitive psychology, mythology, archaeology, and comparative religion, because these fields offer me invaluable analogies with which I can enrich the associations of my patients. Together, we can then find meaning in apparent irrelevancies and thus vastly increase the effectiveness of the dream. For the layman who has done his utmost in the personal and rational sphere of life and yet has found no meaning and no satisfaction there, it is enormously important to be able to enter a sphere of irrational experience. In this way, too, the habitual and the commonplace come to wear an altered countenance, and can even acquire a new glamour. For it all depends on how we look at things, and not on how they are in themselves. The least of things with a meaning is always worth more in life than the greatest of things without it.

97   I do not think I underestimate the risk of this undertaking. It is as if one began to build a bridge out into space. Indeed, the ironist might even allege—and has often done so—that in following this procedure both doctor and patient are indulging in mere fantasy-spinning.

98   This objection is no counter-argument, but is very much to the point. I even make an effort to second the patient in his fantasies. Truth to tell, I have no small opinion of fantasy. To me, it is the maternally creative side of the masculine mind. When all is said and done, we can never rise above fantasy. It is true that there are unprofitable, futile, morbid, and unsatisfying fantasies whose sterile nature is immediately recognized by every person endowed with common sense; but the faulty performance proves nothing against the normal performance. All the works of man have their origin in creative imagination. What right, then, have we to disparage fantasy? In the normal course of things, fantasy does not easily go astray; it is too deep for that, and too closely bound up with the tap-root

45

of human and animal instinct. It has a surprising way of always coming out right in the end. The creative activity of imagination frees man from his bondage to the "nothing but" [5] and raises him to the status of one who plays. As Schiller says, man is completely human only when he is at play.

99   My aim is to bring about a psychic state in which my patient begins to experiment with his own nature—a state of fluidity, change, and growth where nothing is eternally fixed and hopelessly petrified. I can here of course adumbrate only the principles of my technique. Those of you who happen to be acquainted with my works can easily imagine the necessary parallels. I would only like to emphasize that you should not think of my procedure as entirely without aim or limit. In handling a dream or fantasy I make it a rule never to go beyond the meaning which is effective for the patient; I merely try to make him as fully conscious of this meaning as possible, so that he shall also become aware of its supra-personal connections. For, when something happens to a man and he supposes it to be personal only to him, whereas in reality it is a quite universal experience, then his attitude is obviously wrong, that is, too personal, and it tends to exclude him from human society. By the same token we need to have not only a personal, contemporary consciousness, but also a supra-personal consciousness with a sense of historical continuity. However abstract this may sound, practical experience shows that many neuroses are caused primarily by the fact that people blind themselves to their own religious promptings because of a childish passion for rational enlightenment. It is high time the psychologist of today recognized that we are no longer dealing with dogmas and creeds but with the religious attitude *per se,* whose importance as a psychic function can hardly be overrated. And it is precisely for the religious function that the sense of historical continuity is indispensable.

100   Coming back to the question of my technique, I ask myself how far I am indebted to Freud for its existence. At all

5 [The term "nothing but" (*nichts als*) occurs frequently in Jung, and is used to denote the common habit of explaining something unknown by reducing it to something apparently known and thereby devaluing it. For instance, when a certain illness is said to be "nothing but psychic," it is explained as imaginary and is thus devalued.—EDITORS.]

events I learned it from Freud's method of free association, and
I regard it as a direct extension of that.

101 So long as I help the patient to discover the effective elements in his dreams, and so long as I try to get him to see the
general meaning of his symbols, he is still, psychologically
speaking, in a state of childhood. For the time being he is dependent on his dreams and is always asking himself whether
the next dream will give him new light or not. Moreover, he is
dependent on my having ideas about his dreams and on my
ability to increase his insight through my knowledge. Thus he
is still in an undesirably passive condition where everything
is rather uncertain and questionable; neither he nor I know
the journey's end. Often it is not much more than a groping
about in Egyptian darkness. In this condition we must not expect any very startling results—the uncertainty is too great for
that. Besides which there is always the risk that what we have
woven by day the night will unravel. The danger is that nothing permanent is achieved, that nothing remains fixed. It not
infrequently happens in these situations that the patient has
a particularly vivid or curious dream, and says to me, "Do
you know, if only I were a painter I would make a picture of
it." Or the dreams are about photographs, paintings, drawings,
or illuminated manuscripts, or even about the films.

102 I have turned these hints to practical account, urging my
patients at such times to paint in reality what they have seen
in dream or fantasy. As a rule I am met with the objection,
"But I am not a painter!" To this I usually reply that neither
are modern painters, and that consequently modern painting
is free for all, and that anyhow it is not a question of beauty
but only of the trouble one takes with the picture. How true
this is I saw recently in the case of a talented professional por-
traitist; she had to begin my way of painting all over again with
pitiably childish efforts, literally as if she had never held a
brush in her hand. To paint what we see before us is a different
art from painting what we see within.

103 Many of my more advanced patients, then, begin to paint.
I can well understand that everyone will be profoundly impressed with the utter futility of this sort of dilettantism. Do not
forget, however, that we are speaking not of people who still
have to prove their social usefulness, but of those who can no

47

longer see any sense in being socially useful and who have come upon the deeper and more dangerous question of the meaning of their own individual lives. To be a particle in the mass has meaning and charm only for the man who has not yet reached that stage, but none for the man who is sick to death of being a particle. The importance of what life means to the individual may be denied by those who are socially below the general level of adaptation, and is invariably denied by the educator whose ambition it is to breed mass-men. But those who belong to neither category will sooner or later come up against this painful question.

104   Although my patients occasionally produce artistically beautiful things that might very well be shown in modern "art" exhibitions, I nevertheless treat them as completely worthless when judged by the canons of real art. As a matter of fact, it is essential that they should be considered worthless, otherwise my patients might imagine themselves to be artists, and the whole point of the exercise would be missed. It is not a question of art at all—or rather, it should not be a question of art—but of something more and other than mere art, namely the living effect upon the patient himself. The meaning of individual life, whose importance from the social standpoint is negligible, stands here at its highest, and for its sake the patient struggles to give form, however crude and childish, to the inexpressible.

105   But why do I encourage patients, when they arrive at a certain stage in their development, to express themselves by means of brush, pencil, or pen at all?

106   Here again my prime purpose is to produce an effect. In the state of psychological childhood described above, the patient remains passive; but now he begins to play an active part. To start off with, he puts down on paper what he has passively seen, thereby turning it into a deliberate act. He not only talks about it, he is actually doing something about it. Psychologically speaking, it makes a vast difference whether a man has an interesting conversation with his doctor two or three times a week, the results of which are left hanging in mid air, or whether he has to struggle for hours with refractory brush and colours, only to produce in the end something which, taken at its face value, is perfectly senseless. If it were really senseless to

him, the effort to paint it would be so repugnant that he could scarcely be brought to perform this exercise a second time. But because his fantasy does not strike him as entirely senseless, his busying himself with it only increases its effect upon him. Moreover, the concrete shaping of the image enforces a continuous study of it in all its parts, so that it can develop its effects to the full. This invests the bare fantasy with an element of reality, which lends it greater weight and greater driving power. And these rough-and-ready pictures do indeed produce effects which, I must admit, are rather difficult to describe. For instance, a patient needs only to have seen once or twice how much he is freed from a wretched state of mind by working at a symbolical picture, and he will always turn to this means of release whenever things go badly with him. In this way something of inestimable importance is won—the beginning of independence, a step towards psychological maturity. The patient can make himself creatively independent through this method, if I may call it such. He is no longer dependent on his dreams or on his doctor's knowledge; instead, by painting himself he gives shape to himself. For what he paints are active fantasies—that which is active within him. And that which is active within is himself, but no longer in the guise of his previous error, when he mistook the personal ego for the self; it is himself in a new and hitherto alien sense, for his ego now appears as the object of that which works within him. In countless pictures he strives to catch this interior agent, only to discover in the end that it is eternally unknown and alien, the hidden foundation of psychic life.

107   It is impossible for me to describe the extent to which this discovery changes the patient's standpoint and values, and how it shifts the centre of gravity of his personality. It is as though the earth had suddenly discovered that the sun was the centre of the planetary orbits and of its own earthly orbit as well.

108   But have we not always known this to be so? I myself believe that we have always known it. But I may know something with my head which the other man in me is far from knowing, for indeed and in truth I live as though I did not know it. Most of my patients knew the deeper truth, but did not live it. And why did they not live it? Because of that bias which makes us

49

all live from the ego, a bias which comes from overvaluation of the conscious mind.

109   It is of the greatest importance for the young person, who is still unadapted and has as yet achieved nothing, to shape his conscious ego as effectively as possible, that is, to educate his will. Unless he is a positive genius he cannot, indeed he should not, believe in anything active within him that is not identical with his will. He must feel himself a man of will, and may safely depreciate everything else in him and deem it subject to his will, for without this illusion he could not succeed in adapting himself socially.

110   It is otherwise with a person in the second half of life who no longer needs to educate his conscious will, but who, to understand the meaning of his individual life, needs to experience his own inner being. Social usefulness is no longer an aim for him, although he does not deny its desirability. Fully aware as he is of the social unimportance of his creative activity, he feels it more as a way of working at himself to his own benefit. Increasingly, too, this activity frees him from morbid dependence, and he thus acquires an inner stability and a new trust in himself. These last achievements now redound to the good of the patient's social existence; for an inwardly stable and self-confident person will prove more adequate to his social tasks than one who is on a bad footing with his unconscious.

111   I have purposely avoided loading my lecture with theory, hence much must remain obscure and unexplained. But, in order to make the pictures produced by my patients intelligible, certain theoretical points must at least receive mention. A feature common to all these pictures is a primitive symbolism which is conspicuous both in the drawing and in the colouring. The colours are as a rule quite barbaric in their intensity. Often an unmistakable archaic quality is present. These peculiarities point to the nature of the underlying creative forces. They are irrational, symbolistic currents that run through the whole history of mankind, and are so archaic in character that it is not difficult to find their parallels in archaeology and comparative religion. We may therefore take it that our pictures spring chiefly from those regions of the psyche which I have termed the collective unconscious. By this I understand an unconscious psychic functioning common to all men, the source

not only of our modern symbolical pictures but of all similar products in the past. Such pictures spring from, and satisfy, a natural need. It is as if a part of the psyche that reaches far back into the primitive past were expressing itself in these pictures and finding it possible to function in harmony with our alien conscious mind. This collaboration satisfies and thus mitigates the psyche's disturbing demands upon the latter. It must, however, be added that the mere execution of the pictures is not enough. Over and above that, an intellectual and emotional understanding is needed; they require to be not only rationally integrated with the conscious mind, but morally assimilated. They still have to be subjected to a work of synthetic interpretation. Although I have travelled this path with individual patients many times, I have never yet succeeded in making all the details of the process clear enough for publication. So far this has been fragmentary only. The truth is, we are here moving in absolutely new territory, and a ripening of experience is the first requisite. For very important reasons I am anxious to avoid hasty conclusions. We are dealing with a process of psychic life outside consciousness, and our observation of it is indirect. As yet we do not know to what depths our vision will plumb. It would seem to be some kind of centring process, for a great many pictures which the patients themselves feel to be decisive point in this direction. During this centring process what we call the ego appears to take up a peripheral position. The change is apparently brought about by an emergence of the historical part of the psyche. Exactly what is the purpose of this process remains at first sight obscure. We can only remark its important effect on the conscious personality. From the fact that the change heightens the feeling for life and maintains the flow of life, we must conclude that it is animated by a peculiar purposefulness. We might perhaps call this a new illusion. But what is "illusion"? By what criterion do we judge something to be an illusion? Does anything exist for the psyche that we are entitled to call illusion? What we are pleased to call illusion may be for the psyche an extremely important life-factor, something as indispensable as oxygen for the body—a psychic actuality of overwhelming significance. Presumably the psyche does not trouble itself about our categories of reality; for it, everything that *works* is real. The investigator of the psyche must not confuse it with his consciousness, else he veils from his sight the object of his investigation. On the contrary, to recognize it at all, he must learn to see how different it is from consciousness. Nothing is more probable than that what we call illusion is very real for the psyche—for which reason we cannot take psychic reality to be commensurable with conscious reality. To the psychologist there is nothing more fatuous than the attitude of the missionary who pronounces the gods of the "poor heathen" to be mere illusion. Unfortunately we still go blundering along in the same dogmatic way, as though *our* so-called reality were not equally full of illusion. In psychic life, as everywhere in our experience, all things that work are reality, regardless of the names man chooses to bestow on them. To take these realities for what they are—not foisting other names on them—that is our business. To the psyche, spirit is no less spirit for being named sexuality.

112   I must repeat that these designations and the changes rung upon them never even remotely touch the essence of the process we have described. It cannot be compassed by the rational concepts of the conscious mind, any more than life itself; and it is for this reason that my patients consistently turn to the representation and interpretation of symbols as the more adequate and effective course.

113   With this I have said pretty well everything I can say about my therapeutic aims and intentions within the broad framework of a lecture. It can be no more than an incentive to thought, and I shall be quite content if such it has been.

V

PROBLEMS OF MODERN PSYCHOTHERAPY [1]

114   Psychotherapy, or the treatment of the mind by psychological methods, is today identified in popular thought with "psychoanalysis."

115   The word "psychoanalysis" has become so much a part of common speech that everyone who uses it seems to understand what it means. But what the word actually connotes is unknown to most laymen. According to the intention of its creator, Freud, it can be appropriately applied only to the method, inaugurated by himself, of reducing psychic symptoms and complexes to certain repressed impulses; and in so far as this procedure is not possible without the corresponding points of view, the idea of psychoanalysis also includes certain theoretical assumptions, formulated as the Freudian theory of sexuality expressly insisted upon by its author. But, Freud notwithstanding, the layman employs the term "psychoanalysis" loosely for all modern attempts whatsoever to probe the mind by scientific methods. Thus Adler's school must submit to being labelled "psychoanalytic" despite the fact that Adler's viewpoint and method are apparently in irreconcilable opposition to those of Freud. In consequence, Adler does not call his psychology "psychoanalysis" but "individual psychology"; while I prefer to call my own approach "analytical psychology." by which I mean something like a general concept embracing both psychoanalysis and individual psychology as well as other endeavours in the field of "complex psychology."

116   Since, however, there is but one mind, or one psyche, in man, it might seem to the layman that there can be only one psychology, and he might therefore suppose these distinctions to be either subjective quibbles or the commonplace attempts

1 [Published as "Die Probleme der modernen Psychotherapie" in *Schweizerisches Medizinisches Jahrbuch,* 1929, and in *Seelenprobleme der Gegenwart* (Zurich, 1931), pp. 1–39. Previously trans. by C. F. Baynes and W. S. Dell in *Modern Man in Search of a Soul* (London and New York, 1933).—EDITORS.]

of small-minded persons to set themselves up on little thrones. I could easily lengthen the list of "psychologies" by mentioning other systems not included under "analytical psychology." There are in fact many different methods, standpoints, views, and beliefs which are all at war with one another, chiefly because they all misunderstand one another and refuse to give one another their due. The many-sidedness, the diversity, of psychological opinions in our day is nothing less than astonishing, not to say confusing for the layman.

117   If, in a text-book of pathology, we find numerous remedies of the most diverse kind prescribed for a given disease, we may safely conclude that none of these remedies is particularly efficacious. So, when many different ways of approaching the psyche are recommended, we may rest assured that none of them leads with absolute certainty to the goal, least of all those advocated with fanaticism. The very number of present-day psychologies is a confession of perplexity. The difficulty of gaining access to the psyche is gradually being borne in upon us, and the psyche itself is seen to be a "horned problem," to use Nietzsche's expression. It is small wonder therefore that efforts to attack this elusive riddle keep on multiplying, first from one side and then from another. The variety of contradictory standpoints and opinions is the inevitable result.

118   The reader will doubtless agree that in speaking of psychoanalysis we should not confine ourselves to its narrower connotation, but should deal in general with the successes and failures of the various contemporary endeavours, which we sum up under the term "analytical psychology," to solve the problem of the psyche.

119   But why this sudden interest in the human psyche as a datum of experience? For thousands of years it was not so. I wish merely to raise this apparently irrelevant question, not to answer it. In reality it is not irrelevant, because the impulses at the back of our present-day interest in psychology have a sort of subterranean connection with this question.

120   All that now passes under the layman's idea of "psychoanalysis" has its origin in medical practice; consequently most of it is medical psychology. This psychology bears the unmistakable stamp of the doctor's consulting-room, as can be seen not only in its terminology but also in its theoretical set-up.

54

Everywhere we come across assumptions which the doctor has taken over from natural science and biology. It is this that has largely contributed to the divorce between modern psychology and the academic or humane sciences, for psychology explains things in terms of irrational nature, whereas the latter studies are grounded in the intellect. The distance between mind and nature, difficult to bridge at best, is still further increased by a medical and biological nomenclature which often strikes us as thoroughly mechanical, and more often than not severely overtaxes the best-intentioned understanding.

121   Having expressed the hope that the foregoing general remarks may not be out of place in view of the confusion of terms existing in this field, I should now like to turn to the real task in hand and scrutinize the achievements of analytical psychology.

122   Since the endeavours of our psychology are so extraordinarily heterogeneous, it is only with the greatest difficulty that we can take up a broadly inclusive standpoint. If, therefore, I try to divide the aims and results of these endeavours into certain classes, or rather stages, I do so with the express reservation appropriate to a purely provisional undertaking which, it may be objected, is just as arbitrary as the surveyor's triangulation of a landscape. Be that as it may, I would venture to regard the sum total of our findings under the aspect of four stages, namely, confession, elucidation, education, and transformation. I shall now proceed to discuss these somewhat unusual terms.

123   The first beginnings of all analytical treatment of the soul are to be found in its prototype, the confessional. Since, however, the two have no direct causal connection, but rather grow from a common irrational psychic root, it is difficult for an outsider to see at once the relation between the groundwork of psychoanalysis and the religious institution of the confessional.

124   Once the human mind had succeeded in inventing the idea of sin, man had recourse to psychic concealment; or, in analytical parlance, repression arose. Anything concealed is a secret. The possession of secrets acts like a psychic poison that alienates their possessor from the community. In small doses, this poison may be an invaluable medicament, even an essential pre-condition of individual differentiation, so much so that even on the primitive level man feels an irresistible need actu-

ally to invent secrets: their possession safeguards him from dissolving in the featureless flow of unconscious community life and thus from deadly peril to his soul. It is a well known fact that the widespread and very ancient rites of initiation with their mystery cults subserved this instinct for differentiation. Even the Christian sacraments were looked upon as "mysteries" in the early Church, and, as in the case of baptism, were celebrated in secluded spots and only mentioned under the veil of allegory.

125   A secret shared with several persons is as beneficial as a merely private secret is destructive. The latter works like a burden of guilt, cutting off the unfortunate possessor from communion with his fellows. But, if we are conscious of what we are concealing, the harm done is decidedly less than if we do not know what we are repressing—or even that we have repressions at all. In this case the hidden content is no longer consciously kept secret; we are concealing it even from ourselves. It then splits off from the conscious mind as an independent complex and leads a sort of separate existence in the unconscious psyche, where it can be neither interfered with nor corrected by the conscious mind. The complex forms, so to speak, a miniature self-contained psyche which, as experience shows, develops a peculiar fantasy-life of its own. What we call fantasy is simply spontaneous psychic activity, and it wells up wherever the inhibitive action of the conscious mind abates or, as in sleep, ceases altogether. In sleep, fantasy takes the form of dreams. But in waking life, too, we continue to dream beneath the threshold of consciousness, especially when under the influence of repressed or other unconscious complexes. Incidentally, unconscious contents are on no account composed exclusively of complexes that were once conscious and subsequently became unconscious by being repressed. The unconscious, too, has its own specific contents which push up from unknown depths and gradually reach consciousness. Hence we should in no wise picture the unconscious psyche as a mere receptacle for contents discarded by the conscious mind.

126   All unconscious contents, which either approach the threshold of consciousness from below, or have sunk only slightly beneath it, affect the conscious mind. Since the content does not appear as such in consciousness, these effects are necessarily indirect. Most of our "lapses" are traceable to such disturb-

ances, as are all neurotic symptoms, which are nearly always, in medical parlance, of a psychogenic nature, the exceptions being shock effects (shell-shock and the like). The mildest forms of neurosis are the lapses of consciousness mentioned above— e.g., slips of the tongue, suddenly forgetting names and dates, inadvertent clumsiness leading to injuries and accidents, misunderstandings and so-called hallucinations of memory, as when we think we have said something or done something, or faulty apprehension of things heard and said, and so on.

127   In all these instances a thorough investigation can show the existence of some content which, in an indirect and unconscious way, is distorting the performance of the conscious mind.

128   Generally speaking, therefore, an unconscious secret is more injurious than a conscious one. I have seen many patients who, as a result of difficult circumstances that might well have driven weaker natures to suicide, sometimes developed a suicidal tendency but, because of their inherent reasonableness, prevented it from becoming conscious and in this way generated an unconscious suicide-complex. This unconscious urge to suicide then engineered all kinds of dangerous accidents —as, for instance, a sudden attack of giddiness on some exposed place, hesitation in front of a motor-car, mistaking corrosive sublimate for cough mixture, a sudden zest for dangerous acrobatics, and so forth. When it was possible to make the suicidal leaning conscious in these cases, common sense could intervene as a salutary check: the patients could then consciously recognize and avoid the situations that tempted them to self-destruction.

129   All personal secrets, therefore, have the effect of sin or guilt, whether or not they are, from the standpoint of popular morality, wrongful secrets.

130   Another form of concealment is the act of holding something back. What we usually hold back are emotions or affects. Here too it must be stressed that self-restraint is healthy and beneficial; it may even be a virtue. That is why we find self-discipline to be one of the earliest moral arts even among primitive peoples, where it has its place in the initiation ceremonies, chiefly in the form of ascetic continence and the stoical endurance of pain and fear. Self-restraint is here practised within

a secret society as an undertaking shared with others. But if self-restraint is only a personal matter, unconnected with any religious views, it may become as injurious as the personal secret. Hence the well-known bad moods and irritability of the over-virtuous. The affect withheld is likewise something we conceal, something we can hide even from ourselves—an art in which men particularly excel, while women, with very few exceptions, are by nature averse to doing such injury to their affects. When an affect is withheld it is just as isolating and just as disturbing in its effects as the unconscious secret, and just as guilt-laden. In the same way that nature seems to bear us a grudge if we have the advantage of a secret over the rest of humanity, so she takes it amiss if we withhold our emotions from our fellow men. Nature decidedly abhors a vacuum in this respect; hence there is nothing more unendurable in the long run than a tepid harmony based on the withholding of affects. The repressed emotions are often of a kind we wish to keep secret. But more often there is no secret worth mentioning, only emotions which have become unconscious through being withheld at some critical juncture.

131   The respective predominance of secrets or of inhibited emotions is probably responsible for the different forms of neurosis. At any rate the hysterical subject who is very free with his emotions is generally the possessor of a secret, while the hardened psychasthenic suffers from emotional indigestion.

132   To cherish secrets and hold back emotion is a psychic misdemeanour for which nature finally visits us with sickness—that is, when we do these things in private. But when they are done in communion with others they satisfy nature and may even count as useful virtues. It is only restraint practised for oneself alone that is unwholesome. It is as if man had an inalienable right to behold all that is dark, imperfect, stupid, and guilty in his fellow men—for such, of course, are the things we keep secret in order to protect ourselves. It seems to be a sin in the eyes of nature to hide our inferiority—just as much as to live entirely on our inferior side. There would appear to be a sort of conscience in mankind which severely punishes every one who does not somehow and at some time, at whatever cost to his virtuous pride, cease to defend and assert himself, and instead confess himself fallible and human. Until he can do

this, an impenetrable wall shuts him off from the vital feeling that he is a man among other men.

133   This explains the extraordinary significance of genuine, straightforward confession—a truth that was probably known to all the initiation rites and mystery cults of the ancient world. There is a saying from the Greek mysteries: "Give up what thou hast, and then thou wilt receive."

134   We may well take this saying as a motto for the first stage in psychotherapeutic treatment. The beginnings of psychoanalysis are in fact nothing else than the scientific rediscovery of an ancient truth; even the name that was given to the earliest method—catharsis, or cleansing—is a familiar term in the classical rites of initiation. The early cathartic method consisted in putting the patient, with or without the paraphernalia of hypnosis, in touch with the hinterland of his mind, hence into that state which the yoga systems of the East describe as meditation or contemplation. In contrast to yoga, however, the aim here is to observe the sporadic emergence, whether in the form of images or of feelings, of those dim representations which detach themselves in the darkness from the invisible realm of the unconscious and move as shadows before the inturned gaze. In this way things repressed and forgotten come back again. This is a gain in itself, though often a painful one, for the inferior and even the worthless belongs to me as my shadow and gives me substance and mass. How can I be substantial without casting a shadow? I must have a dark side too if I am to be whole; and by becoming conscious of my shadow I remember once more that I am a human being like any other. At any rate, if this rediscovery of my own wholeness remains private, it will only restore the earlier condition from which the neurosis, i.e., the split-off complex, sprang. Privacy prolongs my isolation and the damage is only partially mended. But through confession I throw myself into the arms of humanity again, freed at last from the burden of moral exile. The goal of the cathartic method is full confession—not merely the intellectual recognition of the facts with the head, but their confirmation by the heart and the actual release of suppressed emotion.

135   As may easily be imagined, the effect of such a confession on simple souls is very great, and its curative results are often astonishing. Yet I would not wish to see the main achievement

59

of our psychology at this stage merely in the fact that some sufferers are cured, but rather in the systematic emphasis it lays upon the significance of confession. For this concerns us all. All of us are somehow divided by our secrets, but instead of seeking to cross the gulf on the firm bridge of confession, we choose the treacherous makeshift of opinion and illusion.

136   Now I am far from wishing to enunciate a general maxim. It would be difficult to imagine anything more unsavoury than a wholesale confession of sin. Psychology simply establishes the fact that we have here a sore spot of first-rate importance. As the next stage, the stage of elucidation, will make clear, it cannot be tackled directly, because it is a problem with quite particularly pointed horns.

137   It is of course obvious that the new psychology would have remained at the stage of confession had catharsis proved itself a panacea. First and foremost, however, it is not always possible to bring the patients close enough to the unconscious for them to perceive the shadows. On the contrary, many of them—and for the most part complicated, highly conscious persons—are so firmly anchored in consciousness that nothing can pry them loose. They develop the most violent resistances to any attempt to push consciousness aside; they want to talk with the doctor on the conscious plane and go into a rational explanation and discussion of their difficulties. They have quite enough to confess already, they say; they do not have to turn to the unconscious for that. For such patients a complete technique for approaching the unconscious is needed.

138   This is one fact which at the outset seriously restricts the application of the cathartic method. The other restriction reveals itself later on and leads straight into the problems of the second stage. Let us suppose that in a given case the cathartic confession has occurred, the neurosis has vanished, or rather the symptoms are no longer visible. The patient could now be dismissed as cured—if it depended on the doctor alone. But he —or especially she—cannot get away. The patient seems bound to the doctor through the confession. If this seemingly senseless attachment is forcibly severed, there is a bad relapse. Significantly enough, and most curiously, there are cases where no attachment develops; the patient goes away apparently cured, but he is now so fascinated by the hinterland of his own mind

that he continues to practise catharsis on himself at the expense of his adaptation to life. He is bound to the unconscious, to himself, and not to the doctor. Clearly the same fate has befallen him as once befell Theseus and Peirithous his companion, who went down to Hades to bring back the goddess of the underworld. Tiring on the way, they sat down to rest for a while, only to find that they had grown fast to the rocks and could not rise.

139   These curious and unforeseen mischances need elucidation just as much as the first-mentioned cases, those that proved inaccessible to catharsis. In spite of the fact that the two categories of patients are apparently quite different, elucidation is called for at precisely the same point—that is, where the problem of fixation arises, as was correctly recognized by Freud. This is immediately obvious with patients who have undergone catharsis, especially if they remain bound to the doctor. The same sort of thing had already been observed as the unpleasant result of hypnotic treatment, although the inner mechanisms of such a tie were not understood. It now turns out that the nature of the tie in question corresponds more or less to the relation between father and child. The patient falls into a sort of childish dependence from which he cannot defend himself even by rational insight. The fixation is at times extraordinarily powerful—its strength is so amazing that one suspects it of being fed by forces quite outside ordinary experience. Since the tie is the result of an unconscious process, the conscious mind of the patient can tell us nothing about it. Hence the question arises of how this new difficulty is to be met. Obviously we are dealing with a neurotic formation, a new symptom directly induced by the treatment. The unmistakable outward sign of the situation is that the "feeling-toned" memory-image of the father is transferred to the doctor, so that whether he likes it or not the doctor appears in the role of the father and thus turns the patient into a child. Naturally the patient's childishness does not arise on that account—it was always present, but repressed. Now it comes to the surface, and —the long-lost father being found again—tries to restore the family situation of childhood. Freud gave to this symptom the appropriate name of "transference." That there should be a certain dependence on the doctor who has helped you is a per-

fectly normal and humanly understandable phenomenon. What is abnormal and unexpected is the extraordinary toughness of the tie and its imperviousness to conscious correction.

140   It is one of Freud's outstanding achievements to have explained the nature of this tie, or at least the biological aspects of it, and thus to have facilitated an important advance in psychological knowledge. Today it has been incontestably proved that the tie is caused by unconscious fantasies. These fantasies have in the main what we may call an "incestuous" character, which seems adequately to explain the fact that they remain unconscious, for we can hardly expect such fantasies, barely conscious at best, to come out even in the most scrupulous confession. Although Freud always speaks of incest-fantasies as though they were repressed, further experience has shown that in very many cases they were never the contents of the conscious mind at all or were conscious only as the vaguest adumbrations, for which reason they could not have been repressed intentionally. It is more probable that the incest-fantasies were always essentially unconscious and remained so until positively dragged into the light of day by the analytical method. This is not to say that fishing them out of the unconscious is a reprehensible interference with nature. It is something like a surgical operation on the psyche, but absolutely necessary inasmuch as the incest-fantasies are the cause of the transference and its complex symptoms, which are no less abnormal for being an artificial product.

141   While the cathartic method restores to the ego such contents as are capable of becoming conscious and should normally be components of the conscious mind, the process of clearing up the transference brings to light contents which are hardly ever capable of becoming conscious in that form. This is the cardinal distinction between the stage of confession and the stage of elucidation.

142   We spoke earlier of two categories of patients: those who prove impervious to catharsis and those who develop a fixation after catharsis. We have just dealt with those whose fixation takes the form of transference. But, besides these, there are people who, as already mentioned, develop no attachment to the doctor but rather to their own unconscious, in which they become entangled as in a web. Here the parental imago is not

transferred to any human object but remains a fantasy, although as such it exerts the same pull and results in the same tie as does the transference. The first category, the people who cannot yield themselves unreservedly to catharsis, can be understood in the light of Freudian research. Even before they came along for treatment they stood in an identity-relationship to their parents, deriving from it that authority, independence, and critical power which enabled them successfully to withstand the catharsis. They are mostly cultivated, differentiated personalities who, unlike the others, did not fall helpless victims to the unconscious activity of the parental imago, but rather usurped this activity by unconsciously identifying themselves with their parents.

143   Faced with the phenomenon of transference, mere confession is of no avail; it was for this reason that Freud was driven to substantial modifications of Breuer's original cathartic method. What he now practised he called the "interpretative method."

144   This further step is quite logical, for the transference relationship is in especial need of elucidation. How very much this is the case the layman can hardly appreciate; but the doctor who finds himself suddenly entangled in a web of incomprehensible and fantastic notions sees it all too clearly. He must interpret the transference—explain to the patient what he is projecting upon the doctor. Since the patient himself does not know what it is, the doctor is obliged to submit what scraps of fantasy he can obtain from the patient to analytical interpretation. The first and most important products of this kind are dreams. Freud therefore proceeded to examine dreams exclusively for their stock of wishes that had been repressed because incompatible with reality, and in the process discovered the incestuous contents of which I have spoken. Naturally the investigation revealed not merely incestuous material in the stricter sense of the word, but every conceivable kind of filth of which human nature is capable—and it is notorious that a lifetime would be required to make even a rough inventory of it.

145   The result of the Freudian method of elucidation is a minute elaboration of man's shadow-side unexampled in any previous age. It is the most effective antidote imaginable to

all the idealistic illusions about the nature of man; and it is therefore no wonder that there arose on all sides the most violent opposition to Freud and his school. I will not speak of the inveterate illusionists; I would merely point out that among the opponents of this method of explanation there are not a few who have no illusions about man's shadow-side and yet object to a biased portrayal of man from the shadow-side alone. After all, the essential thing is not the shadow but the body which casts it.

146   Freud's interpretative method rests on "reductive" explanations which unfailingly lead backwards and downwards, and it is essentially destructive if overdone or handled one-sidedly. Nevertheless psychology has profited greatly from Freud's pioneer work; it has learned that human nature has its black side—and not man alone, but his works, his institutions, and his convictions as well. Even our purest and holiest beliefs rest on very deep and dark foundations; after all, we can explain a house not only from the attic downwards, but from the basement upwards, and the latter explanation has the prime advantage of being genetically the more correct, since houses are in fact built bottom-side first, and the beginning of all things is simple and crude. No thinking person can deny that Salomon Reinach's explanation of the Last Supper in terms of primitive totemism is fraught with significance; nor will he reject the application of the incest hypothesis to the myths of the Greek divinities. Certainly it pains our sensibilities to interpret radiant things from the shadow-side and thus in a measure trample them in the sorry dirt of their beginnings. But I hold it to be an imperfection in things of beauty, and a frailty in man, if anything of such a kind permit itself to be destroyed by a mere shadow-explanation. The uproar over Freud's interpretations is entirely due to our own barbarous or childish naïveté, which does not yet understand that high rests on low, and that *les extrêmes se touchent* really is one of the ultimate verities. Our mistake lies in supposing that the radiant things are done away with by being explained from the shadow-side. This is a regrettable error into which Freud himself has fallen. Shadow pertains to light as evil to good, and vice versa. Therefore I cannot lament the shock which this exposure administered to our occidental illusions and pettiness; on the contrary

I welcome it as an historic and necessary rectification of almost incalculable importance. For it forces us to accept a philosophical relativism such as Einstein embodies for mathematical physics, and which is fundamentally a truth of the Far East whose ultimate effects we cannot at present foresee.

147   Nothing, it is true, is less effective than an intellectual idea. But when an idea is a *psychic fact* that crops up in two such totally different fields as psychology and physics, apparently without historical connection, then we must give it our closest attention. For ideas of this kind represent forces which are logically and morally unassailable; they are always stronger than man and his brain. He fancies that he makes these ideas, but in reality they make him—and make him their unwitting mouthpiece.

148   To return to our problem of fixation, I should now like to deal with the effects of elucidation. The fixation having been traced back to its dark origins, the patient's position becomes untenable; he cannot avoid seeing how inept and childish his demands are. He will either climb down from his exalted position of despotic authority to a more modest level and accept an insecurity which may prove very wholesome, or he will realize the inescapable truth that to make claims on others is a childish self-indulgence which must be replaced by a greater sense of responsibility.

149   The man of insight will draw his own moral conclusions. Armed with the knowledge of his deficiencies, he will plunge into the struggle for existence and consume in progressive work and experience all those forces and longings which previously caused him to cling obstinately to a child's paradise, or at least to look back at it over his shoulder. Normal adaptation and forbearance with his own shortcomings: these will be his guiding moral principles, together with freedom from sentimentality and illusion. The inevitable result is a turning away from the unconscious as from a source of weakness and temptation— the field of moral and social defeat.

150   The problem which now faces the patient is his education as a social being, and with this we come to the third stage. For many morally sensitive natures, mere insight into themselves has sufficient motive force to drive them forward, but it is not enough for people with little moral imagination. For them—

to say nothing of those who may have been struck by the analyst's interpretation but still doubt it in their heart of hearts —self-knowledge without the spur of external necessity is ineffective even when they are deeply convinced of its truth. Then again it is just the intellectually differentiated people who grasp the truth of the reductive explanation but cannot tolerate mere deflation of their hopes and ideals. In these cases, too, the power of insight will be of no avail. The explanatory method always presupposes sensitive natures capable of drawing independent moral conclusions from insight. It is true that elucidation goes further than uninterpreted confession alone, for at least it exercises the mind and may awaken dormant forces which can intervene in a helpful way. But the fact remains that in many cases the most thorough elucidation leaves the patient an intelligent but still incapable child. Moreover Freud's cardinal explanatory principle in terms of pleasure and its satisfaction is, as further research has shown, one-sided and therefore unsatisfactory. Not everybody can be explained from this angle. No doubt we all have this angle, but it is not always the most important. We can give a starving man a beautiful painting; he would much prefer bread. We can nominate a languishing lover President of the United States; he would far rather wrap his arms round his adored. On the average, all those who have no difficulty in achieving social adaptation and social position are better accounted for by the pleasure principle than are the unadapted who, because of their social inadequacy, have a craving for power and importance. The elder brother who follows in his father's footsteps and wins to a commanding position in society may be tormented by his desires; while the younger brother who feels himself suppressed and overshadowed by the other two may be goaded by ambition and the need for self-assertion. He may yield so completely to this passion that nothing else can become a problem for him, anyway not a vital one.

151   At this point in Freud's system of explanation there is a palpable gap, into which there stepped his one-time pupil, Adler. Adler has shown convincingly that numerous cases of neurosis can be far more satisfactorily explained by the power instinct than by the pleasure principle. The aim of his interpretation is therefore to show the patient that he "arranges"

66

his symptoms and exploits his neurosis in order to achieve a fictitious importance; and that even his transference and his other fixations subserve the will to power and thus represent a "masculine protest" against imaginary suppression. Obviously Adler has in mind the psychology of the under-dog or social failure, whose one passion is self-assertion. Such individuals are neurotic because they always imagine they are hard done by and tilt at the windmills of their own fancy, thus putting the goal they most desire quite out of reach.

152   Adler's method begins essentially at the stage of elucidation; he explains the symptoms in the sense just indicated, and to that extent appeals to the patient's understanding. Yet it is characteristic of Adler that he does not expect too much of understanding, but, going beyond that, has clearly recognized the need for social education. Whereas Freud is the investigator and interpreter, Adler is primarily the educator. He thus takes up the negative legacy which Freud bequeathed him, and, refusing to leave the patient a mere child, helpless despite his valuable understanding, tries by every device of education to make him a normal and adapted person. He does this evidently in the conviction that social adaptation and normalization are desirable goals, that they are absolutely necessary, the consummation of human life. From this fundamental attitude comes the widespread social activity of the Adlerian school, but also its depreciation of the unconscious, which, it seems, occasionally amounts to its complete denial. This is probably a swing of the pendulum—the inevitable reaction to the emphasis Freud lays on the unconscious, and as such quite in keeping with the natural aversion which we noted in patients struggling for adaptation and health. For, if the unconscious is held to be nothing more than a receptacle for all the evil shadow-things in human nature, including deposits of primeval slime, we really do not see why we should linger longer than necessary on the edge of this swamp into which we once fell. The scientific inquirer may behold a world of wonders in a mud puddle, but for the ordinary man it is something best left alone. Just as early Buddhism had no gods because it had to free itself from an inheritance of nearly two million gods, so psychology, if it is to develop further, must leave behind so entirely negative a thing as Freud's conception of the unconscious. The edu-

67

cational aims of the Adlerian school begin precisely where Freud leaves off; consequently they meet the needs of the patient who, having come to understand himself, wants to find his way back to normal life. It is obviously not enough for him to know how his illness arose and whence it came, for we seldom get rid of an evil merely by understanding its causes. Nor should it be forgotten that the crooked paths of a neurosis lead to as many obstinate habits, and that for all our insight these do not disappear until replaced by other habits. But habits are won only by exercise, and appropriate education is the sole means to this end. The patient must be *drawn out* of himself into other paths, which is the true meaning of "education," and this can only be achieved by an educative will. We can therefore see why Adler's approach has found favour chiefly with clergymen and teachers, while Freud's approach is fancied by doctors and intellectuals, who are one and all bad nurses and educators.

153   Each stage in the development of our psychology has something curiously final about it. Catharsis, with its heart-felt outpourings, makes one feel: "Now we are there, everything has come out, everything is known, the last terror lived through and the last tear shed; now everything will be all right." Elucidation says with equal conviction: "Now we know where the neurosis came from, the earliest memories have been unearthed, the last roots dug up, and the transference was nothing but the wish-fulfilling fantasy of a childhood paradise or a relapse into the family romance; the road to a normally disillusioned life is now open." Finally comes education, pointing out that no amount of confession and no amount of explaining can make the crooked plant grow straight, but that it must be trained upon the trellis of the norm by the gardener's art. Only then will normal adaptation be reached.

154   This curious sense of finality which attends each of the stages accounts for the fact that there are people using cathartic methods today who have apparently never heard of dream interpretation, Freudians who do not understand a word of Adler, and Adlerians who do not wish to know anything about the unconscious. Each is ensnared in the peculiar finality of his own stage, and thence arises that chaos of opinions and views

which makes orientation in these troubled waters so exceedingly difficult.

155   Whence comes the feeling of finality that evokes so much authoritarian bigotry on all sides?

156   I can only explain it to myself by saying that each stage does in fact rest on a final truth, and that consequently there are always cases which demonstrate this particular truth in the most startling way. In our delusion-ridden world a truth is so precious that nobody wants to let it slip merely for the sake of a few so-called exceptions which refuse to toe the line. And whoever doubts this truth is invariably looked on as a faithless reprobate, so that a note of fanaticism and intolerance everywhere creeps into the discussion.

157   And yet each of us can carry the torch of knowledge but a part of the way, until another takes it from him. If only we could understand all this impersonally—could understand that we are not the personal creators of our truths, but only their exponents, mere mouthpieces of the day's psychic needs, then much venom and bitterness might be spared and we should be able to perceive the profound and supra-personal continuity of the human mind.

158   As a rule, we take no account of the fact that the doctor who practises catharsis is not just an abstraction which automatically produces nothing but catharsis. He is also a human being, and although his thinking may be limited to his special field, his actions exert the influence of a complete human being. Without giving it a name and without being clearly conscious of it, he unwittingly does his share of explanation and education, just as the others do their share of catharsis without raising it to the level of a principle.

159   All life is living history. Even the reptile still lives in us *par sous-entendu*. In the same way, the three stages of analytical psychology so far dealt with are by no means truths of such a nature that the last of them has gobbled up and replaced the other two. On the contrary, all three are salient aspects of one and the same problem, and they no more invalidate one another than do confession and absolution.

160   The same is true of the fourth stage, transformation. It too should not claim to be the finally attained and only valid truth.

It certainly fills a gap left by the earlier stages, but in so doing it merely fulfils a further need beyond the scope of the others.

161   In order to make clear what this fourth stage has in view and what is meant by the somewhat peculiar term "transformation," we must first consider what psychic need was not given a place in the earlier stages. In other words, can anything lead further or be higher than the claim to be a normal and adapted social being? To be a normal human being is probably the most useful and fitting thing of which we can think; but the very notion of a "normal human being," like the concept of adaptation, implies a restriction to the average which seems a desirable improvement only to the man who already has some difficulty in coming to terms with the everyday world—a man, let us say, whose neurosis unfits him for normal life. To be "normal" is the ideal aim for the unsuccessful, for all those who are still below the general level of adaptation. But for people of more than average ability, people who never found it difficult to gain successes and to accomplish their share of the world's work—for them the moral compulsion to be nothing but normal signifies the bed of Procrustes—deadly and insupportable boredom, a hell of sterility and hopelessness. Consequently there are just as many people who become neurotic because they are merely normal, as there are people who are neurotic because they cannot become normal. That it should enter anyone's head to educate them to normality is a nightmare for the former, because their deepest need is really to be able to lead "abnormal" lives.

162   A man can find satisfaction and fulfilment only in what he does not yet possess, just as he can never be satisfied with something of which he has already had too much. To be a social and adapted person has no charms for one to whom such an aspiration is child's play. Always to do the right thing becomes a bore for the man who knows how, whereas the eternal bungler cherishes a secret longing to be right for once in some distant future.

163   The needs and necessities of mankind are manifold. What sets one man free is another man's prison. So also with normality and adaptation. Even if it be a biological axiom that man is a herd animal who only finds optimum health in living as a social being, the very next case may quite possibly invert this

axiom and show us that he is completely healthy only when leading an abnormal and unsocial life. It is enough to drive one to despair that in practical psychology there are no universally valid recipes and rules. There are only individual cases with the most heterogeneous needs and demands—so heterogeneous that we can virtually never know in advance what course a given case will take, for which reason it is better for the doctor to abandon all preconceived opinions. This does not mean that he should throw them overboard, but that in any given case he should use them merely as hypotheses for a possible explanation. Not, however, in order to instruct or convince his patient, but rather to show how the doctor reacts to that particular individual. For, twist and turn the matter as we may, the relation between doctor and patient remains a personal one within the impersonal framework of professional treatment. By no device can the treatment be anything but the product of mutual influence, in which the whole being of the doctor as well as that of his patient plays its part. In the treatment there is an encounter between two irrational factors, that is to say, between two persons who are not fixed and determinable quantities but who bring with them, besides their more or less clearly defined fields of consciousness, an indefinitely extended sphere of non-consciousness. Hence the personalities of doctor and patient are often infinitely more important for the outcome of the treatment than what the doctor says and thinks (although what he says and thinks may be a disturbing or a healing factor not to be underestimated). For two personalities to meet is like mixing two different chemical substances: if there is any combination at all, both are transformed. In any effective psychological treatment the doctor is bound to influence the patient; but this influence can only take place if the patient has a reciprocal influence on the doctor. You can exert no influence if you are not susceptible to influence. It is futile for the doctor to shield himself from the influence of the patient and to surround himself with a smoke-screen of fatherly and professional authority. By so doing he only denies himself the use of a highly important organ of information. The patient influences him unconsciously none the less, and brings about changes in the doctor's unconscious which are well known to many psychotherapists: psychic disturbances or even injuries peculiar to the profession, a striking illustration of the patient's almost "chemical" action. One of the best known symptoms of this kind is the counter-transference evoked by the transference. But the effects are often much more subtle, and their nature can best be conveyed by the old idea of the demon of sickness. According to this, a sufferer can transmit his disease to a healthy person whose powers then subdue the demon—but not without impairing the well-being of the subduer.

164   Between doctor and patient, therefore, there are imponderable factors which bring about a mutual transformation. In the process, the stronger and more stable personality will decide the final issue. I have seen many cases where the patient assimilated the doctor in defiance of all theory and of the latter's professional intentions—generally, though not always, to the disadvantage of the doctor.

165   The stage of transformation is grounded on these facts, but it took more than twenty-five years of wide practical experience for them to be clearly recognized. Freud himself has admitted their importance and has therefore seconded my demand for the analysis of the analyst.

166   What does this demand mean? Nothing less than that the doctor is as much "in the analysis" as the patient. He is equally a part of the psychic process of treatment and therefore equally exposed to the transforming influences. Indeed, to the extent that the doctor shows himself impervious to this influence, he forfeits influence over the patient; and if he is influenced only unconsciously, there is a gap in his field of consciousness which makes it impossible for him to see the patient in true perspective. In either case the result of the treatment is compromised.

167   The doctor is therefore faced with the same task which he wants his patient to face—that is, he must become socially adapted or, in the reverse case, appropriately non-adapted. This therapeutic demand can of course be clothed in a thousand different formulae, according to the doctor's beliefs. One doctor believes in overcoming infantilism—therefore he must first overcome his own infantilism. Another believes in abreacting all affects—therefore he must first abreact all his own affects. A third believes in complete consciousness—therefore he must first reach consciousness of himself. The doctor must consistently strive to meet his own therapeutic demand if he wishes

to ensure the right sort of influence over his patients. All these guiding principles of therapy make so many ethical demands, which can be summed up in the single truth: be the man through whom you wish to influence others. Mere talk has always been counted hollow, and there is no trick, however artful, by which this simple truth can be evaded in the long run. The fact of being convinced and not the thing we are convinced of—that is what has always, and at all times, worked.

168   Thus the fourth stage of analytical psychology requires the counter-application to the doctor himself of whatever system is believed in—and moreover with the same relentlessness, consistency, and perseverance with which the doctor applies it to the patient.

169   When one considers with what attentiveness and critical judgment the psychologist must keep track of his patients in order to show up all their false turnings, their false conclusions and infantile subterfuges, then it is truly no mean achievement for him to perform the same work upon himself. We are seldom interested enough in ourselves for that; moreover nobody pays us for our introspective efforts. Again, the common neglect into which the reality of the human psyche has fallen is still so great that self-examination or preoccupation with ourselves is deemed almost morbid. Evidently we suspect the psyche of harbouring something unwholesome, so that any concern with it smells of the sick-room. The doctor has to overcome these resistances in himself, for who can educate others if he is himself uneducated? Who can enlighten others if he is still in the dark about himself? And who purify others if himself impure?

170   The step from education to self-education is a logical advance that completes the earlier stages. The demand made by the stage of transformation, namely that the doctor must change himself if he is to become capable of changing his patient, is, as may well be imagined, a rather unpopular one, and for three reasons. First, because it seems unpractical; second, because of the unpleasant prejudice against being preoccupied with oneself; and third, because it is sometimes exceedingly painful to live up to everything one expects of one's patient. The last item in particular contributes much to the unpopularity of this demand, for if the doctor conscientiously doctors himself he will soon discover things in his own nature which are utterly

73

opposed to normalization, or which continue to haunt him in the most disturbing way despite assiduous explanation and thorough abreaction. What is he to do about these things? He always knows what the patient should do about them—it is his professional duty to do so. But what, in all sincerity, will he do when they recoil upon himself or perhaps upon those who stand nearest to him? He may, in his self-investigations, discover some inferiority which brings him uncomfortably close to his patients and may even blight his authority. How will he deal with this painful discovery? This somewhat "neurotic" question will touch him on the raw, no matter how normal he thinks he is. He will also discover that the ultimate questions which worry him as much as his patients cannot be solved by any treatment, that to expect solutions from others is childish and keeps you childish, and that if no solution can be found the question must be repressed again.

171   I will not pursue any further the many problems raised by self-examination because, owing to the obscurity which still surrounds the psyche, they would be of little interest today.

172   Instead, I would like to emphasize once again that the newest developments in analytical psychology confront us with the imponderable elements in the human personality; that we have learned to place in the foreground the personality of the doctor himself as a curative or harmful factor; and that what is now demanded is his own transformation—the self-education of the educator. Consequently, everything that occurred on the objective level in the history of our psychology—confession, elucidation, education—passes to the subjective level; in other words, what happened to the patient must now happen to the doctor, so that his personality shall not react unfavourably on the patient. The doctor can no longer evade his own difficulty by treating the difficulties of others: the man who suffers from a running abscess is not fit to perform a surgical operation.

173   Just as the momentous discovery of the unconscious shadow-side in man suddenly forced the Freudian school to deal even with questions of religion, so this latest advance makes an unavoidable problem of the doctor's ethical attitude. The self-criticism and self-examination that are indissolubly bound up with it necessitates a view of the psyche radically different from the merely biological one which has prevailed

hitherto; for the human psyche is far more than a mere object of scientific interest. It is not only the sufferer but the doctor as well, not only the object but also the subject, not only a cerebral function but the absolute condition of consciousness itself.

174   What was formerly a method of medical treatment now becomes a method of self-education, and with this the horizon of our psychology is immeasurably widened. The crucial thing is no longer the medical diploma, but the human quality. This is a significant turn of events, for it places all the implements of the psychotherapeutic art that were developed in clinical practice, and then refined and systematized, at the service of our self-education and self-perfection, with the result that analytical psychology has burst the bonds which till then had bound it to the consulting-room of the doctor. It goes beyond itself to fill the hiatus that has hitherto put Western civilization at a psychic disadvantage as compared with the civilizations of the East. We Westerners knew only how to tame and subdue the psyche; we knew nothing about its methodical development and its functions. Our civilization is still young, and young civilizations need all the arts of the animal-tamer to make the defiant barbarian and the savage in us more or less tractable. But at a higher cultural level we must forgo compulsion and turn to self-development. For this we must have a way, a method, which, as I said, has so far been lacking. It seems to me that the findings and experiences of analytical psychology can at least provide a foundation, for as soon as psychotherapy takes the doctor himself for its subject, it transcends its medical origins and ceases to be merely a method for treating the sick. It now treats the healthy or such as have a moral right to psychic health, whose sickness is at most the suffering that torments us all. For this reason analytical psychology can claim to serve the common weal—more so even than the previous stages which are each the bearer of a general truth. But between this claim and present-day reality there lies a gulf, with no bridge leading across. We have yet to build that bridge stone by stone.

VI

PSYCHOTHERAPY AND A PHILOSOPHY OF LIFE[1]

175   So much is psychotherapy the child of practical improvisation that for a long time it had trouble in thinking out its own intellectual foundations. Empirical psychology relied very much at first on physical and then on physiological ideas, and ventured only with some hesitation on the complex phenomena which constitute its proper field. Similarly, psychotherapy was at first simply an auxiliary method; only gradually did it free itself from the world of ideas represented by medical therapeutics and come to understand that its concern lay not merely with physiological but primarily with psychological principles. In other words, it found itself obliged to raise psychological issues which soon burst the framework of the experimental psychology of that day with its elementary statements. The demands of therapy brought highly complex factors within the purview of this still young science, and its exponents very often lacked the equipment needed to deal with the problems that arose. It is therefore not surprising that a bewildering assortment of ideas, theories, and points of view predominated in all the initial discussions of this new psychology which had been, so to speak, forced into existence by therapeutic experience. An outsider could hardly be blamed if he received an impression of babel. This confusion was inevitable, for sooner or later it was bound to become clear that one cannot treat the psyche without touching on man and life as a whole, including the ultimate and deepest issues, any more than one can treat the sick body without regard to the totality of its functions—or rather, as a few representatives of modern medicine maintain, the totality of the sick man himself.

1 [The introductory address to a discussion held by the Swiss Society for Psychology, Zurich, September 26, 1942. Published as "Psychotherapie und Weltanschauung" in the *Schweizerische Zeitschrift für Psychologie und ihre Anwendungen*, I (1943):3, 157–64; and in *Aufsätze zur Zeitgeschichte* (Zurich, 1946), pp. 57–72. Previously trans. by Mary Briner in *Essays on Contemporary Events* (London, 1947).—EDITORS.]

176   The more "psychological" a condition is, the greater its complexity and the more it relates to the whole of life. It is true that elementary psychic phenomena are closely allied to physiological processes, and there is not the slightest doubt that the physiological factor forms at least one pole of the psychic cosmos. The instinctive and affective processes, together with all the neurotic symptomatology that arises when these are disturbed, clearly rest on a physiological basis. But, on the other hand, the disturbing factor proves equally clearly that it has the power to turn physiological order into disorder. If the disturbance lies in a repression, then the disturbing factor—that is, the repressive force—belongs to a "higher" psychic order. It is not something elementary and physiologically conditioned, but, as experience shows, a highly complex determinant, as for example certain rational, ethical, aesthetic, religious, or other traditional ideas which cannot be scientifically proved to have any physiological basis. These extremely complex dominants form the other pole of the psyche. Experience likewise shows that this pole possesses an energy many times greater than that of the physiologically conditioned psyche.

177   With its earliest advances into the field of psychology proper, the new psychotherapy came up against the problem of opposites—a problem that is profoundly characteristic of the psyche. Indeed, the structure of the psyche is so contradictory or contrapuntal that one can scarcely make any psychological assertion or general statement without having immediately to state its opposite.

178   The problem of opposites offers an eminently suitable and ideal battleground for the most contradictory theories, and above all for partially or wholly unrealized prejudices regarding one's philosophy of life. With this development psychotherapy stirred up a hornets' nest of the first magnitude. Let us take as an example the supposedly simple case of a repressed instinct. If the repression is lifted, the instinct is set free. Once freed, it wants to live and function in its own way. But this creates a difficult—sometimes intolerably difficult—situation. The instinct ought therefore to be modified, or "sublimated," as they say. How this is to be done without creating a new repression nobody can quite explain. The little word "ought" always proves the helplessness of the therapist; it is an admis-

77

sion that he has come to the end of his resources. The final appeal to reason would be very fine if man were by nature a rational animal, but he is not; on the contrary, he is quite as much irrational. Hence reason is often not sufficient to modify the instinct and make it conform to the rational order. Nobody can conceive the moral, ethical, philosophical, and religious conflicts that crop up at this stage of the problem—the facts surpass all imagination. Every conscientious and truth-loving psychotherapist could tell a tale here, though naturally not in public. All the contemporary problems, all the philosophical and religious questionings of our day, are raked up, and unless either the psychotherapist or the patient abandons the attempt in time it is likely to get under both their skins. Each will be driven to a discussion of his philosophy of life, both with himself and with his partner. There are of course forced answers and solutions, but in principle and in the long run they are neither desirable nor satisfying. No Gordian knot can be permanently cut; it has the awkward property of always tying itself again.

179   This philosophical discussion is a task which psychotherapy necessarily sets itself, though not every patient will come down to basic principles. The question of the measuring rod with which to measure, of the ethical criteria which are to determine our actions, must be answered somehow, for the patient may quite possibly expect us to account for our judgments and decisions. Not all patients allow themselves to be condemned to infantile inferiority because of our refusal to render such an account, quite apart from the fact that a therapeutic blunder of this kind would be sawing off the branch on which we sit. In other words, the art of psychotherapy requires that the therapist be in possession of avowable, credible, and defensible convictions which have proved their viability either by having resolved any neurotic dissociations of his own or by preventing them from arising. A therapist with a neurosis is a contradiction in terms. One cannot help any patient to advance further than one has advanced oneself. On the other hand, the possession of complexes does not in itself signify neurosis, for complexes are the normal foci of psychic happenings, and the fact that they are painful is no proof of pathological disturbance. Suffering is not an illness; it is the normal counterpole to hap-

piness. A complex becomes pathological only when we think
we have not got it.

180   As the most complex of psychic structures, a man's philosophy of life forms the counterpole to the physiologically conditioned psyche, and, as the highest psychic dominant, it ultimately
determines the latter's fate. It guides the life of the therapist
and shapes the spirit of his therapy. Since it is an essentially
subjective system despite the most rigorous objectivity, it may
and very likely will be shattered time after time on colliding
with the truth of the patient, but it rises again, rejuvenated
by the experience. Conviction easily turns into self-defence
and is seduced into rigidity, and this is inimical to life. The
test of a firm conviction is its elasticity and flexibility; like every
other exalted truth it thrives best on the admission of its errors.

181   I can hardly draw a veil over the fact that we psychotherapists ought really to be philosophers or philosophic doctors—
or rather that we already are so, though we are unwilling to admit it because of the glaring contrast between our work and
what passes for philosophy in the universities. We could also
call it religion *in statu nascendi,* for in the vast confusion that
reigns at the roots of life there is no line of division between
philosophy and religion. Nor does the unrelieved strain of the
psychotherapeutic situation, with its host of impressions and
emotional disturbances, leave us much leisure for the systema-
tization of thought. Thus we have no clear exposition of guiding principles drawn from life to offer either to the philosophers
or to the theologians.

182   Our patients suffer from bondage to a neurosis, they are
prisoners of the unconscious, and if we attempt to penetrate
with understanding into that realm of unconscious forces, we
have to defend ourselves against the same influences to which
our patients have succumbed. Like doctors who treat epidemic
diseases, we expose ourselves to powers that threaten our conscious equilibrium, and we have to take every possible precau-
tion if we want to rescue not only our own humanity but that
of the patient from the clutches of the unconscious. Wise self-
limitation is not the same thing as text-book philosophy, nor
is an ejaculatory prayer in a moment of mortal danger a
theological treatise. Both are the outcome of a religious and

philosophical attitude that is appropriate to the stark dynamism of life.

183   The highest dominant always has a religious or a philosophical character. It is by nature extremely primitive, and consequently we find it in full development among primitive peoples. Any difficulty, danger, or critical phase of life immediately calls forth this dominant. It is the most natural reaction to all highly charged emotional situations. But often it remains as obscure as the semiconscious emotional situation which evoked it. Hence it is quite natural that the emotional disturbances of the patient should activate the corresponding religious or philosophical factors in the therapist. Often he is most reluctant to make himself conscious of these primitive contents, and he quite understandably prefers to turn for help to a religion or philosophy which has reached his consciousness from outside. This course does not strike me as being illegitimate in so far as it gives the patient a chance to take his place within the structure of some protective institution existing in the outside world. Such a solution is entirely natural, since there have always and everywhere been totem clans, cults, and creeds whose purpose it is to give an ordered form to the chaotic world of the instincts.

184   The situation becomes difficult, however, when the patient's nature resists a collective solution. The question then arises whether the therapist is prepared to risk having his convictions dashed and shattered against the truth of the patient. If he wants to go on treating the patient he must abandon all preconceived notions and, for better or worse, go with him in search of the religious and philosophical ideas that best correspond to the patient's emotional states. These ideas present themselves in archetypal form, freshly sprung from the maternal soil whence all religious and philosophical systems originally came. But if the therapist is not prepared to have his convictions called in question for the sake of the patient, then there is some reason for doubting the stability of his basic attitude. Perhaps he cannot give way on grounds of self-defence, which threatens him with rigidity. The margin of psychological elasticity varies both individually and collectively, and often it is so narrow that a certain degree of rigidity really does represent the maximum achievement. *Ultra posse nemo obligatur.*

185   Instinct is not an isolated thing, nor can it be isolated in practice. It always brings in its train archetypal contents of a spiritual nature, which are at once its foundation and its limitation. In other words, an instinct is always and inevitably coupled with something like a philosophy of life, however archaic, unclear, and hazy this may be. Instinct stimulates thought, and if a man does not think of his own free will, then you get compulsive thinking, for the two poles of the psyche, the physiological and the mental, are indissolubly connected. For this reason instinct cannot be freed without freeing the mind, just as mind divorced from instinct is condemned to futility. Not that the tie between mind and instinct is necessarily a harmonious one. On the contrary it is full of conflict and means suffering. Therefore the principal aim of psychotherapy is not to transport the patient to an impossible state of happiness, but to help him acquire steadfastness and philosophic patience in face of suffering. Life demands for its completion and fulfilment a balance between joy and sorrow. But because suffering is positively disagreeable, people naturally prefer not to ponder how much fear and sorrow fall to the lot of man. So they speak soothingly about progress and the greatest possible happiness, forgetting that happiness is itself poisoned if the measure of suffering has not been fulfilled. Behind a neurosis there is so often concealed all the natural and necessary suffering the patient has been unwilling to bear. We can see this most clearly from hysterical pains, which are relieved in the course of treatment by the corresponding psychic suffering which the patient sought to avoid.

186   The Christian doctrine of original sin on the one hand, and of the meaning and value of suffering on the other, is therefore of profound therapeutic significance and is undoubtedly far better suited to Western man than Islamic fatalism. Similarly the belief in immortality gives life that untroubled flow into the future so necessary if stoppages and regressions are to be avoided. Although we like to use the word "doctrine" for these —psychologically speaking—extremely important ideas, it would be a great mistake to think that they are just arbitrary intellectual theories. Psychologically regarded, they are emotional experiences whose nature cannot be discussed. If I may permit myself a banal comparison, when I feel well and content no-

body can prove to me that I am not. Logical arguments simply bounce off the facts felt and experienced. Original sin, the meaning of suffering, and immortality are emotional facts of this kind. But to experience them is a charisma which no human art can compel. Only unreserved surrender can hope to reach such a goal.

187   Not everybody is capable of this surrender. There is no "ought" or "must" about it, for the very act of exerting the will inevitably places such an emphasis on *my* will to surrender that the exact opposite of surrender results. The Titans could not take Olympus by storm, and still less may a Christian take Heaven. The most healing, and psychologically the most necessary, experiences are a "treasure hard to attain," and its acquisition demands something out of the common from the common man.

188   As we know, this something out of the common proves, in practical work with the patient, to be an invasion by archetypal contents. If these contents are to be assimilated, it is not enough to make use of the current philosophical or religious ideas, for they simply do not fit the archaic symbolism of the material. We are therefore forced to go back to pre-Christian and non-Christian conceptions and to conclude that Western man does not possess the monopoly of human wisdom and that the white race is not a species of *Homo sapiens* specially favoured by God. Moreover we cannot do justice to certain contemporary collective phenomena unless we revert to the pre-Christian parallels.

189   Medieval physicians seem to have realized this, for they practised a philosophy whose roots can be traced back to pre-Christian times and whose nature exactly corresponds to our experiences with patients today. These physicians recognized, besides the light of divine revelation, a *lumen naturae* as a second, independent source of illumination, to which the doctor could turn if the truth as handed down by the Church should for any reason prove ineffective either for himself or for the patient.

190   It was eminently practical reasons, and not the mere caperings of a hobby-horse, that prompted me to undertake my historical researches. Neither our modern medical training nor academic psychology and philosophy can equip the doctor with

the necessary education, or with the means, to deal effectively and understandingly with the often very urgent demands of his psychotherapeutic practice. It therefore behoves us, unembarrassed by our shortcomings as amateurs of history, to go to school once more with the medical philosophers of a distant past, when body and soul had not yet been wrenched asunder into different faculties. Although we are specialists par excellence, our specialized field, oddly enough, drives us to universalism and to the complete overcoming of the specialist attitude, if the totality of body and soul is not to be just a matter of words. Once we have made up our minds to treat the soul, we can no longer close our eyes to the fact that neurosis is not a thing apart but the whole of the pathologically disturbed psyche. It was Freud's momentous discovery that the neurosis is not a mere agglomeration of symptoms, but a wrong functioning which affects the whole psyche. The important thing is not the neurosis, but the man who has the neurosis. We have to set to work on the human being, and we must be able to do him justice as a human being.

191   The conference we are holding today proves that our psychotherapy has recognized its aim, which is to pay equal attention to the physiological and to the spiritual factor. Originating in natural science, it applies the objective, empirical methods of the latter to the phenomenology of the mind. Even if this should remain a mere attempt, the fact that the attempt has been made is of incalculable significance.

VII

MEDICINE AND PSYCHOTHERAPY [1]

192   Speaking before an audience of doctors, I always experience a certain difficulty in bridging the differences that exist between medicine on the one hand and psychotherapy on the other
in their conception of pathology. These differences are the
source of numerous misunderstandings, and it is therefore of
the greatest concern to me, in this short talk, to express one or
two thoughts which may serve to clarify the special relationship
that psychotherapy bears to medicine. Where distinctions exist,
well-meaning attempts to stress the common ground are notoriously lacking in point. But it is extremely important, in his
own interests, that the psychotherapist should not in any circumstances lose the position he originally held in medicine,
and this precisely because the peculiar nature of his experience forces upon him a certain mode of thought, and certain
interests, which no longer have—or perhaps I should say, do not
yet have—a rightful domicile in the medicine of today. Both
these factors tend to lead the psychotherapist into fields of study
apparently remote from medicine, and the practical importance
of these fields is generally difficult to explain to the non-psychotherapist. From accounts of case histories and miraculously
successful cures the non-psychotherapist learns little, and that
little is frequently false. I have yet to come across a respectable
specimen of neurosis of which one could give anything like an
adequate description in a short lecture, to say nothing of all
the therapeutic intricacies that are far from clear even to the
shrewdest professional.

193   With your permission I will now examine the three stages
of medical procedure—anamnesis, diagnosis, and therapy—from

1 [Delivered as a lecture to a scientific meeting of the Senate of the Swiss Academy
of Medical Science, Zurich, May 12, 1945. Published as "Medizin und Psychotherapie," *Bulletin der Schweizerischen Akademie der medizinischen Wissenschaften,* I (1945): 5, 315–25.—EDITORS.]

the psychotherapeutic point of view. The pathological material I am here presupposing is pure psychoneurosis.

194   We begin with the anamnesis, as is customary in medicine in general and psychiatry in particular—that is to say, we try to piece together the historical facts of the case as flawlessly as possible. The psychotherapist, however, does not rest content with these facts. He is aware not only of the unreliability of all evidence, but, over and above that, of the special sources of error in statements made on one's own behalf—the statements of the patient who, wittingly or unwittingly, gives prominence to facts that are plausible enough in themselves but may be equally misleading as regards the pathogenesis. The patient's whole environment may be drawn into this system of explanation in a positive or negative sense, as though it were in unconscious collusion with him. At all events one must be prepared *not* to hear the very things that are most important. The psychotherapist will therefore take pains to ask questions about matters that seem to have nothing to do with the actual illness. For this he needs not only his professional knowledge; he has also to rely on intuitions and sudden ideas, and the more widely he casts his net of questions the more likely he is to succeed in catching the complex nature of the case. If ever there were an illness that cannot be localized, because it springs from the whole of a man, that illness is a psychoneurosis. The psychiatrist can at least console himself with diseases of the brain; not so the psychotherapist, even if he privately believes in such a maxim, for the case before him demands the thorough psychological treatment of a disturbance that has nothing to do with cerebral symptoms. On the contrary, the more the psycho-therapist allows himself to be impressed by hereditary factors and the possibility of psychotic complications, the more crippled he will be in his therapeutic action. For better or worse he is obliged to overlook such cogent factors as heredity, the presence of schizophrenic symptoms, and the like, particularly when these dangerous things are put forward with special emphasis. His assessment of anamnestic data may therefore turn out to be very different from a purely medical one.

195   It is generally assumed in medical circles that the examination of the patient should lead to the diagnosis of his illness, so far as this is possible at all, and that with the establishment

of the diagnosis an important decision has been arrived at as regards prognosis and therapy. Psychotherapy forms a startling exception to this rule: the diagnosis is a highly irrelevant affair since, apart from affixing a more or less lucky label to a neurotic condition, nothing is gained by it, least of all as regards prognosis and therapy. In flagrant contrast to the rest of medicine, where a definite diagnosis is often, as it were, logically followed by a specific therapy and a more or less certain prognosis, the diagnosis of any particular psychoneurosis means, at most, that some form of psychotherapy is indicated. As to the prognosis, this is in the highest degree independent of the diagnosis. Nor should we gloss over the fact that the classification of the neuroses is very unsatisfactory, and that for this reason alone a specific diagnosis seldom means anything real. In general, it is enough to diagnose a "psychoneurosis" as distinct from some organic disturbance—the word means no more than that. I have in the course of years accustomed myself wholly to disregard the diagnosing of specific neuroses, and I have sometimes found myself in a quandary when some word-addict urged me to hand him a specific diagnosis. The Greco-Latin compounds needed for this still seem to have a not inconsiderable market value and are occasionally indispensable for that reason.

196   The sonorous diagnosis of neuroses *secundum ordinem* is just a façade, it is not the psychotherapist's real diagnosis. His establishment of certain facts might conceivably be called "diagnosis," though it is psychological rather than medical in character. Nor is it meant to be communicated; for reasons of discretion, and also on account of the subsequent therapy, he usually keeps it to himself. The facts so established are simply perceptions indicating the direction the therapy is to take. They can hardly be reproduced in the sort of Latin terminology that sounds scientific; but there are on the other hand expressions of ordinary speech which adequately describe the essential psychotherapeutic facts. The point is, we are not dealing with clinical diseases but with psychological ones. Whether a person is suffering from hysteria, or an anxiety neurosis, or a phobia, means little beside the much more important discovery that, shall we say, he is *fils à papa*. Here something fundamental has been said about the content of the neurosis and about the difficulties to be expected in the treatment. So that in psycho-

therapy the recognition of disease rests much less on the clinical picture than on the content of complexes. Psychological diagnosis aims at the diagnosis of complexes and hence at the formulation of facts which are far more likely to be concealed than revealed by the clinical picture. The real toxin is to be sought in the complex, and this is a more or less autonomous psychic quantity. It proves its autonomous nature by not fitting into the hierarchy of the conscious mind, or by the resistance it successfully puts up against the will. This fact, which can easily be established by experiment, is the reason why psychoneuroses and psychoses have from time immemorial been regarded as states of *possession,* since the impression forces itself upon the naïve observer that the complex forms something like a shadow-government of the ego.

197   The content of a neurosis can never be established by a single examination, or even by several. It manifests itself only in the course of treatment. Hence the paradox that the true psychological diagnosis becomes apparent only at the end. Just as a sure diagnosis is desirable and a thing to be aimed at in medicine, so, conversely, it will profit the psychotherapist to know as little as possible about specific diagnoses. It is enough if he is reasonably sure of the differential diagnosis between organic and psychic, and if he knows what a genuine melancholy is and what it can mean. Generally speaking, the less the psychotherapist knows in advance, the better the chances for the treatment. Nothing is more deleterious than a routine understanding of everything.

198   We have now established that the anamnesis appears more than usually suspect to the psychotherapist, and that clinical diagnosis is, for his purposes, well-nigh meaningless. Finally, the therapy itself shows the greatest imaginable departures from the views commonly accepted in medicine. There are numerous physical diseases where the diagnosis also lays down the lines for a specific treatment; a given disease cannot be treated just anyhow. But for the psychoneuroses the only valid principle is that their treatment must be psychological. In this respect there is any number of methods, rules, prescriptions, views, and doctrines, and the remarkable thing is that any given therapeutic procedure in any given neurosis can have the desired result. The various psychotherapeutic dogmas about which such a

great fuss is made do not, therefore, amount to very much in the end. Every psychotherapist who knows his job will, consciously or unconsciously, theory notwithstanding, ring all the changes that do not figure in his own theory. He will occasionally use suggestion, to which he is opposed on principle. There is no getting round Freud's or Adler's or anybody else's point of view. Every psychotherapist not only has his own method— he himself is that method. *Ars requirit totum hominem,* says an old master. The great healing factor in psychotherapy is the doctor's personality, which is something not given at the start; it represents his performance at its highest and not a doctrinaire blueprint. Theories are to be avoided, except as mere auxiliaries. As soon as a dogma is made of them, it is evident that an inner doubt is being stifled. Very many theories are needed before we can get even a rough picture of the psyche's complexity. It is therefore quite wrong when people accuse psychotherapists of being unable to reach agreement even on their own theories. Agreement could only spell one-sidedness and desiccation. One could as little catch the psyche in a theory as one could catch the world. Theories are not articles of faith, they are either instruments of knowledge and of therapy, or they are no good at all.

199   Psychotherapy can be practised in a great variety of ways, from psychoanalysis, or something of that kind, to hypnotism, and so on right down to cataplasms of honey and possets of bat's dung. Successes can be obtained with them all. So at least it appears on a superficial view. On closer inspection, however, one realizes that the seemingly absurd remedy was exactly the right thing, not for this particular *neurosis,* but for this particular human being, whereas in another case it would have been the worst thing possible. Medicine too is doubtless aware that sick people exist as well as sicknesses; but psychotherapy knows first and foremost—or rather should know—that its proper concern is not the fiction of a neurosis but the distorted totality of the human being. True, it too has tried to treat neurosis like an *ulcus cruris,* where it matters not a jot for the treatment whether the patient was the apple of her father's eye or whether she is a Catholic, a Baptist, or what not; whether the man she married be old or young, and all the rest of it. Psychotherapy began by attacking the symptom, just as medicine did.

88

Despite its undeniable youthfulness as a scientifically avowable method, it is yet as old as the healing art itself and, consciously or otherwise, has always remained mistress of at least half the medical field. Certainly its real advances were made only in the last half century when, on account of the specialization needed, it withdrew to the narrower field of the psychoneuroses. But here it recognized relatively quickly that to attack symptoms or, as it is now called, symptom analysis was only half the story, and that the real point is the treatment of the whole psychic human being.

200   What does this mean: the whole psychic human being?

201   Medicine in general has to deal, in the first place, with man as an anatomical and physiological phenomenon, and only to a lesser degree with the human being psychically defined. But this precisely is the subject of psychotherapy. When we direct our attention to the psyche from the viewpoint of the natural sciences, it appears as one biological factor among many others. In man this factor is usually identified with the conscious mind, as has mostly been done up to now by the so-called humane sciences as well. I subscribe entirely to the biological view that the psyche is one such factor, but at the same time I am given to reflect that the psyche—in this case, consciousness—occupies an exceptional position among all these biological factors. For without consciousness it would never have become known that there is such a thing as a world, and without the psyche there would be absolutely no possibility of knowledge, since the object must go through a complicated physiological and psychic process of change in order to become a psychic image. This image alone is the immediate object of knowledge. The existence of the world has two conditions: it to exist, and us to know it.

202   Now, whether the psyche is understood as an epiphenomenon of the living body, or as an *ens per se*, makes little difference to psychology, in so far as the psyche knows itself to exist and behaves as such an existent, having its own phenomenology which can be replaced by no other. Thereby it proves itself to be a biological factor that can be described phenomenologically like any other object of natural science. The beginnings of a phenomenology of the psyche lie in psychophysiology and experimental psychology on the one hand, and, on the

other, in descriptions of diseases and the diagnostic methods of psychopathology (e.g., association experiments and Rorschach's irrational ink-blots). But the most convincing evidence is to be found in every manifestation of psychic life, in the humane sciences, religious and political views and movements, the arts, and so forth.

203 The "whole psychic human being" we were asking about thus proves to be nothing less than a world, that is, a microcosm, as the ancients quite rightly thought, though for the wrong reasons. The psyche reflects, and knows, the whole of existence, and everything works in and through the psyche.

204 But, in order to get a real understanding of this, we must very considerably broaden our conventional conception of the psyche. Our original identification of psyche with the conscious mind does not stand the test of empirical criticism. The medical philosopher C. G. Carus had a clear inkling of this and was the first to set forth an explicit philosophy of the unconscious. Today he would undoubtedly have been a psychotherapist. But in those days the psyche was still the anxiously guarded possession of philosophy and therefore could not be discussed within the framework of medicine, although the physicians of the Romantic Age tried all sorts of unorthodox experiments in this respect. I am thinking chiefly of Justinus Kerner. It was reserved for the recent past to fill in the gaps in the conscious processes with hypothetical unconscious ones. The existence of an unconscious psyche is as likely, shall we say, as the existence of an as yet undiscovered planet, whose presence is inferred from the deviations of some known planetary orbit. Unfortunately we lack the aid of the telescope that would make certain of its existence. But once the idea of the unconscious was introduced, the concept of the psyche could be expanded to the formula "psyche = ego-consciousness + unconscious."

205 The unconscious was understood personalistically at first —that is to say, its contents were thought to come exclusively from the sphere of ego-consciousness and to have become unconscious only secondarily, through repression. Freud later admitted the existence of archaic vestiges in the unconscious, but thought they had more or less the significance of anatomical atavisms. Consequently we were still far from an adequate conception of the unconscious. Certain things had yet to be discov-

ered, although actually they lay ready to hand: above all the fact that in every child consciousness grows out of the unconscious in the course of a few years, also that consciousness is always only a temporary state based on an optimum physiological performance and therefore regularly interrupted by phases of unconsciousness (sleep), and finally that the unconscious psyche not only possesses the longer lease of life but is continuously present. From this arises the important conclusion that the real and authentic psyche is the unconscious, whereas the ego-consciousness can be regarded only as a temporary epiphenomenon.

206   In ancient times the psyche was conceived as a microcosm, and this was one of the characteristics attributed to the psychophysical man. To attribute such a characteristic to the ego-consciousness would be boundlessly to overestimate the latter. But with the unconscious it is quite different. This, by definition and in fact, cannot be circumscribed. It must therefore be counted as something boundless: infinite or infinitesimal. Whether it may legitimately be called a microcosm depends simply and solely on whether certain portions of the world beyond individual experience can be shown to exist in the unconscious—certain constants which are not individually acquired but are *a priori* presences. The theory of instinct and the findings of biology in connection with the symbiotic relationship between plant and insect have long made us familiar with these things. But when it comes to the psyche one is immediately seized with the fear of having to do with "inherited ideas." We are not dealing with anything of the sort; it is more a question of *a priori* or prenatally determined modes of behaviour and function. It is to be conjectured that just as the chicken comes out of the egg in the same way all the world over, so there are psychic modes of functioning, certain ways of thinking, feeling, and imagining, which can be found everywhere and at all times, quite independent of tradition. A general proof of the rightness of this expectation lies in the ubiquitous occurrence of parallel mythologems, Bastian's "folk-thoughts" or primordial ideas; and a special proof is the autochthonous reproduction of such ideas in the psyche of individuals where direct transmission is out of the question. The empirical material found in such cases consists of dreams, fantasies, delusions, etc.

207 Mythologems are the aforementioned "portions of the world" which belong to the structural elements of the psyche. They are constants whose expression is everywhere and at all times the same.

208 You may ask in some consternation: What has all this to do with psychotherapy? That neuroses are somehow connected with instinctual disturbances is not surprising. But, as biology shows, instincts are by no means blind, spontaneous, isolated impulses; they are on the contrary associated with typical situational patterns and cannot be released unless existing conditions correspond to the *a priori* pattern. The collective contents expressed in mythologems represent such situational patterns, which are so intimately connected with the release of instinct. For this reason knowledge of them is of the highest practical importance to the psychotherapist.

209 Clearly, the investigation of these patterns and their properties must lead us into fields that seem to lie infinitely far from medicine. That is the fate of empirical psychology, and its misfortune: to fall between all the academic stools. And this comes precisely from the fact that the human psyche has a share in all the sciences, because it forms at least half the ground necessary for the existence of them all.

210 It should be clear from the foregoing discussion that everything psychotherapy has in common with symptomatology clinically understood—i.e., with the medical picture—is, I will not say irrelevant, but of secondary importance in so far as the medical picture of disease is a provisional one. The real and important thing is the psychological picture, which can only be discovered in the course of treatment behind the veil of pathological symptoms. In order to get closer to the sphere of the psyche, the ideas derived from the sphere of medicine are not enough. But, to the extent that psychotherapy, considered as part of the healing art, should never, for many cogent reasons, slip out of the doctor's control and should therefore be taught in medical faculties, it is forced to borrow from the other sciences—which is what other medical disciplines have been doing for a long time. Yet whereas medicine in general can limit its borrowings to the natural sciences, psychotherapy needs the help of the humane sciences as well.

211   In order to complete my account of the differences between medicine and psychotherapy, I ought really to describe
the phenomenology of those psychic processes which manifest
themselves in the course of treatment and do not have their
counterpart in medicine. But such an undertaking would exceed the compass of my lecture, and I must therefore refrain.
I trust, however, that the little I have been privileged to say
has thrown some light on the relations between psychotherapy
and the medical art.

VIII

PSYCHOTHERAPY TODAY[1]

212   It would be a rewarding task to examine in some detail the relationship between psychotherapy and the state of mind in Europe today. Yet probably no one would be blamed for shrinking from so bold a venture, for who could guarantee that the picture he has formed of the present psychological and spiritual plight of Europe is true to reality? Are we, as contemporaries of and participants in these cataclysmic events, at all capable of cool judgment and of seeing clearly amid the indescribable political and ideological chaos of present-day Europe? Or should we perhaps do better to narrow the field of psychotherapy and restrict our science to a modest specialists' corner, remaining indifferent to the ruin of half the world? I fear that such a course, in spite of its commendable modesty, would ill accord with the nature of psychotherapy, which is after all the "treatment of the soul." Indeed, the concept of psychotherapy, however one may choose to interpret it, carries with it very great pretensions: for the soul is the birth-place of all action and hence of everything that happens by the will of man. It would be difficult, if not impossible, to carve out an arbitrarily limited segment of the infinitely vast realm of the psyche and call that the secluded theatre of psychotherapy. Medicine, it is true, has found itself obliged to mark off a specific field, that of the neuroses and psychoses, and this is both convenient and feasible for the practical purpose of treatment. But the artificial restriction must be broken down immediately psychotherapy understands its problems not simply as those of a technique but as

[1] [A lecture delivered to a Section of the Swiss Society for Psychotherapy at its fourth annual meeting (1941). The Section was formed to further the interests of psychotherapists in Switzerland. The lecture was published as "Die Psychotherapie in der Gegenwart" in the *Schweizerische Zeitschrift für Psychologie und ihre Anwendungen,* IV (1945), 1–18; and in *Aufsätze zur Zeitgeschichte* (Zurich, 1946), pp. 25–56, from which the present translation was made. Previously trans. by Mary Briner in *Essays on Contemporary Events* (London, 1947).—EDITORS.]

those of a science. Science *qua* science has no boundaries, and there is no speciality whatever that can boast of complete self-sufficiency. Any speciality is bound to spill over its borders and to encroach on adjoining territory if it is to lay serious claim to the status of a science. Even so highly specialized a technique as Freudian psychoanalysis was unable, at the very outset, to avoid poaching on other, and sometimes exceedingly remote, scientific preserves. It is, in fact, impossible to treat the psyche, and human personality in general, sectionally. In all psychic disturbances it is becoming clear—perhaps even more so than in the case of physical illnesses—that the psyche is a whole in which everything hangs together. When the patient comes to us with a neurosis, he does not bring a part but the whole of his psyche and with it the fragment of world on which that psyche depends, and without which it can never be properly understood. Psychotherapy is therefore less able than any other specialized department of science to take refuge in the sanctuary of a speciality which has no further connection with the world at large. Try as we may to concentrate on the most personal of personal problems, our therapy nevertheless stands or falls with the question: What sort of world does our patient come from and to what sort of world has he to adapt himself? The world is a supra-personal fact to which an essentially personalistic psychology can never do justice. Such a psychology only penetrates to the personal element in man. But in so far as he is also a part of the world, he carries the world in himself, that is, something at once impersonal and supra-personal. It includes his entire physical and psychic basis, so far as this is given from the start. Undoubtedly the personalities of father and mother form the first and apparently the only world of man as an infant; and, if they continue to do so for too long, he is on the surest road to neurosis, because the great world he will have to enter as a whole person is no longer a world of fathers and mothers, but a supra-personal fact. The child first begins to wean itself from the childhood relation to father and mother through its relation to its brothers and sisters. The elder brother is no longer the true father and the elder sister no longer the true mother. Later, husband and wife are originally strangers to one another and come from different families with a different history and often a different social background. When children

95

come, they complete the process by forcing the parents into the role of father and mother, which the parents, in accordance with their infantile attitude, formerly saw only in others, thereby trying to secure for themselves all the advantages of the childhood role. Every more or less normal life runs this enantiodromian course and compels a change of attitude from the extreme of the child to the other extreme of the parent. The change requires the recognition of objective facts and values which a child can dismiss from his mind. School, however, inexorably instils into him the idea of objective time, of duty and the fulfilment of duty, of outside authority, no matter whether he likes or loathes the school and his teacher. And with school and the relentless advance of time, one objective fact after another increasingly forces its way into his personal life, regardless of whether it is welcome or not and whether he has developed any special attitude towards it. Meanwhile it is made overpoweringly clear that any prolongation of the father-and-mother world beyond its allotted span must be paid for dearly. All attempts to carry the infant's personal world over into the greater world are doomed to failure; even the transference which occurs during the treatment of neurosis is at best only an intermediate stage, giving the patient a chance to shed all the fragments of egg-shell still adhering to him from his childhood days, and to withdraw the projection of the parental imagos from external reality. This operation is one of the most difficult tasks of modern psychotherapy. At one time it was optimistically assumed that the parental imagos could be more or less broken down and destroyed through analysis of their contents. But in reality that is not the case: although the parental imagos can be released from the state of projection and withdrawn from the external world, they continue, like everything else acquired in early childhood, to retain their original freshness. With the withdrawal of the projection they fall back into the individual psyche, from which indeed they mainly originated.[2]

213   Before we go into the question of what happens when the parental imagos are no longer projected, let us turn to another question: Is this problem, which has been brought to light by

[2] As we know, the parental imago is constituted on the one hand by the personally acquired image of the personal parents, but on the other hand by the parent archetype which exists *a priori*, i.e., in the pre-conscious structure of the psyche.

modern psychotherapy, a new one in the sense that it was un-known to earlier ages which possessed no scientific psychology as we understand it? How did this problem present itself in the past?

214   In so far as earlier ages had in fact no knowledge of psycho-therapy in our sense of the word, we cannot possibly expect to find in history any formulations similar to our own. But since the transformation of child into parent has been going on everywhere from time immemorial and, with the increase of consciousness, was also experienced subjectively as a difficult process, we must conjecture the existence of various general psychotherapeutic systems which enabled man to accomplish the difficult transition-stages. And we do find, even at the most primitive level, certain drastic measures at all those moments in life when psychic transitions have to be effected. The most im-portant of these are the initiations at puberty and the rites per-taining to marriage, birth, and death. All these ceremonies, which in primitive cultures still free from foreign influence are observed with the utmost care and exactitude, are probably designed in the first place to avert the psychic injuries liable to occur at such times; but they are also intended to impart to the initiand the preparation and teaching needed for life. The existence and prosperity of a primitive tribe are absolutely bound up with the scrupulous and traditional performance of the ceremonies. Wherever these customs fall into disuse through the influence of the white man, authentic tribal life ceases; the tribe loses its soul and disintegrates. Opinion is very much divided about the influence of Christian missionaries in this respect; what I myself saw in Africa led me to take an extremely pessimistic view.

215   On a higher and more civilized level the same work is per-formed by the great religions. There are the christening, con-firmation, marriage, and funeral ceremonies which, as is well known, are much closer to their origins, more living and com-plete, in Catholic ritual than in Protestantism. Here too we see how the father-mother world of the child is superseded by a wealth of analogical symbols: a patriarchal order receives the adult into a new filial relationship through spiritual generation and rebirth. The pope as *pater patrum* and the *ecclesia mater* are the parents of a family that embraces the whole of Christen-

97

dom, except such parts of it as protest. Had the parental imagos been destroyed in the course of development and thus been rendered ineffective, an order of this kind would have lost not only its *raison d'être* but the very possibility of its existence. As it is, however, a place is found for the ever-active parental imagos as well as for that ineradicable feeling of being a child, a feeling which finds meaning and shelter in the bosom of the Church. In addition, a number of other ecclesiastical institutions provide for the steady growth and constant renewal of the bond. Among them I would mention in particular the mass and the confessional. The Communion is, in the proper sense of the word, the family table at which the members foregather and partake of the meal in the presence of God, following a sacred custom that goes far back into pre-Christian times.

216   It is superfluous to describe these familiar things in greater detail. I mention them only to show that the treatment of the psyche in times gone by had in view the same fundamental facts of human life as modern psychotherapy. But how differently religion deals with the parental imagos! It does not dream of breaking them down or destroying them; on the contrary, it recognizes them as living realities which it would be neither possible nor profitable to eliminate. Religion lets them live on in changed and exalted form within the framework of a strictly traditional patriarchal order, which keeps not merely decades but whole centuries in living connection. Just as it nurtures and preserves the childhood psyche of the individual, so also it has conserved numerous and still living vestiges of the childhood psyche of humanity. In this way it guards against one of the greatest psychic dangers—loss of roots—which is a disaster not only for primitive tribes but for civilized man as well. The breakdown of a tradition, necessary as this may be at times, is always a loss and a danger; and it is a danger to the soul because the life of instinct—the most conservative element in man— always expresses itself in traditional usages. Age-old convictions and customs are deeply rooted in the instincts. If they get lost, the conscious mind becomes severed from the instincts and loses its roots, while the instincts, unable to express themselves, fall back into the unconscious and reinforce its energy, causing this in turn to overflow into the existing contents of consciousness. It is then that the rootless condition of consciousness be-

comes a real danger. This secret *vis a tergo* results in a hybris of the conscious mind which manifests itself in the form of exaggerated self-esteem or an inferiority complex. At all events a loss of balance ensues, and this is the most fruitful soil for psychic injury.

217   If we look back over the thousand-odd years of our European civilization, we shall see that the Western ideal of the education and care of the soul has been, and for the most part still is, a patriarchal order based on the recognition of parental imagos. Thus in dealing with the individual, no matter how revolutionary his conscious attitude may be, we have to reckon with a patriarchal or hierarchical orientation of the psyche which causes it instinctively to seek and cling to this order. Any attempt to render the parental imagos and the childhood psyche ineffective is therefore doomed to failure from the outset.

218   At this point we come back to our earlier question of what happens when the parental imagos are withdrawn from projection. The detachment of these imagos from certain persons who carry the projection is undoubtedly possible and belongs to the stock in trade of psychotherapeutic success. On the other hand the problem becomes more difficult when there is a transference of the imagos to the doctor. In these cases the detachment can develop into a crucial drama. For what is to happen to the imagos if they are no longer attached to a human being? The pope as supreme father of Christendom holds his office from God; he is the servant of servants, and transference of the imagos to him is thus a transference to the Father in heaven and to Mother Church on earth. But how fares it with men and women who have been uprooted and torn out of their tradition? Professor Murray[3] of Harvard University has shown on the basis of extensive statistical material—thus confirming my own previously published experience—that the incidence of complexes is, on the average, highest among Jews; second come Protestants; and Catholics third. That a man's philosophy of life is directly connected with the well-being of the psyche can be seen from the fact that his mental attitude, his way of looking at things, is of enormous importance to him and his mental health—so much so that we could almost say that things are less what they

3 In *Explorations in Personality*, 118.

are than how we see them. If we have a disagreeable view of a situation or thing, our pleasure in it is spoiled, and then it does in fact usually disagree with us. And, conversely, how many things become bearable and even acceptable if we can give up certain prejudices and change our point of view. Paracelsus, who was above all a physician of genius, emphasized that nobody could be a doctor who did not understand the art of "theorizing." [4] What he meant was that the doctor must induce, not only in himself but also in his patient, a way of looking at the illness which would enable the doctor to cure and the patient to recover, or at least to endure being ill. That is why he says "every illness is a purgatorial fire." [5] He consciously recognized and made full use of the healing power of a man's mental attitude. When, therefore, I am treating practising Catholics, and am faced with the transference problem, I can, by virtue of my office as a doctor, step aside and lead the problem over to the Church. But if I am treating a non-Catholic, that way out is debarred, and by virtue of my office as a doctor I cannot step aside, for there is as a rule nobody there, nothing towards which I could suitably lead the father-imago. I can, of course, get the patient to recognize with his reason that I am not the father. But by that very act I become the reasonable father and remain despite everything the father. Not only nature, but the patient too, abhors a vacuum. He has an instinctive horror of allowing the parental imagos and his childhood psyche to fall into nothingness, into a hopeless past that has no future. His instinct tells him that, for the sake of his own wholeness, these things must be kept alive in one form or another. He knows that a complete withdrawal of the projection will be followed by an apparently endless isolation within the ego, which is all the more burdensome because he has so little love for it. He found it unbearable enough before, and he is unlikely to bear it now simply out of sweet reasonableness. Therefore at this juncture the Catholic who has been freed from an excessively personal tie to his parents can return fairly easily to the mysteries of the Church, which he is now in a position to understand better and more deeply. There are also Protestants

4 *Labyrinthus medicorum errantium,* 128, Cap. VIII, "Theorica medica." [The word θεωρία originally meant "a looking about one and seeing the world."—TRANS.]
5 *De ente Dei,* 129, Tract. V, Cap. I.

who can discover in one of the newer variants of Protestantism a meaning which appeals to them, and so regain a genuine religious attitude. All other cases—unless there is a violent and sometimes injurious solution—will, as the saying goes, "get stuck" in the transference relationship, thereby subjecting both themselves and the doctor to a severe trial of patience. Probably this cannot be avoided, for a sudden fall into the orphaned, parentless state may in certain cases—namely, where there is a tendency to psychosis—have dangerous consequences owing to the equally sudden activation of the unconscious which always accompanies it. Accordingly the projection can and should be withdrawn only step by step. The integration of the contents split off in the parental imagos has an activating effect on the unconscious, for these imagos are charged with all the energy they originally possessed in childhood, thanks to which they continued to exercise a fateful influence even on the adult. Their integration therefore means a considerable afflux of energy to the unconscious, which soon makes itself felt in the increasingly strong coloration of the conscious mind by unconscious contents. Isolation in pure ego-consciousness has the paradoxical consequence that there now appear in dreams and fantasies impersonal, collective contents which are the very material from which certain schizophrenic psychoses are constructed. For this reason the situation is not without its dangers, since the releasing of the ego from its ties with the projection—and of these the transference to the doctor plays the principal part—involves the risk that the ego, which was formerly dissolved in relationships to the personal environment, may now be dissolved in the contents of the collective unconscious. For, although the parents may be dead in the world of external reality, they and their imagos have passed over into the "other" world of the collective unconscious, where they continue to attract the same ego-dissolving projections as before.

219   But at this point a healthful, compensatory operation comes into play which each time seems to me like a miracle. Struggling against that dangerous trend towards disintegration, there arises out of this same collective unconscious a counter-action, characterized by symbols which point unmistakably to a process of centring. This process creates nothing less than

101

a new centre of personality, which the symbols show from the first to be superordinate to the ego and which later proves its superiority empirically. The centre cannot therefore be classed with the ego, but must be accorded a higher value. Nor can we continue to give it the name of "ego," for which reason I have called it the "self." To experience and realize this self is the ultimate aim of Indian yoga, and in considering the psychology of the self we would do well to have recourse to the treasures of Indian wisdom. In India, as with us, the experience of the self has nothing to do with intellectualism; it is a vital happening which brings about a fundamental transformation of personality. I have called the process that leads to this experience the "process of individuation." If I recommend the study of classical yoga, it is not because I am one of those who roll up their eyes in ecstasy when they hear such magic words as *dhyana* or *buddhi* or *mukti*, but because psychologically we can learn a great deal from yoga philosophy and turn it to practical account. Furthermore, the material lies ready to hand, clearly formulated in the Eastern books and the translations made of them. Here again my reason is not that we have nothing equivalent in the West: I recommend yoga merely because the Western knowledge which is akin to it is more or less inaccessible except to specialists. It is esoteric, and it is distorted beyond recognition by being formulated as an arcane discipline and by all the rubbish that this draws in its wake. In alchemy there lies concealed a Western system of yoga meditation, but it was kept a carefully guarded secret from fear of heresy and its painful consequences. For the practising psychologist, however, alchemy has one inestimable advantage over Indian yoga—its ideas are expressed almost entirely in an extraordinarily rich symbolism, the very symbolism we still find in our patients today. The help which alchemy affords us in understanding the symbols of the individuation process is, in my opinion, of the utmost importance.[6]

220   Alchemy describes what I call the "self" as *incorruptibile*, that is, an indissoluble substance, a One and Indivisible that cannot be reduced to anything else and is at the same time a Universal, to which a sixteenth-century alchemist even gave the

6 Cf. my *Psychology and Alchemy*, 85, and *Psychology and Religion*, 86.

name of *filius macrocosmi.*[7] Modern findings agree in principle with these formulations.

221   I had to mention all these things in order to get to the problem of today. For if we perseveringly and consistently follow the way of natural development, we arrive at the experience of the self, and at the state of being simply what one is. This is expressed as an ethical demand by the motto of Paracelsus, the four-hundredth anniversary of whose birth we celebrated in the autumn of 1941: "Alterius non sit, qui suus esse potest" (That man no other man shall own,/Who to himself belongs alone)—a motto both characteristically Swiss and characteristically alchemical. But the way to this goal is toilsome and not for all to travel. "Est longissima via," say the alchemists. We are still only at the beginning of a development whose origins lie in late antiquity, and which throughout the Middle Ages led little more than a hole-and-corner existence, vegetating in obscurity and represented by solitary eccentrics who were called, not without reason, *tenebriones.* Nevertheless men like Albertus Magnus, Roger Bacon, and Paracelsus were among the fathers of modern science, and their spirit did much to shake the authority of the "total" Church. Our modern psychology grew out of the spirit of natural science and, without realizing it, is carrying on the work begun by the alchemists. These men were convinced that the *donum artis* was given only to the few *electis,* and today our experience shows us only too plainly how arduous is the work with each patient and how few can attain the necessary knowledge and experience. Meanwhile the disintegration and weakening of that salutary institution, the Christian Church, goes on at an alarming rate, and the loss of any firm authority is gradually leading to an intellectual, political, and social anarchy which is repugnant to the soul of European man, accustomed as he is to a patriarchal order. The present attempts to achieve full individual consciousness and to mature the personality are, socially speaking, still so feeble that they carry no weight at all in relation to our historic needs. If our European social order is not to be shaken to its foundations, authority must be restored at all costs.

7 Khunrath, *Von hylealischen . . . Chaos,* 97.

222   This is probably one reason for the efforts now being made in Europe to replace the collectivity of the Church by the collectivity of the State. And just as the Church was once absolute in its determination to make theocracy a reality, so the State is now making an absolute bid for totalitarianism. The mystique of the spirit has not been replaced by a mystique either of nature or of the *lumen naturae,* as Paracelsus named it, but by the total incorporation of the individual in a political collective called the "State." This offers a way out of the dilemma, for the parental imagos can now be projected upon the State as the universal provider and the authority responsible for all thinking and willing. The ends of science are made to serve the social collective and are only valued for their practical utility to the collective's ends. The natural course of psychological development is succeeded, not by a spiritual direction which spans the centuries and keeps cultural values alive, but by a political directorate which ministers to the power struggles of special groups and promises economic benefits to the masses. In this way European man's deep-seated longing for a patriarchal and hierarchical order finds an appropriate concrete expression which accords only too well with the herd instinct, but is fixed at such a low level as to be in every respect detrimental to culture.

223   It is here that opinion is apt to be divided. In so far as psychotherapy claims to stand on a scientific basis and thus by the principle of free investigation, its declared aim is to educate people towards independence and moral freedom in accordance with the knowledge arrived at by unprejudiced scientific research. Whatever the conditions to which the individual wishes to adapt himself, he should always do so consciously and of his own free choice. But, in so far as political aims and the State are to claim precedence, psychotherapy would inevitably become the instrument of a particular political system, and it is to *its* aims that people would have to be educated and at the same time seduced from their own highest destiny. Against this conclusion it will undoubtedly be objected that man's ultimate destiny lies not in his existence as an individual but in the aspirations of human society, because without this the individual could not exist at all. This objection is a weighty one and cannot be lightly dismissed. It is an un-

doubted truth that the individual exists only by virtue of society and has always so existed. That is why among primitive
tribes we find the custom of initiation into manhood, when,
by means of a ritual death, the individual is detached from his
family and indeed from his whole previous identity, and is
reborn as a member of the tribe. Or we find early civilizations,
such as the Egyptian and Babylonian, where all individuality
is concentrated in the person of the king, while the ordinary
person remains anonymous. Or again, we observe whole families in which for generations the individuality of the name has
compensated for the nonentity of its bearers; or a long succession of Japanese artists who discard their own name and adopt
the name of a master, simply adding after it a modest numeral.
Nevertheless, it was the great and imperishable achievement
of Christianity that, in contrast to these archaic systems which
are all based on the original projection of psychic contents,
it gave to each individual man the dignity of an immortal
soul, whereas in earlier times this prerogative was reserved
to the sole person of the king. It would lead me too far to
discuss here just how much this Christian innovation represents an advance of human consciousness and of culture in
general, by putting an end to the projection of the highest
values of the individual soul upon the king or other dignitaries.
The innate will to consciousness, to moral freedom and culture,
proved stronger than the brute compulsion of projections which
keep the individual permanently imprisoned in the dark of
unconsciousness and grind him down into nonentity. Certainly
this advance laid a cross upon him—the torment of consciousness, of moral conflict, and the uncertainty of his own thoughts.
This task is so immeasurably difficult that it can be accomplished, if at all, only by stages, century by century, and it must
be paid for by endless suffering and toil in the struggle against
all those powers which are incessantly at work persuading us
to take the apparently easier road of unconsciousness. Those
who go the way of unconsciousness imagine that the task can
safely be left to "others" or, ultimately, to the anonymous State.
But who are these "others," these obvious supermen who pretend to be able to do what everybody is only too ready to believe
that he cannot do? They are men just like ourselves, who think
and feel as we do, except that they are past masters in the art of

"passing the buck." Exactly *who* is the State?—The agglomeration of all the nonentities composing it. Could it be personified, the result would be an individual, or rather a monster, intellectually and ethically far below the level of most of the individuals in it, since it represents mass psychology raised to the *n*th power. Therefore Christianity in its best days never subscribed to a belief in the State, but set before man a supramundane goal which should redeem him from the compulsive force of his projections upon this world, whose ruler is the spirit of darkness. And it gave him an immortal soul that he might have a fulcrum from which to lift the world off its hinges, showing him that his goal lies not in the mastery of this world but in the attainment of the Kingdom of God, whose foundations are in his own heart.

224   If, then, man cannot exist without society, neither can he exist without oxygen, water, albumen, fat, and so forth. Like these, society is one of the necessary conditions of his existence. It would be ludicrous to maintain that man lives in order to breathe air. It is equally ludicrous to say that the individual exists for society. "Society" is nothing more than a term, a concept for the symbiosis of a group of human beings. A concept is not a carrier of life. The sole and natural carrier of life is the individual, and that is so throughout nature.[8] "Society" or "State" is an agglomeration of life-carriers and at the same time, as an organized form of these, an important condition of life. It is therefore not quite true to say that the individual can exist only as a particle in society. At all events man can live very much longer without the State than without air.

8 Pestalozzi said (*Ideen*, 131, p. 187): "None of the institutions, measures, and means of education established for the masses and the needs of men in the aggregate, whatever shape or form they may take, serve to advance human culture. In the vast majority of cases they are completely worthless for that purpose and are directly opposed to it. Our race develops its human qualities in essence only from face to face, from heart to heart. Essentially it develops only in little intimate circles which gradually grow in graciousness and love, in confidence and trust. All the means requisite for the education of man, which serve to make him truly humane and to bring him to mankindliness, are in their origin and essence the concern of the individual and of such institutions as are closely and intimately attached to his heart and mind. They never were nor will be the concern of the masses. They never were nor will be the concern of civilization." [See note 10 below.—TRANS.]

225   When the political aim predominates there can be no doubt
that a secondary thing has been made the primary thing.
Then the individual is cheated of his rightful destiny and two
thousand years of Christian civilization are wiped out. Consciousness, instead of being widened by the withdrawal of projections, is narrowed, because society, a mere condition of
human existence, is set up as a goal. Society is the greatest
temptation to unconsciousness, for the mass infallibly swallows
up the individual—who has no security in himself—and reduces
him to a helpless particle. The totalitarian State could not
tolerate for one moment the right of psychotherapy to help
man fulfil his natural destiny. On the contrary, it would be
bound to insist that psychotherapy should be nothing but a
tool for the production of manpower useful to the State. In this
way it would become a mere technique tied to a single aim, that
of increasing social efficiency. The soul would forfeit all life of
its own and become a function to be used as the State saw fit.
The science of psychology would be degraded to a study of the
ways and means to exploit the psychic apparatus. As to its
therapeutic aim, the complete and successful incorporation of
the patient into the State machine would be the criterion of
cure. Since this aim can best be achieved by making the individual completely soulless—that is, as unconscious as possible—all
methods designed to increase consciousness would at one stroke
become obsolete, and the best thing would be to bring out of
the lumber-rooms of the past all the methods that have ever
been devised to prevent man from becoming conscious of his
unconscious contents. Thus the art of psychotherapy would
be driven into a complete regression.[9]

9 Ibid., pp. 189f.: "The collective existence of our race can only produce civilization, not culture. [See note 10 below.—Trans.] Is it not true, do we not see every day,
that in proportion as the herd-like aggregations of men become more important,
and in proportion as officialdom, which represents the legal concentration of the
power of the masses, has freer play and wields greater authority, the divine breath
of tenderness is the more easily extinguished in the hearts of the individuals
composing these human aggregations and their officials, and that the receptivity
to truth which lies deep in man's nature perishes within them to the same degree?

"The collectively unified man, if truly he be nothing but that, sinks down in
all his relations into the depths of civilized corruption, and sunk in this corruption, ceases to seek more over the whole earth than the wild animals in the forest
seek."

226 Such, in broad outline, is the alternative facing psychotherapy at this present juncture. Future developments will decide whether Europe, which fancied it had escaped the Middle Ages, is to be plunged for a second time and for centuries into the darkness of an Inquisition. This will only happen if the totalitarian claims of the State are forcibly carried through and become a permanency. No intelligent person will deny that the organization of society, which we call the State, not only feels a lively need to extend its authority but is compelled by circumstances to do so. If this comes about by free consent and the conscious choice of the public, the results will leave nothing to be desired. But if it comes about for the sake of convenience, in order to avoid tiresome decisions, or from lack of consciousness, then the individual runs the certain risk of being blotted out as a responsible human being. The State will then be no different from a prison or an ant-heap.

227 Although the conscious achievement of individuality is consistent with man's natural destiny, it is nevertheless not his whole aim. It cannot possibly be the object of human education to create an anarchic conglomeration of individual existences. That would be too much like the unavowed ideal of extreme individualism, which is essentially no more than a morbid reaction against an equally futile collectivism. In contrast to all this, the natural process of individuation brings to birth a consciousness of human community precisely because it makes us aware of the unconscious, which unites and is common to all mankind. Individuation is an at-one-ment with oneself and at the same time with humanity, since oneself is a part of humanity. Once the individual is thus secured in himself, there is some guarantee that the organized accumulation of individuals in the State—even in one wielding greater authority—will result in the formation no longer of an anonymous mass but of a conscious community. The indispensable condition for this is conscious freedom of choice and individual decision. Without this freedom and self-determination there is no true community, and, it must be said, without such community even the free and self-secured individual cannot in the long run prosper.[10]

10 More than a hundred years ago, in times not so unlike our own, Pestalozzi wrote (ibid., p. 186): "The race of men cannot remain socially united without some ordering power. Culture has the power to unite men as individuals, in independence and

Moreover, the common weal is best served by independent personalities. Whether man today possesses the maturity needed for such a decision is another question. On the other hand, solutions which violently forestall natural development and are forced on mankind are equally questionable. The facts of nature cannot in the long run be violated. Penetrating and seeping through everything like water, they will undermine any system that fails to take account of them, and sooner or later they will bring about its downfall. But an authority wise enough in its statesmanship to give sufficient free play to nature—of which spirit is a part—need fear no premature decline. It is perhaps a humiliating sign of spiritual immaturity that European man needs, and wants, a large measure of authority. The fact has to be faced that countless millions in Europe—with the guilty complicity of reformers whose childishness is only equalled by their lack of tradition—have escaped from the authority of the Church and the *patria potestas* of kings and emperors only to fall helpless and senseless victims to any power that cares to assume authority. The immaturity of man is a fact that must enter into all our calculations.

228   We in Switzerland are not living on a little planetoid revolving in empty space, but on the same earth as the rest of Europe. We are right in the middle of these problems, and if we are unconscious, we are just as likely to succumb to them as the other nations. The most dangerous thing would be for us to imagine that we are on a higher plane of consciousness than our neighbours. There is no question of that. While it would be an impropriety for a handful of psychologists and psychotherapists like ourselves to take our importance too seriously—or I might say, too pompously—I would nevertheless emphasize that just because we are psychologists it is our first task and duty to understand the psychic situation of our time and to see clearly the problems and challenges with which it faces us. Even if our voice

freedom, through law and art. But a cultureless civilization unites them as masses, without regard to independence, freedom, law or art, through the power of coercion." [N.B. Pestalozzi evidently subscribes to the Germanic distinction between *Kultur* and *Zivilisation*, where the latter term is employed in a pejorative sense. The idea is that culture, deriving ultimately from tillage and worship *(cultus)*, is a natural organic growth, whereas civilization is an affair of the city *(civis)* and thus something artificial. Cf. note 9 above.—TRANS.]

is too weak to make itself heard above the tumult of political strife and fades away ineffectively, we may yet comfort ourselves with the saying of the Chinese Master: "When the enlightened man is alone and thinks rightly, it can be heard a thousand miles away."

229 All beginnings are small. Therefore we must not mind doing tedious but conscientious work on obscure individuals, even though the goal towards which we strive seems unattainably far off. But one goal we can attain, and that is to develop and bring to maturity individual personalities. And inasmuch as we are convinced that the individual is the carrier of life, we have served life's purpose if one tree at least succeeds in bearing fruit, though a thousand others remain barren. Anyone who proposed to bring all growing things to the highest pitch of luxuriance would soon find the weeds—those hardiest of perennials—waving above his head. I therefore consider it the prime task of psychotherapy today to pursue with singleness of purpose the goal of individual development. So doing, our efforts will follow nature's own striving to bring life to the fullest possible fruition in each individual, for only in the individual can life fulfil its meaning—not in the bird that sits in a gilded cage.

IX

FUNDAMENTAL QUESTIONS
OF PSYCHOTHERAPY [1]

²³⁰   In the medical text-books of a few years back, under the general heading of "therapy," at the end of a list of cures and pharmaceutical prescriptions, one might find a mysterious item called "psychotherapy." What exactly one was to understand by this remained shrouded in eloquent obscurity. What did it mean? Was it hypnosis, suggestion, persuasion, catharsis, psychoanalysis, Adlerian education, autogenic training, or what? This list amply illustrates the vague multiplicity of opinions, views, theories, and methods that all pass under the name of "psychotherapy."

²³¹   When a new and uninhabited continent is discovered, there are no landmarks, no names, no highways, and every pioneer who sets foot upon it comes back with a different story. Something of this kind seems to have happened when medical men plunged for the first time into the new continent named "psyche." One of the first explorers to whom we are indebted for more or less intelligible reports is Paracelsus. His uncanny knowledge, which is at times not lacking in prophetic vision, was, however, expressed in a language that was informed by the spirit of the sixteenth century. It abounds not only in demonological and alchemical ideas, but in Paracelsian neologisms, whose florid exuberance compensated a secret feeling of inferiority quite in keeping with the self-assertiveness of their much maligned, and not unjustly misunderstood, creator. The scientific era, which began in earnest with the seventeenth century, cast out the pearls of Paracelsus' medical wisdom along with the other lumber. Not until two centuries later did a new and altogether different kind of empiricism arise with Mesmer's theory of animal magnetism, stemming partly from practical experiences which

1 [First published as "Grundfragen der Psychotherapie," *Dialectica* (Neuchâtel), V (1951): 1, 8–24.—EDITORS.]

today we should attribute to suggestion, and partly from the old alchemical lore. Working along these lines, the physicians of the Romantic Age then turned their attention to somnambulism, thus laying the foundations for the clinical discovery of hysteria. But almost another century had to pass before Charcot and his school could begin to consolidate ideas in this field. We have to thank Pierre Janet for a deeper and more exact knowledge of hysterical symptoms, and the two French physicians, Liébeault and Bernheim, later to be joined by August Forel in Switzerland, for a systematic investigation and description of the phenomena of suggestion. With the discovery by Breuer and Freud of the affective origins of psychogenic symptoms, our knowledge of their causation took a decisive step forward into the realm of psychology. The fact that the affectively toned memory images which are lost to consciousness lay at the root of the hysterical symptom immediately led to the postulate of an *unconscious* layer of psychic happenings. This layer proved to be, not "somatic," as the academic psychology of those days was inclined to assume, but *psychic,* because it behaves exactly like any other psychic function from which consciousness is withdrawn, and which thus ceases to be associated with the ego. As Janet showed almost simultaneously with Freud, but independently of him, this holds true of hysterical symptoms generally. But whereas Janet supposed that the reason for the withdrawal of consciousness must lie in some specific weakness, Freud pointed out that the memory images which produce the symptoms are characterized by a disagreeable affective tone. Their disappearance from consciousness could thus easily be explained by *repression.* Freud therefore regarded the aetiological contents as "incompatible" with the tendencies of the conscious mind. This hypothesis was supported by the fact that repressed memories frequently arouse a moral censorship, and do so precisely on account of their traumatic or morally repellent nature.

232   Freud extended the repression theory to the whole field of psychogenic neuroses with great practical success; indeed, he went on to use it as an explanation of culture as a whole. With this he found himself in the sphere of general psychology, which had long been entrusted to the philosophical faculty. Apart from a few technical terms and methodical points of view, psychology, as practised by the doctor, had not so far been able to borrow

much from the philosophers, and so medical psychology, on encountering an unconscious psyche right at the beginning of its career, literally stepped into a vacuum. The concept of the unconscious was, with a few praiseworthy exceptions, anathematized by academic psychology, so that only the phenomena of consciousness were left as a possible object for psychological research. The collision between the medical approach and the general psychology then prevailing was therefore considerable. On the other hand, Freud's discoveries were just as much of a challenge and a stumbling-block to the purely somatic views of the doctors. And so they have remained for the last fifty years. It needed the trend towards psychosomatic medicine that came over from America to put a fresher complexion on the picture. Even so, general psychology has still not been able to draw the necessary conclusions from the fact of the unconscious.

233   Any advance into new territory is always attended by certain dangers, for the pioneer has to rely in all his undertakings upon the equipment he happens to take with him. This, in the present instance, is his training in somatic medicine, his general education, and his view of the world, which is based chiefly on subjective premises, partly temperamental, partly social. His medical premises enable him to size up correctly the somatic and biological aspects of the material he has to deal with; his general education makes it possible for him to form an approximate idea of the nature of the repressive factor; and finally, his view of the world helps him to put his special knowledge on a broader basis and to fit it into a larger whole. But when scientific research moves into a region hitherto undiscovered and therefore unknown, the pioneer must always bear in mind that another explorer, setting foot on the new continent at another place and with other equipment, may well sketch quite another picture.

234   So it happened with Freud: his pupil Alfred Adler developed a view which shows neurosis in a very different light. It is no longer the sexual urge, or the pleasure principle, that dominates the picture, but the urge to power (self-assertion, "masculine protest," "the will to be on top"). As I have shown in a concrete instance,[2] both theories can be successfully applied to one and the same case; moreover it is a well-known psychological fact that the two urges keep the scales balanced, and that

2 *Two Essays*, **88,** pars. 16–55.

the one generally underlies the other. Adler remained as one-sided as Freud, and both agree that not only the neurosis, but the man himself, can be explained from the shadow side, in terms of his moral inferiority.

235   All this points to the existence of a personal equation, a subjective prejudice that was never submitted to criticism. The rigidity with which both men adhered to their position denotes, as always, the compensating of a secret uncertainty and an inner doubt. The facts as described by the two investigators are, if taken with a pinch of salt, right enough; but it is possible to interpret them in the one way as much as in the other, so that both are partially wrong, or rather, they are mutually complementary. The lesson to be drawn from this is that in practice one would do well to consider both points of view.

236   The reason for this first dilemma of medical psychology presumably lies in the fact that the doctors found no cultivated ground under their feet, since ordinary psychology had nothing concrete to offer them. They were therefore thrown back on their own subjective prejudices as soon as they looked round for tools. For me, this resolved itself into the pressing need to examine the kind of attitudes which human beings in general adopt towards the object (no matter what this object may be). Accordingly, I have come to postulate a number of types which all depend on the respective predominance of one or the other orienting function of consciousness, and have devised a tentative scheme into which the various attitudes can be articulated. From this it would appear that there are no less than eight theoretically possible attitudes. If we add to these all the other more or less individual assumptions, it is evident that there is no end to the possible viewpoints, all of which have their justification, at least subjectively. In consequence, criticism of the psychological assumptions upon which a man's theories are based becomes an imperative necessity. Unfortunately, however, this has still not been generally recognized, otherwise certain viewpoints could not be defended with such obstinacy and blindness. One can only understand why this should be so when one considers what the subjective prejudice signifies: it is as a rule a carefully constructed product into whose making has gone the whole experience of a lifetime. It is the individual psyche colliding with the environment. In the majority of cases, therefore, it is a subjective variant

of a universal human experience, and for that very reason careful self-criticism and detailed comparison are needed if we are to frame our judgments on a more universal basis. But the more we rely on the principles of consciousness in endeavouring to perform this essential task, the greater becomes the danger of our interpreting experience in those terms, and thus of doing violence to the facts by excessive theorizing. Our psychological experience is still too recent and too limited in scope to permit of general theories. The investigator needs a lot more facts which would throw light on the nature of the psyche before he can begin to think of universally valid propositions. For the present we must observe the rule that a psychological proposition can only lay claim to significance if the obverse of its meaning can also be accepted as true.

237   Personal and theoretical prejudices are the most serious obstacles in the way of psychological judgment. They can, however, be eliminated with a little good will and insight. Freud himself accepted my suggestion that every doctor should submit to a training analysis before interesting himself in the unconscious of his patients for therapeutic purposes. All intelligent psychotherapists who recognize the need for conscious realization of unconscious aetiological factors agree with this view. Indeed it is sufficiently obvious, and has been confirmed over and over again by experience, that what the doctor fails to see in himself he either will not see at all, or will see grossly exaggerated, in his patient; further, he encourages those things to which he himself unconsciously inclines, and condemns everything that he abhors in himself. Just as one rightly expects the surgeon's hands to be free from infection, so one ought to insist with especial emphasis that the psychotherapist be prepared at all times to exercise adequate self-criticism, a necessity which is all the more incumbent upon him when he comes up against insuperable resistances in the patient which may possibly be justified. He should remember that the patient is there to be treated and not to verify a theory. For that matter, there is no single theory in the whole field of practical psychology that cannot on occasion prove basically wrong. In particular, the view that the patient's resistances are in no circumstances justified is completely fallacious. The resistance might very well prove that the treatment rests on false assumptions.

238   I have dwelt on the theme of training analysis at some length because of late there have been renewed tendencies to build up the doctor's authority as such, and thus to inaugurate another era of *ex cathedra* psychotherapy, a project which differs in no way from the somewhat antiquated techniques of suggestion, whose inadequacy has long since become apparent. (This is not to say that suggestion therapy is never indicated.)

239   The intelligent psychotherapist has known for years that any complicated treatment is an individual, *dialectical* process, in which the doctor, as a person, participates just as much as the patient. In any such discussion the question of whether the doctor has as much insight into his own psychic processes as he expects from his patient naturally counts for a very great deal, particularly in regard to the "rapport," or relationship of mutual confidence, on which the therapeutic success ultimately depends. The patient, that is to say, can win his own inner security only from the security of his relationship to the doctor as a human being. The doctor can put over his authority with fairly good results on people who are easily gulled. But for critical eyes it is apt to look a little too threadbare. This is also the reason why the priest, the predecessor of the doctor in his role of healer and psychologist, has in large measure forfeited his authority, at any rate with the educated public. Difficult cases, therefore, are a veritable ordeal for both patient and doctor. The latter should be prepared for this as far as possible by a thorough training analysis. It is far from being either an ideal or an absolutely certain means of dispelling illusions and projections, but at least it demonstrates the need for self-criticism and can reinforce the psychotherapist's aptitude in this direction. No analysis is capable of banishing all unconsciousness for ever. The analyst must go on learning endlessly, and never forget that each new case brings new problems to light and thus gives rise to unconscious assumptions that have never before been constellated. We could say, without too much exaggeration, that a good half of every treatment that probes at all deeply consists in the doctor's examining himself, for only what he can put right in himself can he hope to put right in the patient. It is no loss, either, if he feels that the patient is hitting him, or even scoring off him: it is his own hurt that gives the measure of his power to heal. This, and nothing else, is the meaning of the Greek myth of the wounded physician.[3]

3 Kerényi, *Der göttliche Arzt*, **95,** p. 84.

240   The problems with which we are concerned here do not occur in the field of "minor" psychotherapy, where the doctor can get along quite well with suggestion, good advice, or an apt explanation. But neuroses or psychotic borderline states in complicated and intelligent people frequently require what is called "major" psychotherapy, that is, the dialectical procedure. In order to conduct this with any prospect of success, all subjective and theoretical assumptions must be eliminated as far as practicable. One cannot treat a Mohammedan on the basis of Christian beliefs, nor a Parsi with Jewish orthodoxy, nor a Christian with the pagan philosophy of the ancient world, without introducing dangerous foreign bodies into his psychic organism. This sort of thing is constantly practised, and not always with bad results; but, for all that, it is an experiment whose legitimacy seems to me exceedingly doubtful. I think a conservative treatment is the more advisable. One should, if possible, not destroy any values that have not proved themselves definitely injurious. To replace a Christian view of the world by a materialistic one is, to my way of thinking, just as wrong as the attempt to argue with a convinced materialist. That is the task of the missionary, not of the doctor.

241   Many psychotherapists, unlike me, hold the view that theoretical problems do not enter into the therapeutic process at all. The aetiological factors, they think, are all questions of purely personal psychology. But if we scrutinize these factors more closely, we find that they present quite a different picture. Take, for example, the sexual urge, which plays such an enormous role in Freudian theory. This urge, like every other urge, is not a personal acquisition, but is an objective and universal datum that has nothing whatever to do with our personal wishes, desires, opinions, and decisions. It is a completely impersonal force, and all we can do is to try to come to terms with it with the help of subjective and theoretical judgments. Of these latter, only the subjective premises (and then only a part of them) belong to the personal sphere; for the rest they are derived from the stream of tradition and from environmental influences, and only a very small fraction of them has been built up personally as a result of conscious choice. Just as I find myself moulded by external and objective social influences, so also I am moulded by internal and unconscious forces, which I have summed up under the term "the subjective factor." The man with the extraverted attitude bases himself primarily on social relationships; the other, the introvert,

primarily on the subjective factor. The former is largely unaware of his subjective determinacy and regards it as insignificant; as a matter of fact, he is frightened of it. The latter has little or no interest in social relationships; he prefers to ignore them, feeling them to be onerous, even terrifying. To the one, the world of relationships is the important thing; for him it represents normality, the goal of desire. The other is primarily concerned with the inner pattern of his life, with his own self-consistency.

242 When we come to analyse the personality, we find that the extravert makes a niche for himself in the world of relationships at the cost of unconsciousness (of himself as a subject); while the introvert, in realizing his personality, commits the grossest mistakes in the social sphere and blunders about in the most absurd way. These two very typical attitudes are enough to show—quite apart from the types of physiological temperament described by Kretschmer—how little one can fit human beings and their neuroses into the strait jacket of a single theory.

243 As a rule these subjective premises are quite unknown to the patient, and also, unfortunately, to the doctor, so that the latter is too often tempted to overlook the old adage *quod licet Jovi, non licet bovi,* or in other words, one man's meat is another man's poison, and in this way to unlock doors that were better shut, and vice versa. Medical theory is just as likely as the patient to become the victim of its own subjective premises, even if to a lesser degree, since it is at least the outcome of comparative work on a large number of cases and has therefore rejected any excessively individual variants. This, however, is only in the smallest degree true of the personal prejudices of its creator. Though the comparative work will do something to mitigate them, they will nevertheless give a certain colouring to his medical activities and will impose certain limits. Accordingly, one urge or the other, one idea or the other, will then impose itself as the limit and become a bogus principle which is the be-all and end-all of research. Within this framework everything can be observed correctly and—according to the subjective premise—logically interpreted, as was undoubtedly the case with Freud and Adler; and yet in spite of this, or perhaps just because of it, very different views will result, in fact to all appearances they will be flatly irreconcilable. The reason obviously lies in the subjective premise, which assimilates what suits it and discards what does not.

244   Such developments are by no means the exception in the history of science, they are the rule. Anyone who accuses modern medical psychology of not even being able to reach agreement on its own theories is completely forgetting that no science can retain its vitality without divergences of theory. Disagreements of this kind are, as always, incentives to a new and deeper questioning. So also in psychology. The Freud-Adler dilemma found its solution in the acceptance of divergent principles, each of which laid stress on one particular aspect of the total problem.

245   Seen from this angle, there are numerous lines of research still waiting to be opened up. One of the most interesting, perhaps, is the problem of the *a priori* attitude-type and of the functions underlying it. This was the line followed by the Rorschach test, Gestalt psychology, and the various other attempts to classify type-differences. Another possibility, which seems to me equally important, is the investigation of the theoretical [4] factors that have proved to be of such cardinal importance when it comes to choosing and deciding. They have to be considered not only in the aetiology of neurosis, but in the evaluation of the analytical findings. Freud himself laid great emphasis on the function of the moral "censor" as one cause of repression, and he even felt obliged to hold up religion as one of the neuroticizing factors which lend support to infantile wish-fantasies. There are, in addition, theoretical assumptions that claim to play a decisive part in "sublimation"—value-categories that are supposed to help or hinder the work of fitting the tendencies revealed by the analysis of the unconscious into the life-plan of the patient. The very greatest significance attaches to the investigation of these so-called theoretical factors, not only in regard to the aetiology but—what is far more important—in regard to the therapy and necessary *reconstruction of the personality,* as Freud himself confirmed, even if only negatively, in his later writings. A substantial part of these factors was termed by him the "super-ego," which is the sum of all the collective beliefs and values consciously handed down by tradition. These, like the Torah for the orthodox Jew, constitute

---

4 [Literally *weltanschaulich,* "pertaining to one's view of the world." *Weltanschauung* is usually translated as "philosophy (of life)," "world-view," etc. In the present context, "theoretical" is used in the precise sense of the Greek ϑεωρία, which meant "looking about the world," "contemplation"; hence "speculation." Cf. p. 100, note 4.—TRANS.]

a solidly entrenched psychic system which is superordinate to the ego and the cause of numerous conflicts.

246   Freud also observed that the unconscious occasionally produces images that can only be described as "archaic." They are found more particularly in dreams and in waking fantasies. He, too, tried to interpret or amplify such symbols "historically," as for example in his study of the dual mother motif in a dream of Leonardo da Vinci.[5]

247   Now it is a well-known fact that the factors composing the "super-ego" correspond to the "collective representations" which Lévy-Bruhl posited as basic to the psychology of primitive man. The latter are general ideas and value-categories which have their origin in the primordial motifs of mythology, and they govern the psychic and social life of the primitive in much the same way as our lives are governed and moulded by the general beliefs, views, and ethical values in accordance with which we are brought up and by which we make our way in the world. They intervene almost automatically in all our acts of choice and decision, as well as being operative in the formation of concepts. With a little reflection, therefore, we can practically always tell why we do something and on what general assumptions our judgments and decisions are based. The false conclusions and wrong decisions of the neurotic have pathogenic effects because they are as a rule in conflict with these premises. Whoever can live with these premises without friction fits into our society as perfectly as the primitive, who takes his tribal teachings as an absolute rule of conduct.

248   But when an individual, as a result perhaps of some anomaly in his personal disposition (no matter what this may be), ceases to conform to the canon of collective ideas, he will very likely find himself not only in conflict with society, but in disharmony with himself, since the super-ego represents another psychic system within him. In that case he will become neurotic: a dissociation of the personality supervenes, which, given the necessary psychopathic foundation, may lead to its complete fragmentation, that is, to the schizoid personality and to schizophrenia. Such a case serves as a model for the *personal neurosis,* for which an explanation in personalistic terms is quite sufficient, as we know from experience that no further procedure is necessary for a cure except the demolition of the subject's false conclusions and wrong deci-

5 Freud, 52.

sions. His wrong attitude having been corrected, the patient can then fit into society again. His illness was in fact nothing but the product of a certain "weakness," either congenital or acquired. In cases of this kind it would be a bad mistake to try to alter anything in the fundamental idea, the "collective representation." That would only thrust the patient still deeper into his conflict with society by countenancing his pathogenic weakness.

249   Clinical observations seem to show that schizophrenes fall into two different groups: an asthenic type (hence the French term *psychasthénie*) and a spastic type, given to active conflict. And the same is true of neurotics. The first type is represented by the kind of neurosis which can be explained purely personalistically, as it is a form of maladjustment based on personal weakness. The second type is represented by individuals who *could* be adjusted without much difficulty, and who have also proved their aptitude for it. But for some reason or other they cannot or will not adjust themselves, and they do not understand why their own particular "adjustment" does not make normal life possible for them, when in their estimation such a life should be well within the bounds of possibility. The reason for their neurosis seems to lie in their having something above the average, an overplus for which there is no adequate outlet. We may then expect the patient to be consciously or—in most cases—unconsciously critical of the generally accepted views and ideas. Freud, too, seems to have come across similar experiences, otherwise he would hardly have felt impelled to attack religion from the standpoint of the medical psychologist, as being the cornerstone of a man's fundamental beliefs. Seen in the light of medical experience, however, this attempt was, in a sense, thoroughly consistent with its own premises, although one can hold a very different view on the manner in which it was conducted; for not only is religion not the enemy of the sick, it is actually a system of psychic healing, as the use of the Christian term "cure of souls" makes clear, and as is also evident from the Old Testament.[6]

250   It is principally the neuroses of the second type that confront the doctor with problems of this kind. There are in addition not a few patients who, although they have no clinically recognizable neurosis, come to consult the doctor on account of psychic conflicts and various other difficulties in their lives, laying before

6 E.g., Psalms 147:3 and Job 5:18.

him problems whose answer inevitably involves a discussion of fundamental questions. Such people often know very well—what the neurotic seldom or never knows—that their conflicts have to do with the fundamental problem of their own attitude, and that this is bound up with certain principles or general ideas, in a word, with their religious, ethical, or philosophical beliefs. It is precisely because of such cases that psychotherapy has to spread far beyond the confines of somatic medicine and psychiatry into regions that were formerly the province of priests and philosophers. From the degree to which priests and philosophers no longer discharge any duties in this respect or their competence to do so has been denied by the public, we can see what an enormous gap the psychotherapist is sometimes called upon to fill, and how remote religion on the one hand and philosophy on the other have become from the actualities of life. The parson is blamed because one always knows in advance what he is going to say; the philosopher, because he never says anything of the slightest practical value. And the odd thing is that both of them—with few and ever fewer exceptions—are distinctly unsympathetic towards psychology.

251   The positive meaning of the religious factor in a man's philosophical outlook will not, of course, prevent certain views and interpretations from losing their force and becoming obsolete, as a result of changes in the times, in the social conditions, and in the development of human consciousness. The old mythologems upon which all religion is ultimately based are, as we now see them, the expression of inner psychic events and experiences; and, by means of a ritualistic "anamnesis," they enable the conscious mind to preserve its link with the unconscious, which continues to send out or "ecphorate" [7] the primordial images just as it did in the remote past. These images give adequate expression to the unconscious, and its instinctive movements can in that way be transmitted to the conscious mind without friction, so that the conscious mind never loses touch with its instinctive roots. If, however, certain of these images become antiquated, if, that is to say, they lose all intelligible connection with our contemporary consciousness, then our conscious acts of choice and decision are sundered from their instinctive roots, and a partial disorientation results, because our judgment then lacks any feeling of

[7] [From ἐκφορέω, "to carry forth."—Trans.]

definiteness and certitude, and there is no emotional driving-force behind decision. The collective representations that connect primitive man with the life of his ancestors or with the founders of his tribe form the bridge to the unconscious for civilized man also, who, if he is a believer, will see it as the world of divine presences. Today these bridges are in a state of partial collapse, and the doctor is in no position to hold those who are worst hit responsible for the disaster. He knows that it is due far more to a shifting of the whole psychic situation over many centuries, such as has happened more than once in human history. In the face of such transformations the individual is powerless.

252   The doctor can only look on and try to understand the attempts at restitution and cure which nature herself is making. Experience has long shown that between conscious and unconscious there exists a compensatory relationship, and that the unconscious always tries to make whole the conscious part of the psyche by adding to it the parts that are missing, and so prevent a dangerous loss of balance. In our own case, as might be expected, the unconscious produces compensating symbols which are meant to replace the broken bridges, but which can only do so with the active co-operation of consciousness. In other words, these symbols must, if they are to be effective, be "understood" by the conscious mind; they must be assimilated and integrated. A dream that is not understood remains a mere occurrence; understood, it becomes a living experience.

253   I therefore consider it my main task to examine the manifestations of the unconscious in order to learn its language. But since, on the one hand, the theoretical assumptions we have spoken of are of eminently historical interest, and, on the other hand, the symbols produced by the unconscious derive from archaic modes of psychic functioning, one must, in carrying out these investigations, have at one's command a vast amount of historical material; and, secondly, one must bring together and collate an equally large amount of empirical material based on direct observation.

254   The practical need for a deeper understanding of the products of the unconscious is sufficiently obvious. In pursuit of this, I am only going further along the path taken by Freud, though I certainly try to avoid having any preconceived metaphysical opinions. I try rather to keep to first-hand experience, and to

leave metaphysical beliefs, either for or against, to look after themselves. I do not imagine for a moment that I can stand above or beyond the psyche, so that it would be possible to judge it, as it were, from some transcendental Archimedean point "outside." I am fully aware that I am entrapped in the psyche and that I cannot do anything except describe the experiences that there befall me. When, for instance, one examines the world of fairytales, one can hardly avoid the impression that one is meeting certain figures again and again, albeit in altered guise. Such comparisons lead on to what the student of folklore calls the investigation of motifs. The psychologist of the unconscious proceeds no differently in regard to the psychic figures which appear in dreams, fantasies, visions, and manic ideas, as in legends, fairytales, myth, and religion. Over the whole of this psychic realm there reign certain motifs, certain typical figures which we can follow far back into history, and even into prehistory, and which may therefore legitimately be described as "archetypes." [8] They seem to me to be built into the very structure of man's unconscious, for in no other way can I explain why it is that they occur universally and in identical form, whether the redeemer-figure be a fish, a hare, a lamb, a snake, or a human being. It is the same redeemer-figure in a variety of accidental disguises. From numerous experiences of this kind I have come to the conclusion that the most individual thing about man is surely his consciousness, but that his shadow, by which I mean the uppermost layer of his unconscious, is far less individualized, the reason being that a man is distinguished from his fellows more by his virtues than by his negative qualities. The unconscious, however, in its principal and most overpowering manifestations, can only be regarded as a collective phenomenon which is everywhere identical, and, because it never seems to be at variance with itself, it may well possess a marvellous unity and self-consistency, the nature of which is at present shrouded in impenetrable darkness. Another fact to be considered here is the existence today of parapsychology, whose proper subject is manifestations that are directly connected with the unconscious. The most important of these are

[8] The concept of the archetype is a specifically psychological instance of the "pattern of behaviour" in biology. Hence it has nothing whatever to do with inherited ideas, but with modes of behaviour.

the E.S.P.[9] phenomena, which medical psychology should on no account ignore. If these phenomena prove anything at all, it is the fact of a certain psychic relativity of space and time, which throws a significant light on the unity of the collective unconscious. For the present, at any rate, only two groups of facts have been established with any certainty: firstly, the congruence of individual symbols and mythologems; and secondly, the phenomenon of extra-sensory perception. The interpretation of these phenomena is reserved for the future.

[9] Extra-sensory perception.

II

SPECIFIC PROBLEMS
OF
PSYCHOTHERAPY

II

I

THE THERAPEUTIC VALUE OF ABREACTION[1]

255   In his discussion of William Brown's paper, "The Revival of Emotional Memories and Its Therapeutic Value," William McDougall, writing in the *British Journal of Psychology*,[2] gave expression to some important considerations which I would like to underline here. The neuroses resulting from the Great War have, with their essentially traumatic aetiology, revived the whole question of the trauma theory of neurosis. During the years of peace this theory had rightly been kept in the background of scientific discussion, since its conception of neurotic aetiology is far from adequate.

256   The originators of the theory were Breuer and Freud. Freud went on to a deeper investigation of the neuroses and soon adopted a view that took more account of their real origins. In by far the greater number of ordinary cases there is no question of a traumatic aetiology.

257   But, in order to create the impression that the neurosis is caused by some trauma or other, unimportant and secondary occurrences must be given an artificial prominence for the sake of the theory. These traumata, when they are not mere products of medical fantasy, or else the result of the patient's own compliancy, are secondary phenomena, the outcome of an attitude that is already neurotic. The neurosis is as a rule a pathological, one-sided development of the personality, the imperceptible beginnings of which can be traced back almost indefinitely into the earliest years of childhood. Only a very arbitrary judgment can say where the neurosis actually begins.

1 [Written in English. First published in the *British Journal of Psychology* (London), *Medical Section*, II (1921): i, 13–22. Revised and published in *Contributions to Analytical Psychology* (London and New York, 1928), pp. 282–94. Some verbal alterations to the revised version have been made here.—EDITORS.]
2 Brown, 31; McDougall, 111.

258   If we were to relegate the determining cause as far back as the patient's prenatal life, thus involving the physical and psychic disposition of the parents at the time of conception and pregnancy—a view that seems not at all improbable in certain cases—such an attitude would be more justifiable than the arbitrary selection of a definite point of neurotic origin in the individual life of the patient.

259   Clearly, in dealing with this question, one should never be influenced too much by the surface appearance of the symptoms, even when both the patient and his family synchronize the first manifestation of these with the onset of the neurosis. A more thorough investigation will almost invariably show that some morbid tendency existed long before the appearance of clinical symptoms.

260   These obvious facts, long familiar to every specialist, pushed the trauma theory into the background until, as a result of the war, there was a regular spate of traumatic neuroses.

261   Now, if we set aside the numerous cases of war neurosis where a trauma—a violent shock—impinged upon an established neurotic history, there still remain not a few cases where no neurotic disposition can be established, or where it is so insignificant that the neurosis could hardly have arisen without a trauma. Here the trauma is more than an agent of release: it is causative in the sense of a *causa efficiens,* especially when we include, as an essential factor, the unique psychic atmosphere of the battlefield.

262   These cases present us with a new therapeutic problem which seems to justify a return to the original Breuer-Freud method and its underlying theory; for the trauma is either a single, definite, violent impact, or a complex of ideas and emotions which may be likened to a psychic wound. Everything that touches this complex, however slightly, excites a vehement reaction, a regular emotional explosion. Hence one could easily represent the trauma as a complex with a high emotional charge, and because this enormously effective charge seems at first sight to be the pathological cause of the disturbance, one can accordingly postulate a therapy whose aim is the complete release of this charge. Such a view is both simple and logical, and it is in apparent agreement with the fact that abreaction —i.e., the dramatic rehearsal of the traumatic moment, its emo-

tional recapitulation in the waking or in the hypnotic state—often has a beneficial therapeutic effect. We all know that a man feels a compelling need to recount a vivid experience again and again until it has lost its affective value. As the proverb says, "What filleth the heart goeth out by the mouth." The unbosoming gradually depotentiates the affectivity of the traumatic experience until it no longer has a disturbing influence.

263   This conception, apparently so clear and simple, is unfortunately—as McDougall rightly objects—no more adequate than many another equally simple and therefore delusive explanation. Views of this kind have to be fiercely and fanatically defended as though they were dogmas, because they cannot hold their own in the face of experience. McDougall is also right to point out that in quite a large number of cases abreaction is not only useless but actually harmful.

264   In reply, it is possible to take up the attitude of an injured theorist and say that the abreactive method never claimed to be a panacea, and that refractory cases are to be met with in every method.

265   But, I would rejoin, it is precisely here, in a careful study of the refractory cases, that we gain the most illuminating insight into the method or theory in question, for they disclose far more clearly than the successes just where the theory is weak. Naturally this does not disprove the efficacy of the method or its justification, but it does at least lead to a possible improvement of the theory and, indirectly, of the method.

266   McDougall, therefore, has laid his finger on the right spot when he argues that the essential factor is the dissociation of the psyche and not the existence of a highly charged affect and, consequently, that the main therapeutic problem is not abreaction but how to integrate the dissociation. This argument advances our discussion and entirely agrees with our experience that a traumatic complex brings about dissociation of the psyche. The complex is not under the control of the will and for this reason it possesses the quality of psychic autonomy.

267   Its autonomy consists in its power to manifest itself independently of the will and even in direct opposition to conscious tendencies: it forces itself tyrannically upon the conscious mind. The explosion of affect is a complete invasion of

the individual, it pounces upon him like an enemy or a wild animal. I have frequently observed that the typical traumatic affect is represented in dreams as a wild and dangerous animal —a striking illustration of its autonomous nature when split off from consciousness.

268   Considered from this angle, abreaction appears in an essentially different light: as an attempt to reintegrate the autonomous complex, to incorporate it gradually into the conscious mind as an accepted content, by living the traumatic situation over again, once or repeatedly.

269   But I rather question whether the thing is as simple as that, or whether there may not be other factors essential to the process. For it must be emphasized that mere rehearsal of the experience does not itself possess a curative effect: the experience must be rehearsed in the presence of the doctor.

270   If the curative effect depended solely upon the rehearsal of experience, abreaction could be performed by the patient alone, as an isolated exercise, and there would be no need of any human object upon whom to discharge the affect. But the intervention of the doctor is absolutely necessary. One can easily see what it means to the patient when he can confide his experience to an understanding and sympathetic doctor. His conscious mind finds in the doctor a moral support against the unmanageable affect of his traumatic complex. No longer does he stand alone in his battle with these elemental powers, but some one whom he trusts reaches out a hand, lending him moral strength to combat the tyranny of uncontrolled emotion. In this way the integrative powers of his conscious mind are reinforced until he is able once more to bring the rebellious affect under control. This influence on the part of the doctor, which is absolutely essential, may, if you like, be called suggestion.

271   For myself, I would rather call it his human interest and personal devotion. These are the property of no method, nor can they ever become one; they are moral qualities which are of the greatest importance in all methods of psychotherapy, and not in the case of abreaction alone. The rehearsal of the traumatic moment is able to reintegrate the neurotic dissociation only when the conscious personality of the patient is so far reinforced by his relationship to the doctor that he can con-

sciously bring the autonomous complex under the control of his will.

272　　Only under these conditions has abreaction a curative value. But this does not depend solely on the discharge of affective tension; it depends, as McDougall shows, far more on whether or not the dissociation is successfully resolved. Hence the cases where abreaction has a negative result appear in a different light.

273　　In the absence of the conditions just mentioned, abreaction by itself is not sufficient to resolve the dissociation. If the rehearsal of the trauma fails to reintegrate the autonomous complex, then the relationship to the doctor can so raise the level of the patient's consciousness as to enable him to overcome the' complex and assimilate it. But it may easily happen that the patient has a particularly obstinate resistance to the doctor, or that the doctor does not have the right kind of attitude to the patient. In either case the abreactive method breaks down.

274　　It stands to reason that when dealing with neuroses which are traumatically determined only to a minor degree, the cathartic method of abreaction will meet with poor success. It has nothing to do with the nature of the neurosis, and its rigid application is quite ludicrous here. Even when a partial success is obtained, it can have no more significance than the success of any other method which admittedly had nothing to do with the nature of the neurosis.

275　　Success in these cases is due to suggestion; it is usually of very limited duration and clearly a matter of chance. The prime cause is always the transference to the doctor, and this is established without too much difficulty provided that the doctor evinces an earnest belief in his method. Precisely because it has as little to do with the nature of neurosis as, shall we say, hypnosis and other such cures, the cathartic method has, with few exceptions, long been abandoned in favour of analysis.

276　　Now it happens that the analytical method is most unassailable just where the cathartic method is most shaky: that is, in the relationship between doctor and patient. It matters little that, even today, the view prevails in many quarters that analysis consists mainly in "digging up" the earliest childhood complex in order to pluck out the evil by the root. This is merely the aftermath of the old trauma theory. Only in so far as they hamper the patient's adaptation to the present have these historical contents any real significance. The painstaking pursuit of all the ramifications of infantile fantasy is relatively unimportant in itself; the therapeutic effect comes from the doctor's efforts to enter into the psyche of his patient, thus establishing a psychologically adapted relationship. For the patient is suffering precisely from the absence of such a relationship. Freud himself has long recognized that the transference is the alpha and omega of psychoanalysis. The transference is the patient's attempt to get into psychological rapport with the doctor. He needs this relationship if he is to overcome the dissociation. The feebler the rapport, i.e., the less the doctor and patient understand one another, the more intensely will the transference be fostered and the more sexual will be its form.

277   To attain the goal of adaptation is of such vital importance to the patient that sexuality intervenes as a function of compensation. Its aim is to consolidate a relationship that cannot ordinarily be achieved through mutual understanding. In these circumstances the transference can well become the most powerful obstacle to the success of the treatment. It is not surprising that violent sexual transferences are especially frequent when the analyst concentrates too much on the sexual aspect, for then all other roads to understanding are barred. An exclusively sexual interpretation of dreams and fantasies is a shocking violation of the patient's psychological material: infantile-sexual fantasy is by no means the whole story, since the material also contains a creative element, the purpose of which is to shape a way out of the neurosis. This natural means of escape is now blocked; the doctor is the only certain refuge in a wilderness of sexual fantasies, and the patient has no alternative but to cling to him with a convulsive erotic transference, unless he prefers to break off the relationship in hatred.

278   In either case the result is spiritual desolation. This is the more regrettable since, obviously, psychoanalysts do not in the least desire such a melancholy result; yet they often bring it about through their blind allegiance to the dogma of sexuality.

279   Intellectually, of course, the sexual interpretation is extremely simple; it concerns itself at most with a handful of elementary facts which recur in numberless variations. One always knows in advance where the matter will end. *Inter faeces*

et urinam nascimur remains an eternal truth, but it is a sterile, a monotonous, and above all an unsavoury truth. There is absolutely no point in everlastingly reducing all the finest strivings of the soul back to the womb. It is a gross technical blunder because, instead of promoting, it destroys psychological understanding. More than anything else neurotic patients need that psychological rapport; in their dissociated state it helps them to adjust themselves to the doctor's psyche. Nor is it by any means so simple to establish this kind of human relationship; it can only be built up with great pains and scrupulous attention. The continual reduction of all projections to their origins —and the transference is made up of projections—may be of considerable historical and scientific interest, but it never produces an adapted attitude to life; for it constantly destroys the patient's every attempt to build up a normal human relationship by resolving it back into its elements.

280   If, in spite of this, the patient does succeed in adapting himself to life, it will have been at the cost of many moral, intellectual, and aesthetic values whose loss to a man's character is a matter for regret. Quite apart from this major loss, there is the danger of perpetually brooding on the past, of looking back wistfully to things that cannot be remedied now: the morbid tendency, very common among neurotics, always to seek the cause of their inferiority in the dim bygone, in their upbringing, the character of their parents, and so forth.

281   This minute scrutiny of minor determinants will affect their present inferiority as little as the existing social conditions would be ameliorated by an equally painstaking investigation of the causes of the Great War. The real issue is the moral achievement of the whole personality.

282   To assert, as a general principle, that a reductive analysis is unnecessary would of course be short-sighted and no more intelligent than to deny the value of all research into the causes of war. The doctor must probe as deeply as possible into the origins of the neurosis in order to lay the foundations of a subsequent synthesis. As a result of reductive analysis, the patient is deprived of his faulty adaptation and led back to his beginnings. The psyche naturally seeks to make good this loss by intensifying its hold upon some human object—generally the doctor, but occasionally some other person, like the pa-

tient's husband or a friend who acts as a counterpole to the doctor. This may effectively balance a one-sided transference, but it may also turn out to be a troublesome obstacle to the progress of the work. The intensified tie to the doctor is a compensation for the patient's faulty attitude to reality. This tie is what we mean by "transference."

283　　The transference phenomenon is an inevitable feature of every thorough analysis, for it is imperative that the doctor should get into the closest possible touch with the patient's line of psychological development. One could say that in the same measure as the doctor assimilates the intimate psychic contents of the patient into himself, he is in turn assimilated as a figure into the patient's psyche. I say "as a figure," because I mean that the patient sees him not as he really is, but as one of those persons who figured so significantly in his previous history. He becomes associated with those memory images in the patient's psyche because, like them, he makes the patient divulge all his intimate secrets. It is as though he were charged with the power of those memory images.

284　　The transference therefore consists in a number of projections which act as a substitute for a real psychological relationship. They create an apparent relationship and this is very important, since it comes at a time when the patient's habitual failure to adapt has been artificially intensified by his analytical removal into the past. Hence a sudden severance of the transference is always attended by extremely unpleasant and even dangerous consequences, because it maroons the patient in an impossibly unrelated situation.

285　　Even if these projections are analysed back to their origins—and all projections can be dissolved and disposed of in this way—the patient's claim to human relationship still remains and should be conceded, for without a relationship of some kind he falls into a void.

286　　Somehow he must relate himself to an object existing in the immediate present if he is to meet the demands of adaptation with any degree of adequacy. Irrespective of the reductive analysis, he will turn to the doctor not as an object of sexual desire, but as an object of purely human relationship in which each individual is guaranteed his proper place. Naturally this is impossible until all the projections have been consciously recognized; consequently they must be subjected to a reductive analysis before all else, provided of course that the legitimacy and importance of the underlying claim to personal relationship is constantly borne in mind.

287   Once the projections are recognized as such, the particular form of rapport known as the transference is at an end, and the problem of individual relationship begins. Every student who has perused the literature and amused himself with interpreting dreams and unearthing complexes in himself and others can easily get as far as this, but beyond it no one has the right to go except the doctor who has himself undergone a thorough analysis, or can bring such passion for truth to the work that he can analyse himself through his patient. The doctor who has no wish for the one and cannot achieve the other should never touch analysis; he will be found wanting, cling as he may to his petty conceit of authority.

288   In the last resort his whole work will be intellectual bluff —for how can he help his patient to conquer his morbid inferiority when he himself is so manifestly inferior? How can the patient learn to abandon his neurotic subterfuges when he sees the doctor playing hide-and-seek with his own personality, as though unable, for fear of being thought inferior, to drop the professional mask of authority, competence, superior knowledge, etc.?

289   The touchstone of every analysis that has not stopped short at partial success, or come to a standstill with no success at all, is always this person-to-person relationship, a psychological situation where the patient confronts the doctor upon equal terms, and with the same ruthless criticism that he must inevitably learn from the doctor in the course of his treatment.

290   This kind of personal relationship is a freely negotiated bond or contract as opposed to the slavish and humanly degrading bondage of the transference. For the patient it is like a bridge; along it, he can make the first steps towards a worthwhile existence. He discovers that his own unique personality has value, that he has been accepted for what he is, and that he has it in him to adapt himself to the demands of life. But this discovery will never be made while the doctor continues to hide behind a method, and allows himself to carp and criticize without question. Whatever method he then adopts, it will be little

different from suggestion, and the results will match the method. In place of this, the patient must have the right to the freest criticism, and a true sense of human equality.

291   I think I have said enough to indicate that, in my view, analysis makes far higher demands on the mental and moral stature of the doctor than the mere application of a routine technique, and also that his therapeutic influence lies primarily in this more personal direction.

292   But if the reader should conclude that little or nothing lay in the method, I would regard that as a total misapprehension of my meaning. Mere personal sympathy can never give the patient that objective understanding of his neurosis which makes him independent of the doctor and sets up a counter-influence to the transference.

293   For the objective understanding of his malady, and for the creation of a personal relationship, science is needed—not a purely medical knowledge that embraces only a limited field, but a wide knowledge of every aspect of the human psyche. The treatment must do more than destroy the old morbid attitude; it must build up a new attitude that is sound and healthy. This requires a fundamental change of vision. Not only must the patient be able to see the cause and origin of his neurosis, he must also see the legitimate psychological goal towards which he is striving. We cannot simply extract his morbidity like a foreign body, lest something essential be removed along with it, something meant for life. Our task is not to weed it out, but to cultivate and transform this growing thing until it can play its part in the totality of the psyche.

II

THE PRACTICAL USE OF DREAM-ANALYSIS [1]

294   The use of dream-analysis in psychotherapy is still a much
debated question. Many practitioners find it indispensable in
the treatment of neuroses, and consider that the dream is a
function whose psychic importance is equal to that of the conscious mind itself. Others, on the contrary, dispute the value
of dream-analysis and regard dreams as a negligible by-product
of the psyche. Obviously, if a person holds the view that the unconscious plays a decisive part in the aetiology of neuroses, he
will attribute a high practical importance to dreams as direct
expressions of the unconscious. Equally obviously, if he denies
the unconscious or at least thinks it aetiologically insignificant,
he will minimize the importance of dream-analysis. It might be
considered regrettable that in this year of grace 1931, more
than half a century after Carus formulated the concept of the
unconscious, more than a century after Kant spoke of the "il-
limitable field of obscure ideas," and nearly two hundred years
after Leibniz postulated an unconscious psychic activity, not to
mention the achievements of Janet, Flournoy, Freud, and many
more—that after all this, the actuality of the unconscious should
still be a matter for controversy. But, since it is my intention to
deal exclusively with practical questions, I will not advance in
this place an apology for the unconscious, although our special
problem of dream-analysis stands or falls with such an hypothesis. Without it, the dream is a mere freak of nature, a meaningless conglomeration of fragments left over from the day.
Were that really so, there would be no excuse for the present
discussion. We cannot treat our theme at all unless we recognize the unconscious, for the avowed aim of dream-analysis is
not only to exercise our wits, but to uncover and realize those

1 [Read at the sixth congress of the International General Medical Society for Psychotherapy, Dresden, 1931. Published as "Die praktische Verwendbarkeit der
Traumanalyse" in *Wirklichkeit der Seele* (Zurich, 1934), pp. 68–103. Previously
trans. by C. F. Baynes and W. S. Dell in *Modern Man in Search of a Soul* (New
York and London, 1933).—EDITORS.]

hitherto unconscious contents which are considered to be of importance in the elucidation or treatment of a neurosis. Anyone who finds this hypothesis unacceptable must simply rule out the question of the applicability of dream-analysis.

295   But since, according to our hypothesis, the unconscious possesses an aetiological significance, and since dreams are the direct expression of unconscious psychic activity, the attempt to analyse and interpret dreams is theoretically justified from a scientific standpoint. If successful, we may expect this attempt to give us scientific insight into the structure of psychic causality, quite apart from any therapeutic results that may be gained. The practitioner, however, tends to consider scientific discoveries as, at most, a gratifying by-product of his therapeutic work, so he is hardly likely to take the bare possibility of theoretical insight into the aetiological background as a sufficient reason for, much less an indication of, the practical use of dream-analysis. He may believe, of course, that the explanatory insight so gained is of therapeutic value, in which case he will elevate dream-analysis to a professional duty. It is well known that the Freudian school is of the firm opinion that very valuable therapeutic results are achieved by throwing light upon the unconscious causal factors—that is, by explaining them to the patient and thus making him fully conscious of the sources of his trouble.

296   Assuming for the moment that this expectation is justified by the facts, then the only question that remains is whether dream-analysis can or cannot be used, alone or in conjunction with other methods, to discover the unconscious aetiology. The Freudian answer to this question is, I may assume, common knowledge. I can confirm this answer inasmuch as dreams, particularly the initial dreams which appear at the very outset of the treatment, often bring to light the essential aetiological factor in the most unmistakable way. The following example may serve as an illustration:

297   I was consulted by a man who held a prominent position in the world. He was afflicted with a sense of anxiety and insecurity, and complained of dizziness sometimes resulting in nausea, heaviness in the head, and constriction of breath—a state that might easily be confused with mountain sickness. He had had an extraordinarily successful career, and had risen,

by dint of ambition, industry, and native talent, from his humble origins as the son of a poor peasant. Step by step he had climbed, attaining at last a leading position which held every prospect of further social advancement. He had now in fact reached the spring-board from which he could have commenced his flight into the empyrean, had not his neurosis suddenly intervened. At this point in his story the patient could not refrain from that familiar exclamation which begins with the stereotyped words: "And just now, when. . . ." The fact that he had all the symptoms of mountain sickness seemed highly appropriate as a drastic illustration of his peculiar impasse. He had also brought to the consultation two dreams from the preceding night. The first dream was as follows: *"I am back again in the small village where I was born. Some peasant lads who went to school with me are standing together in the street. I walk past, pretending not to know them. Then I hear one of them say, pointing at me: 'He doesn't often come back to our village.'"*

298   It requires no feat of interpretation to see in this dream a reference to the humble beginnings of the dreamer's career and to understand what this reference means. The dream says quite clearly: "You forgot how far down you began."

299   Here is the second dream: *"I am in a great hurry because I want to go on a journey. I keep on looking for things to pack, but can find nothing. Time flies, and the train will soon be leaving. Having finally succeeded in getting all my things together, I hurry along the street, only to discover that I have forgotten a brief-case containing important papers. I dash back all out of breath, find it at last, then race to the station, but I make hardly any headway. With a final effort I rush on to the platform only to see the train just steaming out of the station yard. It is very long, and it runs in a curious S-shaped curve, and it occurs to me that if the engine-driver does not look out, and puts on steam when he comes into the straight, the rear coaches will still be on the curve and will be thrown off the rails by the gathering speed. And this is just what happens: the engine-driver puts on steam, I try to cry out, the rear coaches give a frightful lurch and are thrown off the rails. There is a terrible catastrophe. I wake up in terror."*

300   Here again no effort is needed to understand the message of the dream. It describes the patient's frantic haste to advance

himself still further. But since the engine-driver in front steams relentlessly ahead, the neurosis happens at the back: the coaches rock and the train is derailed.

301   It is obvious that, at the present phase of his life, the patient has reached the highest point of his career; the strain of the long ascent from his lowly origin has exhausted his strength. He should have rested content with his achievements, but instead of that his ambition drives him on and on, and up and up into an atmosphere that is too thin for him and to which he is not accustomed. Therefore his neurosis comes upon him as a warning.

302   Circumstances prevented me from treating the patient further, nor did my view of the case satisfy him. The upshot was that the fate depicted in the dream ran its course. He tried to exploit the professional openings that tempted his ambition, and ran so violently off the rails that the catastrophe was realized in actual life.

303   Thus, what could only be inferred from the conscious anamnesis—namely that the mountain sickness was a symbolical representation of the patient's inability to climb any further—was confirmed by the dreams as a fact.

304   Here we come upon something of the utmost importance for the applicability of dream-analysis: the dream describes the inner situation of the dreamer, but the conscious mind denies its truth and reality, or admits it only grudgingly. Consciously the dreamer could not see the slightest reason why he should not go steadily forward; on the contrary, he continued his ambitious climbing and refused to admit his own inability which subsequent events made all too plain. So long as we move in the conscious sphere, we are always unsure in such cases. The anamnesis can be interpreted in various ways. After all, the common soldier carries the marshal's baton in his knapsack, and many a son of poor parents has achieved the highest success. Why should it not be the case here? Since my judgment is fallible, why should my conjecture be better than his? At this point the dream comes in as the expression of an involuntary, unconscious psychic process beyond the control of the conscious mind. It shows the inner truth and reality of the patient as it really is: not as I conjecture it to be, and not as he would like it to be, but *as it is*. I have therefore made it a rule to re-

gard dreams as I regard physiological facts: if sugar appears in the urine, then the urine contains sugar, and not albumen or urobilin or something else that might fit in better with my expectations. That is to say, I take dreams as diagnostically valuable facts.

305 As is the way of all dreams, my little dream example gives us rather more than we expected. It gives us not only the aetiology of the neurosis but a prognosis as well. What is more, we even know exactly where the treatment should begin: we must prevent the patient from going full steam ahead. This is just what he tells himself in the dream.

306 Let us for the time being content ourselves with this hint and return to our consideration of whether dreams enable us to throw light on the aetiology of a neurosis. The dreams I have cited actually do this. But I could equally well cite any number of initial dreams where there is no trace of an aetiological factor, although they are perfectly transparent. I do not wish for the present to consider dreams which call for searching analysis and interpretation.

307 The point is this: there are neuroses whose real aetiology becomes clear only right at the end of an analysis, and other neuroses whose aetiology is relatively unimportant. This brings me back to the hypothesis from which we started, that for the purposes of therapy it is absolutely necessary to make the patient conscious of the aetiological factor. This hypothesis is little more than a hang-over from the old trauma theory. I do not of course deny that many neuroses are traumatic in origin; I simply contest the notion that all neuroses are of this nature and arise without exception from some crucial experience in childhood. Such a view necessarily results in the causalistic approach. The doctor must give his whole attention to the patient's past; he must always ask "Why?" and ignore the equally pertinent question "What for?" Often this has a most deleterious effect on the patient, who is thereby compelled to go searching about in his memory—perhaps for years—for some hypothetical event in his childhood, while things of immediate importance are grossly neglected. The purely causalistic approach is too narrow and fails to do justice to the true significance either of the dream or of the neurosis. Hence an approach that uses dreams for the sole purpose of discovering the aetio-

logical factor is biased and overlooks the main point of the dream. Our example indeed shows the aetiology clearly enough, but it also offers a prognosis or anticipation of the future as well as a suggestion about the treatment. There are in addition large numbers of initial dreams which do not touch the aetiology at all, but deal with quite other matters, such as the patient's attitude to the doctor. As an example of this I would like to tell you three dreams, all from the same patient, and each dreamt at the beginning of a course of treatment under three different analysts. Here is the first: *"I have to cross the frontier into another country, but cannot find the frontier and nobody can tell me where it is."*

308 The ensuing treatment proved unsuccessful and was broken off after a short time. The second dream is as follows: *"I have to cross the frontier, but the night is pitch-black and I cannot find the customs-house. After a long search I see a tiny light far off in the distance, and assume that the frontier is over there. But in order to get there, I have to pass through a valley and a dark wood in which I lose my way. Then I notice that someone is near me. Suddenly he clings to me like a madman and I awake in terror."*

309 This treatment, too, was broken off after a few weeks because the analyst unconsciously identified himself with the patient and the result was complete loss of orientation on both sides.

310 The third dream took place under my treatment: *"I have to cross a frontier, or rather, I have already crossed it and find myself in a Swiss customs-house. I have only a handbag with me and think I have nothing to declare. But the customs official dives into my bag and, to my astonishment, pulls out a pair of twin beds."*

311 The patient had got married while under my treatment, and at first she developed the most violent resistance to her marriage. The aetiology of the neurotic resistance came to light only many months afterwards and there is not a word about it in the dreams. They are without exception anticipations of the difficulties she is to have with the doctors concerned.

312 These examples, like many others of the kind, may suffice to show that dreams are often anticipatory and would lose their specific meaning completely on a purely causalistic view.

They afford unmistakable information about the analytical situation, the correct understanding of which is of the greatest therapeutic importance. Doctor A understood the situation correctly and handed the patient over to Doctor B. Under him she drew her own conclusions from the dream and decided to leave. My interpretation of the third dream was a disappointment to her, but the fact that the dream showed the frontier as already crossed encouraged her to go on in spite of all difficulties.

313 Initial dreams are often amazingly lucid and clear-cut. But as the work of analysis progresses, the dreams tend to lose their clarity. If, by way of exception, they keep it we can be sure that the analysis has not yet touched on some important layer of the personality. As a rule, dreams get more and more opaque and blurred soon after the beginning of the treatment, and this makes the interpretation increasingly difficult. A further difficulty is that a point may soon be reached where, if the truth be told, the doctor no longer understands the situation as a whole. That he does not understand is proved by the fact that the dreams become increasingly obscure, for we all know that their "obscurity" is a purely subjective opinion of the doctor. To the understanding nothing is obscure; it is only when we do not understand that things appear unintelligible and muddled. In themselves dreams are naturally clear; that is, they are just what they must be under the given circumstances. If, from a later stage of treatment or from a distance of some years, we look back at these unintelligible dreams, we are often astounded at our own blindness. Thus when, as the analysis proceeds, we come upon dreams that are strikingly obscure in comparison with the illuminating initial dreams, the doctor should not be too ready to accuse the dreams of confusion or the patient of deliberate resistance; he would do better to take these findings as a sign of his own growing inability to understand—just as the psychiatrist who calls his patient "confused" should recognize that this is a projection and should rather call himself confused, because in reality it is he whose wits are confused by the patient's peculiar behaviour. Moreover it is therapeutically very important for the doctor to admit his lack of understanding in time, for nothing is more unbearable to the patient than to be always understood. He relies far too much anyway on the mysterious powers of the doctor and, by appealing to

his professional vanity, lays a dangerous trap for him. By taking refuge in the doctor's self-confidence and "profound" understanding, the patient loses all sense of reality, falls into a stubborn transference, and retards the cure.

314   Understanding is clearly a very subjective process. It can be extremely one-sided, in that the doctor understands but not the patient. In such a case the doctor conceives it to be his duty to convince the patient, and if the latter will not allow himself to be convinced, the doctor accuses him of resistance. When the understanding is all on my side, I say quite calmly that I do not understand, for in the end it makes very little difference whether the doctor understands or not, but it makes all the difference whether the patient understands. Understanding should therefore be understanding in the sense of an agreement which is the fruit of joint reflection. The danger of a one-sided understanding is that the doctor may judge the dream from the standpoint of a preconceived opinion. His judgment may be in line with orthodox theory, it may even be fundamentally correct, but it will not win the patient's assent, he will not come to an understanding with him, and that is in the practical sense incorrect—incorrect because it anticipates and thus cripples the patient's development. The patient, that is to say, does not need to have a truth inculcated into him—if we do that, we only reach his head; he needs far more to grow up to this truth, and in that way we reach his heart, and the appeal goes deeper and works more powerfully.

315   When the doctor's one-sided interpretation is based on mere agreement as to theory or on some other preconceived opinion, his chances of convincing the patient or of achieving any therapeutic results depend chiefly upon *suggestion*. Let no one deceive himself about this. In itself, suggestion is not to be despised, but it has serious limitations, not to speak of the subsidiary effects upon the patient's independence of character which, in the long run, we could very well do without. A practising analyst may be supposed to believe implicitly in the significance and value of conscious realization, whereby hitherto unconscious parts of the personality are brought to light and subjected to conscious discrimination and criticism. It is a process that requires the patient to face his problems and that taxes his powers of conscious judgment and decision. It is nothing less

than a direct challenge to his ethical sense, a call to arms that must be answered by the whole personality. As regards the maturation of personality, therefore, the analytical approach is of a higher order than suggestion, which is a species of magic that works in the dark and makes no ethical demands upon the personality. Methods of treatment based on suggestion are deceptive makeshifts; they are incompatible with the principles of analytical therapy and should be avoided if at all possible. Naturally suggestion can only be avoided if the doctor is conscious of its possibility. There is at the best of times always enough—and more than enough—unconscious suggestion.

316   The analyst who wishes to rule out conscious suggestion must therefore consider every dream interpretation invalid until such time as a formula is found which wins the assent of the patient.

317   The observance of this rule seems to me imperative when dealing with those dreams whose obscurity is evidence of the lack of understanding of both doctor and patient. The doctor should regard every such dream as something new, as a source of information about conditions whose nature is unknown to him, concerning which he has as much to learn as the patient. It goes without saying that he should give up all his theoretical assumptions and should in every single case be ready to construct a totally new theory of dreams. There are still boundless opportunities for pioneer work in this field. The view that dreams are merely the imaginary fulfilments of repressed wishes is hopelessly out of date. There are, it is true, dreams which manifestly represent wishes or fears, but what about all the other things? Dreams may contain ineluctable truths, philosophical pronouncements, illusions, wild fantasies, memories, plans, anticipations, irrational experiences, even telepathic visions, and heaven knows what besides. One thing we ought never to forget: almost half our life is passed in a more or less unconscious state. The dream is specifically the utterance of the unconscious. Just as the psyche has a diurnal side which we call consciousness, so also it has a nocturnal side: the unconscious psychic activity which we apprehend as dreamlike fantasy. It is certain that the conscious mind consists not only of wishes and fears, but of vastly more besides; and it is highly probable that our dream psyche possesses a wealth of contents and living forms

equal to or even greater than those of the conscious mind, which is characterized by concentration, limitation, and exclusion.

318   This being so, it is imperative that we should not pare down the meaning of the dream to fit some narrow doctrine. We must remember that there are not a few patients who imitate the technical or theoretical jargon of the doctor, and do this even in their dreams, in accordance with the old tag, *Canis panem somniat, piscator pisces.* This is not to say that the fishes of which the fisherman dreams are fishes and nothing more. There is no language that cannot be misused. As may easily be imagined, the misuse often turns the tables on us; it even seems as if the unconscious had a way of strangling the doctor in the coils of his own theory. Therefore I leave theory aside as much as possible when analysing dreams—not entirely, of course, for we always need some theory to make things intelligible. It is on the basis of theory, for instance, that I expect dreams to have a meaning. I cannot prove in every case that this is so, for there are dreams which the doctor and the patient simply do not understand. But I have to make such an hypothesis in order to find courage to deal with dreams at all. To say that dreams add something important to our conscious knowledge, and that a dream which fails to do so has not been properly interpreted —that, too, is a theory. But I must make this hypothesis as well in order to explain to myself why I analyse dreams in the first place. All other hypotheses, however, about the function and the structure of dreams are merely rules of thumb and must be subjected to constant modification. In dream-analysis we must never forget, even for a moment, that we move on treacherous ground where nothing is certain but uncertainty. If it were not so paradoxical, one would almost like to call out to the dream interpreter: "Do anything you like, only don't try to understand!"

319   When we take up an obscure dream, our first task is not to understand and interpret, but to establish the context with minute care. By this I do *not* mean unlimited "free association" starting from any and every image in the dream, but a careful and conscious illumination of the interconnected associations objectively grouped round particular images. Many patients have first to be educated to this, for they resemble the

doctor in their insuperable desire to understand and interpret offhand, especially when they have been primed by ill-digested reading or by a previous analysis that went wrong. They begin by associating in accordance with a theory, that is, they try to understand and interpret, and they nearly always get stuck. Like the doctor, they want to get behind the dream at once in the false belief that the dream is a mere façade concealing the true meaning. But the so-called façade of most houses is by no means a fake or a deceptive distortion; on the contrary, it follows the plan of the building and often betrays the interior arrangement. The "manifest" dream-picture is the dream itself and contains the whole meaning of the dream. When I find sugar in the urine, it is sugar and not just a façade for albumen. What Freud calls the "dream-façade" is the dream's obscurity, and this is really only a projection of our own lack of understanding. We say that the dream has a false front only because we fail to see into it. We would do better to say that we are dealing with something like a text that is unintelligible not because it has a façade—a text has no façade—but simply because we cannot read it. We do not have to get behind such a text, but must first learn to read it.

320   The best way to do this, as I have already remarked, is to establish the context. Free association will get me nowhere, any more than it would help me to decipher a Hittite inscription. It will of course help me to uncover all my own complexes, but for this purpose I have no need of a dream—I could just as well take a public notice or a sentence in a newspaper. Free association will bring out all my complexes, but hardly ever the meaning of a dream. To understand the dream's meaning I must stick as close as possible to the dream images. When somebody dreams of a "deal table," it is not enough for him to associate it with his writing-desk which does not happen to be made of deal. Supposing that nothing more occurs to the dreamer, this blocking has an objective meaning, for it indicates that a particular darkness reigns in the immediate neighbourhood of the dream-image, and that is suspicious. We would expect him to have dozens of associations to a deal table, and the fact that there is apparently nothing is itself significant. In such cases I keep on returning to the image, and I usually say to my patient, "Suppose I had no idea what the words 'deal table' mean. De-

149

scribe this object and give me its history in such a way that I cannot fail to understand what sort of a thing it is."

321   In this way we manage to establish almost the whole context of the dream-image. When we have done this for all the images in the dream we are ready for the venture of interpretation.

322   Every interpretation is an hypothesis, an attempt to read an unknown text. An obscure dream, taken in isolation, can hardly ever be interpreted with any certainty. For this reason I attach little importance to the interpretation of single dreams. A relative degree of certainty is reached only in the interpretation of a series of dreams, where the later dreams correct the mistakes we have made in handling those that went before. Also, the basic ideas and themes can be recognized much better in a dream-series, and I therefore urge my patients to keep a careful record of their dreams and of the interpretations given. I also show them how to work out their dreams in the manner described, so that they can bring the dream and its context with them in writing to the consultation. At a later stage I get them to work out the interpretation as well. In this way the patient learns how to deal correctly with his unconscious without the doctor's help.

323   Were dreams nothing more than sources of information about factors of aetiological importance, the whole work of dream-interpretation could safely be left to the doctor. Again, if their only use was to provide the doctor with a collection of useful hints and psychological tips, my own procedure would be entirely superfluous. But since, as my examples have shown, dreams contain something more than practical helps for the doctor, dream-analysis deserves very special attention. Sometimes, indeed, it is a matter of life and death. Among many instances of this sort, there is one that has remained particularly impressive. It concerns a colleague of mine, a man somewhat older than myself, whom I used to see from time to time and who always teased me about my dream-interpretations. Well, I met him one day in the street and he called out to me, "How are things going? Still interpreting dreams? By the way, I've had another idiotic dream. Does that mean something too?" This is what he had dreamed: *"I am climbing a high mountain, over steep snow-covered slopes. I climb higher and higher, and it is marvellous weather. The higher I climb the better I*

*feel. I think, 'If only I could go on climbing like this for ever!'
When I reach the summit my happiness and elation are so
great that I feel I could mount right up into space. And I discover that I can actually do so: I mount upwards on empty air,
and awake in sheer ecstasy."*

324   After some discussion, I said, "My dear fellow, I know you
can't give up mountaineering, but let me implore you not to
go alone from now on. When you go, take two guides, and
promise on your word of honour to follow them absolutely."
"Incorrigible!" he replied, laughing, and waved good-bye. I
never saw him again. Two months later the first blow fell.
When out alone, he was buried by an avalanche, but was dug
out in the nick of time by a military patrol that happened to be
passing. Three months afterwards the end came. He went on a
climb with a younger friend, but without guides. A guide
standing below saw him literally step out into the air while descending a rock face. He fell on the head of his friend, who was
waiting lower down, and both were dashed to pieces far below.
That was *ecstasis* with a vengeance! [2]

325   No amount of scepticism and criticism has yet enabled me
to regard dreams as negligible occurrences. Often enough they
appear senseless, but it is obviously we who lack the sense and
ingenuity to read the enigmatic message from the nocturnal
realm of the psyche. Seeing that at least half our psychic existence is passed in that realm, and that consciousness acts upon
our nightly life just as much as the unconscious overshadows
our daily life, it would seem all the more incumbent on medical psychology to sharpen its senses by a systematic study of
dreams. Nobody doubts the importance of conscious experience; why then should we doubt the significance of unconscious
happenings? They also are part of our life, and sometimes more
truly a part of it for weal or woe than any happenings of the
day.

326   Since dreams provide information about the hidden inner
life and reveal to the patient those components of his personality which, in his daily behaviour, appear merely as neurotic symptoms, it follows that we cannot effectively treat him
from the side of consciousness alone, but must bring about a
change in and through the unconscious. In the light of our

2 [This dream is discussed at greater length in Jung's "Analytical Psychology and
Education," **79,** pars. 117f.—EDITORS.]

present knowledge this can be achieved only by the thorough and conscious assimilation of unconscious contents.

327   "Assimilation" in this sense means mutual penetration of conscious and unconscious, and not—as is commonly thought and practised—a one-sided evaluation, interpretation, and deformation of unconscious contents by the conscious mind. As to the value and significance of unconscious contents in general, very mistaken views are current. It is well known that the Freudian school presents the unconscious in a thoroughly negative light, much as it regards primitive man as little better than a monster. Its nursery-tales about the terrible old man of the tribe and its teachings about the "infantile-perverse-criminal" unconscious have led people to make a dangerous ogre out of something perfectly natural. As if all that is good, reasonable, worth while, and beautiful had taken up its abode in the conscious mind! Have the horrors of the World War done nothing to open our eyes, so that we still cannot see that the conscious mind is even more devilish and perverse than the naturalness of the unconscious?

328   The charge has recently been laid at my door that my teaching about the assimilation of the unconscious would undermine civilization and deliver up our highest values to sheer primitivity. Such an opinion can only be based on the totally erroneous supposition that the unconscious is a monster. It is a view that springs from fear of nature and the realities of life. Freud invented the idea of sublimation to save us from the imaginary claws of the unconscious. But what is real, what actually exists, cannot be alchemically sublimated, and if anything is apparently sublimated it never was what a false interpretation took it to be.

329   The unconscious is not a demoniacal monster, but a natural entity which, as far as moral sense, aesthetic taste, and intellectual judgment go, is completely neutral. It only becomes dangerous when our conscious attitude to it is hopelessly wrong. To the degree that we repress it, its danger increases. But the moment the patient begins to assimilate contents that were previously unconscious, its danger diminishes. The dissociation of personality, the anxious division of the day-time and the night-time sides of the psyche, cease with progressive assimilation. What my critic feared—the overwhelming of the conscious mind

by the unconscious—is far more likely to ensue when the unconscious is excluded from life by being repressed, falsely interpreted, and depreciated.

330   The fundamental mistake regarding the nature of the unconscious is probably this: it is commonly supposed that its contents have only one meaning and are marked with an unalterable plus or minus sign. In my humble opinion, this view is too naïve. The psyche is a self-regulating system that maintains its equilibrium just as the body does. Every process that goes too far immediately and inevitably calls forth compensations, and without these there would be neither a normal metabolism nor a normal psyche. In this sense we can take the theory of compensation as a basic law of psychic behaviour. Too little on one side results in too much on the other. Similarly, the relation between conscious and unconscious is compensatory. This is one of the best-proven rules of dream interpretation. When we set out to interpret a dream, it is always helpful to ask: What conscious attitude does it compensate?

331   Compensation is not as a rule merely an illusory wish-fulfilment, but an actual fact that becomes still more actual the more we repress it. We do not stop feeling thirsty by repressing our thirst. In the same way, the dream-content is to be regarded with due seriousness as an actuality that has to be fitted into the conscious attitude as a codetermining factor. If we fail to do this, we merely persist in that eccentric frame of mind which evoked the unconscious compensation in the first place. It is then difficult to see how we can ever arrive at a sane judgment of ourselves or at a balanced way of living.

332   If it should occur to anyone to replace the conscious content by an unconscious one—and this is the prospect which my critics find so alarming—he would only succeed in repressing it, and it would then reappear as an unconscious compensation. The unconscious would thus have changed its face completely: it would now be timidly reasonable, in striking contrast to its former tone. It is not generally believed that the unconscious operates in this way, yet such reversals constantly take place and constitute its proper function. That is why every dream is an organ of information and control, and why dreams are our most effective aid in building up the personality.

333   The unconscious does not harbour in itself any explosive materials unless an overweening or cowardly conscious attitude has secretly laid up stores of explosives there. All the more reason, then, for watching our step.

334   From all this it should now be clear why I make it an heuristic rule, in interpreting a dream, to ask myself: What conscious attitude does it compensate? By so doing, I relate the dream as closely as possible to the conscious situation; indeed, I would even assert that without knowledge of the conscious situation the dream can never be interpreted with any degree of certainty. Only in the light of this knowledge is it possible to make out whether the unconscious content carries a plus or a minus sign. The dream is not an isolated event completely cut off from daily life and lacking its character. If it seems so to us, that is only the result of our lack of understanding, a subjective illusion. In reality the relation between the conscious mind and the dream is strictly causal, and they interact in the subtlest of ways.

335   I should like to show by means of an example how important it is to evaluate the unconscious contents correctly. A young man brought me the following dream: *"My father is driving away from the house in his new car. He drives very clumsily, and I get very annoyed over his apparent stupidity. He goes this way and that, forwards and backwards, and manoeuvres the car into a dangerous position. Finally he runs into a wall and damages the car badly. I shout at him in a perfect fury that he ought to behave himself. My father only laughs, and then I see that he is dead drunk."* This dream has no foundation in fact. The dreamer is convinced that his father would never behave like that, even when drunk. As a motorist he himself is very careful and extremely moderate in the use of alcohol, especially when he has to drive. Bad driving, and even slight damage to the car, irritate him greatly. His relation to his father is positive. He admires him for being an unusually successful man. We can say, without any great feat of interpretation, that the dream presents a most unfavourable picture of the father. What, then, should we take its meaning to be for the son? Is his relation to his father good only on the surface, and does it really consist in over-compensated resistances? If so, we should have to give the dream-content a positive sign; we should have to tell the young man:

"That is your real relation to your father." But since I could find nothing neurotically ambivalent in the son's real relation to his father, I had no warrant for upsetting the young man's feelings with such a destructive pronouncement. To do so would have been a bad therapeutic blunder.

336   But, if his relation to his father is in fact good, why must the dream manufacture such an improbable story in order to discredit the father? In the dreamer's unconscious there must be some tendency to produce such a dream. Is that because he has resistances after all, perhaps fed by envy or some other inferior motive? Before we go out of our way to burden his conscience—and with sensitive young people this is always rather a dangerous proceeding—we would do better to inquire not *why* he had this dream, but what its purpose is. The answer in this case would be that his unconscious is obviously trying to take the father down a peg. If we regard this as a compensation, we are forced to the conclusion that his relation to his father is not only good, but actually too good. In fact he deserves the French soubriquet of *fils à papa*. His father is still too much the guarantor of his existence, and the dreamer is still living what I would call a provisional life. His particular danger is that he cannot see his own reality on account of his father; therefore the unconscious resorts to a kind of artificial blasphemy so as to lower the father and elevate the son. "An immoral business," we may be tempted to say. An unintelligent father would probably take umbrage, but the compensation is entirely to the point, since it forces the son to contrast himself with his father, which is the only way he could become conscious of himself.

337   The interpretation just outlined was apparently the correct one, for it struck home. It won the spontaneous assent of the dreamer, and no real values were damaged, either for the father or for the son. But this interpretation was only possible when the whole conscious phenomenology of the father-son relationship had been carefully studied. Without a knowledge of the conscious situation the real meaning of the dream would have remained in doubt.

338   For dream-contents to be assimilated, it is of overriding importance that no real values of the conscious personality

should be damaged, much less destroyed, otherwise there is no one left to do the assimilating. The recognition of the unconscious is not a Bolshevist experiment which puts the lowest on top and thus re-establishes the very situation it intended to correct. We must see to it that the values of the conscious personality remain intact, for unconscious compensation is only effective when it co-operates with an integral consciousness. Assimilation is never a question of "this *or* that," but always of "this *and* that."

339 Just as the interpretation of dreams requires exact knowledge of the conscious status quo, so the treatment of dream symbolism demands that we take into account the dreamer's philosophical, religious, and moral convictions. It is far wiser in practice not to regard dream-symbols semiotically, i.e., as signs or symptoms of a fixed character, but as true symbols, i.e., as expressions of a content not yet consciously recognized or conceptually formulated. In addition, they must be considered in relation to the dreamer's immediate state of consciousness. I say that this procedure is advisable *in practice* because in theory relatively fixed symbols do exist whose meaning must on no account be referred to anything known and formulable as a concept. If there were no such relatively fixed symbols it would be impossible to determine the structure of the unconscious, for there would be nothing that could in any way be laid hold of or described.

340 It may seem strange that I should attribute an as it were indefinite content to these relatively fixed symbols. Yet if their content were not indefinite, they would not be symbols at all, but signs or symptoms. We all know how the Freudian school operates with hard-and-fast sexual "symbols"—which in this case I would call "signs"—and endows them with an apparently definitive content, namely sexuality. Unfortunately Freud's idea of sexuality is incredibly elastic and so vague that it can be made to include almost anything. The word sounds familiar enough, but what it denotes is no more than an indeterminable *x* that ranges from the physiological activity of the glands at one extreme to the sublime reaches of the spirit at the other. Instead of yielding to a dogmatic conviction based on the illusion that we know something because we have a familiar word for it, I prefer to regard the symbol as an unknown quantity,

hard to recognize and, in the last resort, never quite determinable. Take, for instance, the so-called phallic symbols which are supposed to stand for the *membrum virile* and nothing more. Psychologically speaking, the *membrum* is itself—as Kranefeldt points out in a recent work [3]—an emblem of something whose wider content is not at all easy to determine. But primitive people, who, like the ancients, make the freest use of phallic symbols, would never dream of confusing the phallus, as a ritualistic symbol, with the penis. The phallus always means the creative mana, the power of healing and fertility, the "extraordinarily potent," to use Lehmann's expression, whose equivalents in mythology and in dreams are the bull, the ass, the pomegranate, the yoni, the he-goat, the lightning, the horse's hoof, the dance, the magical cohabitation in the furrow, and the menstrual fluid, to mention only a few of the thousand other analogies. That which underlies all the analogies, and sexuality itself, is an archetypal image whose character is hard to define, but whose nearest psychological equivalent is perhaps the primitive mana-symbol.

341 All these symbols are relatively fixed, but in no single case can we have the *a priori* certainty that in practice the symbol must be interpreted in that way.

342 Practical necessity may call for something quite different. Of course, if we had to give an exhaustive scientific interpretation of a dream, in accordance with a theory, we should have to refer every such symbol to an archetype. But in practice that can be a positive mistake, for the patient's psychological state at the moment may require anything but a digression into dream theory. It is therefore advisable to consider first and foremost the meaning of the symbol in relation to the conscious situation—in other words, to treat the symbol as if it were not fixed. This is as much as to say that we must renounce all preconceived opinions, however knowing they make us feel, and try to discover what things mean for the patient. In so doing, we shall obviously not get very far towards a theoretical interpretation; indeed we shall probably get stuck at the very beginning. But if the practitioner operates too much with fixed symbols, there is a danger of his falling into mere routine and pernicious dogmatism, and thus failing his patient. Unfor-

3 "Komplex und Mythos," 102.

tunately I must refrain from illustrating this point, for I should
have to go into greater detail than space here permits. Moreover I have published sufficient material elsewhere in support
of my statements.

343   It frequently happens at the very beginning of the treatment that a dream will reveal to the doctor, in broad perspective, the whole programme of the unconscious. But for practical
reasons it may be quite impossible to make clear to the
patient the deeper meaning of the dream. In this respect, too,
we are limited by practical considerations. Such insight is rendered possible by the doctor's knowledge of relatively fixed symbols. It can be of the greatest value in diagnosis as well as in
prognosis. I was once consulted about a seventeen-year-old
girl. One specialist had conjectured that she might be in the
first stages of progressive muscular atrophy, while another
thought that it was a case of hysteria. In view of the second opinion, I was called in. The clinical picture made me suspect an
organic disease, but there were signs of hysteria as well. I asked
for dreams. The patient answered at once: "Yes, I have terrible dreams. Only recently I dreamt *I was coming home at
night. Everything is as quiet as death. The door into the living-
room is half open, and I see my mother hanging from the
chandelier, swinging to and fro in the cold wind that blows in
through the open windows.* Another time I dreamt that *a terrible noise broke out in the house at night. I get up and discover that a frightened horse is tearing through the rooms. At
last it finds the door into the hall, and jumps through the hall
window from the fourth floor into the street below. I was ter-
rified when I saw it lying there, all mangled.*"

344   The gruesome character of the dreams is alone sufficient to
make one pause. All the same, other people have anxiety dreams
now and then. We must therefore look more closely into the
meaning of the two main symbols, "mother" and "horse." They
must be equivalents, for they both do the same thing: they
commit suicide. "Mother" is an archetype and refers to the
place of origin, to nature, to that which passively creates, hence
to substance and matter, to materiality, the womb, the vegeta-
tive functions. It also means the unconscious, our natural and
instinctive life, the physiological realm, the body in which we
dwell or are contained; for the "mother" is also the matrix, the

hollow form, the vessel that carries and nourishes, and it thus stands psychologically for the foundations of consciousness. Being inside or contained in something also suggests darkness, something nocturnal and fearful, hemming one in. These allusions give the idea of the mother in many of its mythological and etymological variants; they also represent an important part of the Yin idea in Chinese philosophy. This is no individual acquisition of a seventeen-year-old girl; it is a collective inheritance, alive and recorded in language, inherited along with the structure of the psyche and therefore to be found at all times and among all peoples.

345   The word "mother," which sounds so familiar, apparently refers to the best-known, the individual mother—to "my mother." But the mother-symbol points to a darker background which eludes conceptual formulation and can only be vaguely apprehended as the hidden, nature-bound life of the body. Yet even this is too narrow and excludes too many vital subsidiary meanings. The underlying, primary psychic reality is so inconceivably complex that it can be grasped only at the farthest reach of intuition, and then but very dimly. That is why it needs symbols.

346   If we apply our findings to the dream, its interpretation will be: The unconscious life is destroying itself. That is the dream's message to the conscious mind of the dreamer and to anybody who has ears to hear.

347   "Horse" is an archetype that is widely current in mythology and folklore. As an animal it represents the non-human psyche, the subhuman, animal side, the unconscious. That is why horses in folklore sometimes see visions, hear voices, and speak. As a beast of burden it is closely related to the mother-archetype (witness the Valkyries that bear the dead hero to Valhalla, the Trojan horse, etc.). As an animal lower than man it represents the lower part of the body and the animal impulses that rise from there. The horse is dynamic and vehicular power: it carries one away like a surge of instinct. It is subject to panics like all instinctive creatures who lack higher consciousness. Also it has to do with sorcery and magical spells—especially the black night-horses which herald death.

348   It is evident, then, that "horse" is an equivalent of "mother" with a slight shift of meaning. The mother stands for life at its

origin, the horse for the merely animal life of the body. If we apply this meaning to the text of our dream, its interpretation will be: The animal life is destroying itself.

349   The two dreams make nearly identical statements, but, as is usually the case, the second is the more specific. Note the peculiar subtlety of the dream: there is no mention of the death of the individual. It is notorious that one often dreams of one's own death, but that is no serious matter. When it is really a question of death, the dream speaks another language.

350   Both dreams point to a grave organic disease with a fatal outcome. This prognosis was soon confirmed.

351   As for the relatively fixed symbols, this example gives a fair idea of their general nature. There are a great many of them, and all are individually marked by subtle shifts of meaning. It is only through comparative studies in mythology, folklore, religion, and philology that we can evaluate their nature scientifically. The evolutionary stratification of the psyche is more clearly discernible in the dream than in the conscious mind. In the dream, the psyche speaks in images, and gives expression to instincts, which derive from the most primitive levels of nature. Therefore, through the assimilation of unconscious contents, the momentary life of consciousness can once more be brought into harmony with the law of nature from which it all too easily departs, and the patient can be led back to the natural law of his own being.

352   I have not been able, in so short a space, to deal with anything but the elements of the subject. I could not put together before your eyes, stone by stone, the edifice that is reared in every analysis from the materials of the unconscious and finally reaches completion in the restoration of the total personality. The way of successive assimilations goes far beyond the curative results that specifically concern the doctor. It leads in the end to that distant goal which may perhaps have been the first urge to life: the complete actualization of the whole human being, that is, individuation. We physicians may well be the first conscious observers of this dark process of nature. As a rule we see only the pathological phase of development, and we lose sight of the patient as soon as he is cured. Yet it is only after the cure that we would really be in a position to study the normal process, which may extend over years and decades. Had

we but a little knowledge of the ends toward which the unconscious development is tending, and were the doctor's psychological insight not drawn exclusively from the pathological phase, we should have a less confused idea of the processes mediated to the conscious mind by dreams and a clearer recognition of what the symbols point to. In my opinion, every doctor should understand that every procedure in psychotherapy, and particularly the analytical procedure, breaks into a purposeful and continuous process of development, now at this point and now at that, and thus singles out separate phases which seem to follow opposing courses. Each individual analysis by itself shows only one part or one aspect of the deeper process, and for this reason nothing but hopeless confusion can result from comparative case histories. For this reason, too, I have preferred to confine myself to the rudiments of the subject and to practical considerations; for only in closest contact with the everyday facts can we come to anything like a satisfactory understanding.

III

PSYCHOLOGY OF THE TRANSFERENCE [1]

INTERPRETED IN CONJUNCTION WITH
A SET OF ALCHEMICAL ILLUSTRATIONS

> *Quaero non pono, nihil hic determino dictans*
> *Coniicio, conor, confero, tento, rogo. . . .*
>
> (I inquire, I do not assert; I do not here
> determine anything with final assurance; I
> conjecture, try, compare, attempt, ask. . . .)
>
> —Motto to the *Adumbratio Kabbalae*
> *Christianae* (9)

TO MY WIFE

---

[1] [First published, in book form, as *Die Psychologie der Übertragung* (Zurich, 1946).
—EDITORS.]

FOREWORD

Everyone who has had practical experience of psychotherapy knows that the process which Freud called "transference" often presents a difficult problem. It is probably no exaggeration to say that almost all cases requiring lengthy treatment gravitate round the phenomenon of transference, and that the success or failure of the treatment appears to be bound up with it in a very fundamental way. Psychology, therefore, cannot very well overlook or avoid this problem, nor should the psychotherapist pretend that the so-called "dissolution of the transference" is just a matter of course. We meet with a similar optimism in the treatment of "sublimation," a process closely connected with the transference. In discussing these phenomena, people often talk as though they could be dealt with by reason, or by intelligence and will, or could be remedied by the ingenuity and art of a doctor armed with superior technique. This euphemistic and propitiatory approach is useful enough when the situation is the reverse of simple and no easy results are to be had; but it has the disadvantage of disguising the difficulty of the problem and thus preventing or postponing deeper investigation. Although I originally agreed with Freud that the importance of the transference could hardly be overestimated, increasing experience has forced me to realize that its importance is relative. The transference is like those medicines which are a panacea for one and pure poison for another. In one case its appearance denotes a change for the better, in another it is a hindrance and an aggravation, if not a change for the worse, and in a third it is relatively unimportant. Generally speaking, however, it is a critical phenomenon of varying shades of meaning and its absence is as significant as its presence.

In this book I am concerned with the "classical" form of transference and its phenomenology. As it is a form of relationship, it always implies a vis-à-vis. Where it is negative or not there at all, the vis-à-vis plays an unimportant part, as is gen-

erally the case, for instance, when there is an inferiority complex coupled with a compensating need for self-assertion.[2]

It may seem strange to the reader that, in order to throw light on the transference, I should turn to something so apparently remote as alchemical symbolism. But anyone who has read my book Psychology and Alchemy (85) *will know what close connections exist between alchemy and those phenomena which must, for practical reasons, be considered in the psychology of the unconscious. Consequently he will not be surprised to learn that this phenomenon, shown by experience to be so frequent and so important, also has its place in the symbolism and imagery of alchemy. Such images are not likely to be conscious representations of the transference relationship; rather, they unconsciously take that relationship for granted, and for this reason we may use them as an Ariadne thread to guide us in our argument.*

The reader will not find an account of the clinical phenomena of transference in this book. It is not intended for the beginner who would first have to be instructed in such matters, but is addressed exclusively to those who have already gained sufficient experience in their own practice. My object is to provide some kind of orientation in this newly discovered and still unexplored territory, and to acquaint the reader with some of its problems. In view of the great difficulties that beset our understanding here, I would like to stress the provisional character of my investigation. I have tried to put together my observations and ideas, and I recommend them to the reader's consideration in the hope of directing his attention to certain points of view whose importance has forced itself upon me in the course of time. I am afraid that my description will not be easy reading for those who do not possess some knowledge of my earlier works. I have therefore indicated in the footnotes those of my writings which might be of assistance.

The reader who approaches this book more or less unpre-

---

[2] This is not to say that a transference never occurs in such cases. The negative form of transference in the guise of resistance, dislike, or hate endows the other person with great importance from the start, even if this importance is negative; and it tries to put every conceivable obstacle in the way of a positive transference. Consequently the symbolism so characteristic of the latter—the synthesis of opposites—cannot develop.

*pared will perhaps be astonished at the amount of historical
material I bring to bear on my investigation. The reason and
inner necessity for this lie in the fact that it is only possible
to come to a right understanding and appreciation of a contemporary psychological problem when we can reach a point
outside our own time from which to observe it. This point can
only be some past epoch that was concerned with the same
problems, although under different conditions and in other
forms. The comparative analysis here undertaken naturally
demands a correspondingly detailed account of the historical
aspects of the situation. These could be described much more
succinctly if we were dealing with well-known material, where
a few references and hints would suffice. But unfortunately
that is not the case, since the psychology of alchemy here under
review is almost virgin territory. I must therefore take it for
granted that the reader has some knowledge of my* Psychology
and Alchemy, *otherwise it will be hard for him to gain access to
the present volume. The reader whose professional and personal experience has sufficiently acquainted him with the scope
of the transference problem will forgive me this expectation.*

*Although the present study can stand on its own, it forms
at the same time an introduction to a more comprehensive account of the problem of opposites in alchemy, and of their phenomenology and synthesis.*[3] *I would like to express my thanks
here to all those who read my manuscript and drew my attention
to defects. My particular thanks are due to Dr. Marie-Louise von
Franz for her generous help.*

Autumn, 1945   C. G. JUNG

[3] [*Mysterium Coniunctionis,* to be published by Rascher Verlag, Zurich, and subsequently to appear, in translation, as Volume 14 of the *Collected Works.*—EDITORS.]

INTRODUCTION

Bellica pax, vulnus dulce, suave malum.
(A warring peace, a sweet wound, an agreeable
evil.)
—JOHN GOWER, *Confessio amantis*, 57, II, p. 35

1

353 The fact that the idea of the mystic marriage plays such
an important part in alchemy is not so surprising when we
remember that the term most frequently employed for it, *coniunctio,* referred in the first place to what we now call chemical
combination, and that the substances or "bodies" to be combined were drawn together by what we would call affinity. In
days gone by, people used a variety of terms which all expressed
a human, and more particularly an erotic, relationship, such as
nuptiae, matrimonium, coniugium, amicitia, attractio, adulatio.
Accordingly the bodies to be combined were thought of as
agens et patiens, as *vir* or *masculus,* and as *femina, mulier, femi-
neus;* or they were described more picturesquely as dog and
bitch,[1] horse (stallion) and donkey,[2] cock and hen,[3] and as the
winged or wingless dragon.[4] The more anthropomorphic and
theriomorphic the terms become, the more obvious is the part

[1] "Accipe canem corascenum masculum et caniculum Armeniae" (Take a Corascen dog and an Armenian bitch).—Hoghelande, 5, i, p. 163. A quotation from
Kallid (in the *Rosarium*, 2, xiii, p. 248) runs: "Accipe canem coetaneum et catulam
Armeniae" (Take a Coetanean dog and an Armenian bitch). In a magic papyrus,
Selene (moon) is called κύων (bitch).—Paris MS. Z 2280, in Preisendanz, 136, I,
p. 142. In Zosimos, dog and wolf.—Berthelot, 29, III, xii, 9. [No translation of the
words *corascenum* and *coetaneum* has been attempted, as we are advised that they
are probably corrupt, or may indicate geographical names. Cf. par. 458.—EDITORS.]
[2] Zosimos, in 29, III, xii, 9.
[3] The classical passage is to be found in Senior, 164, p. 8: "Tu mei indiges, sicut
gallus gallinae indiget" (You need me as the cock needs the hen).
[4] Numerous pictures of it exist in the literature.

167

played by creative fantasy and thus by the unconscious, and the more we see how the natural philosophers of old were tempted, as their thoughts explored the dark, unknown qualities of matter, to slip away from a strictly chemical investigation and to fall under the spell of the "myth of matter." Since there can never be absolute freedom from prejudice, even the most objective and impartial investigator is liable to become the victim of some unconscious assumption upon going into a region where the darkness has never been illuminated and where he can recognize nothing. This need not necessarily be a misfortune, since the idea which then presents itself as a substitute for the unknown will take the form of an archaic though not inapposite analogy. Thus Kekulé's vision of the dancing couples,[5] which first put him on the track of the structure of certain carbon compounds, namely the benzene ring, was surely a vision of the *coniunctio,* the mating that had preoccupied the minds of the alchemists for seventeen centuries. It was precisely this image that had always lured the mind of the investigator away from the problem of chemistry and back to the ancient myth of the royal or divine marriage; but in Kekulé's vision it reached its chemical goal in the end, thus rendering the greatest imaginable service both to our understanding of organic compounds and to the subsequent unprecedented advances in synthetic chemistry. Looking back, we can say that the alchemists had keen noses when they made this *arcanum arcanorum,*[6] this *donum Dei et secretum altissimi,*[7] this inmost mystery of the art of gold-making, the climax of their work. The subsequent confirmation of the other idea central to gold-making—the transmutability of chemical elements—also takes a worthy place in this belated triumph of alchemical thought. Considering the eminently practical and theoretical importance of these two key ideas, we might well conclude that they were intuitive anticipations whose fascination can be explained in the light of later developments.[8]

5 Kekulé, 94, I, pp. 624f., and Fierz-David, 42, pp. 235f.

6 Zacharias, 5, v, p. 826.

7 "Consilium coniugii," 1, ii, p. 259. Cf. "Aurora consurgens," 19, Part I, Ch. II: "Est namque donum et sacramentum Dei atque res divina" (For it is a gift and sacrament of God and a thing divine).

8 This does not contradict the fact that the *coniunctio* motif owes its fascination primarily to its archetypal character.

354   We find, however, that alchemy did not merely change into chemistry by gradually discovering how to break away from its mythological premises, but that it also became, or had always been, a kind of mystic philosophy. The idea of the *coniunctio* served on the one hand to shed light on the mystery of chemical combination, while on the other it became the symbol of the *unio mystica*, since, as a mythologem, it expresses the archetype of the union of opposites. Now the archetypes do not represent anything external, non-psychic, although they do of course owe the concreteness of their imagery to impressions received from without. Rather, independently of, and sometimes in direct contrast to, the outward forms they may take, they represent the life and essence of a non-individual psyche. Although this psyche is innate in every individual it can neither be modified nor possessed by him personally. It is the same in the individual as it is in the crowd and ultimately in everybody. It is the precondition of each individual psyche, just as the sea is the carrier of the individual wave.

355   The alchemical image of the *coniunctio*, whose practical importance was proved at a later stage of development, is equally valuable from the psychological point of view: that is to say, it plays the same role in the exploration of the darkness of the psyche as it played in the investigation of the riddle of matter. Indeed, it could never have worked so effectively in the material world had it not already possessed the power to fascinate and thus to fix the attention of the investigator along those lines. The *coniunctio* is an *a priori* image which has always occupied an important place in man's mental development. If we trace this idea back we find it has two sources in alchemy, one Christian, the other pagan. The Christian source is unmistakably the doctrine of Christ and the Church, *sponsus* and *sponsa*, where Christ takes the role of Sol and the Church that of Luna.[9] The pagan source is on the one hand the *hieros gamos*,[10] on the other the marital union of the mystic with God.[11] These psychic experiences and the traces they have left behind in tradition explain much that would otherwise

9 Cf. the detailed account in Rahner, 140.
10 A collection of the classical sources is to be found in Klinz, 99.
11 Bousset, 30, pp. 69ff., 263f., 315ff.; Leisegang, 108, I, p. 235.

be totally unintelligible in the strange world of alchemy and its secret language.

356   As we have said above, the image of the *coniunctio* always appears at an important point in the history of the human mind. Recent developments in modern medical psychology have, by observing the mental processes in neuroses and psychoses, forced us to become more and more thorough in our investigation of the psychic background, commonly called the unconscious. It is psychotherapy above all that makes such investigations necessary, because it can no longer be denied that morbid disturbances of the psyche are not to be explained exclusively by the changes going on in the body or in the conscious mind; we must adduce a third factor by way of explanation, namely hypothetical unconscious processes.[12]

357   Practical analysis has shown that unconscious contents are invariably projected at first upon concrete persons and situations. Many projections can ultimately be integrated back into the individual once he has recognized their subjective origin; others resist integration, and although they may be detached from their original objects, they thereupon transfer themselves to the doctor. Among these contents the relation to the parent of opposite sex plays a particularly important part, i.e., the relation of son to mother, daughter to father, and also that of brother to sister.[13] As a rule this complex cannot be integrated completely, since the doctor is nearly always put in the place of the father, the brother, and even (though naturally more rarely) the mother. Experience has shown that this projection persists with all its original intensity (which Freud regarded as aetiological), thus creating a bond that corresponds in every respect to the initial infantile relationship, with a tendency to recapitulate all the experiences of childhood on the doctor. In other words, the neurotic maladjustment of the patient is now

[12] I call unconscious processes "hypothetical" because the unconscious is by definition not amenable to direct observation and can only be inferred.
[13] I leave out of account the so-called homosexual forms, such as father-son, mother-daughter, etc. In alchemy, as far as I know, this variation is alluded to only once, in the "Visio Arislei" (2, i, p. 147): "Domine quamvis rex sis, male tamen imperas et regis: masculos namque masculis coniunxisti, sciens quod masculi non gignunt" (Lord, though thou art king, yet thou rulest and governest badly; for thou hast joined males with males, knowing that males do not produce offspring).

transferred to him.[14] Freud, who was the first to recognize and describe this phenomenon, coined the term "transference neurosis." [15]

358　　This bond is often of such intensity that we could almost speak of a "combination." When two chemical substances combine, both are altered. This is precisely what happens in the transference. Freud rightly recognized that this bond is of the greatest therapeutic importance in that it gives rise to a *mixtum compositum* of the doctor's own mental health and the patient's maladjustment. In Freudian technique the doctor tries to ward off the transference as much as possible—which is understandable enough from the human point of view, though in certain cases it may considerably impair the therapeutic effect. It is inevitable that the doctor should be influenced to a certain extent and even that his nervous health should suffer.[16]

14 Freud says (*Introductory Lectures*, 51, p. 380): "The decisive part of the work is carried through by creating—in the relationship to the physician, in the 'transference'—new editions of those early conflicts, in which the patient strives to behave as he originally behaved. . . . In place of the patient's original illness appears the artificially acquired transference, the transference-disorder; in place of a variety of unreal objects of his libido appears the single object, equally 'fantastic,' namely the person of the physician." It is open to doubt whether the transference is always produced artificially, since it is a phenomenon that can take place quite apart from any treatment, and is moreover a very frequent natural occurrence. Indeed, in any human relationship that is at all intimate, certain transference phenomena will almost always operate as helpful or disturbing factors.

15 "If the patient does but show compliance enough to respect the necessary conditions of the analysis, we can regularly succeed in giving all the symptoms of the illness a new transference-colouring, and in replacing the genuine neurosis by a 'transference-neurosis' . . ." (*Clin. Papers*, 47, p. 374). Freud puts down a little too much to his own account here. A transference is not by any means always the work of the doctor. Often it is in full swing before he has even opened his mouth. Freud's conception of the transference as a "new edition of the old disease," a "newly created and transformed neurosis," or an "artificially acquired neurosis" (51, pp. 371f.), is right in so far as the transference of a neurotic patient is equally neurotic, but this neurosis is neither new nor artificial nor created: it is the same old neurosis, and the only new thing about it is that the doctor is now drawn into the vortex, more as its victim than as its creator.

16 Freud had already discovered the phenomenon of the "counter-transference." Those acquainted with his technique will be aware of its marked tendency to keep the person of the doctor as far as possible beyond the reach of this effect. Hence the doctor's preference for sitting behind the patient, also his pretence that the transference is a product of his technique, whereas in reality it is a perfectly natural phenomenon that can happen to him just as it can happen to the

He quite literally "takes over" the sufferings of his patient and shares them with him. For this reason he runs a risk—and must run it in the nature of things.[17] The enormous importance that Freud attached to the transference phenomenon became clear to me at our first personal meeting in 1907. After a conversation lasting many hours there came a pause. Suddenly he asked me out of the blue, "And what do you think about the transference?" I replied with the deepest conviction that it was the alpha and omega of the analytical method, whereupon he said, "Then you have grasped the main thing."

359   The great importance of the transference has often led to the mistaken idea that it is absolutely indispensable for a cure, that it must be demanded from the patient, so to speak. But a thing like that can no more be demanded than faith, which is only valuable when it is spontaneous. Enforced faith is nothing but spiritual cramp. Anyone who thinks that he must "demand" a transference is forgetting that this is only one of the therapeutic factors, and that the very word "transference" is closely akin to "projection"—a phenomenon that cannot possibly be demanded.[18] I personally am always glad when there is only a mild transference or when it is practically unnoticeable. Far

---

teacher, the clergyman, the general practitioner, and—last but not least—the husband. Freud also uses the expression "transference-neurosis" as a collective term for hysteria, hysterical fears, and compulsion neuroses (Ibid., p. 372).

[17] The effects of this on the doctor or nurse can be very far-reaching. I know of cases where, in dealing with borderline schizophrenics, short psychotic attacks were actually "taken over," and during these moments it happened that the patients were feeling more than ordinarily well. I have even met a case of induced paranoia in a doctor who was analysing a woman patient in the early stages of latent persecution mania. This is not so astonishing since certain psychic disturbances can be extremely infectious if the doctor himself has a latent predisposition in that direction.

[18] Freud himself says (Clin. Papers, 48, p. 380) of this: "I can hardly imagine a more nonsensical proceeding. It robs the phenomenon of that element of spontaneity which is so convincing, and it lays up obstacles ahead which are extremely difficult to overcome." Here Freud stresses the "spontaneity" of the transference, in contrast to his views quoted above. Nevertheless those who "demand" the transference can fall back on the following cryptic utterance of their master (Case Histories, 49, p. 139): "When one goes into the theory of the analytical technique one comes to realize that the transference is something necessarily demanded." [". . . that the transference is an inevitable necessity," as in the authorized translation, is to stretch the meaning of Freud's "etwas notwendig Gefordertes."—TRANS.]

less claim is then made upon one as a person, and one can be satisfied with other effective therapeutic factors. Among these the patient's own insight plays an important part, also his goodwill, the doctor's authority, suggestion,[19] good advice,[20] understanding, sympathy, encouragement, etc. Naturally the more serious cases do not come into this category.

360   Careful analysis of the transference phenomenon yields an extremely complicated picture with such startlingly pronounced features that we are often tempted to pick out one of them as the most important and then exclaim by way of explanation: "Of course, it's nothing but . . .!" I am referring chiefly to the erotic or sexual aspect of transference fantasies. The existence of this aspect is undeniable, but it is not always the only one and not always the essential one. Another is the will to power (described by Adler), which proves to be coexistent with sexuality, and it is often very difficult to make out which of the two predominates. These two aspects alone offer sufficient grounds for a paralysing conflict.

361   There are, however, other forms of instinctive *concupiscentia* that come more from "hunger," from wanting to possess; others again are based on the instinctive negation of desire, so that life seems to be founded on fear or self-destruction. A certain *abaissement du niveau mental,* i.e., a weakness in the hierarchical order of the ego, is enough to set these instinctive urges and desires in motion and bring about a dissociation of personality—in other words, a multiplication of its centres of gravity. (In schizophrenia there is an actual fragmentation of personality.) These dynamic components must be regarded as real or symptomatic, vitally decisive or merely syndromal, according to the degree of their predominance. Although the strongest instincts undoubtedly require concrete realization and generally enforce it, they cannot be considered exclusively biological since the course they actually follow is subject to powerful modifications coming from the personality itself. If a man's temperament inclines him to a spiritual attitude, even

19 Suggestion happens of its own accord, without the doctor's being able to prevent it or taking the slightest trouble to produce it.
20 "Good advice" is often a doubtful remedy, but generally not dangerous because it has so little effect. It is one of the things the public expects in the *persona medici.*

the concrete activity of the instincts will take on a certain symbolical character. This activity is no longer the mere satisfaction of instinctual impulses, for it is now associated with or complicated by "meanings." In the case of purely syndromal instinctive processes, which do not demand concrete realization to the same extent, the symbolical character of their fulfilment is all the more marked. The most vivid examples of these complications are probably to be found in erotic phenomenology. Four stages were known even in the late classical period: Hawwah (Eve), Helen (of Troy), the Virgin Mary, and Sophia. The series is repeated in Goethe's *Faust:* in the figures of Gretchen as the personification of a purely instinctual relationship (Eve); Helen as an anima figure; [21] Mary as the personification of the "heavenly," i.e., Christian or religious, relationship; and the "eternal feminine" as an expression of the alchemical *Sapientia.* The nomenclature shows that we are dealing with the heterosexual Eros- or anima-figure in four stages, and consequently with four stages of the Eros cult. The first stage—Hawwah, Eve, earth—is purely biological; woman is equated with the mother and only represents something to be fertilized. The second stage is still dominated by the sexual Eros, but on an aesthetic and romantic level where woman has already acquired some value as an individual. The third stage raises Eros to the heights of religious devotion and thus spiritualizes him: Hawwah has been replaced by spiritual motherhood. Finally, the fourth stage illustrates something which unexpectedly goes beyond the almost unsurpassable third stage: *Sapientia.* How can wisdom transcend the most holy and the most pure?—Presumably only by virtue of the truth that the less sometimes means the more. This stage represents spiritualization of Helen and consequently of Eros as such. That is why *Sapientia* was regarded as a parallel to the Shulamite in the Song of Solomon.

2

362   Not only are there different instincts which cannot forcibly be reduced to one another, there are also different levels on which they move. In view of this far from simple situation,

[21] Simon Magus' Helen (Selene) is another excellent example.

it is small wonder that the transference—also an instinctive process, in part—is very difficult to interpret and classify. The instincts and their specific fantasy-contents are partly concrete, partly symbolical (i.e., "unreal"), sometimes one, sometimes the other, and they have the same paradoxical character when they are projected. The transference is far from being a simple phenomenon with only one meaning, and we can never make out beforehand what it is all about. The same applies to its specific content, commonly called incest. We know that it is *Incest* possible to interpret the fantasy-contents of the instincts either as *signs,* as self-portraits of the instincts, i.e., reductively; or as *symbols,* as the spiritual meaning of the natural instinct. In the former case the instinctive process is taken to be "real" and in the latter "unreal."

363   In any particular case it is often almost impossible to say what is "spirit" and what is "instinct." Together they form an impenetrable mass, a veritable magma sprung from the depths of primeval chaos. When one meets such contents one immediately understands why the psychic equilibrium of the neurotic is disturbed, and why the whole psychic system is broken up in schizophrenia. They emit a fascination which not only grips— and has already gripped—the patient, but can also have an inductive effect on the unconscious of the impartial spectator, in this case the doctor. The burden of these unconscious and chaotic contents lies heavy on the patient; for, although they are present in everybody, it is only in him that they have become active, and they isolate him in a spiritual loneliness which neither he nor anybody else can understand and which is bound to be misinterpreted. Unfortunately, if we do not feel our way into the situation and if we approach it from the outside, it is only too easy to dismiss it with a light word or to push it in the wrong direction. This is what the patient has long been doing on his own account, giving the doctor every opportunity for misinterpretation. At first the secret seems to lie with his parents, but when this tie has been loosed and the projection withdrawn, the whole weight falls upon the doctor, who is faced with the question: "What are *you* going to do about the transference?"

364   The doctor, by voluntarily and consciously taking over the psychic sufferings of the patient, exposes himself to the

overpowering contents of the unconscious and hence also to their inductive action. The case begins to "fascinate" him. Here again it is easy to explain this in terms of personal likes and dislikes, but one overlooks the fact that this would be an instance of *ignotum per ignotius*. In reality these personal feelings, if they exist at all in any decisive degree, are governed by those same unconscious contents which have become activated. An unconscious tie is established and now, in the patient's fantasies, it assumes all the forms and dimensions so profusely described in the literature. The patient, by bringing an activated unconscious content to bear upon the doctor, constellates the corresponding unconscious material in him, owing to the inductive effect which always emanates from projections in greater or lesser degree. Doctor and patient thus find themselves in a relationship founded on mutual unconsciousness.

365 It is none too easy for the doctor to make himself aware of this fact. One is naturally loath to admit that one could be affected in the most personal way by just any patient. But the more unconsciously this happens, the more the doctor will be tempted to adopt an "apotropaic" attitude, and the *persona medici* he hides behind is, or rather seems to be, an admirable instrument for this purpose. Inseparable from the *persona* is the doctor's routine and his trick of knowing everything beforehand, which is one of the favourite props of the well-versed practitioner and of all infallible authority. Yet this lack of insight is an ill counsellor, for the unconscious infection brings with it the therapeutic possibility—which should not be underestimated—of the illness being transferred to the doctor. We must suppose as a matter of course that the doctor is the better able to make the constellated contents conscious, otherwise it would only lead to mutual imprisonment in the same state of unconsciousness. The greatest difficulty here is that contents are often activated in the doctor which might normally remain latent. He might be so normal as not to need any such unconscious standpoints to compensate for his conscious situation. At least this is often how it looks, though whether it is so in a deeper sense is an open question. Presumably he had good reasons for choosing the profession of psychiatrist and for being particularly interested in the treatment of psychoneuroses; and he cannot very well do that without gaining some insight into

his own unconscious processes. Nor can his concern with the unconscious be explained entirely by a free choice of interests, but rather by a fateful disposition which originally inclined him to the medical profession. The more one sees of human fate and the more one examines its secret springs of action, the more one is impressed by the strength of unconscious motives and by the limitations of free choice. The doctor knows—or at least he should know—that he did not choose this career by chance; and the psychotherapist in particular should clearly understand that psychic infections, however superfluous they seem to him, are in fact the predestined concomitants of his work, and thus fully in accord with the instinctive disposition of his own life. This realization also gives him the right attitude to his patient. The patient then means something to him personally, and this provides the most favourable basis for treatment.

3

366   In the old pre-analytical psychotherapy, going right back to the doctors of the Romantic Age, the transference was already defined as "rapport." It forms the basis of therapeutic influence once the patient's initial projections are broken. During this work it becomes clear that the projections can also obscure the judgment of the doctor—only to a small extent, of course, for otherwise all therapy would be impossible. Although we may justifiably expect the doctor at the very least to be acquainted with the effects of the unconscious on his own person, and may therefore demand that anybody who intends to practise psychotherapy should first submit to a "training analysis," yet even the best preparation will not suffice to teach him everything about the unconscious. A complete "emptying" of the unconscious is out of the question, if only because its creative powers are continually producing new formations. Consciousness, no matter how extensive it may be, must always remain the smaller circle within the greater circle of the unconscious, an island surrounded by the sea; and, like the sea itself, the unconscious yields an endless and self-replenishing abundance of living creatures, a wealth beyond our fathoming. We may long have known the meaning, effects, and characteristics

of unconscious contents without ever having fathomed their depths and potentialities, for they are capable of infinite variation and can never be depotentiated. The only way to get at them in practice is to try to attain a conscious attitude which allows the unconscious to co-operate instead of being driven into opposition.

367   Even the most experienced psychotherapist will discover again and again that he is caught up in a bond, a combination resting on mutual unconsciousness. And though he may believe himself to be in possession of all the necessary knowledge concerning the constellated archetypes, he will in the end come to realize that there are very many things indeed of which his academic knowledge never dreamed. Each new case that requires thorough treatment is pioneer work, and every trace of routine then proves to be a blind alley. Consequently the higher psychotherapy is a most exacting business and sometimes it sets tasks which challenge not only our understanding or our sympathy, but the whole man. The doctor is inclined to demand this total effort from his patient, yet he must realize that this same demand only works if he is aware that it also applies to himself.

368   I said earlier that the contents which enter into the transference were as a rule originally projected upon the parents or other members of the family. Owing to the fact that these contents seldom or never lack an erotic aspect or are genuinely sexual in substance (apart from the other factors already mentioned), an incestuous character does undoubtedly attach to them, and this has given rise to the Freudian theory of incest. Their exogamous transference to the doctor does not alter the situation. He is merely drawn into the peculiar atmosphere of family incest through the projection. This necessarily leads to an unreal intimacy which is highly distressing to both doctor and patient and arouses resistance and doubt on both sides. The violent repudiation of Freud's original discoveries gets us nowhere, for we are dealing with an empirically demonstrable fact which meets with such universal confirmation that only the ignorant still try to oppose it. But the interpretation of this fact is, in the very nature of the case, highly controversial. Is it a genuine incestuous instinct or a pathological variation? Or is the incest one of the "arrangements" (Adler) of the

will to power? Or is it a regression of normal libido [22] to the
infantile level, from fear of an apparently impossible task in
life? [23] Or is all incest-fantasy purely symbolical, and thus a re-
activation of the incest archetype, which plays such an important part in the history of the mind?

369   For all these widely differing interpretations we can marshal more or less satisfactory arguments. The view which probably causes most offence is that incest is a genuine instinct. But,
considering the almost universal prevalence of the incest taboo,
we may legitimately remark that a thing which is not liked and
desired generally requires no prohibition. In my opinion, each
of these interpretations is justified up to a point, because all
the corresponding shades of meaning are present in concrete
instances, though with varying intensity. Sometimes one aspect
predominates and sometimes another. I am far from asserting
that the above list could not be supplemented further.

370   In practice, however, it is of the utmost importance how
the incestuous aspect is interpreted. The explanation will vary
according to the nature of the case, the stage of treatment, the
perspicacity of the patient, and the maturity of his judgment.

371   The existence of the incest element involves not only an
intellectual difficulty but, worst of all, an emotional complication of the therapeutic situation. It is the hiding place for all
the most secret, painful, intense, delicate, shamefaced, timorous,
grotesque, unmoral, and at the same time the most sacred
feelings which go to make up the incredible and inexplicable
wealth of human relationships and give them their compelling
power. Like the tentacles of an octopus they twine themselves
invisibly round parents and children and, through the transference, round doctor and patient. This binding force shows
itself in the irresistible strength and obstinacy of the neurotic
symptom and in the patient's desperate clinging to the world
of infancy or to the doctor. The word "possession" describes
this state in a way that could hardly be bettered.

[22] The reader will know that I do not understand *libido* in the original Freudian
sense as *appetitus sexualis,* but as an *appetitus* which can be defined as psychic
energy. See "On Psychic Energy," 82.
[23] This is the view I have put forward as an explanation of certain processes in
"The Theory of Psychoanalysis," 92.

372   The remarkable effects produced by unconscious contents allow us to infer something about their energy. All unconscious contents, once they are activated—i.e., have made themselves felt—possess as it were a specific energy which enables them to manifest themselves everywhere (like the incest motif, for instance). But this energy is normally not sufficient to thrust the content into consciousness. For that there must be a certain predisposition on the part of the conscious mind, namely a deficit in the form of loss of energy. The energy so lost raises the psychic potency of certain compensating contents in the unconscious. The *abaissement du niveau mental,* the energy lost to consciousness, is a phenomenon which shows itself most drastically in the "loss of soul" among primitive peoples, who also have interesting psychotherapeutic methods for recapturing the soul that has gone astray. This is not the place to go into these things in detail, so a bare mention must suffice.[24] Similar phenomena can be observed in civilized man. He too is liable to a sudden loss of initiative for no apparent reason. The discovery of the real reason is no easy task and generally leads to a somewhat ticklish discussion of things lying in the background. Carelessness of all kinds, neglected duties, tasks postponed, wilful outbursts of defiance, and so on, all these can dam up his vitality to such an extent that certain quanta of energy, no longer finding a conscious outlet, stream off into the unconscious, where they activate other, compensating contents, which in turn begin to exert a compulsive influence on the conscious mind. (Hence the very common combination of extreme neglect of duty and a compulsion neurosis!)

373   This is one way in which loss of energy may come about. The other way causes loss not through a malfunctioning of the conscious mind but through a "spontaneous" activation of unconscious contents, which react secondarily upon the conscious mind. There are moments in human life when a new page is turned. New interests and tendencies appear which have hitherto received no attention, or there is a sudden change of personality (a so-called mutation of character). During the incubation period of such a change we can often observe a loss of conscious energy: the new development has drawn off the energy it needs from consciousness. This lowering of energy can be

24 I refer the reader to Frazer, *Taboo and the Perils of the Soul,* 45, pp. 54ff.

seen most clearly before the onset of certain psychoses and also in the empty stillness which precedes creative work.[25]

374   The remarkable potency of unconscious contents, therefore, always indicates a corresponding weakness in the conscious mind and its functions. It is as though the latter were threatened with impotence. For primitive man this danger is one of the most terrifying instances of "magic." So we can understand why this secret fear is also to be found among civilized people. In serious cases it is the secret fear of going mad; in less serious, the fear of the unconscious—a fear which even the normal person exhibits in his resistance to psychological views and explanations. This resistance borders on the grotesque when it comes to scouting all psychological explanations of art, philosophy, and religion, as though the human psyche had, or should have, absolutely nothing to do with these things. The doctor knows these well-defended zones from his consulting hours: they are reminiscent of island fortresses from which the neurotic tries to ward off the octopus. ("Happy neurosis island," as one of my patients called his conscious state!) The doctor is well aware that the patient needs an island and would be lost without it. It serves as a refuge for his consciousness and as the last stronghold against the threatening embrace of the unconscious. The same is true of the normal person's taboo regions which psychology must not touch. But since no war was ever won on the defensive, one must, in order to terminate hostilities, open negotiations with the enemy and see what his terms really are. Such is the intention of the doctor who volunteers to act as a mediator. He is far from wishing to disturb the somewhat precarious island idyll or pull down the fortifications. On the contrary, he is thankful that somewhere a firm foothold exists that does not first have to be fished up out of the chaos, always a desperately difficult task. He knows that the island is a bit cramped and that life on it is pretty meagre and plagued with all sorts of imaginary wants because too much life has been left outside, and that as a result a terrifying monster is created, or rather roused out of its slumbers. He also knows that this seemingly alarming animal stands in a secret

25 The same phenomenon can be seen on a smaller scale, but no less clearly, in the apprehension and depression which precede any special psychic exertion, such as an examination, a lecture, an important interview, etc.

compensatory relationship to the island and could supply everything that the island lacks.

375   The transference, however, alters the psychological stature of the doctor, though this is at first imperceptible to him. He too becomes affected, and has as much difficulty in distinguishing between the patient and what has taken possession of him as has the patient himself. This leads both of them to a direct confrontation with the daemonic forces lurking in the darkness. The resultant paradoxical blend of positive and negative, of trust and fear, of hope and doubt, of attraction and repulsion, is characteristic of the initial relationship. It is the νεῖκος καὶ φιλία (hate and love) of the elements, which the alchemists likened to the primeval chaos. The activated unconscious appears as a flurry of unleashed opposites and calls forth the attempt to reconcile them, so that, in the words of the alchemists, the great panacea, the *medicina catholica,* may be born.

4

376   It must be emphasized that in alchemy the dark initial state or *nigredo* is often regarded as the product of a previous operation, and that it therefore does not represent the absolute beginning.[26] Similarly, the psychological parallel to the *nigredo* is the result of the foregoing preliminary talk which, at a certain moment, sometimes long delayed, "touches" the unconscious and establishes the unconscious identity [27] of doctor and patient. This moment *may* be perceived and registered consciously, but generally it happens outside consciousness and the bond thus established is only recognized later and indirectly by its results. Occasionally dreams occur about this time,

[26] Where the *nigredo* is identified with the *putrefactio* it does not come at the beginning, as for example in the series of pictures to the *Rosarium philosophorum* (2, xiii, p. 254). In Mylius, 120, p. 116, the *nigredo* only appears in the fifth grade of the work, during the "putrefactio, quae in umbra purgatorii celebratur" (putrefaction which is celebrated in the darkness of Purgatory); but further on (p. 118), we read in contradiction to this: "Et haec denigratio est operis initium, putrefactionis indicium" etc. (And this *denigratio* is the beginning of the work, an indication of the putrefaction).

[27] "Unconscious identity" is the same as Lévy-Bruhl's *participation mystique* (in *How Natives Think,* 109).

announcing the appearance of the transference. For instance, a dream may say that a fire has started in the cellar, or that a burglar has broken in, or that the patient's father has died, or it may depict an erotic or some other ambiguous situation.[28] From the moment when such a dream occurs there may be initiated a queer unconscious time-reckoning, lasting for months or even longer. I have often observed this process and will give a practical instance of it:

377   When treating a lady of over sixty, I was struck by the following passage in a dream she had on October 21, 1938: *"A beautiful little child, a girl of six months old, is playing in the kitchen with her grandparents and myself, her mother. The grandparents are on the left of the room and the child stands on the square table in the middle of the kitchen. I stand by the table and play with the child. The old woman says she can hardly believe we have known the child for only six months. I say that it is not so strange because we knew and loved the child long before she was born."*

378   It is immediately apparent that the child is something special, i.e., a child hero or divine child. The father is not mentioned; his absence is part of the picture.[29] The kitchen, as scene of the happening, points to the unconscious. The square table is the quaternity, the classical basis of the "special" child,[30] for the child is a symbol of the self and the quaternity is a sym-

---

28 A pictorial representation of this moment, in the form of a flash of lightning and a "stone-birth," is to be found in my "Study in Individuation," 90, fig. 2.

29 Because he is the "unknown father," a theme to be met with in Gnosticism. See Bousset, 30, Ch. II, pp. 58–91.

30 Cf. Nicholas of Flüe's vision of the threefold fountain arising in the square container (Lavaud, 105, p. 67, and Stöckli, 154, p. 19). A Gnostic text says: "In the second Father[hood] the five trees are standing and in their midst is a trapeza [τράπεζα]. Standing on the trapeza is an Only-begotten word [λόγος μονογενής]." (Charlotte Baynes, 23, p. 70.) The trapeza is an abbreviation of τετράπεζα, a four-legged table or podium (23, p. 71). Cf. Irenaeus, 72, III, 11, where he compares the "fourfold gospel" with the four cherubim in the vision of Ezekiel, the four regions of the world, and the four winds: "ex quibus manifestum est, quoniam qui est omnium artifex Verbum, qui sedet super Cherubim et continet omnia, dedit nobis quadriforme Evangelium, quod uno spiritu continetur" (from which it is clear that He who is the Maker of all things, the Word [Logos] who sits above the Cherubim and holds all things together, gave unto us the fourfold gospel, which is contained in one spirit). Concerning the kitchen, cf. Lavaud, 105, p. 66, and Stöckli, 154, p. 18.

bolical expression of this. The self as such is timeless and existed before any birth.[31] The dreamer was strongly influenced by Indian writings and knew the Upanishads well, but not the medieval Christian symbolism which is in question here. The precise age of the child made me ask the dreamer to look in her notes to see what had happened in the unconscious six months earlier. Under April 20, 1938, she found the following dream:

379 *"With some other women I am looking at a piece of tapestry, a square with symbolical figures on it. Immediately afterwards I am sitting with some women in front of a marvellous tree. It is magnificently grown, at first it seems to be some kind of conifer, but then I think—in the dream—that it is a monkeypuzzle* [a tree of genus *Araucaria*] *with the branches growing straight up like candles* [a confusion with *Cereus candelabrum*]. *A Christmas tree is fitted into it in such a way that at first it looks like one tree instead of two."*—As the dreamer was writing down this dream immediately on waking, with a vivid picture of the tree before her, she suddenly had a vision of a tiny golden child lying at the foot of the tree (tree-birth motif). She had thus gone on dreaming the sense of the dream. It undoubtedly depicts the birth of the divine ("golden") child.

380 But what had happened nine months previous to April 20, 1938? Between July 19 and 22, 1937, she had painted a picture showing, on the left, a heap of coloured and polished (precious) stones surmounted by a silver serpent, winged and crowned. In the middle of the picture there stands a naked female figure from whose genital region the same serpent rears up towards the heart, where it bursts into a five-pointed, gorgeously flashing golden star. A coloured bird flies down on the right with a little twig in its beak. On the twig five flowers are arranged in a *quaternio*, one yellow, one blue, one red, one green, but the topmost is golden—obviously a mandala structure.[32] The serpent represents the hissing ascent of Kundalini, and in the corresponding yoga this marks the first moment in a process which ends with deification in the divine Self, the syzygy of Shiva and Shakti.[33] It is obviously the moment of

---

31 This is not a metaphysical statement but a psychological fact.
32 As regards the bird with the flowering twig, see the *Rosarium* pictures below.
33 Avalon, *The Serpent Power*, 20, pp. 345f.

symbolical conception, which is both Tantric and—because of the bird—Christian in character, being a contamination of the allegory of the conception with Noah's dove and the sprig of olive.

381   This case, and more particularly the last image, is a classical example of the kind of symbolism which marks the onset of the transference. Noah's dove (the prototype of reconciliation), the *incarnatio Dei,* the union of God with the *materia* for the purpose of begetting the mediator, the serpent path, the Sushumna representing the line midway between sun and moon—all this is the first, anticipatory stage of an as-yet-unfulfilled programme that culminates in the union of opposites. This union is analogous to the "royal marriage" in alchemy. The prodromal events signify the meeting or collision of various opposites and can therefore appropriately be called chaos and blackness. As mentioned above, this may take place at the beginning of the treatment, or it may first have to go through a lengthy analysis, a stage of *rapprochement.* Such is particularly the case when the patient shows violent resistances coupled with fear of the activated contents of the unconscious.[34] There is good reason and ample justification for these resistances and they should never, under any circumstances, be ridden over roughshod or otherwise argued out of existence. Neither should they be belittled, disparaged, or made ridiculous; on the contrary, they should be taken with the utmost seriousness as a vitally important defence mechanism against overpowering contents which are often very difficult to control. The general rule should be that the weakness of the conscious attitude is proportional to the strength of the resistance. When, therefore, there are strong resistances, the conscious rapport with the patient must be carefully watched, and—in certain

[34] Freud, as we know, looks at the transference problem from the standpoint of a personalistic psychology and thus overlooks the very essence of the transference —the collective contents of an archetypal nature. The reason for this is his notoriously negative attitude to the psychic reality of archetypal images, which he dismisses as "illusion." This materialistic bias precludes strict application of the phenomenological principle without which an objective study of the psyche is absolutely impossible. My handling of the transference problem, in contrast to Freud's, includes the archetypal aspect and thus gives rise to a totally different picture. Freud's rational treatment of the problem is quite logical as far as his purely personalistic premises go, but both in theory and in practice they do not go far enough, since they fail to do justice to the obvious admixture of archetypal data.

cases—his conscious attitude must be supported to such a degree that, in view of later developments, one would be bound to charge oneself with the grossest inconsistency. That is inevitable, because one can never be too sure that the weak state of the patient's conscious mind will prove equal to the subsequent assault of the unconscious. In fact, one must go on supporting his conscious (or, as Freud thinks, "repressive") attitude until the patient can let the "repressed" contents rise up spontaneously. Should there by any chance be a latent psychosis [35] which cannot be detected beforehand, this cautious procedure may prevent the devastating invasion of the unconscious or at least catch it in time. At all events the doctor then has a clear conscience, knowing that he has done everything in his power to avoid a fatal outcome.[36] Nor is it beside the point to add that consistent support of the conscious attitude has in itself a high therapeutic value and not infrequently serves to bring about satisfactory results. It would be a dangerous prejudice to imagine that analysis of the unconscious is the one and only panacea which should therefore be employed in every case. It is rather like a surgical operation and we should only resort to the knife when other methods have failed. So long as it does not obtrude itself the unconscious is best left alone. The reader should be quite clear that my discussion of the transference problem is not an account of the daily routine of the psychotherapist, but far more a description of what happens when the check normally exerted on the unconscious by the conscious mind is disrupted, though this need not necessarily occur at all.

382　　Cases where the archetypal problem of the transference becomes acute are by no means always "serious" cases, i.e., grave states of illness. There are of course such cases among them, but there are also mild neuroses, or simply psychological difficulties which we would be at a loss to diagnose. Curiously enough, it is these latter cases that present the doctor with the most difficult problems. Often the persons concerned endure

[35] The numerical proportion of latent to manifest psychoses is about equal to that of latent to active cases of tuberculosis.

[36] The violent resistance, mentioned by Freud, to the rational termination of the transference is often due to the fact that in some markedly sexual forms of transference there are concealed collective unconscious contents which defy all rational solution. Or, if this solution succeeds, the patient is cut off from the collective unconscious and comes to feel this as a loss.

unspeakable suffering without developing any neurotic symptoms that would entitle them to be called ill. We can only call it an intense suffering, a passion of the soul but not a disease of the mind.

5

383   Once an unconscious content is constellated, it tends to break down the relationship of conscious trust between doctor and patient by creating, through projection, an atmosphere of illusion which either leads to continual misinterpretations and misunderstandings, or else produces a most disconcerting impression of harmony. The latter is even more trying than the former, which at worst (though it is sometimes for the best!) can only hamper the treatment, whereas in the other case a tremendous effort is needed to discover the points of difference. But in either case the constellation of the unconscious is a troublesome factor. The situation is enveloped in a kind of fog, and this fully accords with the nature of the unconscious content: it is dark and black—"nigrum, nigrius nigro," [37] as the alchemists rightly say—and in addition it is charged with dangerous polar tensions, with the *inimicitia elementorum*. One finds oneself in an impenetrable chaos, which is indeed one of the synonyms for the mysterious *prima materia*. The latter corresponds to the nature of the unconscious content in every respect, with one exception: this time it does not appear in the alchemical substance but in man himself. In the case of alchemy it is quite evident that the unconscious content is of human origin, as I have shown in my *Psychology and Alchemy*.[37a] Hunted for centuries and never found, the *prima materia* or *lapis philosophorum* is, as a few alchemists rightly suspected, to be discovered in man himself. But it seems that this content can never be found and integrated directly, but only by the circuitous route of projection. For as a rule the unconscious first appears in projected form. Whenever it appears to obtrude itself directly, as in visions, dreams, illuminations, psychoses, etc., these are always preceded by psychic conditions which give clear proof of projection. A classical example of this is Saul's

[37] Cf. Lully, 3, ii, pp. 790ff., and Maier, *Symbola*, 114, pp. 379f.
[37a] 201, pars. 342f.

fanatical persecution of the Christians before Christ appeared to him in a vision.

384   The elusive, deceptive, ever-changing content that possesses the patient like a demon now flits about from patient to doctor and, as the third party in the alliance, continues its game, sometimes impish and teasing, sometimes really diabolical. The alchemists aptly personified it as the wily god of revelation, Hermes or Mercurius; and though they lament over the way he hoodwinks them, they still give him the highest names, which bring him very near to deity.[38] But for all that, they deem themselves good Christians whose faithfulness of heart is never in doubt, and they begin and end their treatises with pious invocations.[39] Yet it would be an altogether unjustifiable suppression of the truth were I to confine myself to the negative description of Mercurius' impish drolleries, his inexhaustible invention, his insinuations, his intriguing ideas and schemes, his ambivalence and—often—his unmistakable malice. He is also capable of the exact opposite, and I can well understand why the alchemists endowed their Mercurius with the highest spiritual qualities, although these stand in flagrant contrast to his exceedingly shady character. The contents of the unconscious are indeed of the greatest importance, for the unconscious is after all the matrix of the human mind and its inventions. Wonderful and ingenious as this other side of the unconscious is, it can be most dangerously deceptive on account of its numinous nature. Involuntarily one thinks of the devils mentioned by St. Athanasius in his life of St. Anthony, who talk

---

[38] Cf. my "The Spirit Mercurius," 89.

[39] Thus the second part of the "Aurora consurgens" (2, iii, pp. 246ff.) closes with the words: "Et haec est probata medicina Philosophorum, quam omni inuestiganti fideli et pio volenti, praestare dignetur Dominus noster Jesus Christus, qui cum Patre et Spiritu Sancto vivit et regnat, Deus per infinita seculorum secula, Amen" (And this is the approved medicine of the philosophers, which our Lord Jesus Christ, who lives and rules with the Father and the Holy Spirit, God through Eternity, may deign to give to every searcher who is faithful, pious, and of good will, Amen). This conclusion no doubt comes from the Offertorium (prayer during the *commixtio*), where it says: ". . . qui humanitatis nostrae fieri dignatus est particeps, Jesus Christus, Filius Tuus, Dominus noster: qui tecum vivit et regnat in unitate Spiritus Sancti Deus per omnia saecula saeculorum. Amen." (. . . who vouchsafed to become partaker of our humanity, Jesus Christ, Thy Son, our Lord: who liveth and reigneth with Thee in the unity of the Holy Ghost, one God, world without end. Amen.)

very piously, sing psalms, read the holy books, and—worst of all—speak the truth. The difficulties of our psychotherapeutic work teach us to take truth, goodness, and beauty where we find them. They are not always found where we look for them: often they are hidden in the dirt or are in the keeping of the dragon. "In stercore invenitur" (it is found in filth)[40] runs an alchemical dictum—nor is it any the less valuable on that account. But, it does not transfigure the dirt and does not diminish the evil, any more than these lessen God's gifts. The contrast is painful and the paradox bewildering. Sayings like

ουρανο ανω	(Heaven above
ουρανο κατω	Heaven below
αστρα ανω	Stars above
αστρα κατω	Stars below
παν ο ανω	All that is above
τουτο κατω	Also is below
ταυτα λαβε	Grasp this
κε ευτυχε	And rejoice)[41]

are too optimistic and superficial; they forget the moral torment occasioned by the opposites, and the importance of ethical values.

385   The refining of the *prima materia,* the unconscious content, demands endless patience, perseverance,[42] equanimity, knowledge, and ability on the part of the doctor; and, on the part of the patient, the putting forth of his best powers and a capacity for suffering which does not leave the doctor altogether unaffected. The deep meaning of the Christian virtues, especially the greatest among these, will become clear even to the unbeliever; for there are times when he needs them all if he is to rescue his consciousness, and his very life, from this pocket of chaos, whose final subjugation, without violence, is no ordi-

---

[40] Cf. *Tractatus aureus,* 1, i, p. 21.

[41] Kircher, 98, II, Class X, Cap. V, p. 414. There is a connection between this text and the "Tabula smaragdina"; cf. Ruska, 149, p. 217.

[42] The *Rosarium* (2, xiii, p. 230) says: "Et scias, quod haec est longissima via, ergo patientia et mora sunt necessariae in nostro magisterio" (And you must know that this is a very long road; therefore patience and perseverance are needful in our magistery). Cf. "Aurora consurgens," 19, Ch. 10: "Tria sunt necessaria videlicet patientia mora et aptitudo instrumentorum" (Three things are necessary, namely: patience, leisure, and skill with the instruments).—Kallid minor.

nary task. If the work succeeds, it often works like a miracle, and one can understand what it was that prompted the alchemists to insert a heartfelt *Deo concedente* in their recipes, or to allow that only if God wrought a miracle could their procedure be brought to a successful conclusion.

6

386   It may seem strange to the reader that a "medical procedure" should give rise to such considerations. Although in illnesses of the body there is no remedy and no treatment that can be said to be infallible in all circumstances, there are still a great many which will probably have the desired effect without either doctor or patient having the slightest need to insert a *Deo concedente*. But we are not dealing here with the body —we are dealing with the psyche. Consequently we cannot speak the language of body-cells and bacteria; we need another language commensurate with the nature of the psyche, and equally we must have an attitude which measures the danger and can meet it. And all this must be genuine or it will have no effect; if it is hollow, it will damage both doctor and patient. The *Deo concedente* is not just a rhetorical flourish; it expresses the firm attitude of the man who does not imagine that he knows better on every occasion and who is fully aware that the unconscious material before him is something *alive,* a paradoxical Mercurius of whom an old master says: "Et est ille quem natura paululum operata est et in metallicam formam formavit, tamen imperfectum relinquit" (And he is that on whom nature hath worked but a little, and whom she hath wrought into metallic form yet left unfinished) [43]—a natural being, therefore, that longs for integration within the wholeness of a man. It is like a fragment of primeval psyche into which no consciousness has as yet penetrated to create division and order, a "united dual nature," as Goethe says—an abyss of ambiguities.

387   Since we cannot imagine—unless we have lost our critical faculties altogether—that mankind today has attained the highest possible degree of consciousness, there must be some poten-

[43] *Rosarium*, 2, xiii, p. 231. What the alchemist sees in "metallic form" the psychotherapist sees in man.

tial unconscious psyche left over whose development would result in a further extension and a higher differentiation of consciousness. No one can say how great or small this "remnant" might be, for we have no means of measuring the possible extent of conscious development, let alone the extent of the unconscious. But there is not the slightest doubt that a *massa confusa* of archaic and undifferentiated contents exists, which not only manifests itself in neuroses and psychoses but also forms the "skeleton in the cupboard" of innumerable people who are not really pathological. We are so accustomed to hear that everybody has his "difficulties and problems" that we simply accept it as a banal fact, without considering what these difficulties and problems really mean. Why is one never satisfied with oneself? Why is one unreasonable? Why is one not always good and why must one ever leave a cranny for evil? Why does one sometimes say too much and sometimes too little? Why does one do foolish things which could easily be avoided with a little forethought? What is it that is always frustrating us and thwarting our best intentions? Why are there people who never notice these things and cannot even admit their existence? And finally, why do people in the mass beget the historical lunacy of the last thirty years? Why couldn't Pythagoras, twenty-four hundred years ago, have established the rule of wisdom once and for all, or Christianity have set up the Kingdom of Heaven upon earth?

388   The Church has the doctrine of the devil, of an evil principle, whom we like to imagine complete with cloven hoofs, horns, and tail, half man, half beast, a chthonic deity apparently escaped from the rout of Dionysus, the sole surviving champion of the sinful joys of paganism. An excellent picture, and one which exactly describes the grotesque and sinister side of the unconscious; for we have never really come to grips with it and consequently it has remained in its original savage state. Probably no one today would still be rash enough to assert that the European is a lamblike creature and not possessed by a devil. The frightful records of our age are plain for all to see, and they surpass in hideousness everything that any previous age, with its feeble instruments, could have hoped to accomplish.

389   If, as many are fain to believe, the unconscious were only nefarious, only evil, then the situation would be simple and the path clear: to do good and to eschew evil. But what is "good" and what is "evil"? The unconscious is not just evil by nature, it is also the source of the highest good: [44] not only dark but also light, not only bestial, semi-human, and demonic but superhuman, spiritual, and, in the classical sense of the word, "divine." The Mercurius who personifies the unconscious [45] is essentially "duplex," paradoxically dualistic by nature, fiend, monster, beast, and at the same time panacea, "the philosophers' son," *sapientia Dei,* and *donum Spiritus Sancti.*[46]

390   Since this is so, all hope of a simple solution is destroyed. All definitions of good and evil become suspect or actually invalid. As moral forces, good and evil remain unshaken, and —as the simple verities for which the penal code, the ten commandments, and conventional Christian morality take them— undoubted. But conflicting loyalties are much more subtle and dangerous things, and a conscience sharpened by worldly wisdom can no longer rest content with precepts, ideas, and fine words. When it has to deal with that remnant of primeval psyche, pregnant with the future and yearning for development, it grows uneasy and looks round for some guiding principle or fixed point. Indeed, once this stage has been reached in our dealings with the unconscious, these desiderata become a pressing necessity. Since the only salutary powers visible in the world today are the great "psychotherapeutic" systems which we call the religions, and from which we expect the soul's salvation, it is quite natural that many people should make the justifiable and often successful attempt to find a niche for themselves in one of the existing faiths and to acquire a deeper insight into the meaning of the traditional saving verities.

[44] Here I must expressly emphasize that I am not dabbling in metaphysics or discussing questions of faith, but am speaking of psychology. Whatever religious experience or metaphysical truth may be in themselves, looked at empirically they are essentially psychic phenomena, that is, they manifest themselves as such and must therefore be submitted to psychological criticism, evaluation, and investigation. Science comes to a stop at its *own* borders.

[45] Cf. my "The Spirit Mercurius," 89.

[46] The alchemists also liken him to Lucifer ("bringer of light"), God's fallen and most beautiful angel. Cf. Mylius, 120, p. 18.

391   This solution is normal and satisfying in that the dog-
matically formulated truths of the Christian Church express,
almost perfectly, the nature of psychic experience. They are the
repositories of the secrets of the soul, and this matchless knowledge is set forth in grand symbolical images. The unconscious
thus possesses a natural affinity with the spiritual values of the
Church, particularly in their dogmatic form, which owes its
special character to centuries of theological controversy—absurd as this seemed in the eyes of later generations—and to the
passionate efforts of many great men.

7

392   The Church would be an ideal solution for anyone seeking a suitable receptacle for the chaos of the unconscious were
it not that everything man-made, however refined, has its im-
perfections. The fact is that a return to the Church, i.e., to a
particular creed, is not the general rule. Much the more frequent is a better understanding of, and a more intense relation
to, religion as such, which is not to be confused with a creed.[47]
This, it seems to me, is mainly because anyone who appreciates
the legitimacy of the two viewpoints, of the two branches into
which Christianity has been split, cannot maintain the exclusive validity of either of them, for to do so would be to deceive
himself. As a Christian, he has to recognize that the Christendom he belongs to has been split for four hundred years and
that his Christian beliefs, far from redeeming him, have exposed him to a conflict and a division that is still rending the
body of Christ. These are the facts, and they cannot be abolished by each creed pressing for a decision in its favour, as
though each were perfectly sure it possessed the absolute truth.
Such an attitude is unfair to modern man; he can see very well
the advantages that Protestantism has over Catholicism and vice
versa, and it is painfully clear to him that this sectarian insistence
is trying to corner him against his better judgment—in other
words, tempting him to sin against the Holy Ghost. He even
understands why the churches are bound to behave in this way,
and knows that it must be so lest any joyful Christian should

[47] Cf. my *Psychology and Religion*, 86, pars. 6ff. (1938 ed., pp. 4ff.).

imagine himself already reposing in Abraham's anticipated bosom, saved and at peace and free from all fear. Christ's passion continues—for the life of Christ in the *corpus mysticum,* or Christian life in both camps, is at loggerheads with itself and no honest man can deny the split. We are thus in the precise situation of the neurotic who must put up with the painful realization that he is in the midst of conflict. His repeated efforts to repress the other side have only made his neurosis worse. The doctor must advise him to accept the conflict just as it is, with all the suffering this inevitably entails, otherwise the conflict will never be ended. Intelligent Europeans, if at all interested in such questions, are consciously or semiconsciously protestant Catholics and catholic Protestants, nor are they any the worse for that. It is no use telling me that no such people exist: I have seen both sorts, and they have considerably raised my hopes about the European of the future.

393   But the negative attitude of the public at large to the Church seems to be less the result of religious convictions than one symptom of the general mental sloth and ignorance of religion. We can wax indignant over man's notorious lack of spirituality, but when one is a doctor one does not invariably think that the disease is intractable or the patient morally inferior; instead, one supposes that the negative results may possibly be due to the remedy applied. Although it may reasonably be doubted whether man has made any marked or even perceptible progress in morality during the known five thousand years of human civilization, it cannot be denied that there has been a notable development in consciousness and its functions. Above all, there has been a tremendous extension of consciousness in the form of *knowledge.* Not only have the individual functions become differentiated, but to a large extent they have been brought under the control of the ego—in other words, man's will has developed. This is particularly striking when we compare our mentality with that of primitives. The security of our ego has, in comparison with earlier times, greatly increased and has even taken such a dangerous leap forward that, although we sometimes speak of "God's will," we no longer know what we are saying, for in the same breath we assert, "Where there's a will there's a way." And who would ever think of appealing to God's help rather than to the goodwill,

the sense of responsibility and duty, the reason or intelligence, of his fellow men?

394   Whatever we may think of these changes of outlook, we cannot alter the fact of their existence. Now when there is a marked change in the individual's state of consciousness, the unconscious contents which are thereby constellated will also change. And the further the conscious situation moves away from a certain point of equilibrium, the more forceful and accordingly the more dangerous become the unconscious contents that are struggling to re-establish the balance. This leads ultimately to a dissociation: on the one hand, ego-consciousness makes convulsive efforts to shake off an invisible opponent (if it does not suspect its next-door neighbour of being the devil!), while on the other hand it increasingly falls victim to the tyrannical will of an internal "Government opposition" which displays all the characteristics of a dæmonic subman and superman combined.

395   When a few million people get into this state, it produces the sort of situation which has afforded us such an edifying object-lesson every day for the last ten years. These contemporary events betray their psychological background by their very singularity. The insensate destruction and devastation are a reaction against the deflection of consciousness from the point of equilibrium. For an equilibrium does in fact exist between the psychic ego and non-ego, and that equilibrium is a *religio,* a "careful consideration" [48] of ever-present unconscious forces which we neglect at our peril. The present crisis has been brewing for centuries because of this shift in man's conscious situation.

396   Have the Churches adapted themselves to this secular change? Their truth may, with more right than we realize, call itself "eternal," but its temporal garment must pay tribute to the evanescence of all earthly things and should take account of psychic changes. Eternal truth needs a human language that alters with the spirit of the times. The primordial images undergo ceaseless transformation and yet remain ever the same, but only in a new form can they be understood anew. Always they require a new interpretation if, as each formulation becomes obsolete, they are not to lose their spellbinding power

48 I use the classical etymology of *religio* and not that of the Church Fathers.

over that *fugax Mercurius* [49] and allow that useful though dangerous enemy to escape. What is that about "new wine in old bottles"? Where are the answers to the spiritual needs and troubles of a new epoch? And where the knowledge to deal with the psychological problems raised by the development of modern consciousness? Never before has "eternal" truth been faced with such a hybris of will and power.

Ottaviani

8

397 Here, apart from motives of a more personal nature, probably lie the deeper reasons for the fact that the greater part of Europe has succumbed to neo-paganism and anti-Christianity, and has set up a religious ideal of worldly power in opposition to the metaphysical ideal founded on love. But the individual's decision not to belong to a Church does not necessarily denote an anti-Christian attitude; it may mean exactly the reverse: a reconsidering of the kingdom of God in the human heart where, in the words of St. Augustine,[49a] the "mysterium paschale" is accomplished "in interioribus ac superioribus suis." The ancient and long obsolete idea of man as a microcosm contains a supreme psychological truth that has yet to be discovered. In former times this truth was projected upon the body, just as alchemy projected the unconscious psyche upon chemical substances. But it is altogether different when the microcosm is understood as that interior world whose inward nature is fleetingly glimpsed in the unconscious. An inkling of this is to be found in the words of Origen: "Intellige te alium mundum esse in parvo et esse intra te Solem, esse Lunam, esse etiam stellas" (Understand that thou art a second world in miniature, and that the sun and the moon are within thee, and also the stars).[50] And just as the cosmos is not a dissolving mass of particles, but rests in the unity of God's embrace, so man must not dissolve into a whirl of warring possibilities and tendencies modelled on the unconscious, but must become the unity that embraces them all. Origen says pertinently: "Vides, quomodo ille,

Chardin

49 Maier, *Symbola*, 114, p. 386.   50 *Hom. in Leviticum*, 126, 5, 2.
49a *Epistula LV*, 18, V, 8.

qui putatur unus esse, non est unus, sed tot in eo personae viden-
tur esse, quot mores" (Thou seest that he who seemeth to be one
is yet not one, but as many persons appear in him as he hath
velleities).[51] Possession by the unconscious means being torn
apart into many people and things, a *disiunctio*. That is why,
according to Origen, the aim of the Christian is to become an
inwardly united human being.[52] The blind insistence on the
outward community of the Church naturally fails to fulfil this
aim; on the contrary, it inadvertently provides the inner
disunity with an outward vessel without really changing the
disiunctio into a *coniunctio*.

398   The painful conflict that begins with the *nigredo* or *tenebrositas* is described by the alchemist as the *separatio* or *divisio
elementorum,* the *solutio, calcinatio, incineratio,* or as dismem-
berment of the body, excruciating animal sacrifices, amputation
of the mother's hands or the lion's paws, atomization of the
bridegroom in the body of the bride, and so on.[53] While this
extreme form of *disiunctio* is going on, there is a transformation of that arcanum—be it substance or spirit—which invariably turns out to be the mysterious Mercurius. In other words,
out of the monstrous animal forms there gradually emerges a
res simplex, whose nature is one and the same and yet consists
of a duality (Goethe's "united dual nature"). The alchemist tries
to get round this paradox or antinomy with his various procedures and formulae, and to make one out of two.[54] But the
very multiplicity of his symbols and symbolic processes proves
that success is doubtful. Seldom do we find symbols of the goal
whose dual nature is not immediately apparent. His *filius
philosophorum,* his *lapis,* his *rebis,* his homunculus, are all
hermaphroditic. His gold is *non vulgi,* his *lapis* is spirit and
body, and so is his tincture, which is a *sanguis spiritualis*—a
spiritual blood.[55] We can therefore understand why the *nuptiae
chymicae,* the royal marriage, occupies such an important place

51 Ibid. ["Velleities" is an attempt to translate the author's rendering of "mores" as
"Eigenwilligkeiten." Possible alternative translations might be "idiosyncrasies" or
"whims."—TRANS.]   52 *Hom. in Librum regnorum,* 127, 1, 4.
53 "Hounded from one bride-chamber to the next."—*Faust,* Part I.
54 For the same process in the individual psyche, see *Psychology and Alchemy,* 85,
pars. 44ff.
55 Cf. Ruska, *Turba,* 150, Sermo XIX, p. 129. The term comes from al-Habib's
book (ibid., p. 43).

in alchemy as a symbol of the supreme and ultimate union, since it represents the magic-by-analogy which is supposed to bring the work to its final consummation and bind the opposites by love, for "love is stronger than death."

9

399   Alchemy describes, not merely in general outline but often in the most astonishing detail, the same psychological phenomenology which can be observed in the analysis of the unconscious process. The individual's specious unity that emphatically says "*I* want, *I* think" breaks down under the impact of the unconscious. So long as the patient can think that somebody else (his father or mother) is responsible for his difficulties, he can save some semblance of unity (*putatur unus esse!*). But once he realizes that he himself has a shadow, that his enemy is in his own heart, then the conflict begins and one becomes two. Since the "other" will eventually prove to be yet another duality, a compound of opposites, the ego soon becomes a shuttlecock tossed between a multitude of "velleities," with the result that there is an "obfuscation of the light," i.e., consciousness is depotentiated and the patient is at a loss to know where his personality begins or ends. It is like passing through the valley of the shadow, and sometimes the patient has to cling to the doctor as the last remaining shred of reality. This situation is difficult and distressing for both parties; often the doctor is in much the same position as the alchemist who no longer knew whether he was melting the mysterious amalgam in the crucible or whether he was the salamander glowing in the fire. Psychological induction inevitably causes the two parties to get involved in the transformation of the third and to be themselves transformed in the process, and all the time the doctor's knowledge, like a flickering lamp, is the one dim light in the darkness. Nothing gives a better picture of the psychological state of the alchemist than the division of his work-room into a "laboratory," where he bustles about with crucibles and alembics, and an "oratory," where he prays to God for the

much needed illumination—"purge the horrible darknesses of our mind," [56] as the author of the "Aurora" quotes.

400   "Ars requirit totum hominem," we read in an old treatise.[57] This is in the highest degree true of psychotherapeutic work. A genuine participation, going right beyond professional routine, is absolutely imperative, unless of course the doctor prefers to jeopardize the whole proceeding by evading his own problems, which are becoming more and more insistent. The doctor must go to the limits of his subjective possibilities, otherwise the patient will be unable to follow suit. Arbitrary limits are no use, only real ones. It must be a genuine process of purification where "all superfluities are consumed in the fire" and the basic facts emerge. Is there anything more fundamental than the realization, "This is what I am"? It reveals a unity which nevertheless is—or was—a diversity. No longer the earlier ego with its make-believes and artificial contrivances, but another, "objective" ego, which for this reason is better called the "self." No longer a mere selection of suitable fictions, but a string of hard facts, which together make up the cross we all have to carry or the fate we ourselves are. These first indications of a future synthesis of personality, as I have shown in my earlier publications, appear in dreams or in "active imagination," where they take the form of the mandala symbols which were also not unknown in alchemy. But the first signs of this symbolism are far from indicating that unity has been attained. Just as alchemy has a great many very different procedures, ranging from the sevenfold to the thousandfold distillation, or from the "work of one day" to "the errant quest" lasting for decades, so the tensions between the psychic pairs of opposites ease off only gradually; and, like the alchemical end-product, which always betrays its essential duality, the united personality will never quite lose the painful sense of innate discord. Complete redemption from the sufferings of this world is and must remain an illusion. The symbolical prototype of Christ's earthly life likewise ended, not in complacent bliss, but on the cross. (It

[56] "Spiritus alme,/illustrator hominum,/horridas nostrae/mentis purga tenebras." (Sublime spirit, enlightener of mankind, purge the horrible darknesses of our mind.)—Pentecostal hymn (124) by Notker Balbulus (d. 912).
[57] Hoghelande, 5, i, p. 139.

is a remarkable fact that in their hedonistic aims materialism and a certain species of "joyful" Christianity join hands like brothers.) The goal is only important as an idea; the essential thing is the *opus* which leads to the goal: *that* is the goal of a lifetime. In its attainment "left and right" [58] are united, and conscious and unconscious work in harmony.

10

401   The *coniunctio oppositorum* in the guise of Sol and Luna, the royal brother-sister or mother-son pair, occupies such an important place in alchemy that sometimes the entire process takes the form of the *hieros gamos* and its mystic consequences. The most complete and the simplest illustration of this is perhaps the series of pictures contained in the *Rosarium philosophorum* of 1550, which series I reproduce in what follows. Its psychological importance justifies closer examination. Everything that the doctor discovers and experiences when analysing the unconscious of his patient coincides in the most remarkable way with the content of these pictures. This is not likely to be mere chance, because the old alchemists were often doctors as well, and thus had ample opportunity for such experiences if, like Paracelsus, they worried about the psychological well-being of their patients or inquired into their dreams (for the purpose of diagnosis, prognosis, and therapy). In this way they could collect information of a psychological nature, not only from their patients but also from themselves, i.e., from the observation of their own unconscious contents which had been activated by induction.[59] Just as the unconscious expresses itself even today in a picture-series, often drawn spontaneously by the patient, so those earlier pictures, such as we find in the Codex Rhenovacensis 172,[59a] in Zurich, and in other treatises, were no doubt produced in a similar way, that is, as the deposit of im-

---

58 Acts of John, 7: . . . καὶ ἁρμονία σοφίας· σοφία δὲ οὖσα ἐν ἁρμονίᾳ ὑπάρχουσιν δεξιοὶ καὶ ἀριστεροί, δυνάμεις, ἐξουσίαι, ἀρχαὶ καὶ δαίμονες, ἐνέργειαι . . . (". . . Harmony of wisdom, but when there is wisdom the left and the right are in harmony: powers, principalities, archons, daemons, forces . . .").
59 Cardan (32) is an excellent example of one who examined his own dreams.
59a 35, iii.

pressions collected during the work and then interpreted or modified by traditional factors.[60] In the modern pictures, too, we find not a few traces of traditional themes side by side with spontaneous repetitions of archaic or mythological ideas. In view of this close connection between picture and psychic content, it does not seem to me out of place to examine a medieval series of pictures in the light of modern discoveries, or even to use them as an Ariadne thread in our account of the latter. These curiosities of the Middle Ages contain the seeds of much that only emerged in clearer form many centuries later.

[60] As regards the work of reinterpretation, see my essay, "Bruder Klaus," 80. Also Lavaud, 105, Ch. III, "La Grande Vision."

Invenit gratiam in deserto populus. . . .
—Jeremias (Vulgate) 31:2
The people . . . found grace in the desert. . . .
—Jeremias (D.V.) 31:2

AN ACCOUNT OF THE TRANSFERENCE PHENOMENA
BASED ON THE ILLUSTRATIONS TO THE
"ROSARIUM PHILOSOPHORUM"

1

THE MERCURIAL FOUNTAIN

We are the metals' first nature and only source/
The highest tincture of the Art is made through us.
No fountain and no water has my like/
I make both rich and poor men whole or sick.
For deadly can I be and poisonous.[1]

[Figure 1]

402   This picture goes straight to the heart of alchemical symbolism, for it is an attempt to depict the mysterious basis of the
opus. It is a quadratic quaternity, characterized by the four
stars in the four corners. These are the four elements. Above,
in the centre, there is a fifth star which represents the fifth
entity, the "One" derived from the four, the *quinta essentia*.
The basin below is the *vas Hermeticum*, where the transformation takes place. It contains the *mare nostrum*, the *aqua permanens* or ὕδωρ θεῖον, the "divine water." This is the *mare tene-
brosum*, the chaos. The vessel is also called the uterus [2] in

[1] [These mottoes, where they appear, translate the verses under the woodcuts in
the figures. Figs. 1–10 are full pages reproduced from the Frankfort first edition
(1550) of the *Rosarium philosophorum*, 144. The textual citations of the *Rosarium*,
however, are drawn from the version printed in the *Artis auriferae* (Basel, 1593),
2, xiii, except for the poem on pp. 307f.—EDITORS.]

[2] The "Consilium coniugii" (I, ii, p. 147) says: "Et locus generationis, licet si
artificialis, tamen imitatur naturalem, quia est concavus, conclusus" etc. (The
place of gestation, even though it is artificial, yet imitates the natural place, since
it is concave and closed). And (p. 204): "Per matricem, intendit fundum cu-
curbitae" (By matrix he means the root of the gourd).

which the *foetus spagyricus* (the homunculus) is gestated.[3] This basin, in contrast to the surrounding square, is circular, because it is the matrix of the perfect form into which the square, as an imperfect form, must be changed. In the square the elements are still separate and hostile to one another and must therefore be united in the circle. The inscription on the rim of the basin bears out this intention. It runs (filling in the abbreviations): "Unus est Mercurius mineralis, Mercurius vegetabilis, Mercurius animalis." (*Vegetabilis* should be translated as "living" and *animalis* as "animate" or even "psychic" in the sense of having a soul.[4]) On the outside of the basin there are six stars which together with Mercurius represent the seven planets or metals. They are all as it were contained in Mercurius, since he is the *pater metallorum*. When personified, he is the unity of the seven planets, an Anthropos whose body is the world, like Gayomart, from whose body the seven metals flow into the earth. Owing to his feminine nature, Mercurius is also the mother of the seven, and not only of the six, for he is his own father and mother.[5]

403   Out of the "sea," then, there rises this Mercurial Fountain, *triplex nomine,* as is said with reference to the three manifestations of Mercurius.[6] He is shown flowing out of three

[3] Cf. Ruska, *Turba,* 150, p. 163.

[4] Cf. Hortulanus (Ruska, *Tabula,* 149, p. 186): "Unde infinitae sunt partes mundi, quas omnes philosophus in tres partes dividit scil. in partem Mineralem Vegetabilem et Animalem. . . . Et ideo dicit habens tres partes philosophiae totius mundi, quae partes continentur in unico lapide scil. Mercurio Philosophorum" (Hence the parts of the world are infinite, all of which the philosopher divides into three parts, namely mineral, vegetable, animal. . . . And therefore he claims to have the three parts of the philosophy of the whole world, which parts are contained in the single stone, namely the Mercurius of the Philosophers). Ch. 13: "Et ideo vocatur lapis iste perfectus, quia in se habet naturam mineralium et vegetabilium et animalium. Est enim lapis triunus et unus, quatuor habens naturas" (And this stone is called perfect because it has in itself the nature of mineral, vegetable, and animal. For the stone is triple and one, having four natures).

[5] Cf. the alchemical doctrine of the *increatum: Psychology and Alchemy,* 85, pars. 430ff.

[6] A quotation based on Rosinus in the *Rosarium,* 2, xiii, p. 249, says: "Triplex in nomine, unus in esse." Cf. the threefold fountain of God in the vision of Brother Klaus (Lavaud, 105, p. 66). The actual Rosinus passage (itself a quotation from Rhazes) runs (2, iv, p. 300): "Lapis noster cum mundi creato[re] nomen habet, qui est trinus et unus" (Our stone has a name common with the Creator of the world who is *triple* and *one*). Senior (164, p. 45) says: "Aes nostrum est sicut homo, habens spiritum, animam et corpus. Propterea dicunt sapientes: Tria et Tria

ROSARIVM

Wyr sindt der metall anfang vnd erste natur /
Die kunst macht durch vns die höchste tinctur.
Reyn brunn noch wasser ist meyn gleych /
Ich mach gesund arm vnd reych.
Vnd bin doch jtzund gyfftig vnd dötlich.

Succus

Figure 1

pipes in the form of *lac virginis, acetum fontis,* and *aqua vitae.*
These are three of his innumerable synonyms. The aforementioned unity of Mercurius is here represented as a triad. It is repeatedly emphasized that he is a trinity, *triunus* or *trinus,* the chthonic, lower, or even infernal counterpart of the Heavenly Trinity, just as Dante's devil is three-headed.[7] For the same reason Mercurius is often shown as a three-headed serpent. Above the three pipes we find the sun and moon, who are the indispensable acolytes and parents of the mystic transformation, and, a little higher, the quintessential star, symbol of the unity of the four hostile elements. At the top of the picture is the *serpens bifidus,* the divided (or two-headed) serpent, the fatal *binarius* which Dorn defines as the devil.[8] This serpent is the *serpens mercurialis,*[9] representing the *duplex natura* of Mercurius. The heads are spitting forth fire, from which Maria the Copt or Jewess derived her "duo fumi." [10] These are the two vapours whose condensation initiates the process [11] which leads to a multiple sublimation or distillation for the purpose of purifying away the *mali odores,* the *foetor sepulcrorum,*[12] and the clinging darkness of the beginning.

---

sunt unum. Deinde dixerunt: in uno sunt tria." (Our copper is like a man, having spirit, soul, and body. Therefore the wise men say: Three and Three are One. Further they said: In One there are Three.) Cf. also Zosimos (Berthelot, 152, III, vi, 18). The mercurial fountain recalls the πηγὴ μεγάλη of the Perates (Hippolytus, 67, V, 12, 2), which forms one part of the threefold world. The three parts correspond to 3 gods, 3 λόγοι, 3 spirits (νοῖ), 3 men. This triad is opposed by a Christ equipped with all the properties of the triad and himself of triadic nature, coming from above, from the ἀγεννησία, before the separation. (Here I prefer Bernays' reading πρὸ τῆς [cf. 67, p. 105] because it makes more sense.)

[7] In al-Iraqi the *lapis* is called *al-shaitan,* "Satan"; cf. Holmyard, 69, p. 422.

[8] The serpent is also *triplex nomine,* as the inscriptions "animalis," "vegetabilis," "mineralis" show.   [9] Jung, *Psychology and Alchemy,* 85.

[10] 2, v, p. 321: "Ipsa sunt duo fumi complectentes duo lumina" (They are the two vapours enveloping the two lights).

[11] We find the same motif in the frontispiece of *Le Songe de Poliphile* (37), as the leaves which fall from the tree rooted in the fire. See *Psychology and Alchemy,* 85, fig. 4.

[12] Cf. "Aurora consurgens," I, 12, Ch. IV: "odores et vapores mali mentem laborantis inficientes" (Bad odours and vapours infecting the mind of the laborant). Also Morienus (2, xii, p. 34): "Hic enim est odor, qui assimilatur odori sepulcrorum . . ." (For this is the odour that is similar to the stench of a graveyard . . .).

404   This structure reveals the tetrameria (fourfold nature) of
the transforming process, already known to the Greeks. It begins with the four separate elements, the state of chaos, and
ascends by degrees to the three manifestations of Mercurius in
the inorganic, organic, and spiritual worlds; and, after attaining the form of Sol and Luna (i.e., the precious metals gold
and silver, but also the radiance of the gods who can overcome
the strife of the elements by love), it culminates in the one and
indivisible (incorruptible, ethereal, eternal) nature of the
anima, the *quinta essentia, aqua permanens,* tincture, or *lapis
philosophorum.* This progression from the number 4 to 3 to 2
to 1 is the "axiom of Maria," and it runs in various forms
through the whole of alchemy like a leitmotiv. If we set aside
the numerous "chemical" explanations we come to the following symbolical ground-plan: the initial state of wholeness is
marked by four mutually antagonistic tendencies—4 being the
minimum number by which a circle can be naturally and
clearly defined. The reduction of this number aims at final
unity. The first to appear in this progression is the number 3,
a masculine number, and out of it comes the feminine number 2.[13] Male and female inevitably constellate the idea of
sexual union as the means to producing the 1, which is then
consistently called the "filius regius" or "filius philosophorum."

405   At bottom, therefore, our symbolical picture is an illustration of the methods and philosophy of alchemy. These are
not warranted by the nature of matter as known to the old
masters; they can only derive from the *unconscious* psyche. No
doubt there was also a certain amount of *conscious* speculation
among the alchemists, but this is no hindrance whatever to unconscious projection, for wherever the mind of the investigator
departs from exact observation of the facts before it and goes
its own way, the unconscious *spiritus rector* will take over the
reins and lead the mind back to the unchangeable, underlying
archetypes, which are then forced into projection by this regression.

406   The quaternity is one of the most widespread archetypes
and has also proved to be one of the most useful diagrams for
representing the arrangement of the functions by which the

[13] The interpretation of uneven numbers as masculine and of even numbers as
feminine is general in alchemy and originated in antiquity.

conscious mind takes its bearings.[14] It is like the crossed threads in the telescope of our understanding. The cross formed by the points of the quaternity is no less universal and has in addition the highest possible moral and religious significance for Western man. Similarly the circle, as the symbol of completeness and perfect being, is a widespread expression for heaven, sun, and God; it also expresses the primordial image of man and the soul.[15] The minimum plural number, 4, represents the plural state of the man who has not yet attained inner unity, hence the state of bondage and disunion, of disintegration, and of being torn in different directions—an agonizing, unredeemed state which longs for union, reconciliation, redemption, healing, and wholeness.

407   The triad appears as "masculine," i.e., as the active resolve or *agens* whose alchemical equivalent is the "upwelling." In relation to it the dyad is "feminine," the receptive, absorbent *patiens,* or the material that still has to be formed and impregnated (*informatio, impraegnatio*). The psychological equivalent of the triad is want, desire, instinct, aggression and determination, whereas the dyad corresponds to the reaction of the psychic system as a whole to the impact or the decisions of the conscious mind. The latter is absolutely impotent by itself, unless it can succeed in overcoming the inertia of the whole human being and in achieving its object despite his laziness and constant resistance. But by dint of compulsion or persuasion the conscious mind can carry through its purpose, and only in the resultant *action* is a man a living whole and a unity ("in the beginning was the deed") [16]—provided, of course, that the action is the mature product of a process embracing the complete psyche and not just a spasm or impulse designed to repress it. We are moving here in familiar waters. These things are described in the most magnificent images in the last and greatest work of alchemy—Goethe's *Faust.* He gives a vivid account of the experience of the alchemist who discovers that what he has projected into

14 Cf. Jacobi, 75, Diagrams IV–VII.

15 For the soul as square, circle, or sphere see *Psychology and Alchemy,* 85, pars. 109 and 439, n. 44.

16 The above remarks should be understood only psychologically and not in the moral sense. The "deed" as such is not the essence of the psychic life-process but only a part of it, although a very important part.

the retort is his own darkness, his unredeemed state, his passion, his struggles to reach the goal, i.e., to become what he really is, to fulfil the purpose for which his mother bore him, and, after the peregrinations of a long life full of confusion and error, to become the *filius regius,* son of the supreme mother. Or we can go even further back to the important forerunner of *Faust,* the *Chymical Wedding* of Christian Rosencreutz (1616), which was assuredly known to Goethe.[17] Fundamentally it is the same theme, the same "Axioma Mariae," telling how Rosencreutz is transformed out of his former unenlightened condition and comes to realize that he is related to "royalty." But in keeping with its period (beginning of the seventeenth century), the whole process is far more projected and the withdrawal of the projection into the hero—which in Faust's case turns him into a superman [18]—is only fleetingly hinted at. Yet the psychological process is essentially the same: the becoming aware of those powerful contents which alchemy sensed in the secrets of matter.

408   The text that follows the picture of the Mercurial Fountain is mainly concerned with the "water" of the art, i.e., mercury. In order to avoid repetition, I would refer the reader to my lecture on "The Spirit Mercurius" (**89**). Here I will only say that this fluid substance, with all its paradoxical qualities, really signifies the unconscious which has been projected into it. The "sea" is its static condition, the "fountain" its activation, and the "process" its transformation. The integration of unconscious contents is expressed in the idea of the elixir, the *medicina catholica* or *universalis,* the *aurum potabile,* the *cibus sempiternus* (everlasting food), the health-giving fruits of the philosophical tree, the *vinum ardens,* and all the other innumerable synonyms. Some of them are decidedly ominous but no less characteristic, such as *succus lunariae* or *lunatica*

17 **145.** Incidentally, Johann Valentin Andreae, the real author of the *Chymical Wedding,* also wrote a Faust drama in Latin entitled *Turbo, sive Moleste et frustra per cuncta divagans ingenium* (1616), the story of a man who knew everything and was finally disappointed, but who found his salvation in the *contemplatio Christi.* The author, a theologian in Württemberg, lived from 1586 to 1654.

18 I have dealt with this psychological process at length in *Two Essays,* **88,** pars. 224f., 380f.

(juice of the moon-plant),[19] *aqua Saturni* (note that Saturn is a baleful deity!), poison, scorpion, dragon, son of the fire, boys' or dogs' urine, brimstone, devil, etc.

409   Although not expressly stated in the text, the gushing up and flowing back of the Mercurial Fountain within its basin completes a circle, and this is an essential characteristic of Mercurius because he is also the serpent that fertilizes, kills, and devours itself and brings itself to birth again. We may mention in this connection that the circular sea with no outlet, which perpetually replenishes itself by means of a spring bubbling up in its centre, is to be found in Nicholas of Cusa as an allegory of God.[20]

[19] An allusion to madness. The *afflictio animae* is mentioned in Olympiodorus (Berthelot, 29, II, iv, 43), Morienus (2, xii, p. 18), and Maier (*Symbola*, 114, p. 568), and in Chinese alchemy (Wei Po-yang, 162, pp. 241–45).

[20] God is the source, river, and sea which all contain the same water. The Trinity is a life "qui va de même au même, en passant par le même."—Vansteensberghe, 158, pp. 296f.

2

KING AND QUEEN

410   The *arcanum artis,* or *coniunctio Solis et Lunae* as supreme
union of hostile opposites, was not shown in our first picture; but now it is illustrated in considerable detail, as its
importance deserves, in a series of pictures. King and Queen,
bridegroom and bride, approach one another for the purpose
of betrothal or marriage. The incest element appears in the
brother-sister relationship of Apollo and Diana. The pair of
them stand respectively on sun and moon, thus indicating their
solar and lunar nature in accordance with the astrological assumption of the importance of the sun's position for man and
the moon's for woman. The meeting is somewhat distant at
first, as the court clothes suggest. The two give each other their
left hands, and this can hardly be unintentional since it is contrary to custom. The gesture points to a closely guarded secret,
to the "left-hand path," as the Indian Tantrists call their Shiva
and Shakti worship. The left-hand (sinister) side is the dark,
the unconscious side. The left is inauspicious and awkward;
also it is the side of the heart, from which comes not only love
but all the evil thoughts connected with it, the moral contradictions in human nature that are expressed most clearly in our
affective life. The contact of left hands could therefore be
taken as an indication of the affective nature of the relationship, of its dubious character, since this is a mixture of "heavenly and earthly" love further complicated by an incestuous
sous-entendu. In this delicate yet altogether human situation
the gesture of the *right* hands strikes us as compensatory. They
are holding a device composed of five (4 + 1) flowers. There
are two flowers on each branch; these four again refer to
the four elements of which two—fire and air—are active and
two—water and earth—passive, the former being ascribed to
the man and the latter to the woman. The fifth flower comes
from above and presumably represents the *quinta essentia;* it

211

is brought by the dove of the Holy Ghost, an analogy of Noah's dove that carried the olive branch of reconciliation in its beak. The bird descends from the quintessential star (cf. fig. 1).

411 But the real secret lies in the union of *right* hands, for, as the picture shows, this is mediated by the *donum Spiritus Sancti,* the royal art. The "sinister" left-handed contact here becomes associated with the union, effected from above, of the two quaternities (the masculine and feminine manifestations of the four elements), in the form of an ogdoad consisting of five flowers and three branches. These masculine numbers point to action, decision, purpose, and movement. The 5 is shown as superior to the 4 in that it is brought by the dove. The three branches correspond to the upwelling of Mercurius *triplex nomine* or to the three pipes of the fountain. So once again we have an abbreviated recapitulation of the *opus,* i.e., of its deeper meaning as shown in the first picture. The text to figure 2 begins significantly with the words: "Mark well, in the art of our magisterium nothing is concealed by the philosophers except the secret of the art which may not be revealed to all and sundry. For were that to happen, that man would be accursed; he would incur the wrath of God and perish of the apoplexy. Wherefore all error in the art arises because men do not begin with the proper substance,[1] and for this reason you should employ the venerable Nature, because from her and through her and in her is our art born and in naught else: and so our magisterium is the work of Nature and not of the worker." [2]

412 If we take the fear of divine punishment for betrayal at its face value, the reason for this must lie in something that is thought to endanger the soul's salvation, i.e., a typical "peril of the soul." The causal "wherefore" with which the next sentence begins can only refer to the secret that must not be revealed; but because the *prima materia* remains unknown in consequence, all those who do not know the secret fall into error,

[1] *Debita materia,* meaning the *prima materia* of the process.
[2] *Rosarium,* 2, xiii, p. 219: "Nota bene: In arte nostri magisterii nihil est celatum a Philosophis excepto secreto artis, quod non licet cuiquam revelare: quodsi fieret, ille malediceretur et indignationem Domini incurreret et apoplexia moreretur. Quare omnis error in arte existit ex eo quod debitam materiam non accipiunt. Igitur venerabili utimini natura, quia ex ea et per eam et in ea generatur ars nostra et non in alio: et ideo magisterium nostrum est opus naturae et non opificis."

PHILOSOPHORVM.

Qu. Star Fig. 1

3 branches
3 pipes
of fig 1

Nota bene: In arte noſtri magiſterij nihil eſt *Secretum*
celatũ à Philoſophis excepto ſecreto artis, quod *artis*
non licet cuiquam reuelare, quod ſi fieret ille ma
lediceretur, & indignationem domini incurreret, & apoplexia moreretur. ✠ Quare omnis error in arte exiſtit, ex eo, quod debitam

C ij

Figure 2

and this happens because, as said, they choose something arbitrary and artificial instead of pure Nature. The emphasis laid on the *venerabilis natura* [3] gives us some idea of that passion for investigation which ultimately gave birth to natural science, but which so often proved inimical to faith. Worship of nature, a legacy from the past, stood in more or less secret opposition to the views of the Church and led the mind and heart in the direction of a "left-hand path." What a sensation Petrarch's ascent of Mont Ventoux caused! St. Augustine had warned in his *Confessions* (16, X, viii): "And men go forth to admire the high mountains and the great waves of the sea and the broad torrent of the rivers and the vast expanse of the ocean and the orbits of the stars, and to turn away from themselves. . . ."

413   The exclusive emphasis on nature as the one and only basis of the art is in flagrant contrast to the ever-recurring protestation that the art is a *donum Spiritus Sancti,* an arcanum of the *sapientia Dei,* and so forth, from which we would have to conclude that the alchemists were unshakably orthodox in their beliefs. I do not think that this can be doubted as a rule. On the contrary, their belief in illumination through the Holy Ghost seems to have been a psychological necessity in view of the ominous darkness of nature's secrets.

414   Now if a text which insists so much on pure nature is explained or illustrated by a picture like figure 2, we must assume that the relationship between king and queen was taken to be something perfectly natural. Meditation and speculation about the mystery of the *coniunctio* were inevitable, and this would certainly not leave the erotic fantasy untouched, if only because these symbolical pictures spring from the corresponding unconscious contents—half spiritual, half sexual—and are also intended to remind us of that twilit region, for only from indistinguishable night can the light be born. This is what nature and natural experience teach, but the spirit believes in the *lumen de lumine*—the light born of light.[4] Somehow the artist was entangled in this game of unconscious projection and was

---

[3] Cf. Ruska, *Turba,* 150, Sermo XXIX, p. 137.

[4] Cf. "Aurora consurgens," I, where the parables "Of the black earth," "Of the deluge and death," "Of the Babylonian captivity," are followed by the parable "Of the philosophical faith" with its creed of the *lumen de lumine.* Cf. also Avicenna, 5, xii, p. 990.

bound to experience the mysterious happening with shudders of fear, as a *tremendum*. Even that scoffer and blasphemer Agrippa von Nettesheim displays a remarkable reticence when criticizing the "Alkumistica." [5] After saying a great deal about this dubious art, he adds: [6] "Permulta adhuc de hoc arte (mihi tamen non ad modum inimica) dicere possem, nisi iuratum esset (quod facere solent, qui mysteriis initiantur) de silentio" (I could say much more about this art (which I do not find so disagreeable) were it not for the oath of silence usually taken by initiates into mysteries).[7] Such a mitigation of his criticism, most unexpected in Agrippa, makes one think that he is on the defensive: somehow he was impressed by the royal art.

415   It is not necessary to think of the secret of the art as anything very lurid. Nature knows nothing of moral squalor, indeed her truth is alarming enough. We need only bear in mind one fact: that the desired *coniunctio* was not a legitimate union but was always—one could almost say, on principle—incestuous. The fear that surrounds this complex—the "fear of incest"—is quite typical and has already been stressed by Freud. It is further exacerbated by fear of the compulsive force which emanates from most unconscious contents.

416   The left-handed contact and crosswise union of the right hands—*sub rosa*—is a startlingly concrete and yet very subtle hint of the delicate situation in which "venerable nature" has placed the adept. Although the Rosicrucian movement cannot be traced further back than the *Fama* and *Confessio fraternitatis*

5 A corruption of "alchymia."

6 *De incertitudine et vanitate omnium scientiarum,* 10, Ch. XC.

7 Later, Agrippa (ibid.) says one or two other things about the stone: "As to that unique and blessed substance, besides which there is no other although you may find it everywhere, as to that most sacred stone of the philosophers—almost I had broken my oath and made myself a desecrator of temples by blurting out its name —I shall nevertheless speak in circumlocutions and dark hints, so that none but the sons of the art and the initiates of this mystery shall understand. The thing is one which hath neither too fiery nor too earthen a substance. . . . More I am not permitted to say, and yet there be greater things than these. However, I consider this art—with which I have a certain familiarity—as being the most worthy of that honour which Thucydides pays to an upright woman, when he says that the best is she of whom least is said either in praise or blame." Concerning the oath of secrecy, see also Senior, 164, p. 92: "Hoc est secretum, super quo iuraverunt, quod non indicarent in aliquo libro" (This is the secret which they promised on oath not to divulge in any book).

of Andreae at the beginning of the seventeenth century,[8] we are nevertheless confronted with a "rosie cross" in this curious bouquet of three flowering branches, which evidently originated sometime before 1550 but, equally obviously, makes no claim to be a true *rosicrux*.[9] As we have already said, its threefold structure is reminiscent of the Mercurial Fountain, while at the same time it points to the important fact that the "rose" is the product of three *living* things: the king, the queen, and between them the dove of the Holy Ghost. Mercurius *triplex nomine* is thus converted into three figures, and he can no longer be thought of as a metal or mineral, but only as "spirit." In this form also he is triple-natured—masculine, feminine, and divine. His coincidence with the Holy Ghost as the third person in the Trinity certainly has no foundation in dogma, but "venerable nature" evidently enabled the alchemist to provide the Holy Ghost with a most unorthodox and distinctly earth-bound partner, or rather to complement Him with that divine spirit which had been imprisoned in all creatures since the day of Creation. This "lower" spirit is the Primordial Man, hermaphroditic by nature and of Iranian origin, who was imprisoned in physis.[10] He is the spherical, i.e., perfect, man who appears at the beginning and end of time and is man's own beginning and end. He is man's totality, which is beyond the division of the sexes and can only be reached when male and female come together in one. The revelation of this higher meaning solves the problems created by the "sinister" contact and produces from the chaotic darkness the *lumen quod superat omnia lumina.*

417   If I did not know from ample experience that such developments also occur in modern man, who cannot possibly be suspected of having any knowledge of the Gnostic doctrine of the Anthropos, I should be inclined to think that the alchemists were keeping up a secret tradition, although the evidence for this (the hints contained in the writings of Zosimos of Panopolis) is so scanty that Waite, who knows medieval alchemy

---

[8] Both texts are supposed to have been in circulation in manuscript from about 1610, according to F. Maack, editor, in Rosencreutz, 145, pp. xxxviif. [They are found in 145, pp. 47–84.—EDITORS.]

[9] A kind of "rosie cross" can also be seen in Luther's crest.

[10] Cf. *Psychology and Alchemy*, 85, par. 436, and Reitzenstein and Schaeder, 142.

relatively well, doubts whether a secret tradition existed at all.[10a]
I am therefore of the opinion, based on my professional work,
that the Anthropos idea in medieval alchemy was largely "autochthonous," i.e., the outcome of subjective experience. It is
an "eternal" idea, an archetype that can appear spontaneously
at any time and in any place. We meet the Anthropos even in
ancient Chinese alchemy, in the writings of Wei Po-yang, about
A.D. 142. There he is called *chen-jen* (the true man).[11]

418   The revelation of the Anthropos is associated with no ordinary religious emotion; it signifies much the same thing as the
vision of Christ for the believing Christian. Nevertheless it does
not appear *ex opere divino* but *ex opere naturae;* not from
above but from the transformation of a shade from Hades,
akin to evil itself and bearing the name of the pagan god of
revelation. This dilemma throws a new light on the secret of
the art: the very serious danger of heresy. Consequently the
alchemists found themselves between Scylla and Charybdis:
on the one hand they ran the conscious risk of being misunderstood and suspected of fraudulent gold-making, and on the
other of being burned at the stake as heretics. As to the gold,
right at the beginning of the text to figure 2, the *Rosarium*
quotes the words of Senior: "Aurum nostrum non est aurum
vulgi." But, as history shows, the alchemist would rather risk
being suspected of gold-making than of heresy. It is still an
open question, which perhaps can never be answered, how far
the alchemist was conscious of the true nature of his art. Even
texts as revealing as the *Rosarium* or the "Aurora consurgens"
do not help us in this respect.

419   As regards the psychology of this picture, we must stress
above all else that it depicts a human encounter where love
plays the decisive part. The conventional dress of the pair suggests an equally conventional attitude in both of them. Con-
vention still separates them and hides their natural reality, but
the crucial contact of left hands points to something "sinister,"
illegitimate, morganatic, emotionally instinctive, i.e., the fatal
touch of incest and its "perverse" fascination. At the same time
the intervention of the Holy Ghost reveals the hidden meaning
of the incest, whether of brother and sister or of mother and son.
as a repulsive symbol for the *unio mystica.* Although the union

10a Waite, *The Secret Tradition,* 161.   11 Wei Po-yang, 162, p. 241.

of close blood-relatives is everywhere taboo, it is yet the prerogative of kings (witness the incestuous marriages of the Pharaohs, etc.). Incest symbolizes union with one's own being, it means individuation or becoming a self, and, because this is so vitally important, it exerts an unholy fascination—not, perhaps, as a crude reality, but certainly as a psychic process controlled by the unconscious, a fact well known to anybody who is familiar with psychopathology. It is for this reason, and not because of occasional cases of human incest, that the first gods were believed to propagate their kind incestuously. Incest is simply the union of like with like, which is the next stage in the development of the primitive idea of self-fertilization.[12]

420   This psychological situation sums up what we can all see for ourselves if we analyse a transference carefully. The conventional meeting is followed by an unconscious "familiarization" of one's partner, brought about by the projection of archaic, infantile fantasies which were originally vested in members of the patient's own family and which, because of their positive or negative fascination, attach him to parents, brothers, and sisters.[13] The transference of these fantasies to the doctor draws him into the atmosphere of family intimacy, and although this is the last thing he wants, it nevertheless provides a workable *prima materia*. Once the transference has appeared, the doctor must accept it as part of the treatment and try to understand it, otherwise it will be just another piece of neurotic stupidity. The transference itself is a perfectly natural phenomenon which does not by any means happen only in the consulting-room—it can be seen everywhere and may lead to all sorts of nonsense, like all unrecognized projections. Medical treatment of the transference gives the patient a priceless opportunity to withdraw his projections, to make good his losses, and to integrate his personality. The impulses underlying it certainly show their dark side to begin with, however much one may try to whitewash them; for an integral part of the work is

12 The union of "like with like" in the form of homosexual relationships is to be found in the "Visio Arislei," marking the stage preceding the brother-sister incest.
13 According to Freud, these projections are infantile wish-fantasies. But a more thorough examination of neuroses in childhood shows that such fantasies are largely dependent on the psychology of the parents, that is, are caused by the parents' wrong attitude to the child. Cf. my "Analytical Psychology and Education," 79, pars. 216f.

the *umbra solis* or *sol niger* of the alchemists, the black shadow
which everybody carries with him, the inferior and therefore
hidden aspect of the personality, the weakness that goes with
every strength, the night that follows every day, the evil in the
good.[14] The realization of this fact is naturally coupled with the
danger of falling victim to the shadow, but the danger also
brings with it the possibility of consciously deciding not to become its victim. A visible enemy is always better than an invisible one. In this case I can see no advantage whatever in behav-
ing like an ostrich. It is certainly no ideal for people always to
remain childish, to live in a perpetual state of delusion about
themselves, foisting everything they dislike on to their neighbours and plaguing them with their prejudices and projections.
How many marriages are wrecked for years, and sometimes forever, because he sees his mother in his wife and she her father
in her husband, and neither ever recognizes the other's reality!
Life has difficulties enough without that; we might at least
spare ourselves the stupidest of them. But, without a fundamental discussion of the situation, it is often simply impossible
to break these infantile projections. As this is the legitimate aim
and real meaning of the transference, it inevitably leads, whatever method of rapprochement be used, to discussion and
understanding and hence to a heightened consciousness, which
is a measure of the personality's integration. During this discussion the conventional disguises are dropped and the true
man comes to light. He is in very truth reborn from this psychological relationship, and his field of consciousness is rounded
into a circle.

421   It would be quite natural to suppose that the king and
queen represent a transference relationship in which the king
stands for the masculine partner and the queen for the feminine partner. But this is by no means the case, because the
figures represent contents which have been projected from the
unconscious of the adept (and his *soror mystica*). Now the adept
is conscious of himself as a man, consequently his masculinity
cannot be projected, since this only happens to unconscious
contents. As it is primarily a question of man and woman here,

14 Hence the "Aurora consurgens," I, Ch. VI, says: ". . . et a facie iniquitatis meae
conturbata sunt omnia ossa mea." Compare Psalm 37:4 (D.V.): ". . . there is
no peace for my bones, because of my sins."

the projected fragment of personality can only be the feminine component of the man, i.e., his anima.[15] Similarly, in the woman's case, only the masculine component can be projected. There is thus a curious crossing of the sexes: the man (in this case the adept) is represented by the queen, and the woman (the *soror mystica*) by the king. It seems to me that the flowers forming the "symbol" suggest this crossing. The reader should therefore bear in mind that the picture shows two archetypal figures meeting, and that Luna is secretly in league with the adept, and Sol with his woman helper. The fact that the figures are royal expresses, like real royalty, their archetypal character; they are collective figures common to large numbers of people. If the main ingredient of this mystery were the enthronement of a king or the deification of a mortal, then the figure of the king might possibly be a projection and would in that case correspond to the adept. But the further development of the drama has quite another meaning, so we can discount this possibility.[16]

422   The fact that, for reasons which can be proved empirically, king and queen play cross roles and represent the unconscious contra-sexual side of the adept and his soror leads to a painful complication which by no means simplifies the problem of transference. Scientific integrity, however, forbids all simplification of situations that are not simple, as is obviously the case here. The pattern of relationship is simple enough, but, when

---

15 Cf. *Two Essays*, **88,** pars. 296ff., where the relevant literature is also given.

16 It may be helpful to remind the reader that in Rider Haggard's *She* (61) there is a description of this "royal" figure. Leo Vincey, the hero, is young and handsome, the acme of perfection, a veritable Apollo. Beside him there stands his fatherly guardian, Holly, whose resemblance to a baboon is described in great detail. But inwardly Holly is a paragon of wisdom and moral rectitude—even his name hints at "holy." In spite of their banality both of them have superhuman qualities, Leo as well as the devout "baboon." (Together they correspond to the *sol et umbra eius*.) The third figure is the faithful servant who bears the significant name of Job. He stands for the long-suffering but loyal companion who has to endure both superhuman perfection and subhuman baboonishness. Leo may be regarded as the sun-god; he goes in quest of "She" who "dwells among the tombs" and who is reputed to kill her lovers one by one—a characteristic also ascribed by Benoît (24) to his "Atlantide"—and to rejuvenate herself by periodically bathing in a pillar of fire. She stands for Luna, and particularly for the dangerous new moon. (It is at the *synodus* of the *novilunium*—i.e., at the *coniunctio* of the Sun and Moon at the time of the new moon—that the bride kills her lover.) The story eventually leads, in *Ayesha* (60), another novel of Haggard's, to the mystical *hieros gamos*.

it comes to detailed description in any given case, it is extremely difficult to see from which angle it is being described and what aspect we are describing. The pattern is as follows:

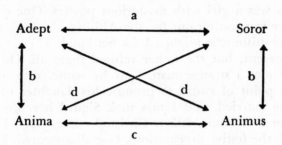

423   The direction of the arrows indicates the pull from masculine to feminine and vice versa, and from the unconscious of one person to the conscious of the other, thus denoting a positive transference relationship. The following relationships have therefore to be distinguished, although in certain cases they can all merge into each other, and this naturally leads to the greatest possible confusion:

(a) An uncomplicated personal relationship.

(b) A relationship of the man to his anima and of the woman to her animus.

(c) A relationship of anima to animus and vice versa.

(d) A relationship of the feminine animus to the man (which happens when the woman is identical with her animus), and of the masculine anima to the woman (which happens when the man is identical with his anima).

424   In describing the transference problem with the help of this series of illustrations, I have not always kept these different possibilities apart; for in real life they are invariably mixed up and it would have put an intolerable strain on the explanation had I attempted a rigidly schematic exposition. Thus the king and queen each display every conceivable shade of meaning from the superhuman to the subhuman, sometimes appearing as a transcendental figure, sometimes hiding in the figure of the adept. The reader should bear this in mind if he comes across any real or supposed contradictions in the remarks which follow.

425   These intercrossing transference relationships are foreshadowed in folklore: the archetype of the crossed marriage, which I call the "marriage quaternity," [17] can also be found in fairytales. An Icelandic fairytale [18] tells the following story:

426   Finna was a girl with mysterious powers. One day, when her father was setting out for the Althing, she begged him to refuse any suitor who might ask for her hand. There were many suitors present, but the father refused them all. On the way home he met a strange man, Geir by name, who forced the father at point of sword to promise his daughter to him. So they were married, and Finna took Sigurd her brother with her to her new home. About Christmas-time, when Finna was busy with the festive preparations, Geir disappeared. Finna and her brother went out to look for him and found him on an island with a beautiful woman. After Christmas, Geir suddenly appeared in Finna's bedroom. In the bed lay a child. Geir asked her whose child it was, and Finna answered that it was her child. And so it happened for three years in succession, and each time Finna accepted the child. But at the third time, Geir was released from the spell. The beautiful woman on the island was Ingeborg, his sister. Geir had disobeyed his stepmother, a witch, and she had laid a curse on him: he was to have three children by his sister, and unless he found a wife who knew everything and held her peace, he would be changed into a snake and his sister into a filly. Geir was saved by the conduct of his wife; and he married his sister Ingeborg to Sigurd.

427   Another example is the Russian fairytale "Prince Danila Govorila": [19] There is a young prince who is given a lucky ring by a witch. But its magic will work only on one condition: he must marry none but the girl whose finger the ring fits. When he grows up he goes in search of a bride, but all in vain, because the ring fits none of them. So he laments his fate to his sister, who asks to try on the ring. It fits perfectly. Thereupon her brother wants to marry her, but she thinks it would be a sin and sits at the door of the house weeping. Some old beggars who are passing comfort her and give her the following advice: "Make four dolls and put them in the four corners of the room.

17 The alchemical pairs of opposites are often arranged in such quaternities. Cf. my *Symbols of Transformation*, 91.
18 44, i, No. 8, pp. 47ff.   19 44, iii, pp. 351ff.

If your brother summons you to the wedding, go, but if he summons you to the bedchamber, do not hurry! Trust in God and follow our advice."

428   After the wedding her brother summons her to bed. Then the four dolls begin to sing:

> Cuckoo, Prince Danila,
> Cuckoo, Govorila,
> Cuckoo, he takes his sister,
> Cuckoo, for a wife,
> Cuckoo, earth open wide,
> Cuckoo, sister fall inside.

429   The earth opens and swallows her up. Her brother calls her three times, but by the third time she has already vanished. She goes along under the earth until she comes to the hut of Baba Yaga,[20] whose daughter kindly shelters her and hides her from the witch. But before long the witch discovers her and heats up the oven. The two girls then seize the old woman and put her in the oven instead, thus escaping the witch's persecution. They reach the prince's castle, where the sister is recognized by her brother's servant. But her brother cannot tell the two girls apart, they are so alike. So the servant advises him to make a test: the prince is to fill a skin with blood and put it under his arm. The servant will then stab him in the side with a knife and the prince is to fall down as if dead. The sister will then surely betray herself. And so it happens: the sister throws herself upon him with a great cry, whereupon the prince springs up and embraces her. But the magic ring also fits the finger of the witch's daughter, so the prince marries her and gives his sister to a suitable husband.

430   In this tale the incest is on the point of being committed, but is prevented by the peculiar ritual with the four dolls. The four dolls in the four corners of the room form the marriage quaternity, the aim being to prevent the incest by putting four in place of two. The four dolls form a magic simulacrum which stops the incest by removing the sister to the underworld, where she discovers her alter ego. Thus we can say that the witch who gave the young prince the fatal ring is his mother-in-law-to-be,

20 The Russian arch-witch.

for, as a witch, she must certainly have known that the ring would fit not only his sister but her own daughter.

431   In both tales the incest is an evil fate that cannot easily be avoided. Incest, as an endogamous relationship, is an expression of the libido which serves to hold the family together. One could therefore define it as "kinship libido," a kind of instinct which, like a sheep-dog, keeps the family group intact. This form of libido is the diametrical opposite of the exogamous form. The two forms together hold each other in check: the endogamous form tends towards the sister and the exogamous form towards some stranger. The best compromise is therefore a first cousin. There is no hint of this in our fairy-stories, but the marriage quaternity is clear enough. In the Icelandic story we have the pattern:

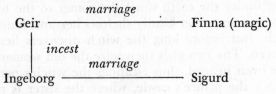

In the Russian:

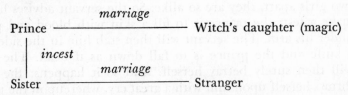

432   The two patterns agree in a remarkable way. In both cases the hero wins a bride who has something to do with magic or the world beyond. Assuming that the archetype of the marriage *quaternio* described above is at the bottom of these quaternities which are authenticated by folklore, the stories are obviously based on the following pattern:

	marriage	
Adept	———————	Anima
	marriage	
Soror	———————	Animus

433   Marriage with the anima is the psychological equivalent of absolute identity between conscious and unconscious. But

since such a condition is only possible in the complete absence
of psychological self-knowledge, it must be more or less primitive, i.e., the man's relationship to the woman is essentially an
anima projection. The only sign that the whole thing is "unconscious" is the remarkable fact that the carrier of the anima-
image is distinguished by magical characteristics. These characteristics are missing from the soror-animus relationship in the
stories; that is, the unconscious does not make itself felt at all
as a separate experience. From this we must conclude that the
symbolism of the stories rests on a much more primitive frame
of mind than the alchemical *quaternio* and its psychological
equivalent. Therefore we must expect that on a still more primitive level the anima too will lose her magical attributes, the
result being an uncomplicated, purely matter-of-fact marriage
quaternity. And we do find a parallel to the two crossed pairs in
the so-called "cross-cousin marriage." In order to explain this
primitive form of marriage I must go into some detail. The
marriage of a man's sister to his wife's brother is a relic of the
"sister-exchange marriage," characteristic of the structure of
many primitive tribes. But at the same time this double marriage is the primitive parallel to the problem which concerns us
here: the conscious and unconscious dual relationship between
adept and soror on the one hand and king and queen (or animus and anima) on the other. John Layard's important study,
"The Incest Taboo and the Virgin Archetype" (**106**), put me in
mind of the sociological aspects of our psychologem. The primitive tribe falls into two halves, of which Howitt says: "It is
upon the division of the whole community into two exogamous
intermarrying classes, that the whole social structure is built
up." [21] These "moieties" show themselves in the lay-out of set-
tlements [22] as well as in many strange customs. At ceremonies,
for instance, the two moieties are strictly segregated and neither
may trespass on the other's territory. Even when going out on
a hunt, they at once divide into two halves as soon as they set
up camp, and the two camps are so arranged that there is a
natural obstacle between them, e.g., the bed of a stream. On
the other hand the two halves are connected by what Hocart
calls "the ritual interdependence of the two sides" or "mutual

[21] *The Native Tribes of S.E. Australia,* **71**, p. 157; cf. Frazer, *Totemism and Exogamy,* **46**, I, p. 306.　　　　[22] Layard, *Stone Men of Malekula,* **107**, pp. 62ff.

ministration." In New Guinea one side breeds and fattens pigs and dogs, not for themselves but for the other side, and vice versa. Or when there is a death in the village and the funeral feast is prepared, this is eaten by the other side, and so on.[23] The division also shows itself in the widespread institution of "dual kingship." [24]

434   The names given to the two sides are particularly enlightening, such as—to mention only a few—east and west, high and low, day and night, male and female, water and land, left and right. It is not difficult to see from these names that the two halves are felt to be antithetical and thus the expression of an endopsychic antithesis. The antithesis can be formulated as the masculine ego versus the feminine "other," i.e., conscious versus unconscious personified as anima. The primary splitting of the psyche into conscious and unconscious seems to be the cause of the division within the tribe and the settlement. It is a division founded on fact but not consciously recognized as such.

435   The social split is by origin a matrilineal division into two, but in reality it represents a division of the tribe and settlement into four. The quartering comes about through the crossing of the matrilineal by a patrilineal line of division.[25] The practical purpose of this quartering is the separation and differentiation of marriage classes. (Marriage on this level amounts to "group marriage.") The entire population is divided into moieties, and a man can take a wife only from the opposite moiety. The basic pattern is a square or circle divided by a cross; it forms the ground-plan of the primitive settlement and the archaic city, also of monasteries, convents, etc., as can be seen in Europe, Asia, and prehistoric America.[26] The Egyptian hieroglyph for "city" is a St. Andrews's cross in a circle.[27]

436   In specifying the marriage classes, it should be mentioned that every man belongs to his father's patrilineal moiety and can only take a wife from his mother's matrilineal moiety. In order to avoid the possibility of incest, he marries his mother's brother's daughter and gives his sister to his wife's brother (sister-exchange marriage). This results in the cross-cousin marriage.[28]

437   This form of union, consisting of two brother-and-sister marriages crossing each other, seems to be the original pattern

23 Hocart, 68, p. 265.   25 Layard, 107, pp. 85ff.   27 Ibid., p. 250.
24 Ibid., pp. 157, 193.   26 Hocart, 68, pp. 244ff.   28 Layard, 106, pp. 270ff.

of the peculiar psychologem which we find in alchemy:

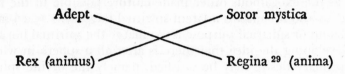

Adept — Soror mystica

Rex (animus) — Regina [29] (anima)

When I say "pattern" I do not mean that the system of marriage classes was the cause and our psychologem the effect. I merely wish to point out that this system predated the alchemical quaternity. Nor can we assume that the primitive marriage *quaternio* is the absolute origin of this archetype, for the latter is not a human invention at all but a fact that existed long before consciousness, as is true of all ritual symbols among primitives as well as among civilized peoples today. We do certain things simply without thinking, because they have always been done like that.[30]

438   The difference between the primitive and the cultural marriage *quaternio* consists in the fact that the former is a sociological and the latter a mystical phenomenon. While marriage classes have all but disappeared among civilized peoples, they nevertheless re-emerge on a higher cultural level as spiritual ideas. In the interests of the welfare and development of the tribe, the exogamous social order thrust the endogamous tendency into the background so as to prevent the dangerous formation of small and ever smaller groups. It insisted on the introduction of "new blood" both physically and spiritually, and it thus proved to be a powerful instrument in the development of culture. In the words of Spencer and Gillen: "This system of what has been called group marriage, serving as it does to bind more or less closely together groups of individuals who are mutually interested in one another's welfare, has been one of the most powerful agents in the early stages of the upward development of the human race." [31] Layard has amplified this idea in his above-mentioned study. He regards the endogamous (incest) tendency as a genuine instinct which, if

29 I would remind the reader that Rex and Regina are usually brother and sister or sometimes mother and son.
30 If we think at all when doing these things, it must be a preconscious or rather an unconscious act of thought. Psychological explanations cannot very well get on without such an hypothesis.
31 *The Northern Tribes of Central Australia,* 152, p. 74.

denied realization in the flesh, must realize itself in the spirit. Just as the exogamous order made culture possible in the first place, so also it contains a latent spiritual purpose. Layard says: "Its latent or spiritual purpose is to enlarge the spiritual horizon by developing the idea that there is after all a sphere in which the primary desire may be satisfied, namely the divine sphere of the gods together with that of their semi-divine counterparts, the culture heroes." [32] The idea of the incestuous *hieros gamos* does in fact appear in the civilized religions and blossoms forth in the supreme spirituality of Christian imagery (Christ and the Church, *sponsus* and *sponsa,* the mysticism of the Song of Solomon, etc.). "Thus the incest taboo," says Layard, "leads in full circle out of the biological sphere into the spiritual." [33] On the primitive level the feminine image, the anima, is still completely unconscious and therefore in a state of latent projection. Through the differentiation of the "four-class marriage system" into the eight-class,[34] the degree of kinship between marriage partners is considerably diluted, and in the twelve-class system it becomes almost negligible. These "dichotomies" [35] obviously serve to enlarge the framework of the marriage classes and thus to draw more and more groups of people into the kinship system. Naturally such an enlargement was possible only where a sizeable population was expanding.[36] The eight-class and particularly the twelve-class systems mean a great advance for the exogamous order, but an equally severe repression of the endogamous tendency, which is thereby stimulated to a new advance in its turn. Whenever an instinctive force—i.e., a certain sum of psychic energy—is driven into the background through a one-sided (in this case, exogamous) attitude on the part of the conscious mind, it leads to a dissociation of personality. The conscious personality with its single (exogamous) line of thought comes up against an invisible (endogamous) opponent, and because this is unconscious it is felt to be a stranger and therefore manifests itself in projected form. At first it makes its appearance in human figures who have the power to do what others may not do—kings and

32 Layard, 106, p. 284.   33 Ibid., p. 293.
34 In this system a man marries his grandmother's brother's granddaughter.
35 Hocart, 68, p. 259.
36 In China, for instance, one can still find vestiges of the twelve-class system.

princes, for example. This is probably the reason for the royal
incest prerogative, as in ancient Egypt. To the extent that the
magical power of royalty was derived increasingly from the
gods, the incest prerogative shifted to the latter and so gave
rise to the incestuous *hieros gamos*. But when the numinous
aura surrounding the person of the king is taken over by the
gods, it has been transferred to a spiritual authority, which results in the projection of an autonomous psychic complex—in
other words, psychic life becomes a reality. Thus Layard logically derives the anima from the numen of the goddess.[37] The
anima is manifestly *projected* in the shape of the goddess, but
in her proper (psychological) shape she is *introjected;* she is, as
Layard says, the "anima within." She is the natural *sponsa,*
man's mother or sister or daughter or wife from the beginning,
the companion whom the endogamous tendency vainly seeks
to win in the form of mother and sister. She represents that
longing which has always had to be sacrificed since the grey
dawn of history. Layard therefore speaks very rightly of "inter-
nalization through sacrifice." [38]

439   The endogamous tendency finds an outlet in the exalted
sphere of the gods and in the higher world of the spirit. Here it
shows itself to be an instinctive force of a spiritual nature; and,
regarded in this light, the life of the spirit on the highest level
is a return to the beginnings, so that man's development becomes a recapitulation of the stages that lead ultimately to the
perfection of life in the spirit.

440   The specifically alchemical projection looks at first sight
like a regression: god and goddess are reduced to king and
queen, and these in turn look like mere allegories of chemical
substances which are about to combine. But the regression is
only apparent. In reality it is a highly remarkable development: the conscious mind of the medieval investigator was still
under the influence of metaphysical ideas, but because he could
not derive them from nature he projected them into nature.
He tried to find them in matter, because he supposed that they
were most likely to be found there. It was really a question

---

37 Layard, **106**, pp. 281ff.

38 Ibid., p. 284. Perhaps I may note the similar conclusions reached in my earlier
Psychology of the Unconscious, **87**, Part II, Ch. VIII, "The Sacrifice." (**91**, pt. ii,
Ch. VII.)

of a transference of numen similar to that from the king to the god. The numen seemed to have migrated in some mysterious way from the world of the spirit to the realm of matter. But the descent of the projection into matter had led some of the old alchemists, for example Morienus Romanus, to the distinct realization that this matter was not just the human body (or something in it) but the human personality itself. These prescient masters had already got beyond the inevitable stage of obtuse materialism which had yet to be born from the womb of time. But it was not until the discoveries of modern psychology that this human "matter" of the alchemists could be recognized as the *psyche.*

441   On the psychological level, the tangle of relationships in the cross-cousin marriage reappears in the transference problem. The dilemma here consists in the fact that anima and animus are projected upon their human counterparts and thus create by suggestion a primitive relationship which evidently goes back to the time of group marriages. But in so far as anima and animus undoubtedly represent the contrasexual components of the personality, their kinship character does not point backwards to group marriage but "forwards" to the integration of personality, i.e., to individuation.

442   Our present-day civilization with its cult of consciousness—if this can be called civilization—has a Christian stamp, which means that neither anima nor animus is integrated but is still in the state of projection, i.e., expressed by dogma. On this level both these figures are unconscious as components of personality, though their effectiveness is still apparent in the numinous aura surrounding the dogmatic ideas of bridegroom and bride. Our "civilization," however, has turned out to be a very doubtful proposition, a distinct falling away from the lofty ideal of Christianity; and, in consequence, the projections have largely fallen away from the divine figures and have necessarily settled in the human sphere. This is understandable enough, since the "enlightened" intellect cannot imagine anything greater than man except those tin gods with totalitarian presumptions who call themselves State or Fuehrer. This regression has made itself as plain as could be wished in Germany and other countries. And even where it is not so apparent, the lapsed projections have a disturbing effect on human relationships and

230

wreck at least a quarter of the marriages. If we decline to measure the vicissitudes of the world's history by the standards of right and wrong, true and false, good and evil, but prefer to see the retrograde step in every advance, the evil in every good, the error in every truth, we might compare the present regression with the apparent retreat which led from scholasticism to the mystical trend of natural philosophy and thence to materialism. Just as materialism led to empirical science and thus to a new understanding of the soul, so the totalitarian psychosis with its frightful consequences and the intolerable disturbance of human relationships is forcing us to pay attention to the psyche and our abysmal unconsciousness of it. Never before has mankind as a whole experienced the numen of the psychological factor on so vast a scale. In one sense this is a catastrophe and a retrogression without parallel, but it is not beyond the bounds of possibility that such an experience also has its positive aspects and might become the seed of a nobler culture in a regenerated age. It is possible that ultimately the endogamous tendency is not aiming at projection at all; it may be trying to unite the different components of the personality on the pattern of the cross-cousin marriage, but on a higher plane where "spiritual marriage" becomes an inner experience that is not projected. Such an experience has long been depicted in dreams as a mandala divided into four, and it seems to represent the goal of the individuation process, i.e., the self.[39]

443   Following the growth of population and the increasing dichotomy of the marriage classes, which led to a further extension of the exogamous order, all barriers gradually broke down and nothing remained but the incest-taboo. The original social order made way for other organizing factors culminating in the modern idea of the State. Now, everything that is past sinks in time into the unconscious, and this is true also of the original social order. As an archetype, it combined exogamy and endogamy in the most fortunate way, for while it prevented marriage between brother and sister it provided a substitute in the cross-cousin marriage. This relationship is still close enough to satisfy the endogamous tendency more or less, but distant enough to include other groups and to extend the orderly cohesion of the tribe. But with the gradual abolition

[39] Cf. my *Psychology and Religion*, 86.

of exogamous restrictions through increasing dichotomy, the endogamous tendency was bound to gain strength in order to give due weight to consanguineous relationships and so hold them together. This reaction was chiefly felt in the religious and then in the political field, with the growth on the one hand of religious societies and sects—we have only to think of the brotherhoods and the Christian ideal of "brotherly love"—and of nations on the other. Increasing internationalism and the weakening of religion have largely abolished or bridged over these last remaining barriers and will do so still more in the future, only to create an amorphous mass whose preliminary symptoms can already be seen in the modern phenomenon of the mass psyche. Consequently the original exogamous order is rapidly approaching a condition of chaos painfully held in check. For this there is but one remedy: the inner consolidation of the individual, who is otherwise threatened with inevitable stultification and dissolution in the mass psyche. The recent past has given us the clearest possible demonstration of what this would mean. No religion has afforded any protection, and our organizing factor, the State, has proved to be the most efficient machine for turning out mass-men. In these circumstances the immunizing of the individual against the toxin of the mass psyche is the only thing that can help. As I have already said, it is just conceivable that the endogamous tendency will intervene compensatorily and restore the consanguineous marriage, or the union of the divided components of the personality, on the psychic level—that is to say, *within* the individual. This would form a counterbalance to the progressive dichotomy, the psychic dissociation of collective man.

444   It is of supreme importance that this process should take place *consciously*, otherwise the psychic consequences of mass-mindedness will harden and become permanent. For, if the inner consolidation of the individual is not conscious, it will occur spontaneously and will then take the well-known form of that incredible hard-heartedness which collective man displays towards his fellow men. He becomes a soulless herd animal governed only by panic and lust: his soul, which can live only in and from human relationships, is irretrievably lost. But the conscious achievement of inner unity clings desperately to human relationships as to an indispensable condition, for without

232

the conscious acknowledgment and acceptance of our kinship with those around us there can be no synthesis of personality. That mysterious something in which the inner union takes place is nothing personal, has nothing to do with the ego, is in fact superior to the ego because, as the self, it is the synthesis of the ego and the supra-personal unconscious. The inner consolidation of the individual is not just the hardness of collective man on a higher plane, in the form of spiritual aloofness and inaccessibility: it emphatically includes our fellow man.

445   To the extent that the transference is projection and nothing more, it divides quite as much as it connects. But experience teaches that there is one connection in the transference which does not break off with the severance of the projection. That is because there is an extremely important instinctive factor behind it: the kinship libido. This has been pushed so far into the background by the unlimited expansion of the exogamous tendency that it can find an outlet, and a modest one at that, only within the immediate family circle, and sometimes not even there, because of the quite justifiable resistance to incest. While exogamy was limited by endogamy, it resulted in a natural organization of society which has entirely disappeared today. Everyone is now a stranger among strangers. Kinship libido—which could still engender a satisfying feeling of belonging together, as for instance in the early Christian communities—has long been deprived of its object. But, being an instinct, it is not to be satisfied by any mere substitute such as a creed, party, nation, or state. It wants the *human* connection. That is the core of the whole transference phenomenon, and it is impossible to argue it away, because relationship to the self is at once relationship to our fellow man, and no one can be related to the latter until he is related to himself.

446   If the transference remains at the level of projection, the connection it establishes shows a tendency to regressive concretization, i.e., it reverts to the primitive order of society. This tendency has no possible foothold in our modern world, so that every step in this direction only leads to a deeper conflict, and ultimately to a real transference neurosis. Analysis of the transference is therefore an absolute necessity, because the projected contents must be reintegrated if the patient is to gain the broader view he needs for free decision.

447   If, however, the projection is broken, the connection—whether it be negative (hate) or positive (love)—may collapse for the time being so that nothing seems to be left but the politeness of a professional tête-à-tête. One cannot begrudge either doctor or patient a sigh of relief when this happens, although one knows full well that the problem has only been postponed for both of them. Sooner or later, here or in some other place, it will present itself again, for behind it there stands the restless urge towards individuation.

448   Individuation has two principal aspects: in the first place it is an internal and subjective process of integration, and in the second it is an equally indispensable process of objective relationship. Neither can exist without the other, although sometimes the one and sometimes the other predominates. This double aspect has two corresponding dangers. The first is the danger of the patient's using the opportunities for spiritual development arising out of the analysis of the unconscious as a pretext for evading the deeper human responsibilities, and for affecting a certain "spirituality" which cannot stand up to moral criticism; the second is the danger that atavistic tendencies may gain the ascendency and drag the relationship down to a primitive level. Between this Scylla and that Charybdis there is a narrow passage, and both medieval Christian mysticism and alchemy have contributed much to its discovery.

449   Looked at in this light, the bond established by the transference—however hard to bear and however unintelligible it may seem—is vitally important not only for the individual but also for society, and indeed for the moral and spiritual progress of mankind. So, when the psychotherapist has to struggle with difficult transference problems, he can at least take comfort in these reflections. He is not just working for this particular patient, who may be quite insignificant, but for himself as well and his own soul, and in so doing he is perhaps laying an infinitesimal grain in the scales of humanity's soul. Small and invisible as this contribution may be, it is yet an *opus magnum,* for it is accomplished in a sphere but lately visited by the numen, where the whole weight of mankind's problems has settled. The ultimate questions of psychotherapy are not a private matter—they represent a supreme responsibility.

THE NAKED TRUTH

450 The text to this picture (fig. 3) is, with a few alterations, a quotation from the *Tractatus aureus.*[1] It runs: "He who would be initiated into this art and secret wisdom must put away the vice of arrogance, must be devout, righteous, deep-witted, humane towards his fellows, of a cheerful countenance and a happy disposition, and respectful withal. Likewise he must be an observer of the eternal secrets that are revealed to him. My son, above all I admonish thee to fear God who seeth thine actions [*in quo dispositionis tuae visus est*] and in whom is help for the solitary, whosoever he may be [*adiuvatio cuius-libet sequestrati*]."[2] And the *Rosarium* adds from Pseudo-Aristotle: "Could God but find a man of faithful understanding, He would open His secret to him."[3]

451 This appeal to obviously moral qualities makes one thing quite clear: the *opus* demands not only intellectual and technical ability as in the study and practice of modern chemistry; it is a moral as well as a psychological undertaking. The texts are full of such admonitions, and they indicate the kind of attitude that is required in the execution of a religious work. The alchemists undoubtedly understood the *opus* in this sense, though it is difficult to square our picture with such an exordium. The chaste disguises have fallen away.[4] Man and woman confront one another in unabashed naturalness. Sol says, "O Luna, let[4a] me be thy husband," and Luna, "O Sol, I

[1] An Arabic treatise whose origin is still obscure. It is to be found in the *Ars chemica*, 1, and (with scholia) in the *Bibliotheca chemica curiosa*, 3.
[2] This passage is rather different in the original text (1, i, p. 14): "in quo est nisus tuae dispositionis, et adunatio cuiuslibet sequestrati." Cf. *Psychology and Alchemy*, 85, par. 385 and footnote. [3] 2, xiii, pp. 227–28.
[4] Cf. Cant. 5:3 (Vulg.): "Exspoliavi me tunica mea" (D.V.: "I have put off my garment"). [4a] Original is illegible: ?vgan.

must submit to thee." The dove bears the inscription: "Spiritus est qui unificat." [5] This remark hardly fits the unvarnished eroticism of the picture, for if what Sol and Luna say—who, be it noted, are brother and sister—means anything at all, it must surely mean earthly love. But since the spirit descending from above is stated to be the mediator,[6] the situation acquires another aspect: it is supposed to be a union in the spirit. This is borne out admirably by one important detail in the picture: the contact of left hands has ceased. Instead, Luna's left hand and Sol's right hand now hold the branches (from which spring the *flores Mercurii,* corresponding to the three pipes of the fountain), while Luna's right and Sol's left hand are touching the flowers. The left-handed relationship is no more: the two hands of both are now connected with the "uniting symbol." This too has been changed: there are only three flowers instead of five, it is no longer an ogdoad but a hexad,[7] a six-rayed figure. The double quaternity has thus been replaced by a double triad. This simplification is evidently the result of the fact that two elements have each paired off, presumably with their opposites, for according to alchemical theory each element

---

[5] This is the reading of the 1593 edition. The first edition of 1550 has "vivificat."

[6] The dove is also the attribute of the goddess of love and was a symbol of *amor coniugalis* in ancient times.

[7] Cf. Joannes Lydus, 110, II, 11: "The sixth day they ascribe to Phosphorus [morning star], who is the begetter of warmth and generative moisture [γονίμως ὑγραίνοντι]. Perhaps this is the son of Aphrodite, like Hesperus the evening star, as appeared to the Greeks. Aphrodite we could call the nature of the visible universe, the first-born Hyle which the oracle names star-like ['Αστερίαν] as well as heavenly. The number 6 is most skilled in begetting [γεννητικώτατος], for it is even and uneven, partaking both of the active nature on account of the uneven [περιττὸν also means "superfluous" or "excessive"], and of the hylical nature on account of the even, for which reason the ancients also named it marriage and harmony. For among those that follow the number 1, it is the only number perfect in all its parts, being composed of these: its halves of the number 3, its thirds of the number 2, and its sixths of the number 1 [6 = 3 + 2 + 1]. And they say also that it is both male and female, like Aphrodite herself, who is of male and female nature and is accordingly called hermaphroditic by the theologians. And another says that the number 6 is soul-producing [or belongs to the ψυχογονία, ψυχογονικός], because it multiplies itself into the world-sphere [ἐπιπεδούμενος = πολλαπλασιασμός], and because in it the opposites are mingled. It leads to like-mindedness [ὁμόνοιαν] and friendship, giving health to the body, harmony to songs and music, virtue to the soul, prosperity to the state, and forethought [πρόνοιαν] to the universe."

PHILOSOPHORVM.

seipsis secundum equalitatē inspissentur. Solus
enim calor tēperatus est humiditatis inspissatiuus
et mixtionis perfectiuus, et non super excedens.
Nā generatiōes et procreationes rerū naturaliū
habent solū fieri per tēperatissimū calorē et equa
lē, vti est solus simus equinus humidus et calidus.

Figure 3

contains its opposite "within" it. Affinity, in the form of a "lov-ing" approach, has already achieved a partial union of the ele-ments, so that now only one pair of opposites remains: mascu-line-feminine or *agens-patiens,* as indicated by the inscription. In accordance with the axiom of Maria, the elementary quater-nity has become the active triad, and this will lead to the *con-iunctio* of the two.

452 Psychologically we can say that the situation has thrown off the conventional husk and developed into a stark encounter with reality, with no false veils or adornments of any kind. Man stands forth as he really is and shows what was hidden under the mask of conventional adaptation: the shadow. This is now raised to consciousness and integrated with the ego, which means a move in the direction of wholeness. Wholeness is not so much perfection as completeness. Assimilation of the shadow gives a man body, so to speak; the animal sphere of instinct, as well as the primitive or archaic psyche, emerge into the zone of consciousness and can no longer be repressed by fictions and illusions. In this way man becomes for himself the difficult problem he really is. He must always remain conscious of the fact that he is such a problem if he wants to develop at all. Repression leads to a one-sided development if not to stag-nation, and eventually to neurotic dissociation. Today it is no longer a question of "How can I get rid of my shadow?"—for we have seen enough of the curse of one-sidedness. Rather we must ask ourselves: "How can man live with his shadow with-out its precipitating a succession of disasters?" Recognition of the shadow is a reason for humility, for genuine fear of the abysmal depths in man. This caution is most expedient, since the man without a shadow thinks himself harmless precisely because he is ignorant of his shadow. The man who recognizes his shadow knows very well that he is not harmless, for it brings the archaic psyche, the whole world of the archetypes, into direct contact with the conscious mind and saturates it with archaic influences. This naturally adds to the dangers of "af-finity," with its deceptive projections and its urge to assimilate the object in terms of the projection, to draw it into the family circle in order to actualize the hidden incest situation, which seems all the more attractive and fascinating the less it is under-stood. The advantage of the situation, despite all its dangers, is

that once the naked truth has been revealed the discussion can get down to essentials; ego and shadow are no longer divided but are brought together in an—admittedly precarious—unity. This is a great step forward, but at the same time it shows up the "differentness" of one's partner all the more clearly, and the unconscious usually tries to close the gap by increasing the attraction, so as to bring about the desired union somehow or other. All this is borne out by the alchemical idea that the fire which maintains the process must be temperate to begin with and must then gradually be raised to the highest intensity.

239

4

IMMERSION IN THE BATH

453   A new motif appears in this picture: the bath. In a sense this takes us back to the first picture of the Mercurial Fountain, which represents the "upwelling." The liquid is Mercurius, not only of the three but of the "thousand" names. He stands for the mysterious psychic substance which nowadays we would call the unconscious psyche. The rising fountain of the unconscious has reached the king and queen, or rather they have descended into it as into a bath. This is a theme with many variations in alchemy. Here are a few of them: the king is in danger of drowning in the sea; he is a prisoner under the sea; the sun drowns in the mercurial fountain; the king sweats in the glass-house; the green lion swallows the sun; Gabricus disappears in the body of his sister Beya, where he is dissolved into atoms; and so forth. Interpreted on the one hand as a harmless bath and on the other hand as the perilous encroachment of the "sea," the earth-spirit Mercurius in his watery form now begins to attack the royal pair from *below*, just as he had previously descended from above in the shape of the dove. The contact of left hands in figure 2 has evidently roused the spirit of the deep and called up a rush of water.

454   The immersion in the "sea" signifies the *solutio*—"dissolution" in the physical sense of the word and at the same time, according to Dorn, the solution of a problem.[1] It is a return to the dark initial state, to the amniotic fluid of the gravid uterus. The alchemists frequently point out that their stone grows like the child in its mother's womb; they call the *vas*

---

[1] Dorn, 5, ii, p. 303: "Studio philosophorum comparatur putrefactio chemica. . . . Ut per solutionem corpora solvuntur, ita per cognitionem resolvuntur philosophorum dubia" (The chemical putrefaction can be compared with the study of the philosophers. . . . As bodies are dissolved through the *solutio*, so the doubts of the philosophers are resolved through the [acquisition of] knowledge).

ROSARIVM

corrūpitur, neꝗ ex imperfecto penitus fecundũ artem aliquid fieri poteſt. Ratio eſt quia ars primas diſpoſitiones inducere non poteſt, fed lapis noſter eſt res media inter perfecta & imperfecta corpora, & quod natura ipſa incepit hoc per artem ad perfectionẽ deducitur. Si in ipſo Mercurio operari inceperis vbi natura reliquit imperfectum, inuenies in eo perfectione et gaudebis.

Perfectum non alteratur, fed corrumpitur. Sed imperfectum bene alteratur, ergo corruptio vnius eſt generatio alterius.

Speculum

Figure 4

hermeticum the uterus and its content the foetus. What is said of the *lapis* is also said of the water: "This stinking water contains everything it needs." [2] It is sufficient unto itself, like the Uroboros, the tail-eater, which is said to beget, kill, and devour itself. *Aqua est, quae occidit et vivificat*—the water is that which kills and vivifies.[3] It is the *aqua benedicta*, the lustral water,[4] where the birth of the new being is prepared. As the text to our picture explains: "Our stone is to be extracted from the nature of the two bodies." It also likens the water to the *ventus* of the "Tabula smaragdina," where we read: "Portavit eum ventus in ventre suo" (The wind hath carried it in his belly). The *Rosarium* adds: "It is clear that wind is air, and air is life, and life is soul, that is, oil and water." [5] The curious idea that the soul (i.e., the breath-soul) is oil and water derives from the dual nature of Mercurius. The *aqua permanens* is one of his many synonyms, and the terms *oleum, oleaginitas, unctuosum, unctuositas,* all refer to the arcane substance which is likewise Mercurius. The idea is a graphic reminder of the ecclesiastical use of various unguents and of the consecrated water. The dual substance mentioned above is represented by the king and queen, a possible reference to the *commixtio* of the two substances in the chalice of the Mass. A similar *coniunctio* is shown in the "Grandes heures du duc de Berry," [6] where a naked "little man and woman" are being anointed by two saintly servitors in the baptismal bath of the chalice. There can be no doubt of the connections between the alchemical *opus* and the Mass, as the treatise of Melchior Cibinensis (5, x) proves. Our text says: "Anima est Sol et Luna." The alchemist thought in strictly

---

2 Instead of the meaningless "aqua foetum" I read "aqua foetida" (*Rosarium*, 2, xiii, p. 241). Cf. "Consilium coniugii," p. 64: Leo viridis, id est . . . aqua foetida, quae est mater omnium ex qua et per quam et cum qua praeparant . . ." (The green lion, that is . . . the stinking water, which is the mother of all things, and out of it and through it and with it, they prepare . . .).

3 *Rosarium*, 2, xiii, p. 214. Cf. "Aurora consurgens," I, Ch. XII, where the bride says of herself in God's words (Vulg., Deut. 32:39): ". . . ego occidam, et ego vivere faciam . . . et non est qui de manu mea possit eruere." (D.V.: "I will kill and I will make to live . . . and there is none that can deliver out of my hand").

4 *Rosarium*, 2, xiii, p. 213.

5 Ibid., p. 237. This goes back to Senior, 164, pp. 19, 31, 33.

6 35, ii. Cf. *Psychology and Alchemy*, 85, fig. 159.

medieval trichotomous terms: [7] anything alive—and his *lapis* is undoubtedly alive—consists of corpus, anima, and spiritus. The *Rosarium* remarks (p. 239) that "the body is Venus and feminine, the spirit is Mercurius and masculine"; hence the anima, as the "vinculum," the link between body and spirit, would be hermaphroditic,[8] i.e., a *coniunctio Solis et Lunae*. Mercurius is the hermaphrodite par excellence. From all this it may be gathered that the queen stands for the body [9] and the king for the spirit, but that both are unrelated without the soul, since this is the *vinculum* which holds them together.[10] If no bond of love exists, they have no soul. In our pictures the bond is effected by the dove from above and by the water from below. These constitute the link—in other words, they are the soul.[11] Thus the underlying idea of the psyche proves it to be a half bodily, half spiritual substance, an *anima media natura*,[12] as the alchemists call it,[13] an hermaphroditic being [14] capable of uniting the opposites, but who is never complete in the individual unless related to another individual. The unrelated human being lacks wholeness, for he can achieve wholeness only through the soul, and the soul cannot exist without its other side, which is always found in a "You." Wholeness is a combi-

[7] Cf. "Aurora consurgens," I, Ch. IX, "qualis pater talis filius, talis et Spiritus Sanctus et hi tres unum sunt, corpus, spiritus et anima, quia omnis perfectio in numero ternario consistit, hoc est mensura, numero et pondere" (As the Father, such is the Son, and such is also the Holy Spirit; and these three are One, body, spirit, and soul, since all perfection consists in the number Three, i.e., in measure, number, and weight).

[8] "Anima vocatur Rebis."—2, ii, p. 180.

[9] According to Firmicus Maternus (43, p. 3), Luna is "humanorum corporum mater."

[10] Sometimes the spirit is the *vinculum,* or else the latter is a *natura ignea* (Zacharias, 5, v, p. 887).

[11] Psychologically one should read *mens* for *spiritus.*

[12] Cf. "De arte chymica," 2, xi, pp. 584ff., and Mylius, 120, p. 9.

[13] "Turba," 2, ii, p. 180: ". . . Spiritus et corpus unum sunt mediante anima, quae est apud spiritum et corpus. Quod si anima non esset, tunc spiritus et corpus separarentur ab invicem per ignem, sed anima adiuncta spiritui et corpori, hoc totum non curat ignem nec ullam rem mundi." (. . . The spirit and the body are one, the soul acting as a mediator which abides with the spirit and the body. If there were no soul, the spirit and the body would separate from each other by the fire, but because the soul is joined to the spirit and the body, this whole is unaffected by fire or by any other thing in the world.)

[14] Cf. the observations of Winthuis, 163.

243

nation of I and You, and these show themselves to be parts of a transcendent unity[15] whose nature can only be grasped symbolically, as in the symbols of the *rotundum,* the rose, the wheel,[16] or the *coniunctio Solis et Lunae.* The alchemists even go so far as to say that the *corpus, anima,* and *spiritus* of the arcane substance are one, "because they come from the One, and of the One, and with the One, which is its own root" (Quia ipsa omnia sunt ex uno et de uno et cum uno, quod est radix ipsius."—*Rosarium,* p. 369). A thing which is the cause and origin of itself can only be God, unless we adopt the implied dualism of the Paracelsists, who were of the opinion that the *prima materia* is an *increatum.*[17] Similarly, the pre-Paracelsist *Rosarium* maintains (p. 251) that the quintessence is a "self-subsistent body, differing from all the elements and from everything composed thereof."

455   Coming now to the psychology of the picture, it is clearly a descent into the unconscious. The immersion in the bath is another "night sea journey,"[18] as the "Visio Arislei" (2, i) proves. There the philosophers are shut up with the brother-sister pair in a triple glass-house at the bottom of the sea by the Rex Marinus. Just as, in the primitive myths, it is so stiflingly hot in the belly of the whale that the hero loses his hair, so the philosophers suffer very much from the intense heat[19] during their confinement. The hero-myths deal with rebirth and apocatastasis, and the "Visio" likewise tells of the resuscitation of the dead Thabritius (Gabricus) or, in another version, of his rebirth.[20] The night sea journey is a kind of

[15] I do not, of course, mean the synthesis or identification of two individuals, but the conscious union of the ego with everything that has been projected into the "You." Hence wholeness is the result of an intrapsychic process which depends essentially on the relation of one individual to another. Such a relationship paves the way for individuation and makes it possible, but is itself no proof of wholeness. The projection upon the feminine partner contains the anima and sometimes the self.   [16] Cf. *Psychology and Alchemy,* 85, index.

[17] Ibid., pars. 430ff.   [18] Cf. Frobenius, *Das Zeitalter des Sonnengottes,* 53.

[19] 2, i, p. 148: "Mansimus in tenebris undarum et intenso aestatis calore ac maris perturbatione" (We remained in the darknesses of the waves and in the intense heat of summer and in the perturbation of the sea).

[20] Cf. the birth of Mithras: "de solo aestu libidinis" (Jerome, 76, col. 246). In Arabic alchemy, too, the fire that causes the fusion is called "libido." Cf. "Turba," 2, ii, Exercitatio XV, p. 181: "Inter supradicta tria (scil., corpus anima, spiritus) in est libido," etc. (Between the aforementioned three, i.e., body, soul, spirit, there is a libido).

descensus ad inferos—a descent into Hades and a journey to the
land of ghosts somewhere beyond this world, beyond consciousness, hence an immersion in the unconscious. In our picture the
immersion is effected by the rising up of the fiery, chthonic
Mercurius, presumably the sexual libido which engulfs the
pair [21] and is the obvious counterpart to the heavenly dove. The
latter has always been regarded as a love-bird, but it also has a
purely spiritual significance in the Christian tradition accepted
by the alchemists. Thus the pair are united *above* by the symbol
of the Holy Ghost, and it looks as if the immersion in the bath
were also uniting them *below,* i.e., in the water which is the
counterpart of spirit ("It is death for souls to become water,"
says Heraclitus). Opposition and identity at once—a philosophical problem only when taken as a psychological one!

456   This development recapitulates the story of how the original
man (Nous) stepped down from heaven to earth and was
wrapped in the embrace of Physis—a primordial image that runs
through the whole of alchemy. The modern equivalent of this
stage is the conscious realization of sexual fantasies which colour
the transference accordingly. It is significant that even in this
quite unmistakable situation the pair are still holding on with
both hands to the starry symbol brought by the Holy Ghost,
which signalizes the meaning of their relationship: man's longing for transcendent wholeness.

21 See the inscription to fig. 5a:
     "But here King Sol is tight shut in,
       And *Mercurius philosophorum* pours over him."
The sun drowning in the mercurial fountain (*Rosarium,* **2, xiii,** p. 315) and the
lion swallowing the sun (p. 367) both have this meaning, which is also an allusion
to the *ignea natura* of Mercurius (Leo is the House of the Sun) . For this aspect of
Mercurius see my "The Spirit Mercurius," **89,** pars. 113f. (1948 ed., pp. 120f.).

5

THE CONJUNCTION

O Luna, folded in my sweet embrace/
Be you as strong as I, as fair of face.
O Sol, brightest of all lights known to men/
And yet you need me, as the cock the hen.

[*Figure 5*]

457   The sea has closed over the king and queen, and they have
gone back to the chaotic beginnings, the *massa confusa*. Physis
has wrapped the "man of light" in a passionate embrace. As the
text says: "Then Beya [the maternal sea] rises up over Gabricus
and encloses him in her womb, so that nothing more of him is
to be seen. And she embraced Gabricus with so much love that
she utterly consumed him in her own nature and dissolved him
into atoms." These verses from Merculinus are then quoted:

Candida mulier, si rubeo sit nupta marito,
Mox complexantur, complexaque copulantur,
Per se solvuntur, per se quoque conficiuntur,
Ut duo qui fuerant, unum quasi corpore fiant.

(White-skinned lady, lovingly joined to her ruddy-limbed husband,
Wrapped in each other's arms in the bliss of connubial union,
Merge and dissolve as they come to the goal of perfection:
They that were two are made one, as though of one body.)

458   In the fertile imagination of the alchemists the *hieros
gamos* of Sol and Luna continues right down to the animal kingdom, as is shown by the following instructions: "Take a Coetanean dog and an Armenian bitch, mate them, and they
will bear you a son in the likeness of a dog." [1] The symbolism
is about as crass as it could be. On the other hand the *Rosarium*
says (p. 247): "In hora coniunctionis maxima apparent mirac-

1 *Rosarium*, 2, xiii, p. 248. Quotation after Kallid, 2, vi, p. 340. [Cf. par. 353, n. 1;
also n. 2 supra.—EDITORS.]

CONIVNCTIO SIVE
Coitus.

O Luna durch meyn vmbgeben/vnd susse mynne/
Wirstu schön/starck/vnd gewaltig als ich byn.
O Sol/ du bist vber alle liecht zu erkennen/
So bedarsstu doch mein als der han der hennen.

ARISLEVS IN VISIONE.

Coniunge ergo filium tuum Gabricum dile=
ctiorem tibi in omnibus filijs tuis cum sua sorore
Beya

Figure 5

Physis has wrapped the "man of light"
in a passionate embrace.
Filius philosophorum or lapis
is begotten:
miraculous Son in likeness of a dog begotten.

ula" (In the hour of conjunction the greatest marvels appear). For this is the moment when the *filius philosoporum* or *lapis* is begotten. A quotation from Alfidius adds (p. 248): "Lux moderna ab eis gignitur" (The new light is begotten by them). Kallid says of the "son in the likeness of a dog" that he is "of a celestial hue" and that "this son will guard you . . . in this world and in the next." [2] Likewise Senior: "She hath borne a son who served his parents in all things, save that he is more splendid and refulgent than they," [3] i.e., he outshines sun and moon. The real meaning of the *coniunctio* is that it brings to birth something that is one and united. It restores the vanished "man of light" who is identical with the Logos in Gnostic and Christian symbolism and who was there before the creation; we also meet him at the beginning of the Gospel of St. John. Consequently we are dealing with a cosmic idea, and this amply explains the alchemists' use of superlatives.

459   The psychology of this central symbol is not at all simple. On a superficial view it looks as if natural instinct had triumphed. But if we examine it more closely we note that the coitus is taking place in the water, the *mare tenebrositatis*, i.e., the unconscious. This idea is borne out by a variant of the picture (fig. 5a). There again Sol and Luna are in the water, but both are winged. They thus represent spirit—they are aerial beings, creatures of thought. The texts indicate that Sol and Luna are two *vapores* or *fumi* which gradually develop as the fire increases in heat, and which then rise as on wings from the

---

[2] Kallid, 2, vi, p. 340: "Et dixit Hermes patri suo: Pater timeo ab inimico in mea mansione. Et dixit: Fili, accipe canem masculum Corascenem et caniculam Armeniae et iunge in simul et parient canem coloris coeli et imbibe ipsum una siti ex aqua maris: quia ipse custodiet tuum amicum et custodiet te ab inimico tuo et adiuvabit te ubicumque sis, semper tecum existendo in hoc mundo et in alio." (And Hermes said to his father: Father, I am afraid of the enemy in my house. And he said: My son, take a Corascen dog and an Armenian bitch, join them together, and they will beget a dog of a celestial hue, and if ever he is thirsty, give him sea water to drink: for he will guard your friend, and he will guard you from your enemy, and he will help you wherever you may be, always being with you, in this world and in the next.)

[3] 2, xiii, p. 248. The radiant quality (στίλβων) is characteristic of Mercurius and also of the first man, Gayomart or Adam. Cf. Christensen, 33, pp. 22ff., and Kohut, 101, pp. 68, 72, 87.

FERMENTATIO.

Hye wird Sol aber verschlossen
Vnd mit Mercurio philosophorum ybergossen.

Figure 5a

[handwritten annotations:]

Water =
Fire =

Boiling solution in which the two
substances unite
Sol & Luna
Winged, representing spirit
Brings to birth vanished "man of
light, identical with the Logos in Gnostic
& Christian symbolism.

(uncon . . .)

decoctio and *digestio* of the *prima materia*.[4] That is why the paired opposites are sometimes represented as two birds fighting[5] or as winged and wingless dragons.[6] The fact that two aerial creatures should mate on or beneath the water does not disturb the alchemist in the least, for he is so familiar with the changeable nature of his synonyms that for him water is not only fire but all sorts of astonishing things besides. If we interpret the water as steam we may be getting nearer the truth. It refers to the boiling solution in which the two substances unite.

460   As to the frank eroticism of the pictures, I must remind the reader that they were drawn for medieval eyes and that consequently they have a symbolical rather than a pornographic meaning. Medieval hermeneutics and meditation could contemplate even the most delicate passages in the Song of Solomon without taking offence and view them through a veil of spirituality. Our pictures of the *coniunctio* are to be understood in this sense: union on the biological level is a symbol of the *unio oppositorum* at its highest. This proves that the union of opposites in the royal art is just as real as coitus in the common acceptation of the word, so that the *opus* becomes an analogy of the natural process by means of which instinctive energy is transformed, at least in part, into symbolical activity. The creation of such analogies frees instinct and the biological sphere as a whole from the pressure of unconscious contents. Absence of symbolism, however, overloads the sphere of instinct.[7] The analogy contained in figure 5 is a little too obvious for our modern taste, so that it almost fails of its object.

461   As every specialist knows, the psychological parallels encountered in medical practice often take the form of fantasy-

4 The "Practica Mariae" (2, v, p. 321) makes the two into four: "(Kibrich et Zubech) . . . ipsa sunt duo fumi complectentes duo luminaria" (They are the two vapours enveloping the two lights). These four evidently correspond to the four elements, since we read on p. 320: ". . . si sunt apud homines omnia 4 elementa, dixit compleri possent et complexionari et coagulari eorum fumi . . ." (He said that if there are in men all 4 elements their vapours could, as he says, be completed and intermingled and coagulated).   5 See Lambspringk, 4 iii.
6 Frontispiece to *Le Songe de Poliphile*, 37. See *Psychology and Alchemy*, 85, fig. 4.
7 Hence the ambivalent saying in Mylius, 120, p. 182: "In habentibus symbolum facilis est transitus" (For those that have the symbol the passage is easy).

images which, when drawn, differ hardly at all from our pictures. The reader may remember the typical case I mentioned earlier (par. 377ff.), where the act of conception was represented symbolically and, exactly nine months later, the unconscious, as though influenced by a *suggestion à échéance,* produced the symbolism of a birth, or of a new-born child, without the patient's being conscious of the preceding psychological conception or having consciously reckoned the period of her "pregnancy." As a rule the whole process passes off in a series of dreams and is discovered only retrospectively, when the dream material comes to be analysed. Many alchemists compute the duration of the *opus* to be that of a pregnancy, and they liken the entire procedure to such a period of gestation.[8]

462   The main emphasis falls on the *unio mystica,* as is shown quite clearly by the retention of the uniting symbol in the earlier pictures. It is perhaps not without deeper significance that this symbol has disappeared in the pictures of the *coniunctio.* For at this juncture the meaning of the symbol is fulfilled: the partners have themselves become symbolic. At first each represented two elements; then each of them united into one (integration of the shadow!); and finally the two together with the third become a whole—"ut duo qui fuerant, unum quasi corpore fiant." Thus the axiom of Maria is fulfilled. In this union the Holy Ghost disappears as well, but to make up for that, Sol and Luna themselves become spirit. The real meaning, therefore, is Goethe's "higher copulation,"[9] a union in unconscious identity, which could be compared with the primitive, initial state of chaos, the *massa confusa,* or rather with the state of *participation mystique* where heterogeneous factors merge in an unconscious relationship. The *coniunctio* differs from this not as a mechanism but because it is by nature never an initial state: it is always the product of a process or the goal of endeavour. This is equally the case in psychology, though here the *coniunctio* comes about unintentionally and is opposed to the bitter end by all biologically minded and conscientious

---

[8] Cf. Kallid, 2, vii, pp. 355f.

[9] "No more shall you stay a prisoner
Wrapped in darkest obfuscation;
New desires call you upwards
To the higher copulation."—*West-östlicher Divan.*

doctors. That is why they speak of "severing the transference." The detachment of the patient's projections from the doctor is desirable for both parties and, if successful, may be counted as a positive result. This is a practical possibility when, owing to the patient's immaturity, or his fate, or because of some misunderstanding arising out of the projection, or because reason and plain common sense demand it, the continued transformation of projected unconscious contents comes to a hopeless standstill, and at the same time an opportunity presents itself from outside for the projection to be switched to another "object." This solution has about the same merit as persuading a person not to go into a monastery or not to set out on a dangerous expedition or not to make a marriage which everybody agrees would be stupid. We cannot rate reason highly enough, but there are times when we must ask ourselves: do we really know enough about the destinies of individuals to enable us to give good advice under *all* circumstances? Certainly we must act according to our best convictions, but are we so sure that our convictions are for the best as regards the other person? Very often we do not know what is best for ourselves, and in later years we may come to thank God from the bottom of our hearts that his kindly hand preserved us from the "reasonableness" of our former plans. It is easy for the critic to say after the event, "Ah, but that wasn't the right sort of reason!" Who can know with unassailable certainty when he has the right sort? Moreover, is it not essential to the true art of living, sometimes, in defiance of all reason and fitness, to include the unreasonable and the unfitting within the ambience of the possible?

463   Therefore it should not surprise us to find that there are not a few cases where, despite every effort, no possibility presents itself of severing the transference, although the patient is—from the rational point of view—equipped with the necessary understanding and neither he nor the doctor can be accused of any technical negligence or oversight. Both of them may be so deeply impressed by the vast irrationality of the unconscious as to come to the conclusion that the best thing is to cut the Gordian knot with a drastic decision. But the surgical partition of these Siamese twins is a perilous operation. There may be successes, though in my experience they are few and far between. I am all for a conservative solution of the

problem. If the situation really is such that no other possibilities of any kind can be considered, and the unconscious obviously insists on the retention of the tie, then the treatment must be continued hopefully. It may be that the severance will only occur at a later stage, but it may also be a case of psychological "pregnancy" whose natural outcome must be awaited with patience, or again it may be one of those fatalities which, rightly or wrongly, we take on our own shoulders or else try to avoid. The doctor knows that always, wherever he turns, man is dogged by his fate. Even the simplest illness may develop surprising complications; or, equally unexpectedly, a condition that seemed very serious may take a turn for the better. Sometimes the doctor's art helps, sometimes it is useless. In the domain of psychology especially, where we still know so little, we often stumble upon the unforeseen, the inexplicable—something of which we can make neither head nor tail. Things cannot be forced, and wherever force seems to succeed it is generally regretted afterwards. Better always to be mindful of the limitations of one's knowledge and ability. Above all one needs forbearance and patience, for often time can do more than art. Not everything can and must be cured. Sometimes dark moral problems or inexplicable twists of fate lie hidden under the cloak of a neurosis. One patient suffered for years from depressions and an unaccountable phobia about Paris. She managed to rid herself of the depressions, but the phobia proved inaccessible. However, she felt so well that she was prepared to risk ignoring her phobia. She succeeded in getting to Paris, and the next day she lost her life in a car smash. Another patient had a peculiar and abiding horror of flights of steps. One day he got caught up in some street-rioting and shots were fired. He found himself in front of a public building with a broad flight of steps leading up to it. In spite of his phobia he dashed up them to seek shelter inside the building, and fell on the steps, mortally wounded by a stray bullet.

464   These examples show that psychic symptoms need to be judged with the greatest caution. This is also true of the various forms of transference and its contents. They sometimes set the doctor almost insoluble problems or cause him all manner of worries which may go to the limits of the endurable and even beyond. Particularly if he has a marked ethical personality

253

and takes his psychological work seriously, this may lead to moral conflicts and divided loyalties whose real or supposed incompatibility has been the occasion of more than one disaster. On the basis of long experience I would therefore like to warn against too much therapeutic enthusiasm. Psychological work is full of snags, but it is just here that incompetents swarm. The medical faculties are largely to blame for this, because for years they refused to admit the psyche among the aetiological factors of pathology, even though they had no other use for it. Ignorance is certainly never a recommendation, but often the best knowledge is not enough either. Therefore I say to the psychotherapist: let no day pass without humbly remembering that everything has still to be learned.

465   The reader should not imagine that the psychologist is in any position to explain what "higher copulation" is, or the *coniunctio,* or "psychic pregnancy," let alone the "soul's child." Nor should one feel annoyed if the newcomer to this delicate subject, or one's own cynical self, gets disgusted with these—as he thinks them—phoney ideas and brushes them aside with a pitying smile and an offensive display of tact. The unprejudiced scientific inquirer who seeks the truth and nothing but the truth must guard against rash judgments and interpretations, for here he is confronted with *psychological facts* which the intellect cannot falsify and conjure out of existence. There are among one's patients intelligent and discerning persons who are just as capable as the doctor of giving the most disparaging interpretations, but who cannot avail themselves of such a weapon in the face of these insistent facts. Words like "nonsense" only succeed in banishing little things—not the things that thrust themselves tyrannically upon you in the stillness and loneliness of the night. The images welling up from the unconscious do precisely that. What we choose to call this fact does not affect the issue in any way. If it is an illness, then this *morbus sacer* must be treated according to its nature. The doctor can solace himself with the reflection that he, like the rest of his colleagues, does not only have patients who are curable, but chronic patients too, where curing becomes nursing. At all events the empirical material gives us no sufficient grounds for always talking about "illness"; on the contrary, one comes to realize that it is a moral problem and often one wishes for a

priest who, instead of confessing and proselytizing, would just
listen, obey, and put this singular matter before God so that He
could decide.

466   *Patientia et mora* are absolutely necessary in this kind of
work. One must be able to wait on events. Of work there is
plenty—the careful analysis of dreams and other unconscious
contents. Where the doctor fails, the patient will fail too, which
is why the doctor should possess a real knowledge of these
things and not just opinions, the offscourings of our modern
philosophy for everyman. In order to augment this much-
needed knowledge, I have carried my researches back to those
earlier times when naïve introspection and projection were
still at work, mirroring a psychic hinterland that is virtually
blocked for us today. In this way I have learned much for my
own practice, especially as regards understanding the formid-
able fascination of the contents in question. These may not always strike the patient as particularly fascinating, so he suffers
instead from a proportionately strong compulsive tie in whose
intensity he can rediscover the force of those subliminal images. He will, however, try to interpret the tie rationalistically,
in the spirit of the age, and consequently does not perceive
and will not admit the irrational foundations of his transference, namely the archetypal images.

6

DEATH

Here King and Queen are lying dead/
In great distress the soul is sped.

[Figure 6]

467   *Vas hermeticum,* fountain, and sea have here become sarcophagus and tomb. King and queen are dead and have melted
into a single being with two heads. The feast of life is followed
by the funereal threnody. Just as Gabricus dies after becoming
united with his sister, and the son-lover always comes to an early
end after consummating the *hieros gamos* with the mother-
goddess of the Near East, so, after the *coniunctio oppositorum,*
deathlike stillness reigns. When the opposites unite, all energy
ceases: there is no more flow. The waterfall has plunged to its
full depth in that torrent of nuptial joy and longing; now only
a stagnant pool remains, without wave or current. So at least it
appears, looked at from the outside. As the legend tells us, the
picture represents the *putrefactio,* the corruption, the decay of a
once living creature. Yet the picture is also entitled "Concep-
tio." The text says: "Corruptio unius generatio est alterius"—
the corruption of one is the genesis of the other,[1] an indication
that this death is an interim stage to be followed by a new life.
No new life can arise, say the alchemists, without the death of
the old. They liken the art to the work of the sower, who buries
the grain in the earth: it dies only to waken to new life.[2] Thus

[1] Avicenna, **2, x,** p. 426.

[2] Cf. "Aurora," I, **12,** Ch. XII (after John 12:24). Hortulanus (Ruska, *Tabula,*
149, p. 186): "Vocatur [lapis] etiam granum frumenti, quod nisi mortuum fuerit,
ipsum solum manet," etc. (It [the stone] is also called "grain of wheat," since it
remains itself alone, unless it dies). Equally unfortunate is the other comparison,
also a favourite: "Habemus exemplum in ovo quod putrescit primo, et tunc gignitur pullus, qui post totum corruptum est animal vivens" (We have an example in
the egg: first it decays and then the chicken is born, a living animal coming after
the decay of the whole).—*Rosarium,* **2, xiii,** p. 255.

PHILOSOPHORVM.

CONCEPTIO SEV PVTRE
factio

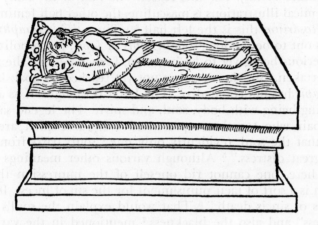

Hye ligen könig vnd königin dot/
Die sele scheydt sich mit grosser not.

ARISTOTELES REX ET
Philosophus.

Nunquam vidi aliquod animatum crescere
sine putrefactione, nisi autem fiat putri-
dum inuanum erit opus alchimicum.

Figure 6

with their *mortificatio, interfectio, putrefactio, combustio, incineratio, calcinatio,* etc., they are imitating the work of nature. Similarly they liken their labours to human mortality, without which the new and eternal life cannot be attained.[3]

468   The corpse left over from the feast is already a new body, a *hermaphroditus* (a compound of Hermes-Mercurius and Aphrodite-Venus). For this reason one half of the body in the alchemical illustrations is masculine, the other half feminine (in the *Rosarium* this is the left half [3a]). Since the *hermaphroditus* turns out to be the long-sought *rebis* or *lapis,* it symbolizes that mysterious being yet to be begotten, for whose sake the *opus* is undertaken. But the *opus* has not yet reached its goal, because the *lapis* has not come alive. The latter is thought of as animal, a living being with body, soul, and spirit. The legend says that the pair who together represented body and spirit are dead, and that the soul (evidently only *one* [4] soul) parts from them "in great distress." [5] Although various other meanings play a part here, one cannot rid oneself of the impression that the death is a sort of tacit punishment for the sin of incest, for "the wages of sin is death." [6] That would explain the soul's "great distress" and also the blackness [7] mentioned in the variant of our picture ("Here is Sol turned black").[8] This blackness is

3 Cf. Ruska, *Turba.* 150, p. 139: "Tunc autem, doctrinae filii, illa res igne indiget, quousque illius corporis spiritus vertatur et per noctes dimittatur, ut homo in suo tumulo, et pulvis fiat. His peractis reddet ei Deus et animam suam et spiritum, ac infirmitate ablata confortatur illa res . . . quemadmodum homo post resurrectionem fortior fit," etc. (But, sons of the doctrine, that thing will need fire, until the spirit of its body is changed and is sent away through the nights, like a man in his grave, and becomes dust. When this has happened, God will give back to it its soul and its spirit and, with all infirmity removed, that thing is strengthened . . . as man becomes stronger after the resurrection.)

3a 2, xiii, p. 291.

4 Cf. Senior, 164, p. 16: ". . . et reviviscit, quod fuerat morti deditum, post inopiam magnam" (What had been given over to death, comes to life again after great tribulation).

5 Cf. par. 451, n. 7, the ψυχογονία in Lydus' account of the hexad.

6 For the alchemist, this has a precedent in Gen. 2:17: "for in the day that thou eatest thereof thou shalt surely die." Adam's sin is part of the drama of the creation. "Cum peccavit Adam, eius est anima mortua" (When Adam sinned his soul died), says Gregory the Great (58, Epist. CXIV).

7 *Rosarium,* 2, xiii, p. 324.

8 The *nigredo* appears here not as the initial state but as the product of a prior process. The time-sequence of phases in the *opus* is very uncertain. We see the

Herzog
J.

the *immunditia* (uncleanliness), as is proved by the *ablutio* that subsequently becomes necessary. The *coniunctio* was incestuous and therefore sinful, leaving pollution behind it. The *nigredo* always appears in conjunction with *tenebrositas*, the darkness of the tomb and of Hades, not to say of Hell. Thus the descent that began in the marriage-bath has touched rock-bottom: death, darkness, and sin. For the adept, however, the hopeful side of things is shown in the anticipated appearance of the hermaphrodite, though the psychological meaning of this is at first obscure.

469   The situation described in our picture is a kind of Ash Wednesday. The reckoning is presented, and a dark abyss yawns. Death means the total extinction of consciousness and the complete stagnation of psychic life, so far as this is capable of consciousness. So catastrophic a consummation, which has been the object of annual lamentations in so many places (e.g., the laments for Linus, Tammuz,[9] and Adonis), must surely correspond to an important archetype, since even today we have our Good Friday. An archetype always stands for some typical event. As we have seen, there is in the *coniunctio* a union of two figures, one representing the daytime principle, i.e., lucid consciousness, the other a nocturnal light, the unconscious. Because the latter cannot be seen directly, it is always projected; for, unlike the shadow, it does not belong to the ego but is collective. For this reason it is felt to be something alien to us, and we suspect it of belonging to the particular person with whom we have emotional ties. In addition a man's unconscious has a feminine character; it hides in the feminine side of him which he naturally does not see in himself but in the woman who fascinates him. That is probably why the soul (anima) is feminine. If, therefore, man and woman are merged in some kind of unconscious identity, he will take over the traits of her animus and she the traits of his anima. Neither anima nor animus

___

same uncertainty in the individuation process, so that a typical sequence of stages can only be constructed in very general terms. The deeper reason for this "disorder" is probably the "timeless" quality of the unconscious, where conscious succession becomes simultaneity, a phenomenon I have called "synchronicity." From another point of view we would be justified in speaking of the "elasticity of unconscious time" on the analogy of the equally real "elasticity of space." For the relations between psychology and atomic physics, see Meier, "Moderne Physik," 115.   9 Ezek. 8:14: ". . . behold, there sat women weeping for Tammuz."

can be constellated without the intervention of the personality to whom each corresponds, but this is not to say that the resultant situation is nothing but a personal relationship and a personal entanglement. The personal side of it is a fact, but not the main fact. The main fact is the *subjective experience* of the situation—in other words, it is a mistake to believe that one's personal dealings with one's partner play the most important part. Quite the reverse: the most important part falls to the man's dealings with the anima and the woman's dealings with the animus. Nor does the *coniunctio* take place with the personal partner; it is a royal game played out between the active, masculine side of the woman (the animus) and the passive, feminine side of the man (the anima). Although the two figures are always tempting the ego to identify itself with them, a real understanding even on the personal level is possible only if the identification is refused. Non-identification demands considerable moral effort. Moreover it is only legitimate when not used as a pretext to avoid the necessary degree of personal understanding. On the other hand, if we approach this task with psychological views that are too personalistic, we fail to do justice to the fact that we are dealing with an archetype which is anything but personal. It is, on the contrary, a postulate so universal in scope and incidence that it often seems advisable to speak less of *my* anima or *my* animus and more of *the* anima and *the* animus. As archetypes, these figures are semi-collective and impersonal quantities, so that when we identify ourselves with them and fondly imagine that we are then most truly ourselves, we are in fact most estranged from ourselves and most like the average type of *Homo sapiens*. The personal protagonists in the royal game should steadfastly bear in mind that at bottom it represents the "trans-subjective" union of archetypal figures, and it should never be forgotten that it is a *symbolical* relationship whose goal is complete individuation. In our series of pictures this idea is suggested *sub rosa*. Hence, if the *opus* interposes itself in the form of the rose or wheel, the unconscious and purely personal relationship becomes a psychological problem which, while it prevents a descent into complete darkness, does not in any way cancel out the operative force of the archetype. The right way, like the wrong way, must be paid for, and however much the alchemist may extol the *venerabilis natura,*

it is in either case an *opus contra naturam*. It goes against
nature to commit incest, and it goes against nature not to yield
to an ardent desire. And yet it is nature that prompts such
an attitude in us, because of the kinship libido. So it is as
Pseudo-Democritus says: "Nature rejoices in nature, nature
subdues nature, nature rules over nature." [10] Man's instincts are
not all harmoniously arranged, they are perpetually jostling
each other out of the way. The ancients were optimistic enough
to see this struggle not as a chaotic muddle but as aspiring to
some higher order.

470 Thus the encounter with anima and animus means conflict and brings us up against the hard dilemma in which nature herself has placed us. Whichever course one takes, nature
will be mortified and must suffer, even to the death; for the
merely natural man must die in part during his own lifetime.
The Christian symbol of the crucifix is therefore a prototype
and an "eternal" truth. There are medieval pictures showing
how Christ is nailed to the Cross by his own virtues. Other
people meet the same fate at the hands of their vices. Nobody
who finds himself on the road to wholeness can escape that characteristic suspension which is the meaning of crucifixion. For
he will infallibly run into things that thwart and "cross" him:
first, the thing he has no wish to be (the shadow); second, the
thing he is not (the "other," the individual reality of the
"You"); and third, his psychic non-ego (the collective unconscious). This being at cross purposes with ourselves is suggested
by the crossed branches held by the king and queen, who are
themselves man's cross in the form of the anima and woman's
cross in the form of the animus. The meeting with the collective
unconscious is a fatality of which the natural man has no inkling until it overtakes him. As Faust says: "You are conscious
only of the single urge/ O may you never know the other!"

471 This process underlies the whole *opus*, but to begin with
it is so confusing that the alchemist tries to depict the conflict,
death, and rebirth figuratively, on a higher plane, first—in his
practica—in the form of chemical transformations and then—
in his *theoria*—in the form of conceptual images. The same
process may also be conjectured to underlie certain religious

10 Berthelot, 28, II, i, 3: Ἡ φύσις τῇ φύσει τέρπεται, καὶ ἡ φύσις τὴν φύσιν
νικᾷ, καὶ ἡ φύσις τὴν φύσιν κρατεῖ.

261

opera, since notable parallels exist between ecclesiastical symbolism and alchemy. In psychotherapy and in the psychology of neuroses it is recognized as the psychic process par excellence, because it typifies the content of the transference neurosis. The supreme aim of the *opus psychologicum* is conscious realization, and the first step is to make oneself conscious of contents that have hitherto been projected. This endeavour gradually leads to knowledge of one's partner and to self-knowledge, and so to the distinction between what one really is and what is projected into one, or what one imagines oneself to be. Meanwhile, one is so taken up with one's own efforts that one is hardly conscious of the extent to which "nature" acts not only as a driving-force but as a helper—in other words, how much instinct insists that the higher level of consciousness be attained. This urge to a higher and more comprehensive consciousness fosters civilization and culture, but must fall short of the goal unless man voluntarily places himself in its service. The alchemists are of the opinion that the *artifex* is the servant of the work, and that not he but nature brings the work to fruition. All the same, there must be will as well as ability on man's part, for unless both are present the urge remains at the level of merely natural symbolism and produces nothing but a perversion of that instinct for wholeness which, if it is to fulfil its purpose, needs all parts of the whole, including those that are projected into a "You." Instinct seeks them there, in order to re-create that royal pair which every human being has in his wholeness, i.e., that bisexual First Man who "has no need of anything but himself." Whenever this instinct for wholeness appears, it begins by disguising itself under the symbolism of incest, for, unless he seeks it in himself, a man's nearest feminine counterpart is to be found in his mother, sister, or daughter.

472   With the integration of projections—which the merely natural man in his unbounded naïveté can never recognize as such—the personality becomes so vastly enlarged that the normal ego-personality is almost extinguished. In other words, if the individual identifies himself with the contents awaiting integration, a positive or negative inflation results. Positive inflation comes very near to a more or less conscious megalomania; negative inflation is felt as an annihilation of the ego. The two conditions may alternate. At all events the integration

of contents that were always unconscious and projected involves a serious lesion of the ego. Alchemy expresses this through the symbols of death, mutilation, or poisoning, or through the curious idea of dropsy, which in the *Aenigma Merlini* [11] is represented as the king's desire to drink inordinate quantities of water. He drinks so much that he melts away and has to be cured by the Alexandrian physicians.[12] He suffers from a surfeit of the unconscious and becomes dissociated—"ut mihi videtur omnia membra mea ab invicem dividuntur" (so that all my limbs seem divided one from another).[13] As a matter of fact, even Mother Alchemia is dropsical in her lower limbs.[14] In alchemy, inflation evidently develops into a psychic oedema.[15]

473   The alchemists assert that death is at once the conception of the *filius philosophorum,* a peculiar variation of the doctrine of the Anthropos.[16] Procreation through incest is a royal or divine prerogative whose advantages the ordinary man is forbidden to enjoy. The ordinary man is the natural man, but the king or hero is the "supernatural" man, the *pneumatikos* who is "baptized with spirit and water," i.e., begotten in the *aqua benedicta* and born from it. He is the Gnostic Christ who descends upon the human Jesus during his baptism and departs from him again before the end. This "son" is the new man, the product of the union of king and queen—though here he is not

[11] Merlinus probably has as little to do with Merlin the magician as "King Artus" with King Arthur. It is more likely that Merlinus is "Merculinus," a diminutive form of Mercurius and the pseudonym of some Hermetic philosopher. "Artus" is the Hellenistic name for Horus. The form "Merqûlius" and "Marqûlius" for Mercurius is substantiated in Arabic sources. Jûnân ben Marqûlius is the Greek Ion, who according to Byzantine mythology is a son of Mercurius (Chwolsohn, 34, I, p. 796). al-Maqrîzi says: "The Merqûlians . . . are the Edessenes who were in the neighbourhood of Harran," obviously the Sabians (ibid., II, p. 615). The Ion in Zosimos (Berthelot, 28, III, i, 2) probably corresponds to the above Ion.

[12] Merlinus, **2,** ix: "Rex autem . . . bibit et rebibit, donec omnia membra sua repleta sunt, et omnes venae eius *inflatae*" (But the king drinks and drinks again until all his limbs are full and all his veins *inflated*).

[13] In the *Tractatus aureus* (**4, i,** p. 51), the king drinks the "aqua pernigra," here described as "pretiosa et sana," for strength and health. He represents the new birth, the self that has assimilated the "black water," i.e., the unconscious. In the Apocalypse of Baruch (**22**) the black water signifies the sin of Adam, the coming of the Messiah, and the end of the world.   [14] "Aurora," **2,** iii, p. 196.

[15] Hence the warning: "Cave ab hydropisi et diluvio Noe" (Beware of dropsy and the flood of Noah).—Ripley, **143,** p. 69.

[16] Cf. *Psychology and Alchemy,* **85,** pars. 456f.

born of the queen, but queen and king are themselves transformed into the new birth.[17]

474   Translated into the language of psychology, the mythologem runs as follows: the union of the conscious mind or ego-personality with the unconscious personified as anima produces a new personality compounded of both—"ut duo qui fuerant, unum quasi corpore fiant." Not that the new personality is a third thing midway between conscious and unconscious, it is both together. Since it transcends consciousness it can no longer be called "ego" but must be given the name of "self." Reference must be made here to the Indian idea of the atman, whose personal and cosmic modes of being form an exact parallel to the psychological idea of the self and the *filius philosophorum*.[18] The self too is both ego and non-ego, subjective and objective, individual and collective. It is the "uniting symbol" which epitomizes the total union of opposites.[19] As such and in accordance with its paradoxical nature, it can only be expressed by means of symbols. These appear in dreams and spontaneous fantasies and find visual expression in the mandalas that occur in the patient's dreams, drawings, and paintings. Hence, properly understood, the self is not a doctrine or theory but an image born of nature's own workings, a natural symbol far removed from all conscious intention. I must stress this obvious fact because certain critics still believe that unconscious phenomena can be written off as pure speculation. But they are matters of observed fact, as every doctor knows who has to deal with such cases. The integration of the self is a fundamental problem which arises in the second half of life. Dream symbols having all the characteristics of mandalas may occur long beforehand without the development of the inner man becoming an immediate problem. Isolated incidents of this kind can easily be overlooked, so that it then seems as if the phenomena I have described were rare curiosities. They are in fact nothing of the sort; they occur wherever the individuation process becomes the object of conscious scrutiny, or where, as in psychoses, the collective unconscious peoples the conscious mind with archetypal figures.

17 One of several versions.

18 This is meant only as a psychological and not as a metaphysical parallel.

19 Cf. my *Psychological Types*, 84, Part I, pars. 405f. (1946 edn.: pp. 320f.).

7

THE ASCENT OF THE SOUL

Here is the division of the four elements/
As from the lifeless corpse the soul ascends.

[Figure 7]

475   This picture carries the *putrefactio* a stage further. Out of the decay the soul mounts up to heaven. Only *one* soul departs from the two, for the two have indeed become one. This brings out the nature of the soul as a vinculum or *ligamentum:* it is a function of relationship. As in real death, the soul departs from the body and returns to its heavenly source. The One born of the two represents the metamorphosis of both, though it is not yet fully developed and is still a "conception" only. Yet, contrary to the usual meaning of conception, the soul does not come down to animate the body, but leaves the body and mounts heavenwards. The "soul" evidently represents the *idea* of unity which has still to become a concrete fact and is at present only a potentiality. The idea of a wholeness made up of *sponsus* and *sponsa* has its correlate in the *rotundus globus coelestis.*[1]

476   This picture corresponds psychologically to a dark state of disorientation. The decomposition of the elements indicates dissociation and the collapse of the existing ego-consciousness. It is closely analogous to the schizophrenic state, and it should be taken very seriously because this is the moment when latent psychoses may become acute, i.e., when the patient becomes aware of the collective unconscious and the psychic non-ego. This collapse and disorientation of consciousness may last a considerable time and it is one of the most difficult transitions the analyst has to deal with, demanding the greatest patience, courage, and faith on the part of both doctor and patient. It is a sign that the patient is being driven along willy-nilly without

1 *Tractatus aureus,* 4, i, p. 47.

any sense of direction, that, in the truest sense of the word, he is in an utterly *soulless* condition, exposed to the full force of autoerotic affects and fantasies. Referring to this state of deadly darkness, an alchemist says: "Hoc est ergo magnum signum, in cuius investigatione nonnulli perierunt" (This is a great sign, in the investigation of which not a few have perished).[2]

477   This critical state, where the conscious mind is liable to be submerged at any moment in the unconscious, is akin to the "loss of soul" that frequently attacks primitives. It is a sudden *abaissement du niveau mental*, a slackening of the conscious tension, to which primitive man is especially prone because his consciousness is still relatively weak and means a considerable effort for him. Hence his lack of will-power, his inability to concentrate and the fact that, mentally, he tires so easily, as I have experienced to my cost during "palavers." The widespread practice of yoga and dhyana in the East is a similar *abaissement* deliberately induced for the purpose of relaxation, a technique for releasing the soul. With certain patients, I have even been able to establish the existence of subjectively experienced levitations in moments of extreme derangement.[3] Lying in bed, the patients felt that they were floating horizontally in the air a few feet above their bodies. This is a suggestive reminder of the phenomenon called the "witch's trance," and also of the parapsychic levitations reported of many saints.

478   The corpse in our picture is the residue of the past and represents the man who is no more, who is destined to decay. The "torments" which form part of the alchemist's procedure belong to this stage of the *iterum mori*—the reiterated death. They consisted in "membra secare, arctius sequestrare ac partes mortificare et in naturam, quae in eo [lapide] est, vertere" (cutting up the limbs, dividing them into smaller and smaller pieces, mortifying the parts, and changing them into the nature which is in [the stone]), as the *Rosarium* says, quoting from Hermes. The passage continues: "You must guard the water and fire dwelling in the arcane substance and contain those waters with the permanent water, even though this be no water,

2 Quotation from a source unknown to me, given as "Sorin" in the *Rosarium*, 2, xiii, p. 264.
3 One such case is described in Meier, "Spontanmanifestationen," 116, p. 290.

ROSARIVM
ANIMÆ EXTRACTIO VEL
imprægnatio.

Hye teylen sich die vier element/
Aus dem leyb scheydt sich die sele behendt.

De

Figure 7

but the fiery form of the true water." [4] For the precious substance, the soul, is in danger of escaping from the bubbling solution in which the elements are decomposed. This precious substance is a paradoxical composite of fire and water, i.e., Mercurius, the *servus* or *cervus fugitivus* who is ever about to flee—or who, in other words, resists integration (into consciousness). He has to be "contained" by the "water," whose paradoxical nature corresponds to the nature of Mercurius and actually contains him within itself. Here we seem to have a hint about the treatment required: faced with the disorientation of the patient, the doctor must hold fast to his own orientation; that is, he must know what the patient's condition means, he must understand what is of value in the dreams, and do so moreover with the help of that *aqua doctrinae* which alone is appropriate to the nature of the unconscious. In other words, he must approach his task with views and ideas capable of grasping unconscious symbolism. Intellectual or supposedly scientific theories are not adequate to the nature of the unconscious, because they make use of a terminology which has not the remotest connection with its pregnant symbolism. The waters must be drawn together and held fast by the one water, by the *forma ignea verae aquae*. The kind of approach that makes this possible must therefore be plastic and symbolical, and itself the outcome of personal experience with unconscious contents. It should not stray too far in the direction of abstract intellectualism; hence we are best advised to remain within the framework of traditional mythology, which has already proved comprehensive enough for all practical purposes. This does not preclude the satisfaction of theoretical requirements, but these should be reserved for the private use of the doctor.

470   Therapy aims at strengthening the conscious mind, and whenever possible I try to rouse the patient to mental activity and get him to subdue the *massa confusa* of his mind with his own understanding,[5] so that he can reach a vantage-point *au-*

---

[4] 2, xiii, p. 264: "Et eorum aquas sua aqua continere, si qua non est aqua, forma ignea verae aquae."

[5] Remembering the rule that every proposition in psychology may be inverted with advantage, I would point out that it is always a bad thing to accentuate the conscious attitude when this has shown itself to be so strong in the first place as to violently suppress the unconscious.

dessus de la mêlée. Nobody who ever had any wits is in danger of losing them in the process, though there are people who never knew till then what their wits are for. In such a situation, understanding acts like a life-saver. It integrates the unconscious, and gradually there comes into being a higher point of view where both conscious and unconscious are represented. It then proves that the invasion by the unconscious was rather like the flooding of the Nile: it increases the fertility of the land. The panegyric addressed by the *Rosarium* to this state is to be taken in that sense: "O natura benedicta et benedicta est tua operatio, quia de imperfecto facis perfectum cum vera putrefactione quae est nigra et obscura. Postea facis germinare novas res et diversas, cum tua viriditate facis diversos colores apparere." (O blessed Nature, blessed are thy works, for that thou makest the imperfect to be perfect through the true putrefaction, which is dark and black. Afterwards thou makest new and multitudinous things to grow, causing with thy verdure the many colours to appear.)[6] It is not immediately apparent why this dark state deserves special praise, since the *nigredo* is universally held to be of a sombre and melancholy humour reminiscent of death and the grave. But the fact that medieval alchemy had connections with the mysticism of the age, or rather was itself a form of mysticism, allows us to adduce as a parallel to the *nigredo* the writings of St. John of the Cross[6a] concerning the "dark night." This author conceives the "spiritual night" of the soul as a supremely positive state, in which the invisible—and therefore dark—radiance of God comes to pierce and purify the soul.

480   The appearance of the colours in the alchemical vessel, the so-called *cauda pavonis,* denotes the spring, the renewal of life—*post tenebras lux.* The text continues: "This blackness is called earth." The Mercurius in whom the sun drowns is an earth-spirit, a *Deus terrenus,*[7] as the alchemists say, or the *Sapientia Dei* which took on body and substance in the creature

---

[6] 2, xiii, p. 265.   [6a] *The Dark Night of the Soul,* 78.

[7] Ventura, 5, ix, p. 260. There is in the gold a "quiddam essentiale Divinum" (something of Divine essence) ("Tractatus Aristotelis," 5, xvi, p. 892). "Natura est vis quaedam insita rebus. . . . Deus est natura et natura Deus, a Deo oritur aliquid proximum ei" (Nature is a certain force innate in things. . . . God is Nature and Nature is God, and from God originates something very near to him).—Penotus, 5, vii, p. 153. God is known in the *linea in se reducta* of the gold (Maier, 112, p. 16).

— by creating it. The unconscious is the spirit of chthonic nature
and contains the archetypal images of the *Sapientia Dei*. But
the intellect of modern civilized man has strayed too far in the
world of consciousness, so that it received a violent shock when
it suddenly beheld the face of its mother, the earth.

481   The fact that the soul is depicted as a homunculus in our
picture indicates that it is on the way to becoming the *filius
regius*, the undivided and hermaphroditic First Man, the Anthropos. Originally he fell into the clutches of Physis, but now
he rises again, freed from the prison of the mortal body. He is
caught up in a kind of ascension, and, according to the *Tabula
smaragdina*, unites himself with the "upper powers." He is the
essence of the "lower power" which, like the "third filiation"
in the doctrine of Basilides, is ever striving upwards from the
depths,[8] not with the intention of staying in heaven, but solely
in order to reappear on earth as a healing force, as an agent of
immortality and perfection, as a mediator and saviour. The connection with the Christian idea of the Second Coming is unmistakable.

482   The psychological interpretation of this process leads into
regions of inner experience which defy our powers of scientific description, however unprejudiced or even ruthless we
may be. At this point, unpalatable as it is to the scientific
temperament, the idea of mystery forces itself upon the mind
of the inquirer, not as a cloak for ignorance but as an admission of his inability to translate what he knows into the
everyday speech of the intellect. I must therefore content myself with a bare mention of the archetype which is inwardly
experienced at this stage, namely the birth of the "divine child"
or—in the language of the mystics—the inner man.[9]

8 Hippolytus, 67, VII, 26, 10.
9 Angelus Silesius, 13, Book IV, p. 194: "The work that God loves best and most
wants done/ Is this: that in you he can bear his son." Book II, p. 103: "There
where God bends on you his spirit mild/ Is born within the everlasting child."

PURIFICATION

*Here falls the heavenly dew, to lave/
The soiled black body in the grave.*

[*Figure 8*]

483   The falling dew is a portent of the divine birth now at hand. *Ros Gedeonis* (Gideon's dew)[1] is a synonym for the *aqua permanens,* hence for Mercurius.[2] A quotation from Senior at this point in the *Rosarium* text says: "But the water I have spoken of is something [*res*] that comes down from heaven, and the earth's humidity absorbs it, and the water of heaven is retained with the water of the earth, and the water of the earth honours that water with its lowliness and its sand, and water consorts with water and water will hold fast to water and Albira is whitened with Astuna." [3]

484   The whitening (*albedo* or *dealbatio*) is likened to the *ortus solis,* the sunrise; it is the light, the illumination, that follows the darkness. Hermes says: "Azoth et ignis latonem abluunt et nigredinem ab eo auferunt" (Azoth and fire cleanse the lato and remove the blackness).[4] The spirit Mercurius descends in his heavenly form as *sapientia* and as the fire of the Holy Ghost, to purify the blackness. Our text continues: "Deal-

---

1 Judges 6:36ff.

2 My "The Spirit Mercurius," 89, pars. 89f. (1948 Swiss edn., pp. 90f.).

3 2, xiii, pp. 275f. Cf. Senior, 164, pp. 17–18: "Dixit iterum Maria: Aqua, quam iam memoravi, est rex de coelo descendens et terra cum humore suo suscepit eum et retinetur aqua coeli cum aqua terrae propter servitium suum et propter arenam suam honorat eam et congregatur aqua in aquam, Alkia in Alkiam et dealbatur Alkia cum Astuam." In the Arabic text "Astua" appears also as "Alkia"; "al-kiyān"="life principle" (Stapleton, 153, p. 152). "Alkia" occurs in the "Liber Platonis quartorum" (5, xiii, p. 152) in the sense of "life principle" or "libido."

4 Azoth is the arcane substance (cf. Senior, 164, p. 95) and the lato is the black substance, a mixture of copper, cadmium, and orichalcum (ἐλατρόν; see Du Cange, 40).

bate latonem et libros rumpite, ne corda vestra rumpantur.[5] Haec est enim compositio omnium Sapientum et etiam tertia pars totius operis.[6] Jungite ergo, ut dicitur in Turba, siccum humido: id est terram nigram cum aqua sua et coquite donec dealbatur. Sic habes aquam et terram per se et terram cum aqua dealbatam: illa albedo dicitur aer." (Whiten the lato and rend the books lest your hearts be rent asunder.[5] For this is the synthesis of the wise and the third part of the whole *opus*.[6] Join therefore, as is said in the Turba,[7] the dry to the moist, the black earth with its water, and cook till it whitens. In this manner you will have the essence of water and earth, having whitened the earth with water: but that whiteness is called air.) So that the reader may know that the "water" is the *aqua sapientiae*, and the dew falling from heaven the divine gift of illumination and wisdom, there follows a long disquisition on wisdom, entitled "Septimum Sapientiae Salomonis": "Solomon has shown men how to use this wisdom as a light, and he set it above all beauty and fortune and said that it had no equal among precious stones. For in comparison with the stone all gold is but sand, and silver but clay. Hence the acquisition of the stone is better than the fruits of purest gold and silver. Its fruits are more precious than all the riches of this world, and everything that seems desirable in this world is not to be compared with it. Long life and health are at its right hand, and at its left hand renown and wealth without end. Its ways are fair and praiseful operations, not to be contemned, and its

---

[5] *Rosarium*, 2, xiii, p. 277. This oft-repeated quotation is to be found in the treatise of Morienus (2, xii, pp. 7ff.), which appears to have been translated from the Arabic by Robert of Chartres in the 12th century. Morienus attributes it to the obsolete author Elbo Interfector. It must be of very early origin, but hardly earlier than the 8th century.

[6] Reference to the *Tabula smaragdina*: "Itaque vocatus sum Hermes Trismegistus habens tres partes philosophiae totius mundi" (Therefore I am called Hermes Trismegistus, having the three parts of the philosophy of the whole world).

[7] A classic of Arabic origin, put into Latin between the 11th and 12th centuries. The *Turba* quotation in the *Rosarium* comes from Zosimos, 2, iv, pp. 284f. Ruska, 150, p. 158, has only: "Siccum igitur humido miscete, quae sunt terra et aqua; ac igne et aere coquite, unde spiritus et anima desiccantur" (Therefore mix the dry with the moist, which are earth and water, and cook them with fire and air, whence spirit and soul are dried out).

PHILOSOPHORVM

ABLVTIO VEL
Mundificatio

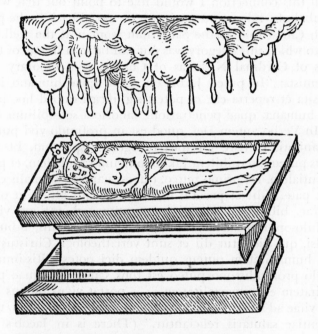

Hie felt der Tauw von Himmel herab/
Vnnd wascht den schwarßen leyb im grab ab·

K iij

Figure 8

paths are measured and not hurried,[8] but are joined with the steadfastness of persevering labour. A tree of life is this [*Sapientia* or *Scientia Dei*] for all them that grasp it, and an unfailing light. Blessed are those that have understood it, for God's wisdom shall never pass away, as Alfidius testifies when he says: Whoever has found this wisdom, for him it will be his rightful and eternal food." [9]

485   In this connection I would like to point out that water as a symbol of wisdom and spirit can be traced back to the parable which Christ told to the Samaritan woman at the well.[10] The uses to which this allegory was put can be seen in one of the sermons of Cardinal Nicholas of Cusa, a contemporary of our alchemists: "In puteo Jacob est aqua, quae humano ingenio quaesita et reperta est, et potest significari quoad hoc philosophia humana, quae penetratione laboriosa sensibilium quaeritur. In Verbo autem Dei, quod est in profundo vivi putei, scl. humanitatis Christi, est fons refrigerans spiritum. Et ita notemus puteum sensibilem Jakob, puteum rationalem, et puteum sapientialem. De primo puteo, qui est naturae animalis et altus, bibit pater, filii et pecora; de secundo, qui altior in orizonte naturae, bibunt filii hominum tantum, scl. ratione vigentes, et philosophi vocantur; de tertio, qui altissimus, bibunt filii excelsi, qui dicuntur dii et sunt veri theologi. Christus secundum humanitatem puteus quidem dici potest altissimus. . . . In illo profundissimo puteo est fons sapientiae, quae praestat felicitatem et immortalitatem . . . portat vivus puteus fontem suae vitae ad sitientes, vocat sitientes ad aquas salutares, ut aqua sapientiae salutaris reficiantur." (There is in Jacob's well a water which human ingenuity has sought and found. Philosophy is its name, and it is found through laborious investigation

---

[8] A reference to the saying of Morienus (**2, xii,** p. 21): ". . . omnis festinatio [scil. festinantia] ex parte Diaboli est" (. . . all haste is of the devil). Hence the *Rosarium* says (p. 352): "Ergo qui patientiam non habet ab opere manum suspendat, quia impedit eum ob festinantiam credulitas" (Therefore, he who has not patience, let him keep his hands from the work, for rash credulity hinders him because of his haste).

[9] *Rosarium*, **2, xiii,** p. 277. Cf. "Aurora consurgens," I, 12, Ch. I.

[10] John 4:13-14: ". . . Whosoever drinketh of this water shall thirst again: But whosoever drinketh of the water that I shall give him shall never thirst; but the water that I shall give him shall be in him a well of water springing up into everlasting life."

of the world of the senses. But in the Word of God, which dwells in the depths of the living well of Christ's humanity, there is a fountain for the refreshment of the spirit. Here, then, we have Jacob's well of the senses, the well of reason and the well of wisdom. From the first well, which is of animal nature and deep, the father drinks, together with his children and cattle; from the second, which is yet deeper and on the very margin of nature, there drink only the children of men, namely those whose reason has awakened and whom we call philosophers; from the third, the deepest of all, drink the sons of the All-Highest, whom we call gods and true theologians. Christ in his humanity may be called the deepest well. . . . In this deepest well is the source which brings wisdom, bliss, and immortality. . . . The living well bears the source of its own life, it calls the thirsty to the waters of salvation that they may be quickened with the water of healing wisdom.) Another passage in the same sermon says: "Whosoever drinks the spirit, drinks of a bubbling spring." Finally, Cusanus says: "Adhuc nota, quod intellectus nobis datus est cum virtute seminis intellectualis: unde in se habet principium fontale, mediante quo in seipso generat aquam intelligentiae, et fons ille non potest nisi aquam suae naturae producere, scl. humanae intelligentiae, sicut intellectus principii, 'quodlibet est vel non est' producit aquas metaphysicales, ex quibus alia flumina scientiarum emanant indesinenter." (Mark well, our reason is given to us with the power of a spiritual seed; wherefore it contains a welling principle through which it generates in itself the water of understanding. And this well can yield naught but water of a like nature, namely, the water of human understanding; just as the understanding of the principle 'each thing is or is not' yields the metaphysical water from which all the other streams of science flow without cease.) [11]

486   After all this there can be no more doubt that the black darkness is washed away by the *aqua sapientiae* of "our science," namely the God-given gift of the royal art and the knowledge it bestows. The *mundificatio* (purification) means, as we have seen, the removal of the superfluities that always cling to merely natural products, and especially to the symbolic unconscious contents which the alchemist found projected into matter. He

[11] See Koch, 100, pp. 124, 132, 134.

therefore acted on Cardan's rule that the object of the work of interpretation is to reduce the dream material to its lowest common denominator.[12] This is what the laboratory worker called the *extractio animae,* and what in the psychological field we would call the working out of the idea contained in the dream. We all know that this requires a necessary premise or hypothesis, a certain intellectual structure by means of which "apperceptions" can be made. In the case of the alchemist, such a premise was ready to hand in the *aqua (doctrinae),* or the God-inspired *sapientia* which he could also acquire through a diligent study of the "books," the alchemical classics. Hence the reference to the books; but, at this stage of the work, they must be destroyed or avoided "lest your hearts be rent asunder." This singular exhortation, altogether inexplicable from the "chemical" point of view, has a profound significance here. The absolvent water or *aqua sapientiae* had been established in the teachings and sayings of the masters as the *donum Spiritus Sancti* which enables the philosopher to understand the *miracula operis.* Therefore he might easily be tempted to assume that philosophical knowledge is the highest good, as the above quotation shows. The psychological equivalent of this situation is when people imagine that they have reached the goal of the work once the unconscious contents have been made conscious and theoretically appreciated. In both cases this would be arbitrarily to define "spirit" as a mere matter of thinking and intuition. Both disciplines, it is true, are aiming at a "spiritual" goal: the alchemist undertakes to produce a new, volatile (hence aerial or "spiritual") essence endowed with *corpus, anima, et spiritus,* where *corpus* is naturally understood as a "subtle" body or "breath body"; the analyst tries to bring about a certain attitude or frame of mind, a certain "spirit" therefore. But because the body, even when conceived as the *corpus glorificationis,* is grosser than *anima* and *spiritus,* a "remnant of earth" necessarily clings to it, albeit a very subtle one.[13] Hence an at-

[12] Cardan, 32: "Unumquodque somnium ad sua generalia deducendum est" (Every dream must be reduced to its common denominator).
[13] ". . . subtilietur lapis, donec in ultimam subtilitatis puritatem deveniat et ultimo volatilis fiat" (The stone should be refined until it reaches the ultimate purity of refinement and becomes, in the end, volatile).—*Rosarium,* 2, xiii, p. 351. Or again (ibid., p. 285): "Sublimatio est duplex: Prima est remotio superfluitatis, ut remaneant partes purissimae a faecibus elementaribus segregatae sicque virtutem

titude that seeks to do justice to the unconscious as well as to one's fellow human beings cannot possibly rest on knowledge alone, in so far as this consists merely of intellect and intuition. It would lack the function that perceives values, i.e., feeling, as well as the *fonction du réel*, i.e., sensation, the sensible perception of reality.[14]

487   Thus if books and the knowledge they impart are given exclusive value, man's emotional and affective life is bound to suffer. That is why the purely intellectual attitude must be abandoned. "Gideon's dew" is a sign of divine intervention, it is the moisture that heralds the return of the soul.

488   The alchemists seem to have perceived the danger that the work and its realization may get stuck in one of the conscious functions. Consequently they stress the importance of *theoria,* i.e., intellectual understanding as opposed to the *practica,* which consisted merely of chemical experiments. We might say that the *practica* corresponds to pure perception, and that this must be supplemented by apperception. But this second stage still does not bring complete realization. What is still lacking is heart or feeling, which imparts an abiding value to anything we have understood. The books must therefore be "destroyed" lest thinking impair feeling and thus hinder the return of the soul.

489   These difficulties are familiar ground to the psychotherapist. It often happens that the patient is quite satisfied with merely registering a dream or fantasy, especially if he has pretensions to aestheticism. He will then fight against even intellectual understanding because it seems an affront to the reality of his psychic life. Others try to understand with their brains only, and want to skip the purely practical stage. And when they have understood, they think they have done their full share of realization. That they should also have a *feeling-relationship* to the contents of the unconscious seems strange to them or

---

quintae essentiae possideant. Et haec sublimatio est corporum in spiritum reductio cum scilicet corporalis densitas transit in spiritus subtilitatem." (Sublimation is twofold: The first is the removal of the superfluous so that the purest parts shall remain, free from elementary dregs, and shall possess the quality of the quintessence. The other sublimation is the reduction of the bodies to spirit, i.e., when the corporeal density is transformed into spiritual thinness.)

14 Cf. my *Psychological Types,* 84, part ii, defs. 13, 20, 22, 36.

even ridiculous. Intellectual understanding and aestheticism both produce the deceptive, treacherous sense of freedom and superiority which is liable to collapse if feeling intervenes. Feeling always binds one to the reality and meaning of symbolic contents, and these in turn impose binding standards of ethical behaviour from which aestheticism and intellectualism are only too ready to emancipate themselves.

490   Owing to the almost complete lack of psychological differentiation in the age of alchemy, it is hardly surprising that such considerations as these are only hinted at in the treatises. But hints do exist, as we have seen. Since then the differentiation of the functions has increased apace, with the result that they have become more and more segregated from one another. Consequently it is very easy for the modern mind to get stuck in one or other of the functions and to achieve only an incomplete realization. It is hardly necessary to add that in time this leads to a neurotic dissociation. To this we owe the further differentiation of the individual functions as well as the discovery of the unconscious, but at the price of psychological disturbance. Incomplete realization explains much that is baffling both in the individual and in the contemporary scene. It is the crux of the matter for the psychotherapist, particularly for those who still believe that intellectual insight and routine understanding, or even mere recollection, are enough to effect a cure. The alchemists thought that the *opus* demanded not only laboratory work, the reading of books, meditation, and patience, but also love.

491   Nowadays we would speak of "feeling-values" and of realization through feeling. One is often reminded of Faust's shattering experience when he was shaken out of the "deadly dull rut" of his laboratory and philosophical work by the revelation that "feeling is all." In this we can already see the modern man who has got to the stage of building his world on a single function and is not a little proud of his achievement. The medieval philosophers would certainly never have succumbed to the idea that the demands of feeling had opened up a new world. The pernicious and pathological slogan *l'art pour l'art* would have struck them as absurd, for when they contemplated the mysteries of nature, sensation, creation, thinking, cognition and feeling were all one to them. Their state of mind was not

yet split up into so many different functions that each stage of the realization process would have needed a new chapter of life. The story of Faust shows how unnatural our condition is: it required the intervention of the devil—in anticipation of Stein-ach—to transform the ageing alchemist into a young gallant and make him forget himself for the sake of the all-too-youthful feelings he had just discovered! That is precisely the risk modern man runs: he may wake up one day to find that he has missed half his life.

492   Nor is realization through feeling the final stage. Although it does not really belong to this chapter, yet it might not be out of place to mention the fourth stage after the three already discussed, particularly since it has such a very pronounced symbolism in alchemy. This fourth stage is the anticipation of the *lapis*. The imaginative activity of the fourth function—intuition, without which no realization is complete—is plainly evident in this anticipation of a possibility whose fulfilment could never be the object of empirical experience at all: already in Greek alchemy it was called λίθος οὐ λίθος "the stone that is no stone." Intuition gives outlook and insight; it revels in the garden of magical possibilities as if they were real. Nothing is more charged with intuitions than the *lapis philosophorum*. This keystone rounds off the work into an experience of the totality of the individual. Such an experience is completely foreign to our age, although no previous age has ever needed wholeness so much. It is abundantly clear that this is the prime problem confronting the art of psychic healing in our day, as a consequence of which we are now trying to loosen up our rigid *psychologie à compartiments* by putting in a few communicating doors.

493   After the ascent of the soul, with the body left behind in the darkness of death, there now comes an enantiodromia: the *nigredo* gives way to the *albedo*. The black or unconscious state that resulted from the union of opposites reaches the nadir and a change sets in. The falling dew signals resuscitation and a new light: the ever deeper descent into the unconscious suddenly becomes illumination from above. For, when the soul vanished at death, it was not lost; in that other world it formed the living counterpole to the state of death in this world. Its reappearance from above is already indicated by the dewy mois-

ture. This dewiness partakes of the nature of the psyche, for ψυχή is cognate with ψυχρός (cold) and ψυχόω (to freshen and animate), while on the other hand dew is synonymous with the *aqua permanens,* the *aqua sapientiae,* which in turn signifies illumination through the realization of meaning. The preceding union of opposites has brought light, as always, out of the darkness of night, and by this light it will be possible to see what the real meaning of that union was.

9

THE RETURN OF THE SOUL

Here is the soul descending from on high/
To quick the corpse we strove to purify.

[Figure 9]

494   Here the reconciler, the soul, dives down from heaven to breathe life into the dead body. The two birds at the bottom left of the picture represent the allegorical winged and wingless dragons in the form of fledged and unfledged birds.[1] This is one of the many synonyms for the double nature of Mercurius, who is both a chthonic and a pneumatic being. The presence of this divided pair of opposites means that although the hermaphrodite appears to be united and is on the point of coming alive, the conflict between them is by no means finally resolved and has not yet disappeared: it is relegated to the "left" and to the "bottom" of the picture, i.e., banished to the sphere of the unconscious. The fact that these still unintegrated opposites are represented theriomorphically (and not anthropomorphically as before) bears out this supposition.

495   The text of the *Rosarium* continues with a quotation from Morienus: "Despise not the ashes, for they are the diadem of thy heart." These ashes, the inert product of incineration, refer to the dead body, and the admonition establishes a curious

---

1 Cf. Lambspringk's Symbols, **4, iii,** p. 355, with the verses:

"Nidus in sylva reperitur   (A nest is found in the forest
In quo Hermes suos pullos habet,   In which Hermes has his birds.
Unus semper conatur volatum,   One always tries to fly away,
Alter in nido manere gaudet,   The other rejoices in the nest to stay
Et alter alterum non dimittit."   And will not let the other go.)

This image comes from Senior, **164,** p. 15: "Abscissae sunt ab eo alae et pennae et est manens, non recedens ad superiora" (Its wings are cut off and its feathers, and it is stationary, not returning to the heights). Likewise Stolcius de Stolcenberg, **155,** Fig. XXXIII. In Maier, *De circulo,* **113,** p. 127, the opposites are represented as "vultur in cacumine montis et corvus sine alis" (a vulture on the peak of the mountain and a raven without wings). Cf. **1, i,** pp. 11–12, and **2, iv,** p. 316.

connection between body and heart which at that time was regarded as the real seat of the soul.[2] The "diadem" refers of course to the supreme kingly ornament. Coronation plays some part in alchemy—the *Rosarium philosophorum,* for instance, has a picture [3] of the *Coronatio Mariae,* signifying the glorification of the white, moonlike (purified) body. The text then quotes Senior as follows: "De Tinctura alba: Si parentes dilecti mei de vita gustaverint et lacte mero lactati fuerint et meo albo inebriati fuerint et in lectulo meo nupserint, generabunt filium Lunae, qui totam parentelam suam praevalebit. Et si dilectus meus de tumulo rubeo petrae potaverit et fontem matris suae gustaverit et inde copulatus fuerit et vino meo rubeo et mecum inebriatus fuerit et in lecto [meo] mihi amicabiliter concubuerit, et in amore meo sperma suum cellulam meam subintraverit, concipiam et ero praegnans et tempore meo pariam filium potentissimum, dominantem et regnantem prae cunctis regibus et principibus terrae, coronatum aurea corona victoriae, ad omnia a Deo altissimo, qui vivit et regnat in seculorum secula" (Concerning the white tincture: When my beloved parents have tasted of life, have been nourished with pure milk and become drunk with my white substance, and have embraced each other in my bed, they shall bring forth the son of the moon, who will excel all his kindred. And when my beloved has drunk from the red rock sepulchre and tasted the maternal fount in matrimony, and has drunk with me of my red wine and lain with me in my bed in friendship, then I, loving him and receiving his seed into my cell, shall conceive and become pregnant and when my time is come shall bring forth a most mighty son, who shall rule over and govern all the kings and princes of the earth, crowned with the golden crown of victory by the supreme God who liveth and reigneth for ever more).[4]

496   The coronation picture that illustrates this text [5] proves that the resuscitation of the purified corpse is at the same time a glorification, since the process is likened to the crowning of

---

[2] Cf. my "Paracelsus as a Spiritual Phenomenon," 83, par. 238 (or 1942 Swiss edn., p. 138).   [3] *Psychology and Alchemy,* 85, fig. 235.

[4] 2, xiii, p. 377. Cf. "Consilium coniugii," 1, ii, p. 129, and Zosimos, 2, iv, pp. 291ff.
[5] The style of the pictures derives from the 16th century, but the text may be a century older. Ruska (*Tabula,* 149, p. 193) relegates the text to the 14th century. The later dating, 15th century (Ruska, *Turba,* 150, p. 342), is probably the more accurate.

PHILOSOPHORVM

ANIMÆ IVBILATIO SEV
Ortus seu Sublimatio.

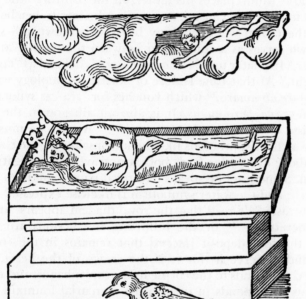

hie schwingt sich die sele hernidder/
Vnd erquickt den gereinigten leychnam wider-

L iij

Figure 9

the Virgin.[6] The allegorical language of the Church supports such a comparison. The connections of the Mother of God with the moon,[7] water, and fountains are so well known that I need not substantiate them further. But whereas it is the Virgin who is crowned here, in the Senior text it is the son who receives the "crown of victory"—which is quite in order since he is the *filius regius* who replaces his father. In the "Aurora" the crown is given to the *regina austri*, Sapientia, who says to her beloved: "I am the crown wherewith my beloved is crowned," so that the crown serves as a connection between the mother and her son-lover.[8] In a later text [9] the *aqua amara* is defined as "crowned with light." At that time Isidore of Seville's etymology was still valid: *mare ab amaro*,[10] which vouches for "sea" as synonymous with the *aqua permanens*. It is also an allusion to the water symbolism of Mary (πηγή, "fountain").[11] Always we must note that the alchemist proceeds like the unconscious in the choice of his symbols: every idea finds both a positive and a negative expression. Sometimes he speaks of a royal pair, sometimes of dog and bitch; and the water symbolism is likewise expressed in violent contrasts. We read that the royal diadem appears "in menstruo meretricis," [12] or the following instructions are given: "Take the foul deposit [*fecem*] that remains in the cooking-vessel and preserve it, for it is the crown of the heart." The deposit corresponds to the corpse in the sarcophagus, and the sarcophagus corresponds in turn to the mercurial fountain or the *vas hermeticum*.

---

6 See *Psychology and Alchemy*, **85**, par. 499.   7 See ibid., fig. 220.

8 Vulgate, Cant. 3:11: ". . . videte . . . regem Salomonem in diademate, quo coronavit illum mater sua in die desponsationis illius," etc. (D.V.: . . . see king Solomon in the diadem, wherewith his mother crowned him in the day of his espousals . . .). Gregory the Great comments that the mother is Mary "quae coronavit eum diademate, quia humanitatem nostram ex ea ipsa assumpsit. . . . Et hoc in die desponsationis eius . . . factum esse dicitur: quia quando unigenitus filius Dei divinitatem suam humanitati nostrae copulare voluit, quando. . . . Ecclesiam sponsam suam sibi assumere placuit: tunc . . . carnem nostram ex matre Virgine suscipere voluit" (who crowned him with the crown because he assumed our human nature from her. . . . And that is said to have been done on the day of his espousals: Since, when the only-begotten son of God wished to join His divinity with our human nature, He decided to take unto Himself, as His bride, the Church. Then it was that He wished to assume our flesh out of His virgin mother).—St. Gregory, "Cantica," 59, Ch. III.   9 "Gloria mundi," **4**, ii, p. 213.   10 74, XIII, 14.

11 *Psychology and Alchemy*, **85**, par. 92.   12 Philalethes, **4**, iv, p. 654.

497   The soul descending from heaven is identical with the
dew, the *aqua divina,* which, as the *Rosarium,* quoting Hermes,
explains, is "Rex de coelo descendens." [13] Hence this water is
itself crowned and forms the "diadem of the heart," [14] in apparent contradiction to the earlier statement that the ashes were
the diadem. It is difficult to tell whether the alchemists were
so hopelessly muddled that they did not notice these flat contradictions, or whether their paradoxes were sublimely deliberate. I suspect it was a bit of both, since the *ignorantes, stulti,
fatui* would take the texts at their face value and get bogged in
the welter of analogies, while the more astute reader, realizing
the necessity for symbolism, would handle it like a virtuoso with
no trouble at all. Intellectual responsibility seems always to
have been the alchemists' weak spot, though a few of them tell
us plainly enough how we are to regard their peculiar language.[15] The less respect they showed for the bowed shoulders

[13] This appears as a quotation from Maria, not Hermes, in Senior, 164, p. 17.
[14] It is just possible that the idea of the *diadema* is connected with the cabalistic
Kether (corona). The *Diadema purpureum* is *Malchuth,* "the female," "the
bride." Purple relates to the *vestimentum,* an attribute of the Shekhina (the Divine Presence), which "enim est Vestis et Palatium Modi Tiphereth, non enim
potest fieri mentio Nominis Tetragrammati nisi in Palatio eius, quod est Adonai.
Appellaturque nomine *Diadematis,* quia est Corona in capite mariti sui" (. . . is
the Garment and the Palace of the Modus Tiph'ereth [Glory], for no mention
can be made of the Four-Letter Name which is Adonai, except in His Palace.
And it is called by the name of Diademe because it is the crown on the head of
the husband).—*Kabbala denudata,* 93, I, p. 131. ". . . Malchuth vocatur Kether
nempe corona legis," etc. (Malchuth is called Kether since it is the crown of the
Law). "Sephirah decima vocatur Corona: quia est mundus Dilectionum, quae
omnia circumdant," etc. (The tenth Sephira [number] is called the crown, because it
is the world of delights which surround all things).—Ibid., p. 487. "[Corona] sicut
vocatur Malchuth, quando ascendit usque ad Kether; ibi enim existens est Corona
super caput mariti sui" [The Crown] is called Malchuth when it ascends up to
Kether; for there is the crown upon the head of the husband).—Ibid., p. 624.
[15] Norton's "Ordinall" (6, i, p. 40) says:
     "For greatly doubted evermore all suche,
     That of this Scyence they may write too muche:
     Every each of them tought but one pointe or twayne,
     Whereby his fellowes were made certayne:
     How that he was to them a Brother,
     For every of them understoode each other;
     Alsoe they wrote not every man to teache,
     But to shew themselves by a secret speache: *[continued]*

of the sweating reader, the greater was their obligation, willing or unwilling, to the unconscious, for the infinite variety of their

Trust not therefore to reading of one Boke,
But in many Auctors works ye may looke;
Liber librum apperit saith Arnolde the great Clerke."

"The Book of Krates" (Berthelot, 29, III, p. 52) says: "Tes intentions sont excellentes, mais ton âme ne se résoudra jamais à divulguer la vérité, à cause des diversités des opinions et des misères de l'orgueil." Hoghelande (5, i, p. 155) says: "At haec [scientia] . . . tradit opus suum immiscendo falsa veris et vera falsis, nunc diminute nimium, nunc superabundanter, et sine ordine, et saepius praepostero ordine, et nititur obscure tradere et occultare quantum potest" (This [science] transmits its work by mixing the false with the true and the true with the false, sometimes very briefly, at other times in a most prolix manner, without order and quite often in the reverse order; and it endeavours to transmit [the work] obscurely, and to hide it as much as possible). Senior (164, p. 55) says: "Verum dixerunt per omnia, Homines vero non intelligunt verba eorum . . . unde falsificant veridicos, et verificant falsificos opinionibus suis. . . . Error enim eorum est ex ignorantia intentionis eorum, quando audiunt diversa verba, sed ignota intellectui eorum, cum sint in intellectu occulto." (They told the truth by means of all things, but men do not understand their words . . . whence through their assumptions they falsify the verities and verify the falsities. . . . The error springs from ignorance of their [the writers'] meaning, when they hear divers words unknown to their understanding, since these have a hidden meaning.) Of the secret hidden in the words of the wise, Senior says: "Est enim illud interius subtiliter perspicientis et cognoscentis" (For this belongs to him who subtly perceives and is cognizant of the inner meaning). The *Rosarium* (2, xiii, p. 230) explains: "Ergo non dixi omnia apparentia et necessaria in hoc opere, quia sunt aliqua quae non licet homini loqui" (So I did not declare all that appears and is necessary in this work, because there are things which one must not tell to a human being). Again (p. 274): "Talis materia debet tradi mystice, sicut poësis fabulose et parabolice" (Such matters must be transmitted in mystical terms, like poetry employing fables and parables). Khunrath (*Chaos*, 97, p. 21) mentions the saying: "Arcana publicata vilescunt" (secrets that are published become cheap)—words which Andreae used as a motto for his *Chymical Wedding*. Abu'l Qāsim Muhammad ibn Ahmad al-Simawi, known as al-Iraqi, says in his "Book of the Seven Climes" (see 69, p. 410) regarding Jābir ibn Hayyān's method of instruction: "Then he spoke enigmatically concerning the composition of the External and the Internal. . . . Then he spoke darkly . . . that in the External there is no complete tincture and that the complete tincture is to be found only in the Internal. Then he spoke darkly . . . saying, Verily we have made the External nothing more than a veil over the Internal . . . that the Internal is like this and like that and he did not cease from this kind of behaviour until he had completely confused all except the most quick-witted of his pupils. . . ." Wei Po-yang (*c*. 142 B.C.) says: "It would be a great sin on my part not to transmit the Tao which would otherwise be lost to the world forever. I shall not write on silk lest the divine secret be unwittingly spread abroad. In hesitation I sigh . . ." (162, p. 243).

images and paradoxes points to a psychological fact of prime importance, namely the indefiniteness of the archetype with its multitude of meanings, all presenting different facets of a single, simple truth. The alchemists were so steeped in their inner experiences that their sole concern was to devise fitting images and expressions regardless of whether these were intelligible or not. Although in this respect they remained behind the times, they nevertheless performed the inestimable service of having constructed a phenomenology of the unconscious long before the advent of psychology. We, as heirs to these riches, do not find our heritage at all easy to enjoy. Yet we can comfort ourselves with the reflection that the old masters were equally at a loss to understand one another, or that they did so only with difficulty. Thus the author of the *Rosarium* says that the "antiqui Philosophi tam obscure quam confuse scripserunt," so that they only baffled the reader or put him off altogether. For his part, he says, he would make the "experimentum verissimum" plain for all eyes to see and reveal it "in the most certain and human manner"—and then proceeds to write exactly like all the others before him. This was inevitable, as the alchemists did not really know what they were writing about. Whether we know today seems to me not altogether sure. At any rate we no longer believe that the secret lies in chemical substances, but that it is rather to be found in one of the darker and deeper layers of the psyche, although we do not know the nature of this layer. Perhaps in another century or so we shall discover a new darkness from which there will emerge something we do not understand, but whose presence we sense with the utmost certainty.

498 The alchemist saw no contradiction in comparing the diadem with a "foul deposit" and then, in the next breath, saying that it is of heavenly origin. He follows the rule laid down in the "Tabula smaragdina": "Quod est inferius, est sicut quod est superius. Et quod est superius, est sicut quod est inferius." [16] His faculty for conscious discrimination was not as acute as modern man's, and was distinctly blunter than the scholastic thought of his contemporaries. This apparent regression cannot be explained by any mental backwardness on the part of the alchemist; it is more the case that his main in-

16 The parallel to this is the paradoxical relation of Malchuth to Kether, the lowest to the highest (see note 14 above).

terest was focussed on the unconscious itself and not at all on the powers of discrimination and formulation which mark the concise conceptual thinking of the schoolmen. He is content if he succeeds in finding expressions to delineate afresh the secret he feels. How these expressions relate to and differ from one another is of the smallest account to him, for he never supposes that anybody could reconstruct the art from his ideas about it, but that those who approach the art at all are already fascinated by its secret and are guided by sure intuition, or are actually elected and dedicated thereto by God. Thus the *Rosarium* says, quoting Hortulanus: [17] "Solus ille, qui scit facere lapidem Philosophorum, intelligit verba eorum de lapide" (Only he who knows how to make the philosophers' stone can understand their words concerning it) (p. 270). The darkness of the symbolism scatters before the eyes of the enlightened philosopher. Hortulanus says again: "Nihil enim prodest occultatio philosophorum in sermonibus, ubi doctrina Spiritus sancti operatur" [18] (The mystification in the sayings of the philosophers is of no avail where the word of the Holy Ghost is at work).

499   The alchemist's failure to distinguish between *corpus* and *spiritus* is here assisted by the assumption that, owing to the preceding *mortificatio* and *sublimatio,* the body has taken on "quintessential" or spiritual form and consequently, as a *corpus mundum* (pure substance), is not so very different from spirit. It may shelter spirit or even draw it down to itself.[19] All these ideas lead one to conclude that not only the *coniunctio* but the reanimation of the "body" is an altogether transmundane event, a process occurring in the psychic non-ego. This would explain why the process is so easily projected,

[17] He is thought to be identical with Joannes de Garlandia, who lived in the second half of the 12th century and wrote the "Commentariolus in Tabulam smaragdinam," 70.

[18] Ibid., p. 365. Since the alchemists were, as "philosophers," the empiricists of the psyche, their terminology is of secondary importance compared with their experience, as is the case with empiricism generally. The discoverer is seldom a good classifier.

[19] Thus Dorn (5, iii, p. 409) says: "Spagirica foetura terrestris caelicam naturam induat per ascensum, et deinceps suo descensu centri naturam terreni recipiat" (The terrestrial spagiric offspring shall assume heavenly nature through ascent, and in turn by its descent shall assume the nature of the centre of the earth).

for if it were of a personal nature its liability to projection would be considerably reduced, because it could then be made conscious without too much difficulty. At any rate this liability would not have been sufficient to cause a projection upon inanimate matter, which is the polar opposite of the living psyche. Experience shows that the carrier of the projection is not just *any* object but is always one that proves adequate to the nature of the content projected—that is to say, it must offer the content a "hook" to hang on.[20]

500   Although the process is essentially transcendental, the projection brings it down to reality by violently affecting the conscious and personal psyche. The result is an inflation, and it then becomes clear that the *coniunctio* is a *hieros gamos* of the gods and not a mere love-affair between mortals. This is very subtly suggested in the *Chymical Wedding*, where Rosencreutz, the hero of the drama, is only a guest at the feast and, though forbidden to do so, slips into the bedchamber of Venus in order to gaze admiringly on the naked beauty of the sleeper. As a punishment for this intrusion Cupid wounds him in the hand with an arrow.[21] His own personal, secret connection with the royal marriage is only fleetingly indicated right at the end: the king, alluding to Rosencreutz, says that he (Rosencreutz) was his father.[22] Andreae, the author, must have been a man of some wit, since at this point he tries to extricate himself from the affair with a jest. He gives a clear hint that he himself is the father of his characters and gets the king to confirm this. The voluntarily proffered information about the paternity of this "child" is the familiar attempt of a creative artist to bolster up the prestige of his ego against the suspicion that he is the victim of the creative urge welling out of the unconscious. Goethe could not shake off the grip of Faust—his "main business"—half so easily. (Lesser men have correspondingly more need of greatness, hence they must make others think more highly of them.) Andreae was as fascinated by the secret of the art as any alchemist; the serious attempt he made to found the

[20] This explains why the projection usually has some influence on the carrier, which is why the alchemists in their turn expected the "projection" of the stone to bring about a transmutation of base metals.
[21] The alchemists regarded the arrow as the *telum passionis* of Mercurius.
[22] Rosencreutz, 145.

Rosicrucian Order is proof of this, and it was largely for reasons of expediency, owing to his position as a cleric, that he was led to adopt a more distant attitude in later years.[23]

501   If there is such a thing as an unconscious that is not personal—i.e., does not consist of individually acquired contents, whether forgotten, subliminally perceived, or repressed—then there must also be processes going on in this non-ego, spontaneous archetypal events which the conscious mind can only perceive when they are projected. They are immemorially strange and unknown, and yet we seem to have known them from everlasting; they are also the source of a remarkable fascination that dazzles and illuminates at once. They draw us like a magnet and at the same time frighten us; they manifest themselves in fantasies, dreams, hallucinations, and in certain kinds of religious ecstasy.[24] The *coniunctio* is one of these archetypes. The absorptive power of the archetype explains not only the widespread incidence of this theme but also the passionate intensity with which it seizes upon the individual, often in defiance of all reason and understanding. To the *peripeteia* of the *coniunctio* also belong the processes illustrated in the last few pictures. They deal with the after-effects of the fusion of opposites, which have involved the conscious personality in their union. The extreme consequence of this is the dissolution of the ego in the unconscious, a state resembling death. It results from the more or less complete identification of the ego with unconscious factors, or, as we would say, from contamination. This is what the alchemists experienced as *immunditia*, pollution. They saw it as the defilement of something transcendent by the gross and opaque body which had for that reason to undergo sublimation. But the body, psychologically speaking, is the expression of our individual and conscious existence, which, we then feel, is in danger of being swamped or poisoned by the unconscious. We therefore try to separate the ego-consciousness from the unconscious and free it from that perilous embrace. Yet, although the power of the unconscious is feared as something sinister, this feeling is only partially justified by the facts, since we also

---

23 Waite, *Real History of the Rosicrucians*, 160.

24 Intoxicants that induce delirious states can also release these processes, for which purpose datura (Jimson weed) and peyotl are used in primitive rites. See Hastings, *Encyclopedia*, 65, IV, pp. 735f.

know that the unconscious is capable of producing beneficial effects. The kind of effect it will have depends to a large extent on the attitude of the conscious mind.

502   Hence the *mundificatio*—purification—is an attempt to discriminate the mixture, to sort out the *coincidentia oppositorum* that has overwhelmed the individual. The rational man, in order to live in this world, has to make a distinction between "himself" and what we might call the "eternal man." Although he is a unique individual, he also stands for "man" as a species, and thus he has a share in all the movements of the collective unconscious. In other words, the "eternal" truths become dangerously disturbing factors when they suppress the unique ego of the individual and live at his expense. If our psychology is forced, owing to the special nature of its empirical material, to stress the importance of the unconscious, that does not in any way diminish the importance of the conscious mind. It is merely the one-sided over-valuation of the latter that has to be checked by a certain relativization of values. But this relativization should not be carried so far that the ego is completely fascinated and overpowered by the archetypal truths. The ego lives in space and time and must adapt itself to their laws if it is to exist at all. If it is absorbed by the unconscious to such an extent that the latter alone has the power of decision, then the ego is stifled, and there is no longer any medium in which the unconscious could be integrated and in which the work of realization could take place. The separation of the empirical ego from the "eternal" and universal man is therefore of vital importance, particularly today, when mass-degeneration of the personality is making such threatening strides. Mass-degeneration does not come only from without: it also comes from within, from the collective unconscious. Against the outside, some protection was afforded by the *droits de l'homme* which at present are lost to the greater part of Europe,[25] and even where they are not actually lost we see political parties, as naïve as they are powerful, doing their best to abolish them in favour of the slave state, with the bait of social security. Against the daemonism from within, the Church offers some protection so long as it wields authority. But protection and security are

25 As this book was written in 1943, I leave this sentence as it stands, in the hope of a better world to come.

only valuable when not excessively cramping to our existence; and in the same way the superiority of consciousness is desirable only if it does not suppress and shut out too much life. As always, life is a voyage between Scylla and Charybdis.

503   The process of differentiating the ego from the unconscious,[26] then, has its equivalent in the *mundificatio,* and, just as this is the necessary condition for the return of the soul to the body, so the body is necessary if the unconscious is not to have destructive effects on the ego-consciousness, for it is the body that gives bounds to the personality. The unconscious can only be integrated if the ego holds its ground. Consequently, the alchemist's endeavour to unite the *corpus mundum,* the purified body, with the soul is also the endeavour of the psychologist once he has succeeded in freeing the ego-conscious from contamination with the unconscious. In alchemy the purification is the result of numerous distillations; in psychology too it comes from an equally thorough separation of the ordinary ego-personality from all inflationary admixtures of unconscious material. This task entails the most painstaking self-examination and self-education, which can, however, be passed on to others by one who has acquired the discipline himself. The process of psychological differentiation is no light work; it needs the tenacity and patience of the alchemist, who must purify the body from all superfluities in the fiercest heat of the furnace, and pursue Mercurius "from one bride chamber to the next." As alchemical symbolism shows, a radical understanding of this kind is impossible without a human partner. A general and merely academic "insight into one's mistakes" is ineffectual, for then the mistakes are not really seen at all, only the idea of them. But they show up acutely when a human relationship brings them to the fore and when they are noticed by the other person as well as by oneself. Then and then only can they really be felt and their true nature recognized. Similarly, confessions made to one's secret self generally have little or no effect, whereas confessions made to another are much more promising.

504   The "soul" which is reunited with the body is the One born of the two, the vinculum common to both.[27] It is therefore the

26 This process is described in the second of my *Two Essays,* 88.
27 Cf. Pseudo-Aristotle, 2, viii, p. 371.

very essence of relationship. Equally the psychological anima, as representative of the collective unconscious, has a "collective" character. The collective unconscious is a natural and universal datum and its manifestation always causes an unconscious identity, a state of *participation mystique*. If the conscious personality becomes caught up in it and offers no resistance, the relationship is personified by the anima (in dreams, for instance) which then, as a more or less autonomous part of the personality, generally has a disturbing effect. But if, as the result of a long and thorough analysis and the withdrawal of projections, the ego has been successfully separated from the unconscious, the anima will gradually cease to act as an autonomous personality and will become a function of relationship between conscious and unconscious. So long as it is projected it leads to all sorts of illusions about people and things and thus to endless complications. The withdrawal of projections makes the anima what it originally was: an archetypal image which, in its right place, functions to the advantage of the individual. Interposed between the ego and the world, it acts like an ever-changing Shakti, who weaves the veil of Maya and dances the illusion of existence. But, functioning between the ego and the unconscious, the anima becomes the matrix of all the divine and semi-divine figures, from the pagan goddess to the Virgin, from the messenger of the Holy Grail to the saint.[28] The "unconscious" anima is a creature without relationships, an autoerotic being whose one aim is to take total possession of the individual. When this happens to a man he becomes strangely womanish in the worst sense, with a moody and uncontrolled disposition which, in time, has a deleterious effect even on the hitherto reliable functions—e.g., his intellect—and gives rise to the kind of ideas and opinions we rightly find so objectionable in animus-possessed women.[29]

[28] A good example of this is to be found in Angelus Silesius, 13, Book III, no. 238:
"God is made man and now is born—rejoice!
Where then? In me, the mother of his choice.
How should that be? My soul that Virgin Maid,
My heart the manger and my limbs the shed. . . ."
[29] In woman the animus produces very similar illusions, the only difference being that they consist of dogmatic opinions and prejudices which are taken over at random from somebody else and are never the product of her own reflection.

505   Here I must point out that very different rules apply in feminine psychology, since in this case we are not dealing with a function of relationship but, on the contrary, with a *discriminative* function, namely the animus. Alchemy was, as a philosophy, mainly a masculine preoccupation and in consequence of this its formulations are for the most part masculine in character. But we should not overlook the fact that the feminine element in alchemy is not so inconsiderable since, even at the time of its beginnings in Alexandria, we have authentic proof of female philosophers like Theosebeia,[30] the *soror mystica* of Zosimos, and Paphnutia and Maria Prophetissa. From later times we know of the pair of alchemists, Nicolas Flamel and his wife Peronelle. The *Mutus liber* of 1677 gives an account of a man and wife performing the *opus* together,[31] and finally in the nineteenth century we have the pair of English alchemists, Thomas South and his daughter, who later became Mrs. Atwood. After busying themselves for many years with the study of alchemy, they decided to set down their ideas and experiences in book form. To this end they separated, the father working in one part of the house and his daughter in another. She wrote a thick, erudite tome while he versified. She was the first to finish and promptly sent the book to the printer. Scarcely had it appeared when her father was overcome with scruples, fearing lest they had betrayed the great secret. He succeeded in persuading his daughter to withdraw the book and destroy it. In the same spirit, he sacrificed his own poetic labours. Only a few lines are preserved in her book, of which it was too late to withdraw all the copies. A reprint,[32] prepared after her death in 1910, appeared in 1918. I have read the book: no secrets are betrayed. It is a thoroughly medieval production garnished with would-be theosophical explanations as a sop to the syncretism of the new age.

506   A remarkable contribution to the role of feminine psychology in alchemy is furnished by the letter which the English

---

[30] She is the Euthicia of the treatise by Zosimos, **2, iv.**

[1] 119. The *Mutus liber* is reproduced as an appendix to Vol. I of the *Bibliotheca chemica curiosa*, 1702 (**3, iii;** for illustrations from the *Mutus liber,* see figs. 11–13 of the present volume, and *Psychology and Alchemy,* **85,** index). We might mention John Pordage and Jane Leade (17th century) as another pair of alchemists.

[32] *A Suggestive Inquiry into the Hermetic Mystery,* **14.**

theologian and alchemist, John Pordage,[33] wrote to his *soror mystica* Jane Leade. In it [34] he gives her spiritual instruction concerning the *opus:*

507   This sacred furnace, this *Balneum Mariae,* this glass phial, this secret furnace, is the place, the matrix or womb, and the centre from which the divine Tincture flows forth from its source and origin. Of the place or abode where the Tincture has its home and dwelling I need not remind you, nor name its name, but I exhort you only to knock at the foundation. Solomon tells us in his Song that its inner dwelling is not far from the navel, which resembles a round goblet filled with the sacred liquor of the pure Tincture.[35] You know the fire of the philosophers, it was the key they kept concealed. . . . The fire is the love-fire, the life that flows forth from the Divine Venus, or the Love of God; the fire of Mars is too choleric, too sharp, and too fierce, so that it would dry up and burn the *materia:* wherefore the love-fire of Venus alone has the qualities of the right true fire.

508   This true philosophy will teach you how you should know yourself, and if you know yourself rightly, you will also know the pure nature; for the pure nature is in yourself. And when you know the pure nature which is your true selfhood, freed from all wicked, sinful selfishness, then also you will know God, for the Godhead is concealed and wrapped in the pure nature like a kernel in the nutshell. . . . The true philosophy will teach you who is the father and who is the mother of this magical child. . . . The father of this child is Mars, he is the fiery life which proceeds from Mars as the father's quality. His mother is Venus, who is the gentle

33 John Pordage (1607–1681) studied theology and medicine in Oxford. He was a disciple of Jakob Böhme and a follower of his alchemical theosophy. He became an accomplished alchemist and astrologer. One of the chief figures in his mystical philosophy is Sophia. ("She is my divine, eternal, essential self-sufficiency. She is my wheel within my wheel," etc.—Pordage's *Sophia,* 135, p. 21.)

34 The letter is printed in Roth-Scholz, *Deutsches Theatrum chemicum,* 148, I, pp. 557–97. The first German edition of this "Philosophisches Send-Schreiben vom Stein der Weissheit" seems to have been published in Amsterdam in 1698. [The letter was evidently written in English, since the German version in Roth-Scholz, 1728–32, is stated to be "aus dem Englischen übersetzet." But no English edition or MS. can be traced at the British Museum, the Library of Congress, or any of the other important British and American libraries. Pordage's name does not occur among the alumni at Oxford.—EDITORS.]

35 One of the favourite allusions to the Song of Solomon 7:2: "Thy navel is like a round goblet, which wanteth not liquor." Cf. also "Aurora consurgens" I, 19, Ch. XII.

love-fire proceeding from the son's quality. Here then, in the qualities and forms of nature, you see male and female, man and wife,
bride and bridegroom, the first marriage or wedding of Galilee,
which is celebrated between Mars and Venus when they return
from their fallen state. Mars, or the husband, must become a godly
man, otherwise the pure Venus will take him neither into the con-
jugal nor into the sacred marriage bed. Venus must become a pure
virgin, a virginal wife, otherwise the wrathful jealous Mars in his
wrath-fire will not wed with her nor live with her in union; but
instead of agreement and harmony, there will be naught but strife,
jealousy, discord, and enmity among the qualities of nature. . . .

509   Accordingly, if you think to become a learned artist, look with
earnestness to the union of your own Mars and Venus, that the
nuptial knot be rightly tied and the marriage between them well
and truly consummated. You must see to it that they lie together
in the bed of their union and live in sweet harmony; then the virgin Venus will bring forth her pearl, her water-spirit, in you, to
soften the fiery spirit of Mars, and the wrathful fire of Mars will
sink quite willingly, in mildness and love, into the love-fire of
Venus, and thus both qualities, *as fire and water,* will mingle together, agree, and flow into one another; and from their agreement
and union there will proceed the first conception of the magical
birth which we call Tincture, the love-fire Tincture. Now although
the Tincture is conceived in the womb of your humanity and is
awakened to life, yet there is still a great danger, and it is to be
feared that, because it is still in the body or womb, it may yet be
spoiled by neglect before it be brought in due season into the light.
On this account you must look round for a good nurse, who will
watch it in its childhood and will tend it properly: and such must
be your own pure heart and your own virginal will. . . .

510   This child, this tincturing life, must be assayed, proved, and
tried in the qualities of nature; and here again great anxiety and
danger will arise, seeing that it must suffer the damage of temptation in the body and womb, and you may thus lose the birth. For the
delicate Tincture, this tender child of life, must descend into the
forms and qualities of nature, that it may suffer and endure temptation and overcome it; it must needs descend into the Divine Darkness,
into the darkness of Saturn, wherein no light of life is to be seen:
there it must be held captive, and be bound with the chains of
darkness, and must live from the food which the prickly Mercurius
will give it to eat, which to the Divine Tincture of life is naught
but dust and ashes, poison and gall, fire and brimstone. It must
enter into the fierce wrathful Mars, by whom (as happened to
Jonah in the belly of hell) it is swallowed, and must experience the

curse of God's wrath; also it must be tempted by Lucifer and the million devils who dwell in the quality of the wrathful fire. And here the divine artist in this philosophical work will see the first colour, where the Tincture appears in its blackness, and it is the blackest black; the learned philosophers call it their black crow, or their black raven, or again their blessed and blissful black; for in the darkness of this black is hidden the light of lights in the quality of Saturn; and in this poison and gall there is hidden in Mercurius the most precious medicament against the poison, namely the life of life. And the blessed Tincture is hidden in the fury or wrath and curse of Mars.

511   Now it seems to the artist that all his work is lost. What has become of the Tincture? Here is nothing that is apparent, that can be perceived, recognized, or tasted, but darkness, most painful death, a hellish fearful fire, nothing but the wrath and curse of God; yet he does not see that the Tincture of Life is in this putrefaction or dissolution and destruction, that there is light in this darkness, life in this death, love in this fury and wrath, and in this poison the highest and most precious Tincture and medicament against all poison and sickness.

512   The old philosophers named this work or labour their descension, their cineration, their pulverization, their death, their putrefaction of the *materia* of the stone, their corruption, their *caput mortuum*. You must not despise this blackness, or black colour, but persevere in it in patience, in suffering, and in silence, until its forty days of temptation are over, until the days of its tribulations are completed, when the seed of life shall waken to life, shall rise up, sublimate or glorify itself, transform itself into whiteness, purify and sanctify itself, give itself the redness, in other words, transfigure and fix its shape. When the work is brought thus far, it is an easy work: for the learned philosophers have said that the making of the stone is then woman's work and child's play. Therefore, if the human will is given over and left, and becomes patient and still and as a dead nothing, the Tincture will do and effect everything in us and for us, if we can keep our thoughts, movements, and imaginations still, or can leave off and rest. But how difficult, hard, and bitter this work appears to the human will, before it can be brought to this shape, so that it remains still and calm even though all the fire be let loose in its sight, and all manner of temptations assail it!

513   Here, as you see, there is great danger, and the Tincture of life can easily be spoiled and the fruit wasted in the womb, when it is thus surrounded on all sides and assailed by so many devils and so many tempting essences. But if it can withstand and overcome this fiery trial and sore temptation, and win the victory: then you

will see the beginning of its resurrection from hell, death, and the mortal grave, appearing first in the quality of Venus; and then the Tincture of life will itself burst forth mightily from the prison of the dark Saturn, through the hell of the poisonous Mercurius, and through the curse and direful death of God's wrath that burns and flames in Mars, and the gentle love-fire of the Venus quality will gain the upper hand, and the love-fire Tincture will be preferred in the government and have supreme command. And then the gentleness and love-fire of Divine Venus will reign as lord and king in and over all qualities.

514   Nevertheless there is still another danger that the work of the stone may yet miscarry. Therefore the artist must wait until he sees the Tincture covered over with its other colour, as with the whitest white, which he may expect to see after long patience and stillness, and which truly appears when the Tincture rises up in the lunar quality: illustrious Luna imparts a beautiful white to the Tincture, the most perfect white hue and a brilliant splendour. And thus is the darkness transformed into light, and death into life. And this brilliant whiteness awakens joy and hope in the heart of the artist, that the work has gone so well and fallen out so happily. For now the white colour reveals to the enlightened eye of the soul cleanliness, innocence, holiness, simplicity, heavenly-mindedness, and righteousness, and with these the Tincture is henceforth clothed over and over as with a garment. She is radiant as the moon, beautiful as the dawn. Now the divine virginity of the tincturing life shines forth, and no spot or wrinkle nor any other blemish is to be seen.

515   The old masters were wont to call this work their white swan, their albification, or making white, their sublimation, their distillation, their circulation, their purification, their separation, their sanctification, and their resurrection, because the Tincture is made white like a shining silver. It is sublimed or exalted and transfigured by reason of its many descents into Saturn, Mercurius, and Mars, and by its many ascents into Venus and Luna. This is the distillation, the *Balneum Mariae:* because the Tincture is purified in the qualities of nature through the many distillations of the water, blood, and heavenly dew of the Divine Virgin Sophia, and, through the manifold circulation in and out of the forms and qualities of nature, is made white and pure, like brilliantly polished silver. And all uncleanliness of the blackness, all death, hell, curse, wrath, and all poison which rise up out of the qualities of Saturn, Mercury, and Mars are separated and depart, wherefore they call it their separation, and when the Tincture attains its whiteness and brilliance in Venus and Luna they call it their sanctification, their

purification and making white. They call it their resurrection, because the white rises up out of the black, and the divine virginity and purity out of the poison of Mercurius and out of the red fiery rage and wrath of Mars. . . .

516   Now is the stone shaped, the elixir of life prepared, the love-child or the child of love born, the new birth completed, and the work made whole and perfect. Farewell! fall, hell, curse, death, dragon, beast, and serpent! Good night! mortality, fear, sorrow, and misery! For now redemption, salvation, and recovery of everything that was lost will again come to pass within and without, for now you have the great secret and mystery of the whole world; you have the Pearl of Love; you have the unchangeable eternal essence of Divine Joy from which all healing virtue and all multiplying power come, from which there actively proceeds the active power of the Holy Ghost. You have the seed of the woman who has trampled on the head of the serpent. You have the seed of the virgin and the blood of the virgin in one essence and quality.

517   O wonder of wonders! You have the tincturing Tincture, the pearl of the virgin, which has three essences or qualities in one; it has body, soul, and spirit, it has fire, light, and joy, it has the Father's quality, it has the Son's quality, and has also the Holy Ghost's quality, even all these three, in one fixed and eternal essence and being. This is the Son of the Virgin, this is her first-born, this is the noble hero, the trampler of the serpent, and he who casts the dragon under his feet and tramples upon him. . . . For now the Man of Paradise is become clear as a transparent glass, in which the Divine Sun shines through and through, like gold that is wholly bright, pure, and clear, without blemish or spot. The soul is henceforth a most substantial seraphic angel, she can make herself doctor, theologian, astrologer, divine magician, she can make herself whatsoever she will, and do and have whatsoever she will: for all qualities have but one will in agreement and harmony. And this same one will is God's eternal infallible will; and from henceforth the Divine Man is in his own nature become one with God.[36]

518   This hymn-like myth of love, virgin, mother, and child sounds extremely feminine, but in reality it is an archetypal conception sprung from the masculine unconscious, where the Virgin Sophia corresponds to the anima (in the psychological

---

[36] The concluding passages are very reminiscent of the teachings of the "secta liberi spiritus," which were propagated as early as the 13th century by the Béguines and Beghards.

sense).[37] As is shown by the symbolism and by the not very clear distinction between her and the son, she is also the "paradisal" or "divine" being, i.e., the self. The fact that these ideas and figures were still mystical for Pordage and more or less undifferentiated is explained by the emotional nature of the experiences which he himself describes.[38] Experiences of this kind leave little room for critical understanding. They do, however, throw light on the processes hidden behind the alchemical symbolism and pave the way for the discoveries of modern medical psychology. Unfortunately we possess no original treatises that can with any certainty be ascribed to a woman author. Consequently we do not know what kind of alchemical symbolism a woman's view would have produced. Nevertheless, modern medical practice tells us that the feminine unconscious produces a symbolism which, by and large, is compensatory to the masculine. In that case, to use Pordage's terms, the leitmotiv would not be gentle Venus but fiery Mars, not Sophia but Hecate, Demeter, and Persephone, or the matriarchal Kali of southern India in her brighter and darker aspects.[38a]

519   In this connection I would like to draw attention to the curious pictures of the *arbor philosophica* in the fourteenth-century Codex Ashburnham.[39] One picture shows Adam struck by an arrow,[40] and the tree growing out of his genitals; in the other picture the tree grows out of Eve's head. Her right hand covers her genitals, her left points to a skull. Plainly this is a hint that the man's *opus* is concerned with the erotic aspect of the anima, while the woman's is concerned with the animus,

---

[37] Hence Pordage's view is more or less in agreement with woman's conscious psychology, but not with her unconscious psychology.

[38] Pordage, *Sophia,* 135, Ch. I.

[38a] There is a modern work that gives an excellent account of the feminine world of symbols: Esther Harding's *Woman's Mysteries* (64).

[39] 35, i. They are reproduced as figs. 131 and 135 in *Psychology and Alchemy,* 85.

[40] The arrow refers to the *telum passionis* of Mercurius (cf. "Cantilena Riplaei" in 143, p. 423). Cf. also my "Spirit Mercurius," 89, pars. 113f. (Swiss edn., pp. 120f.), and St. Bernard of Clairvaux, 26, XXX, 8: "Est et sagitta sermo Dei vivus et efficax et penetrabilior omni gladio ancipiti. . . . Est etiam sagitta electa amor Christi, quae Mariae animam non modo confixit, sed etiam pertransivit, ut nullam in pectore virginali particulam vacuam amore relinqueret." (God's word is an arrow; it is lively and effective and more penetrating than a double-edged sword. . . . And the love of Christ is a choice arrow too, which not only entered, but transfixed, the soul of Mary, so that it left no particle of her virgin heart free of love.)—Trans. from 27, I, p. 346.

which is a "function of the head." [41] The *prima materia*, i.e., the unconscious, is represented in man by the "unconscious" anima, and in woman by the "unconscious" animus. Out of the *prima materia* grows the philosophical tree, the unfolding *opus*. In their symbolical sense, too, the pictures are in accord with the findings of psychology, since Adam would then stand for the woman's animus who generates "philosophical" ideas with his member (λόγοι σπερματικοί), and Eve for the man's anima who, as Sapientia or Sophia, produces out of her head the intellectual content of the work.

520   Finally, I must point out that a certain concession to feminine psychology is also to be found in the *Rosarium*, in so far as the first series of pictures is followed by a second—less complete, but otherwise analogous—series, at the end of which there appears a masculine figure, the "emperor," and not, as in the first, an "empress," the "daughter of the philosophers." The accentuation of the feminine element in the Rebis (fig. 10) is consistent with a predominantly male psychology, whereas the addition of an "emperor" in the second version is a concession to woman (or possibly to the male consciousness).

521   In its primary "unconscious" form the animus is a compound of spontaneous, unpremeditated opinions which exercise a powerful influence on the woman's emotional life, while the anima is similarly compounded of feelings which thereafter influence or distort the man's understanding ("she has turned his head"). Consequently the animus likes to project itself upon "intellectuals" and all kinds of "heroes," including tenors, artists, sporting celebrities, etc. The anima has a predilection for everything that is unconscious, dark, equivocal, and at a loose end in woman, and also for her vanity, frigidity, helplessness, and so forth. In both cases the incest element plays an important part: there is a relation between the young woman and her father, the older woman and her son, the young man and his mother, the older man and his daughter.

522   It will be clear from all this that the "soul" which accrues to ego-consciousness during the *opus* has a feminine character in the man and a masculine character in the woman. His anima

41 Cf. the Alaskan Eskimo tale "The Woman Who Became a Spider," in Rasmussen, 141, pp. 121ff., and the Siberian tale "The Girl and the Skull," in 44, ii, No. 31, where a woman marries a skull.

wants to reconcile and unite; her animus tries to discern and discriminate. This strict antithesis is depicted in the alchemists' Rebis, the symbol of transcendental unity, as a coincidence of opposites; but in conscious reality—once the conscious mind has been cleansed of unconscious impurities by the preceding *mundificatio*—it represents a conflict even though the conscious relations between the two individuals may be quite harmonious. Even when the conscious mind does not identify itself with the inclinations of the unconscious, it still has to face them and somehow take account of them in order that they may play their part in the life of the individual, however difficult this may be. For if the unconscious is not allowed to express itself through word and deed, through worry and suffering, through our consideration of its claims and resistance to them, then the earlier, divided state will return with all the incalculable consequences which disregard of the unconscious may entail. If, on the other hand, we give in to the unconscious too much, it leads to a positive or negative inflation of the personality. Turn and twist this situation as we may, it always remains an inner and outer conflict: one of the birds is fledged and the other not. We are always in doubt: there is a pro to be rejected and a contra to be accepted. All of us would like to escape from this admittedly uncomfortable situation, but we do so only to discover that what we left behind us was ourselves. To live in perpetual flight from ourselves is a bitter thing, and to live with ourselves demands a number of Christian virtues which we then have to apply to our own case, such as patience, love, faith, hope, and humility. It is all very fine to make our neighbour happy by applying them to him, but the demon of self-admiration so easily claps us on the back and says, "Well done!" And because this is a great psychological truth, it must be stood on its head for an equal number of people so as to give the devil something to carp at. But—does it make *us* happy when we have to apply these virtues to ourselves? when I am the recipient of my own gifts, the least among my brothers whom I must take to my bosom? when I must admit that I need all my patience, my love, my faith, and even my humility, and that I myself am my own devil, the antagonist who always wants the opposite in everything? Can we ever really endure ourselves? "Do unto others . . ."—this is as true of evil as of good.

523   In John Gower's *Confessio amantis* (57) there is a saying
which I have used as a motto to the Introduction of this book:
"Bellica pax, vulnus dulce, suave malum" (a warring peace, a
sweet wound, an agreeable evil).[42] Into these words the old alchemist put the quintessence of his experience. I can add nothing to their incomparable simplicity and conciseness. They contain all that the ego can reasonably demand of the *opus,* and
illuminate for it the paradoxical darkness of human life. Sub-
mission to the fundamental contrariety of human nature
amounts to an acceptance of the fact that the psyche is at cross
purposes with itself. Alchemy teaches that the tension is fourfold, forming a cross which stands for the four warring elements.
The quaternity is the minimal aspect under which such a state
of total opposition can be regarded. The "cross" as a form of
suffering expresses psychic reality, and carrying the cross is
therefore an apt symbol for the wholeness and the passion which
the alchemist saw in his work. Hence the *Rosarium* ends, not
unfittingly, with the picture of the risen Christ and the verses:

> After my many sufferings and great martyry
> I rise again transfigured, of all blemish free.

524   An exclusively rational analysis and interpretation of alchemy, and of the unconscious contents projected into it, must
necessarily stop short at the above parallels and antinomies,
for in a total opposition there is no third—*tertium non datur!*
Science comes to a stop at the frontiers of logic, but nature
does not—she thrives on ground as yet untrodden by theory.
Venerabilis natura does not halt at the opposites; she uses them
to create, out of opposition, a new birth.

42 72, II, p. 35: motto of Book I. Cf. St. Bernard of Clairvaux, 26, XXIX, 8 (of
Mary): "Et illa quidem in tota se grande et suave amoris vulnus accepit . . ." (And
she indeed received a great and sweet wound of love in all her being).

10

THE NEW BIRTH

Here is born the Empress of all honour/
The philosophers name her their daughter.
She multiplies/ bears children ever again/
They are incorruptibly pure and without any stain.

[*Figure 10*]

525   Our last picture is the tenth in the series, and this is certainly no accident, for the denarius is supposed to be the perfect number.[1] We have shown that the axiom of Maria consists of 4, 3, 2, 1; the sum of these numbers is 10, which stands for unity on a higher level. The unarius represents unity in the form of the *res simplex*, i.e., God as *auctor rerum*,[2] while

[1] "Numerus perfectus est denarius" (the perfect number is ten).—Mylius, 120, p. 134. The Pythagoreans regarded the δεκάς as the τέλειος ἀριθμός.—Hippolytus, 67, I, 2, 8. Cf. Joannes Lydus, 110, 3, 4, and Proclus, 137, 21 AB. This view was transmitted to alchemy through the *Turba* (pp. 300ff., "Sermo Pythagorae"). Dorn (5, iv, p. 622) says: "Quando quidem ubi Quaternarius et Ternarius ad Denarium ascendunt, eorum fit ad unitatem regressus. In isto concluditur arcano omnis occulta rerum sapientia." (When the number four and the number three ascend to the number ten, they return to the One. In this secret all the hidden wisdom of things is contained.) But he denies (ibid., p. 545) that $1 + 2 + 3 + 4 = 10$, since 1 is not a number, maintaining that the denarius comes from $2 + 3 + 4 = 9 + 1$. He insists on the elimination of the devilish binarius (ibid., pp. 542ff.). John Dee (5, viii, p. 220) derives the denarius in the usual way: the *antiquissimi Latini philosophi* assumed that the *crux rectilinea* meant the denarius. The old author Artefius (probably an Arab) also derives the denarius by adding together the four first numbers (5, xi, p. 222). But later he says that 2 is the first number, and he proceeds to make the following operation: $2 + 1 = 3, 2 + 2 = 4, 4 + 1 = 5, 4 + 3 = 7, 7 + 1 = 8, 8 + 1 = 9, 8 + 2 = 10$, and says that "eodem modo centenarii ex denariis, millenarii vero ex centenariis procreantur" (in the same way the hundreds are produced out of the tens, and the thousands out of the hundreds). This operation can be regarded as either enigmatic or childish.

[2] According to Hippolytus (67, IV, 43, 4), the Egyptians said that God was a μονὰς ἀδιαίρετος (an indivisible unity), and that 10 was a monad, the beginning and end of all number.

304

PHILOSOPHORVM.

hie ist geboren die eddele Keyserin reich/
Die meister nennen sie jhrer dochter gleich.
Die vermeret sich/gebiert kinder ohn zal/
Sein vnd tlich rein/vnnd ohn alles mahl·

Die

Figure 10

the denarius is the result of the completed work. Hence the real meaning of the denarius is the Son of God.[3] Although the alchemists call it the *filius philosophorum*,[4] they use it as a Christ-symbol and at the same time employ the symbolic qualities of the ecclesiastical Christ-figure to characterize their Rebis.[5] It is probably correct to say that the medieval Rebis had these Christian characteristics, but for the Hermaphroditus of Arabic and Greek sources we must conjecture a partly pagan tradition. The Church symbolism of *sponsus* and *sponsa* leads to the mystic union of the two, i.e., to the *anima Christi* which lives in the *corpus mysticum* of the Church. This unity underlies the idea of Christ's androgyny, which medieval alchemy exploited for its own ends. The much older figure of the Hermaphroditus, whose outward aspect probably derives from a Cyprian *Venus barbata*, encountered in the Eastern Church the already extant idea of an androgynous Christ, which is no doubt connected with the Platonic conception of the bisexual First Man, for Christ is ultimately the Anthropos.

526   The denarius forms the *totius operis summa*, the culminating point of the work beyond which it is impossible to go except by means of the *multiplicatio*. For, although the denarius represents a higher stage of unity, it is also a multiple of 1 and can therefore be multiplied to infinity in the ratio of 10, 100, 1000, 10,000, etc., just as the mystical body of the Church is composed of an indefinitely large number of believers and is capable of multiplying that number without limit. Hence the Rebis is described as the *cibus sempiternus* (everlasting food), *lumen indeficiens*, and so forth; hence also the assumption that the tincture replenishes itself and that the

[3] The denarius as an *allegoria Christi* is to be found in Rabanus Maurus, 139.
[4] "Audi atque attende: Sal antiquissimum Mysterium! Cuius nucleum in Denario, Harpocratice. sile." (Listen and pay heed: Salt is the oldest mystery. Hide its nucleus in the number ten, after the manner of Harpocrates.)—Khunrath, *Amphitheatrum*, 96, p. 194. The salt is the salt of wisdom. Harpocrates is the genius of the secret mysteries.
[5] There is a parallel to this in the system of Monoïmos (Hippolytus, 67, VIII, 12, 2ff.). The son of Oceanus (the Anthropos) is an undivisible monad and yet divisible: he is mother and father, a monad that is also a decad. "Ex denario divino statues unitatem" (Out of the divine number ten you will constitute unity).— Quotation from Joh. Daustin in Aegidius de Vadis, 5, vi, p. 115. Dausten, or Dastyne, was probably an Englishman; certain authorities date him at the beginning of the 14th century, others much later. See Ferguson, 41, s.v. "Dausten."

work need only be completed once and for all time.[6] But, since the *multiplicatio* is only an attribute of the denarius, 100 is no different from and no better than 10.[7]

527   The *lapis,* understood as the cosmogonic First Man, is the *radix ipsius,* according to the *Rosarium:* everything has grown from this One and through this One.[8] It is the Uroboros, the serpent that fertilizes and gives birth to itself, by definition an *increatum,* despite a quotation from Rosarius to the effect that "Mercurius noster nobilissimus" was created by God as a "res nobilis." This *creatum increatum* can only be listed as another paradox. It is useless to rack our brains over this extraordinary attitude of mind. Indeed we shall only continue to do so while we assume that the alchemists were not being consciously and intentionally paradoxical. It seems to me that theirs was a perfectly natural view: anything unknowable could best be described in terms of opposites.[9] A long German poem, evidently written about the time of its printing in the 1550 *Rosarium,* explains the nature of the Hermaphroditus as follows:

528   Here is born the Empress of all honour/
                       The philosophers name her their daughter.
                       She multiplies/ bears children ever again/
                       They are incorruptibly pure and without any stain.
                            The Queen hates death and poverty
                       She surpasses gold silver and jewellery/
                       All medicaments great and small.
                       Nothing upon earth is her equal/
                       Wherefore we say thanks to God in heaven.
                            O force constrains me naked woman that I am/
                       For unblest was my body when I first began.

[6] Norton's "Ordinall" **6, i,** p. 48; Philalethes (**4, v,** p. 802) says: "Qui semel adeptus est, ad Autumnum sui laboris pervenit" (He who has once found it has reached the harvest time of his work). This is a quotation from Johannes Pontanus, who lived about 1550 and was a physician and professor of philosophy at Königsberg. Cf. Ferguson, **41, II,** p. 212.

[7] It is worth noting that St. John of the Cross pictures the ascent of the soul in ten stages.

[8] "Ipsa omnia sunt ex uno et de uno et cum uno, quod est radix ipsius" (They are all from the One, and of the One, and with the One, which is the root of itself).—**2,** xiii, p. 369.

[9] Nicholas of Cusa, in his *De Docta ignorantia* (**62**), regarded antinomial thought as the highest form of reasoning.

And never did I become a mother/
Until the time when I was born another.
Then the power of roots and herbs did I possess/
And I triumphed over all sickness.
Then it was that I first knew my son/
And we two came together as one.
There I was made pregnant by him and gave birth
Upon a barren stretch of earth.
I became a mother yet remained a maid/
And in my nature was establishèd.
Therefore my son was also my father/
As God ordained in accordance with nature.
I bore the mother who gave me birth/
Through me she was born again upon earth.
To regard as one what nature hath wed/
Is in our mountain most masterfully hid.
Four come together in one/
In this our magisterial Stone.
And six when seen as a trinity/
Is brought to essential unity.
To him who thinks on these things aright/
God giveth the power to put to flight
All such sicknesses as pertain
To metals and the bodies of men.
None can do that without God's help/
And then only if he see through himself.
Out of my earth a fountain flows/
And into two streams it branching goes.
One of them runs to the Orient/
The other towards the Occident.
Two eagles fly up with feathers aflame/
Naked they fall to earth again.
Yet in full feather they rise up soon/
That fountain is Lord of sun and moon.
O Lord Jesu Christ who bestow'st
The gift through the grace of thy Holy Ghost:
He unto whom it is given truly/
Understands the masters' sayings entirely.
That his thoughts on the future life may dwell/
Body and soul are joined so well.
And to raise them up to their father's kingdom/
Such is the way of the art among men.

529   This poem is of considerable psychological interest. I have already stressed the anima nature of the androgyne. The "unblessedness" of the "first body" has its equivalent in the disagreeable, daemonic, "unconscious" anima which we considered in the last chapter. At its second birth, that is, as a result of the opus, this anima becomes fruitful and is born together with her son, in the shape of the Hermaphroditus, the product of mother-son incest. Neither fecundation nor birth impairs her virginity.[10] This essentially Christian paradox is connected with the extraordinary *timeless* quality of the unconscious: everything has already happened and is yet unhappened, is already dead and yet unborn.[11] Such paradoxical statements illustrate the potentiality of unconscious contents. In so far as comparisons are possible at all, they are objects of memory and knowledge, and in this sense belong to the remote past; we therefore speak of "vestiges of primordial mythological ideas." But, in so far as the unconscious manifests itself in a sudden incomprehensible invasion, it is something that was never there before, something altogether strange, new, and belonging to the future. The unconscious is thus the mother as well as the daughter, and the mother has given birth to her own mother (*increatum*), and her son was her father.[11a] It seems to have dawned on the alchemists that this most monstrous of paradoxes was somehow connected with the self, for no man can practise such an art unless it be with God's help, and unless "he sees through himself." The old masters were aware of this, as we can see from the dialogue between Morienus and King Kallid. Morienus relates how Hercules (the Byzantine Emperor Heraclius) told his pupils: "O sons of wisdom, know that God, the supreme and glorious

10 Cf. Zosimos, **2,** iv, p. 309: "Cuius [lapidis] mater virgo est, et pater non concubuit" (Its [the stone's] mother is a virgin, and the father lay not with her).

11 Cf. Petrus Bonus, **5, xv,** p. 649: "Cuius mater virgo est, cuius pater foeminam nescit. Adhuc etiam noverunt, quod Deus fieri debet homo, quia in die novissima huius artis, in qua est operis complementum, generans et generatum fiunt omnino unum: et senex et puer et pater et filius fiunt omnino unum. Ita quod omnia vetera fiunt nova." (Whose mother is a virgin and whose father did not know his wife. They also know that God must become man because, on the last day of this work, when the completion of this work takes place, the begetter and the begotten become altogether one. Old man and youth, father and son, become altogether one. So that all things old become new.)

11a Cf. Dante, *Paradiso*, XXXIII, i: "O Virgin Mother, daughter of thy son.'

Creator, has made the world out of four unequal elements and set man as an ornament between them." When the King begged for further explanation, Morienus answered: "Why should I tell you many things? For this substance [i.e., the arcanum] is extracted from you, and you are its mineral; in you the philosophers find it, and, that I may speak more plainly, from you they take it. And when you have tested it, its love will increase in you. And know that this will remain true and indubitable. . . . For in this stone the four elements are bound together, and men liken it to the world and its structure." [12]

530   One gathers from this discourse that, owing to his position between the four world-principles, man contains within himself a replica of the world in which the unequal elements are united. This is the microcosm in man, corresponding to the "firmament" or "Olympus" of Paracelsus: that unknown quantity in man which is as universal and wide as the world itself, which is in him by nature and cannot be acquired. Psychologically, this corresponds to the collective unconscious, whose projections are to be found everywhere in alchemy. I must refrain from adducing more proofs of the psychological insight of the alchemists, since this has already been done elsewhere. [13]

531   The end of the poem hints at immortality—at the great hope of the alchemists, the *elixir vitae*. As a transcendental idea, immortality cannot be the object of experience, hence there is no argument either for or against. But immortality as an *experience of feeling* is rather different. A feeling is as indisputable a reality as the existence of an idea, and can be experienced to exactly the same degree. On many occasions I have observed that the spontaneous manifestations of the self, i.e., the appearance of certain symbols relating thereto, bring with them something of the timelessness of the unconscious which expresses itself in a feeling of eternity or immortality. Such experiences can be extraordinarily impressive. The idea of the *aqua permanens*, the *incorruptibilitas lapidis*, the *elixir vitae*, the *cibus immortalis*, etc., is not so very strange, since it fits

---

[12] 2, xii, p. 37.

[13] Cf. my *Psychology and Religion*, 86, pars. 95ff., 153ff. (1938 edn., pp. 69ff., other lacking); my Paracelsus study, 83, pars. 214ff. (Swiss edn., pp. 89ff.); and my *Psychology and Alchemy*, 85, pars. 342ff.

in with the phenomenology of the collective unconscious.[14] It might seem a monstrous presumption on the part of the alchemist to imagine himself capable, even with God's help, of producing an everlasting substance. This claim gives many treatises an air of boastfulness and humbug on account of which they have deservedly fallen into disrepute and oblivion. All the same, we should beware of emptying out the baby with the bath water. There are treatises that look deep into the nature of the *opus* and put another complexion on alchemy. Thus the anonymous author of the *Rosarium* says: "Patet ergo quod Philosophorum Magister lapis est, quasi diceret, quod naturaliter etiam per se facit quod tenetur facere: et sic Philosophus non est Magister lapidis, sed potius minister. Ergo qui quaerit per artem extra naturam per artificium inducere aliquid in rem, quod in ea naturaliter non est, errat et errorem suum deflebit." (It is therefore clear that the stone is the master of the philosophers, as if [the philosopher] were to say that he does of his own nature that which he is compelled to do. Therefore the philosopher is not the master of the stone but rather its minister. Consequently, whoever tries, by means of the art and by unnatural artifice, to introduce into it anything which does not by nature exist in the arcanum, he will fall into error and repent of his error.) [15] This tells us plainly enough that the artist does not act from his own creative whim, but is driven to act by the stone. This almighty taskmaster is none other than the self. The self wants to be made manifest in the work, and for this reason the *opus* is a process of individuation, of becoming a self. The self is the total, timeless man and as such corresponds to the original, spherical,[16] bisexual being who stands for the mutual integration of conscious and unconscious.

532   From the foregoing we can see how the *opus* ends with the idea of a highly paradoxical being that defies rational analysis. The work could hardly end in any other way, since the *complexio oppositorum* cannot possibly lead to anything but a baf-

---

14 It goes without saying that these concepts offer no solution of any metaphysical problem. They neither prove nor disprove the immortality of the soul.

15 2, xiii, pp. 356f. Cf. *Psychology and Alchemy*, 85, par. 142.

16 The Persian Gayomart is as broad as he is long, hence spherical in shape like the world-soul in Plato's *Timaeus*. He is supposed to dwell in each individual soul and in it to return to God. See Reitzenstein and Schaeder, 142, p. 25.

fling paradox. Psychologically, this means that human wholeness can only be described in antinomies, which is always the
case when dealing with a transcendental idea. By way of comparison, we might mention the equally paradoxical corpuscular
theory and wave theory of light, although these do at least
hold out the possibility of a mathematical synthesis, which the
psychological idea naturally lacks. Our paradox, however, offers
the possibility of an *intuitive* and *emotional* experience, because the unity of the self, unknowable and incomprehensible,
irradiates even the sphere of our discriminating, and hence
divided, consciousness, and, like all unconscious contents, does
so with very powerful effects. This inner unity, or experience of
unity, is expressed most forcibly by the mystics in the idea
of the *unio mystica,* and above all in the philosophy and religion of India, in Chinese Taoism, and in the Zen Buddhism of
Japan. From the point of view of psychology, the names we
give to the self are quite irrelevant, and so is the question of
whether or not it is "real." Its psychological reality is enough
for all practical purposes. The intellect is incapable of knowing
anything beyond that anyway, and therefore its Pilate-like
questionings are devoid of meaning.

533   To come back to our picture: it shows an apotheosis of
the Rebis, the right side of the body being male, the left female. The figure stands on the moon, which in this case corresponds to the feminine lunar vessel, the *vas Hermeticum.* Its
wings betoken volatility, i.e., spirituality. In one hand it
holds a chalice with three snakes in it, or possibly one snake
with three heads; in the other, a single snake. This is an obvious allusion to the axiom of Maria and the old dilemma of 3
and 4, and also to the mystery of the Trinity. The three snakes
in the chalice are the chthonic equivalent of the Trinity, and
the single snake represents, firstly, the unity of the three as expressed by Maria and, secondly, the "sinister" *serpens Mercurialis* with all its subsidiary meanings.[17] Whether pictures of
this kind are in any way related to the Baphomet [18] of the
Templars is an open question, but the snake symbolism [19] cer-

[17] Cf. "The Spirit Mercurius," 89.
[18] From βαφή (*tinctura*) and μῆτις (skill, sagacity), roughly corresponding to
the Krater of Hermes filled with νοῦς. Cf. Nicolai, 123, p. 120; Hammer, *Mysterium Baphometis,* 63, pp. 3ff.
[19] Cf. *Psychology and Alchemy,* 85, fig. 70, showing a snake ritual. There is no certain connection with the Templars (Hammer, *Mémoire sur coffrets gnostiques,* 62).

tainly points to the problem of evil, which, although outside the Trinity, is yet somehow connected with the work of redemption. Moreover to the left of the Rebis we also find the raven, a synonym for the devil.[20] The unfledged bird has disappeared: its place is taken by the winged Rebis. To the right, there stands the "sun and moon tree," the *arbor philosophica*, which is the conscious equivalent of the unconscious process of development suggested on the opposite side. The corresponding picture of the Rebis in the second version [21] has, instead of the raven, a pelican plucking its breast for its young, a well-known allegory of Christ. In the same picture a lion is prowling about behind the Rebis and, at the bottom of the hill on which the Rebis stands, there is the three-headed snake.[22] The alchemical hermaphrodite is a problem in itself and really needs special elucidation. Here I will say only a few words about the remarkable fact that the fervently desired goal of the alchemist's endeavours should be conceived under so monstrous and horrific an image. We have proved to our satisfaction that the antithetical nature of the goal largely accounts for the monstrosity of the corresponding symbol. But this rational explanation does not alter the fact that the monster is a hideous abortion and a perversion of nature. Nor is this a mere accident undeserving of further scrutiny; it is on the contrary highly significant and the outcome of certain psychological facts fundamental to alchemy. The symbol of the hermaphrodite, it must be remembered, is one of the many synonyms for the goal of the art. In order to avoid unnecessary repetition I would refer the reader to the material collected in *Psychology and Alchemy,* and particularly to the *lapis-Christus* parallel, to which we must add the rarer and, for obvious rea-

---

20 Anastasius Sinaïta, 12, Lib. XII: "Et cum vel suffocatus esset et periisset tenebrosus corvus Satan . . ." (And when the dark raven Satan [or "of Satan"] was either suffocated or had perished . . .). St. Ambrose, 11, Lib. I, Cap. VIII: "Siquidem omnis impudentia atque culpa tenebrosa est et mortuis pascitur sicut corvus . . ." (If indeed all shamelessness and guilt is dark and feeds on the dead like a raven . . .). Again, the raven signifies the peccatores: St. Augustine, *Annotationes in Job,* 15, Lib. I, Cap. XXXVIII, v. 41: "Significantur ergo nigri [scl. corvi] hoc est peccatores nondum dealbati remissione peccatorum" (They signify the black [raven], i.e., the sinners not yet whitened by remission of their sins). Paulinus of Aquileia, 130: "anima peccatoris . . . quae nigrior corvo est" (The soul of a sinner . . . which is blacker than a raven).

21 *Rosarium,* 2, xiii, p. 359. See *Psychology and Alchemy,* 85, fig. 54.

22 For further pictures of the Rebis see ibid., Index, s.v. "hermaphrodite."

sons, generally avoided comparison of the *prima materia* with God.[23] Despite the closeness of the analogy, the *lapis* is not to be understood simply as the risen Christ and the *prima materia* as God; the *Tabula smaragdina* hints, rather, that the alchemical mystery is a "lower" equivalent of the higher mysteries, a sacrament not of the paternal "mind" but of maternal "matter." The disappearance of theriomorphic symbols in Christianity is here compensated by a wealth of allegorical animal forms which tally quite well with *mater natura*. Whereas the Christian figures are the product of spirit, light, and good, the alchemical figures are creatures of night, darkness, poison, and evil. These dark origins do much to explain the misshapen hermaphrodite, but they do not explain everything. The crude, embryonic features of this symbol express the immaturity of the alchemist's mind, which was not sufficiently developed to equip him for the difficulties of his task. He was underdeveloped in two senses: firstly he did not understand the real nature of chemical combinations, and secondly he knew nothing about the psychological problem of projection and the unconscious. All this lay as yet hidden in the womb of the future. The growth of natural science has filled the first gap, and the psychology of the unconscious is endeavouring to fill the second. Had the alchemists understood the psychological aspects of their work, they would have been in a position to free their "uniting symbol" from the grip of instinctive sexuality where, for better or worse, mere nature, unsupported by the critical intellect, was bound to leave it. Nature could say no more than that the combination of supreme opposites was a hybrid thing. And there the statement stuck, in sexuality, as always when the

[23] The identification of the *prima materia* with God occurs not only in alchemy but in other branches of medieval philosophy as well. It derives from Aristotle and its first appearance in alchemy is in the "Harranite Treatise of Platonic Tetralogies" (5, xiii). Mennens (5, xiv, p. 334) says: "Nomen itaque quadriliterum Dei sanctissimam Trinitatem designare videtur et materiam, quae et umbra eius dicitur et a Moyse Dei posteriora vocatur" (Therefore the four-letter name seems to signify the Most Holy Trinity and the Materia, which is also called His Shadow, and which Moses called Dei posteriora). Subsequently this idea crops up in the philosophy of David of Dinant, who was attacked by Albertus Magnus: "Sunt quidam haeretici dicentes Deum et materiam primam et νοῦν sive mentem idem esse" (There are some heretics who say that God and the prima materia and the Nous or mind are the same thing).—*Summa Theologica*, I, 6, quaest. 39. Further details in Krönlein, 104, pp. 303ff.

potentialities of consciousness do not come to the assistance of nature—which could hardly have been otherwise in the Middle Ages owing to the complete absence of psychology.[24] So things remained until, at the end of the nineteenth century, Freud dug up this problem again. There now ensued what usually happens when the conscious mind collides with the unconscious: the former is influenced and prejudiced in the highest degree by the latter, if not actually overpowered by it. The problem of the union of opposites had been lying there for centuries in its sexual form, yet it had to wait until scientific enlightenment and objectivity had advanced far enough for people to mention "sexuality" in scientific conversation. The sexuality of the unconscious was instantly taken with great seriousness and elevated to a sort of religious dogma, which has been fanatically defended right down to the present time: such was the fascination emanating from those contents which had last been nurtured by the alchemists! The natural archetypes that underlie the mythologems of incest, the *hieros gamos,* the divine child, etc., blossomed forth—in the age of science— into the theory of infantile sexuality, perversions, and incest, while the *coniunctio* was rediscovered in the transference neurosis.[25]

534   The sexualism of the hermaphrodite-symbol completely overpowered consciousness and gave rise to an attitude of mind which is just as unsavoury as the old hybrid symbolism. The task that defeated the alchemists presented itself anew: how is the profound cleavage in man and the world to be understood, how are we to respond to it and, if possible, abolish it? So runs the question when stripped of its natural sexual symbolism, in which it had got stuck only because the problem could not push its way over the threshold of the unconscious. The sexualism of these contents always denotes an unconscious identity of the ego with some unconscious figure (either anima or animus), and because of this the ego is obliged, willing and

24 The idea of the hermaphrodite is seemingly to be met with in later Christian mysticism. Thus Pierre Poiret (1646–1719), the friend of Mme Guyon, was accused of believing that, in the millennium, propagation would take place hermaphroditically. The accusation was refuted by Cramer (writing in Hauck, **66, XV,** p. 496), who showed that there was nothing of this in Poiret's writings.

25 It is interesting to see how this theory once more joined forces with alchemy in Herbert Silberer's book, *Problems of Mysticism and Its Symbolism,* **151.**

reluctant at once, to be a party to the *hieros gamos,* or at least to believe that it is simply and solely a matter of an erotic consummation. And sure enough it increasingly becomes so the more one believes it—the more exclusively, that is to say, one concentrates on the sexual aspect and the less attention one pays to the archetypal patterns. As we have seen, the whole question invites fanaticism because it is so painfully obvious that we are in the wrong. If, on the other hand, we decline to accept the argument that because a thing is fascinating it is the absolute truth, then we give ourselves a chance to see that the alluring sexual aspect is but one among many—the very one that deludes our judgment. This aspect is always trying to deliver us into the power of a partner who seems compounded of all the qualities we have failed to realize in ourselves. Hence, unless we prefer to be made fools of by our illusions, we shall, by carefully analysing every fascination, extract from it a portion of our own personality, like a quintessence, and slowly come to recognize that we meet ourselves time and again in a thousand disguises on the path of life. This, however, is a truth which only profits the man who is temperamentally convinced of the individual and irreducible reality of his fellow men.

535   We know that in the course of the dialectical process the unconscious produces certain images of the *goal.* In *Psychology and Alchemy* I have described a long series of dreams which contain such images (including even a shooting target). They are mostly concerned with ideas of the mandala type, that is, the circle and the quaternity. The latter are the plainest and most characteristic representations of the goal. Such images unite the opposites under the sign of the *quaternio,* i.e., by combining them in the form of a cross, or else they express the idea of wholeness through the circle or sphere. The superior type of personality may also figure as a goal-image, though more rarely. Occasionally special stress is laid on the luminous character of the centre. I have never come across the hermaphrodite as a personification of the goal, but more as a symbol of the initial state, expressing an identity with anima or animus.

536   These images are naturally only anticipations of a wholeness which is, in principle, always just beyond our reach. Also, they do not invariably indicate a subliminal readiness on the part of the patient to realize that wholeness consciously, at a

316

later stage; often they mean no more than a temporary compensation for chaotic confusion and lack of orientation. Fundamentally, of course, they always point to the self, the container and organizer of all opposites. But at the moment of their appearance they merely wish to indicate the possibility of order in wholeness.

537   What the alchemist tried to express with his Rebis and his squaring of the circle, and what the modern man also tries to express when he draws patterns of circles and quaternities, is wholeness—a wholeness that resolves all opposition and puts an end to conflict, or at least draws its sting. The symbol of this is a *coincidentia oppositorum* which, as we know, Nicholas of Cusa identified with God. It is far from my intention to cross swords with this great man. My business is merely the natural science of the psyche, and my main concern to establish the facts. How these facts are named and what further interpretation is then placed upon them is of secondary importance. Natural science is not a science of words and ideas, but of facts. I am no terminological rigorist—call the existing symbols "wholeness," "self," "consciousness," "higher ego," or what you will, it makes little difference. I for my part only try not to give any false or misleading names. All these terms are simply names for the facts that alone carry weight. The names I give do not imply a philosophy, although I cannot prevent people from barking at these terminological phantoms as if they were scientific postulates. The facts are sufficient in themselves, and it is well to know about them. But their interpretation should be left to the individual's discretion. "Maximum autem est, cui nihil opponitur, ubi et Minimum est Maximum" (The maximum is that to which nothing is opposed, and in which the minimum is also the maximum),[26] says Nicholas of Cusa. Yet God is also above the opposites: "Ultra hanc coincidentiam creare cum creari es tu Deus" (Beyond this coincidence of creating and being created art Thou God).[27] Man is an analogy of God: "Homo enim Deus est, sed non absolute, quoniam homo. Humane igitur est Deus. Homo etiam mundus est, sed non contracte omnia, quoniam homo. Est igitur homo μικρόκοσμος." (Man is God, but not in an absolute sense, since he is man. He is therefore in a human way God. Man is also a world, but he is not

[26] *De docta ignorantia*, 122, II, 3.   [27] Ibid., XII.

all things at once in contracted form, since he is man. He is therefore a microcosm.) [28] Hence the *complexio oppositorum* becomes a possibility as well as an ethical duty: "Debet autem in his profundis omnis nostri humani ingenii conatus esse, ut ad illam se elevet simplicitatem, ubi contradictoria coincidunt" (All the endeavour of our human intellect must be concerned with these deep problems, that it may rise to that simplicity where the opposites coincide).[29] The alchemists are as it were the empiricists of the great problem of the union of opposites, whereas Nicholas of Cusa is its philosopher.

[28] *De conjecturis*, 121, II, 14.
[29] 122, I, Ch. X. (Cited in Vansteenberghe, 158, pp. 310, 346, 283.)

EPILOGUE

538   To give any description of the transference phenomenon is a very difficult and delicate task, and I did not know how to set about it except by drawing upon the symbolism of the alchemical *opus*. The *theoria* of alchemy, as I think I have shown, is for the most part a projection of unconscious contents, of those archetypal forms which are the characteristic features of all pure fantasy-products, such as are to be met with in myths and fairytales, or in the dreams, visions, and the manias of individual men and women. The important part played in the history of alchemy by the *hieros gamos* and the mystical marriage, and also by the *coniunctio,* corresponds to the central significance of the transference in psychotherapy on the one hand and in the field of normal human relationships on the other. For this reason, it did not seem to me too rash an undertaking to use an historical document, whose substance derives from centuries of intellectual effort, as the basis and guiding thread of my argument. The gradual unfolding of the symbolic drama presented me with a welcome opportunity to bring together the countless individual experiences I have had in the course of many years' study of this theme—experiences which, I readily admit, I did not know how to arrange in any other way. This venture, therefore, must be regarded as a mere experiment; I have no desire to attribute any conclusive significance to it. The problems connected with the transference are so complicated and so various that I lack the categories necessary for a systematic account. There is in such cases always an urge to simplify things, but this is dangerous because it so easily violates the facts by seeking to reduce incompatibles to a common denominator. I have resisted this temptation as much as possible and allow myself to hope that the reader will not run away with the idea that the process I have described here is a working model of the average course of events. Experience shows, in fact, that not only were the alchemists exceedingly vague as to the sequence of the various stages, but that in our observation

of individual cases there is a bewildering number of variations as well as the greatest arbitrariness in the sequence of states, despite all agreement in principle as to the basic facts. A logical order, as we understand it, or even the possibility of such an order, seems to lie outside the bounds of our subject at present. We are moving here in a region of individual and unique happenings that have no parallel. A process of this kind can, if our categories are wide enough, be reduced to an order of sorts and described, or at least adumbrated, with the help of analogies; but its inmost essence is the uniqueness of a life individually lived—and this nobody can grasp from outside, rather, the individual concerned is grasped by it. The series of pictures that served as our "Ariadne thread" is one of many,[1] so that we could easily set up several other working models which would display the process of transference each in a different light. But no single model would be capable of fully expressing the endless wealth of individual variations which all have their *raison d'être*. Such being the case, it is clear to me that even this attempt to give a comprehensive account of the phenomenon is a bold undertaking. Yet its practical importance is so great that the attempt surely justifies itself, even if its defects give rise to misunderstandings.

539   We live today in a time of confusion and disintegration. Everything is in the melting pot. As is usual in such circumstances, unconscious contents thrust forward to the very borders of consciousness for the purpose of compensating the crisis in which it finds itself. It is therefore well worth our while to examine all such borderline phenomena with the greatest care, however obscure they seem, with a view to discovering the seeds of

[1] Of these I would only draw attention to the series contained in the *Mutus liber*, 119, where the adept and his *soror mystica* are shown performing the *opus*. The first picture (fig. 11) shows an angel waking the sleeper with a trumpet; in the second picture (fig. 12), the pair of alchemists kneel on either side of the Athanor (furnace) with the sealed phial inside it, and above them are two angels holding the same phial, which now contains Sol and Luna, the spiritual equivalents of the two adepts. The third picture (fig. 13) shows, among other things, the soror catching birds in a net and the adept hooking a nixie with rod and line: birds, being volatile creatures, stand for thoughts or the pluralistic animus, and the nixie corresponds to the anima. The undisguisedly psychic character of this portrayal of the *opus* is probably due to the fact that the book was written comparatively late—1677.

Figure 11

Figure 12

Figure 13

new and potential orders. The transference phenomenon is without doubt one of the most important syndromes in the process of individuation; its wealth of meanings goes far beyond mere personal likes and dislikes. By virtue of its collective contents and symbols it transcends the individual personality and extends into the social sphere, reminding us of those higher human relationships which are so painfully absent in our present social order, or rather disorder. The symbols of the circle and the quaternity, the hallmarks of the individuation process, point back, on the one hand, to the original and primitive order of human society, and forward on the other to an inner order of the psyche. It is as though the psyche were the indispensable instrument in the reorganization of a civilized community as opposed to the collectivities which are so much in favour today, with their aggregations of half-baked mass-men. This type of organization has a meaning only if the human material it purports to organize is good for something. But the mass-man is good for nothing—he is a mere particle that has forgotten what it is to be human and has lost its soul. What our world lacks is the *psychic connection;* and no clique, no community of interests, no political party, and no State will ever be able to replace this. It is therefore small wonder that it was the doctors and not the sociologists who were the first to feel more clearly than anybody else the true needs of man, for, as psychotherapists, they have the most direct dealings with the sufferings of the soul. If my general conclusions sometimes coincide almost word for word with the thoughts of Pestalozzi, the deeper reason for this does not lie in any special knowledge I might possess of this great educator's writings but in the nature of the subject itself, that is, in insight into the reality of man.

BIBLIOGRAPHY

BIBLIOGRAPHY

The items of the bibliography are arranged alphabetically under two headings: *A*. Ancient volumes containing collections of alchemical tracts by various authors; *B*. General bibliography, including cross-references to the material in section *A*. Short titles of the ancient volumes are printed in capital letters.

A. ANCIENT VOLUMES CONTAINING COLLECTIONS OF ALCHEMICAL TRACTS BY VARIOUS AUTHORS

1 *ARS CHEMICA, quod sit licita recte exercentibus, probationes doctissimorum iurisconsultorum.* . . . . Argentorati [Strasbourg], 1566.

> *Contents quoted in this volume:*

    i   Septem tractatus seu capitula Hermetis Trismegisti aurei [pp. 7–31; usually referred to as "Tractatus aureus"]

    ii Studium Consilii coniugii de massa solis et lunae [pp. 48–263; usually referred to as "Consilium coniugii"]

2 *ARTIS AURIFERAE quam chemiam vocant.* . . . . Basileae [Basel], [1593]. 2 vols.

> *Contents quoted in this volume:*

VOLUME I

    i   Aenigmata ex visione Arislei philosophi et allegoriis sapientum [pp. 146–54; usually referred to as "Visio Arislei"]

    ii In Turbam philosophorum exercitationes [pp. 154–82]

    iii Aurora consurgens, quae dicitur Aurea hora [pp. 185–246]

    iv [Zosimus:] Rosinus ad Sarratantam episcopum [pp. 277–319]

v   Maria Prophetissa: Practica . . . in artem alchemicam
    [pp. 319–24]
vi [Kallid:] Liber secretorum alchemiae compositus per
    Calid filium Iazichi [pp. 325–51; see also 21 (Bacon)]
vii Liber trium verborum Kallid [pp. 352–61; authorship
    doubtful]
viii Tractatulus Aristotelis de practica lapidis philosophici
    [pp. 361–73]
ix Merlinus: Allegoria de arcano lapidis [pp. 392–96]
x   Tractatulus Avicennae [pp. 405–37]
xi Liber de arte chymica [pp. 575–631]

VOLUME II

xii Morienus Romanus: Sermo de transmutatione metal-
     lica [pp. 7–54]
xiii Rosarium philosophorum [pp. 204–384]

3 MANGETUS, JOANNES JACOBUS (ed.). *BIBLIOTHECA CHEM-
  ICA CURIOSA, seu Rerum ad alchemiam pertinentium
  thesauraus instructissimus.* . . . Geneva [Colonia Allobro-
  gum], 1702. 2 vols.

    Contents quoted in this volume:

    i   Hermes Trismegistus: Tractatus aureus de lapidis
        physici secreto [pp. 400–445]
    ii Lully: Testamentum novissimum, Carolo regi dicatum
        [pp. 790–806]
    iii Mutus Liber in quo tamen tota Philosophia Hermetica
        figuris hieroglyphicis depingitur [unpaged, follow-
        ing p. 938]

4 *MUSAEUM HERMETICUM reformatum et amplificatum
  . . . continens tractatus chimicos XXI praestantissimos.* . . .
  Francofurti [Frankfort], 1678. For translation, see 158
  (Waite).

    Contents quoted in this volume:

    i   [Hermes Trismegistus:] Tractatus aureus de philoso-
        phorum lapide [pp. 8–52]
    ii [Barcius (F. von Sternberg):] Gloria mundi, alias Para-
        dysi tabula [pp. 203–304]
    iii Lambspringk: De lapide philosophico figurae et em-
        blemata [pp. 337–71]

iv   Philalethes: Introitus apertus ad occlusum regis palatium [pp. 647–700]

v   Philalethes: Fons chemicae philosophiae [pp. 799–814]

5 *THEATRUM CHEMICUM, praecipuos selectorum auctorum
tractatus . . . continens.* Ursellis [Ursel], 1602. 3 vols. (Vol.
IV, Argentorati [Strasbourg], 1613; Vol. V, Argentorati, 1622.)

Contents quoted in this volume:

VOLUME I

i   Hoghelande: Liber de alchemiae difficultatibus [pp.
121–215]

ii   Dorn: Speculativae philosophiae, gradus septem vel
decem continens [pp. 255–310]

iii   Dorn: Physica Trismegisti [pp. 405–37]

iv   Dorn: Congeries Paracelsicae chemicae de transmuta-
tionibus metallorum [pp. 557–646]

v   Zacharias: Opusculum philosophiae naturalis metallorum [pp. 804–48]

VOLUME II

vi   Aegidius de Vadis: Dialogus inter naturam et filium
philosophiae [pp. 95–123]

vii   Penotus: Quinquaginta septem canones de opere
physico [pp. 150–54]

viii   Dee: Monas hieroglyphica [pp. 218–43]

ix   Ventura: De ratione conficiendi lapidis [pp. 244–356]

VOLUME III

x   [Melchior:] Addam et processum sub forma missae, a
Nicolao [Melchiori] Cibiensi, Transilvano, ad Ladis-
laum Ungariae et Bohemiae regem olim missum
[pp. 853–60]

VOLUME IV

xi   Artefius: Clavis majoris sapientiae [pp. 221–40]

xii   Avicenna: Declaratio lapidis physici filio suo Aboali
[pp. 986–94]

VOLUME V

xiii   Liber Platonis quartorum . . . [pp. 114–208]

xiv   Mennens: Aurei velleris . . . libri tres [pp. 267–470]

xv   Bonus: Preciosa margarita novella [pp. 589–794]

xvi Tractatus Aristotelis alchymistae ad Alexandrum Magnum, de lapide philosophico [pp. 880–92]

6 *THEATRUM CHEMICUM BRITANNICUM. Containing Severall Poeticall Pieces of Our Famous English Philosophers, Who Have Written the Hermetique Mysteries in Their Owne Ancient Language.* Collected with annotations by Elias Ashmole. London, 1652.

Contents quoted in this volume:

i Norton: The Ordinall of Alchimy [pp. 13–106; for a facsimile reproduction see:

i-a THOMAS NORTON OF BRISTOLL. *The Ordinall of Alchimy.* With an introduction by E. J. Holmyard. London, 1928; Baltimore, 1929.]

B. GENERAL BIBLIOGRAPHY

ABUL KASIM. See **69** (Holmyard).

7 Acta Joannis. In: *Acta apostolorum apocrypha.* Edited by Richard Adalbert Lipsius and Maximilian Bonnet after Constantine Tischendorf. Leipzig, 1891, 1903. 2 vols. (Vol. II.) For translation, see:

8 Acts of John. In: MONTAGUE RHODES JAMES (trans.). *The Apocryphal New Testament.* Oxford, 1924. (Pp. 228ff.)

9 *Adumbratio Kabbalae Christianae.* Frankfort on the Main, 1684.

AEGIDIUS DE VADIS. See **5** (Theatrum chemicum), vi.

10 AGRIPPA VON NETTESHEIM, HEINRICH CORNELIUS. *De incertitudine et vanitate omnium scientiarum.* The Hague, 1653.

11 AMBROSE, SAINT. *De Noe et Arca.* See **117** (Migne, *P.L.*), vol. 14, col. 391.

12 ANASTASIUS SINAÏTA. *Anagogicae contemplationes in hexaemeron ad Theophilum.* See **117** (Migne, *P.G.*), vol. 89, cols. 851–1078.

ANDREAE, JOHANN VALENTIN. See **145** (Rosencreutz).

13 ANGELUS SILESIUS (Johannes Scheffler). *Cherubinischer Wandersmann.* In: *Sämtliche poetische Werke.* Edited by H. L. Held. Munich, 1924.

ARISTOTLE, pseud. See 2 (*Artis auriferae*), **viii**; 5 (*Theatrum chemicum*), **xvi**.

ARTEFIUS. See 5 (*Theatrum chemicum*), **xi**.

ASHMOLE, ELIAS. See 6 (*Theatrum chemicum Britannicum*).

14 ATWOOD, MARY ANNE. *A Suggestive Inquiry into the Hermetic Mystery*. Belfast, 1918.

15 AUGUSTINE, SAINT. *Annotationes in Job*. See 117 (Migne, *P.L.*), vol. 34, col. 880.

16 ——. *Confessiones*. See 117 (Migne, *P.L.*), vol. 32, col. 784. For translation, see:

17 [——.] *The Confessions of Saint Augustine*. Translated by Francis Joseph Sheed. London, 1943.

18 ——. *Epistula LV*. See 117 (Migne, *P.L.*), vol. 33, cols. 208–209.

19 "Aurora consurgens."
   Part I. See 35, **iii** (Codex Rhenovacensis 172).
   Part II. See 2 (*Artis auriferae*), **iii**.

20 AVALON, ARTHUR, pseud. (Sir John Woodroffe) (ed. and trans.). *The Serpent Power*. Translated from the Sanskrit. 3rd revised edition, Madras and London, 1931.

AVICENNA. See 5 (*Theatrum chemicum*), **xii**.

21 BACON, ROGER. *The Mirror of Alchimy . . . with Certaine Other Worthie Treatises of the Like Argument. (The Smaragdine Table of Hermes Trismegistus, a Commentarie of Hortulanus, The Booke of the Secrets of Alchemie by Calid the Son of Jazich.)* London, 1597.

22 Baruch, Apocalypse of. In: ROBERT HENRY CHARLES (ed.). *The Apocrypha and Pseudepigrapha of the Old Testament in English*. Oxford, 1913. 2 vols. (Vol. II, pp. 470ff.)

23 BAYNES, CHARLOTTE AUGUSTA. *A Coptic Gnostic Treatise Contained in the Codex Brucianus—Bruce MS. 96, Bodleian Library, Oxford*. Cambridge, 1933.

24 BENOÎT, PIERRE. *L'Atlantide*. Paris, 1920. For translation, see:

25 ——. *Atlantida*. Translated by Mary C. Tongue and Mary Ross. New York, 1920.

26 BERNARD OF CLAIRVAUX, SAINT. *Sermo in Cantica canticorum*. See 117 (Migne, *P.L.*), vol. 183, cols. 932–33. For translation, see:

27 ———. *Sermons on the Canticle of Canticles.* Translated by a Priest of Mount Melleray. Dublin, 1920. 2 vols.

BÉROALDE DE VERVILLE, FRANÇOIS. See 37.

28 BERTHELOT, MARCELLIN. *La Chimie au moyen âge. (Histoire des sciences.)* Paris, 1893. 3 vols.

29 ———. *Collection des anciens alchimistes grecs.* Paris, 1887–88. 3 vols.: Introduction, Textes, Traductions.

BONUS, PETRUS. See 5 (*Theatrum chemicum*), xv.

30 BOUSSET, WILHELM. *Hauptprobleme der Gnosis.* (Forschungen zur Religion und Literatur des Alten und Neuen Testaments, X.) Göttingen, 1907.

31 BROWN, WILLIAM. "The Revival of Emotional Memories and Its Therapeutic Value," *British Journal of Psychology* (London), *Medical Section*, I (1920–21), 16–18.

32 CARDAN, JEROME (Hieronymus Cardanus). *Somniorum synesiorum omnis generis insomnia explicantes libri IV.* Basel, 1652. 2 vols.

33 CHRISTENSEN, ARTHUR. *Les Types du premier homme et du premier roi dans l'histoire légendaire des iraniens.* (Archives d'Études orientales, XIV, Parts 1–2.) Stockholm, 1917; Leiden, 1934.

34 CHWOLSOHN, DANIEL ABRAMOVICH. *Die Ssabier und der Ssabismus.* St. Petersburg, 1856. 2 vols.

35 Codices and manuscripts:
    i Florence. Biblioteca Medicea-Laurenziana. MS. (Ashburnham 1166). "Miscellanea d'alchimia." 14th cent.
    ii Paris. Bibliothèque nationale. MS. (Latin 919). "Grandes heures dú duc de Berry." 1413.
    iii Zurich. Zentralbibliothek. Codex Rhenovacensis 172. 15th cent. Abh. 1: "Aurora consurgens." (Note: Mutilated manuscript beginning at the fourth parable.)

36 COLONNA, FRANCESCO. *Hypnerotomachia Poliphili.* . . . Venice, 1499. For French translation, see 37; for paraphrase, see 38.

37 [———.] *Le Songe de Poliphile.* Translated by François Béroalde de Verville. Paris, 1600.

38 [———.] *The Dream of Poliphilo.* Related and interpreted by Linda Fierz-David. Translated by Mary Hottinger. (Bollingen Series XXV.) New York, 1950.

"Consilium coniugii." See 1 (*Ars chemica*), **ii.**

DEE, JOHN. See 5 (*Theatrum chemicum*), **viii.**

39 DEMOCRITUS, pseudo. *Physica et mystica.* See "Questions naturelles et mystérieuses" in 29 (Berthelot), II, i (Textes: pp. 41–53; Traductions: pp. 43–57).

DORN, GERHARD. See 5 (*Theatrum chemicum*), **ii–iv.**

40 DU CANGE, CHARLES DU FRESNE, SIEUR. *Glossarium ad scriptores mediae et infimae graecitatis.* Lyons, 1688. 2 vols.

41 FERGUSON, JOHN. *Bibliotheca Chemica.* Glasgow, 1906. 2 vols.

42 FIERZ-DAVID, HANS EDUARD. *Die Entwicklungsgeschichte der Chemie.* Basel, 1945.

43 FIRMICUS MATERNUS, JULIUS. *Mathesis V. praefat.* In: *Julii Firmici Materni Matheseos Libri VIII.* Edited by W. Kroll and F. Skutsch. Leipzig, 1897–1913. 2 vols. (Vol. II, pp. 1–66.)

44 Folktales collections:
    i   *Isländische Volksmärchen.* Translated (into German) by Hans and Ida Naumann. (Die Märchen der Weltliteratur.) Jena, 1923.
    ii *Märchen aus Sibirien.* Edited by Hugo Kunike. (Die Märchen der Weltliteratur.) Jena, 1940.
    iii *Russian Fairy Tales.* Translated by Norbert Guterman. London and New York, 1946. (Derived from the original collection of A. N. Afanasiev.)
    See also 141 (Rasmussen).

45 FRAZER, SIR JAMES GEORGE. *Taboo and the Perils of the Soul.* (*The Golden Bough,* 3rd edition, Vol. III.) London, 1911.

46 ———. *Totemism and Exogamy.* London, 1910. 4 vols.

47 FREUD, SIGMUND. "Further Recommendations in the Technique of Psycho-Analysis: Recollection, Repetition and Working Through." In: *Collected Papers,* Vol. II: "Clinical Papers; Papers on Technique." Translated under the supervision of Joan Riviere. (International Psycho-Analytical Library, edited by Ernest Jones, 8.) New York and London, 1924–25. (Pp. 366–76.)

48 ———. "Further Recommendations in the Technique of Psycho-Analysis: Observations on Transference-Love." In: Ibid. (Pp. 377–91.)

49 ———. "Fragment of an Analysis of a Case of Hysteria." In: *Collected Papers*, Vol. III: "Case Histories." Authorized translation by Alix and James Strachey. (International Psycho-Analytical Library, edited by Ernest Jones, 9.) New York and London, 1924–25. (Pp. 13–146.)

50 ———. *The Interpretation of Dreams.* Authorized translation by A. A. Brill. Revised edition, London, 1932.

51 ———. *Introductory Lectures on Psycho-Analysis.* Authorized translation by Joan Riviere. London, 1923.

52 ———. *Leonardo da Vinci. A Psychosexual Study of an Infantile Reminiscence.* Authorized translation by A. A. Brill. London and New York, 1947.

53 FROBENIUS, LEO. *Das Zeitalter des Sonnengottes.* Berlin, 1904.

54 GOETHE, JOHANN WOLFGANG VON. *Faust.*

55 ———. *West-östlicher Divan.* For translation see:

56 ———. *West-Easterly Divan.* Translated with an introduction and notes by J. Weiss. Boston, 1877.

57 GOWER, JOHN. *Confessio amantis.* In: *The Complete Works of John Gower.* Edited by G. C. Macaulay. Oxford, 1899–1902. 4 vols. (Vols. II and III.)

58 GREGORY THE GREAT, SAINT. "Epistolae." In: *Opera.* Paris, 1586. (Pp. 575ff.) See also 117 (Migne, *P.L.*), vol. 77, col. 806.

59 ———. "Super Cantica Canticorum expositio." In: Ibid. (Pp. 6ff.) See also 117 (Migne, *P.L.*), vol. 79, col. 507.

60 HAGGARD, SIR HENRY RIDER. *Ayesha, or The Return of She.* London, 1905.

61 ———. *She.* London, 1887.

62 HAMMER-PURGSTALL, JOSEPH. *Mémoire sur deux coffrets gnostiques du moyen âge.* Paris, 1835.

63 ———. *Mysterium Baphometis revelatum seu Fratres militiae Templi.* (Fundgruben des Orients, VI.) Vienna, 1818.

64 HARDING, M. ESTHER. *Woman's Mysteries, Ancient and Modern.* London and New York, 1935.

65 HASTINGS, JAMES (ed.). *Encyclopedia of Religion and Ethics.* Edinburgh and New York, 1908–27. 13 vols.

66 HAUCK, ALBERT (ed.). *Realencyklopädie für protestantische Theologie und Kirche.* Leipzig, 1896–1913. 24 vols.

67 HIPPOLYTUS. *Elenchos.* In: *Hippolytus Werke,* Vol. III: *Refutatio omnium haeresium.* Edited by Paul Wendland. (Preussische Akademie der Wissenschaften, Kirchenväter Commission: Die griechischen christlichen Schriftsteller der ersten drei Jahrhunderte, XXVI.) Leipzig, 1916.

68 HOCART, ARTHUR MAURICE. *Kings and Councillors.* Cairo, 1936.

69 HOLMYARD, ERIC JOHN. "Abû' l-Qâsim al-Irâqî," *Isis* (Bruges), VIII (1926): 3, 403–26. (Pp. 408–16: preamble of "The Book of the Seven Climes"; pp. 417–24: concerning the "Al-Kanz al-Afkhar" (The Most Glorious Treasure).)

———. See also **6, i–a.**

70 HORTULANUS, pseud. (Joannes de Garlandia). "Commentariolus in Tabulam smaragdinam Hermetis Trismegisti." In: *De Alchemia.* Nuremberg, 1541. (Pp. 364–73.) See also **149** (Ruska), pp. 180–86. For translation, see **21** (Bacon).

71 HOWITT, ALFRED WILLIAM. *The Native Tribes of South-East Australia.* London and New York, 1904.

72 IRENAEUS, SAINT. *Contra haereses.* See **117** (Migne, *P.G.*), vol. 7, cols. 879–92. For translation see:

73 [———.] *Five Books of S. Irenaeus . . . against Heresies.* Translated by John Keble. Oxford, 1872.

74 ISIDORE OF SEVILLE, SAINT. *Liber ethymologiarum Isidori Hyspalensis epi[scopi].* Basel, 1489. See also **117** (Migne, *P.L.*), vol. 82, cols. 73–728.

75 JACOBI, JOLANDE. *The Psychology of C. G. Jung.* Translated by K. W. Bash. Revised editions, London, 1951, and New Haven, 1951 (separate printings differing in pagination).

76 JEROME, SAINT. *Adversus Jovinianum liber primus.* See **117** (Migne, *P.L.*), vol. 23, cols. 219ff. For translation see:

77 ———. *Letters and Select Works.* Translated by W. H. Freemantle and others. (Select Library of Nicene and Post-Nicene Fathers of the Christian Church, 2nd series, edited by Philip Schaff and Henry Wace, VI.) New York, Oxford, and London, 1893.

John, Acts of. See **7** (Acta Joannis).

78 JOHN OF THE CROSS, SAINT. "The Dark Night of the Soul." In: *The Complete Works of St John of the Cross.* Translated by

E. Allison Peers. London, 1934–35. 3 vols. (Vol. I, pp. 335–486.)

79 JUNG, C. G. "Analytical Psychology and Education." In: *The Development of Personality. Collected Works,** Vol. 17. (Alternate source: *Psychologie und Erziehung,* Zurich, 1946.)

80 ——. "Bruder Klaus." In: *Collected Works,** Vol. 11. (Alternate source: "Brother Klaus," translated by Horace Gray, *Journal of Nervous and Mental Disease* (London), CIII:4 (April, 1946), 359–77.)

81 ——. "AION: Contributions to the Symbolism of the Self." In: *Collected Works,** Vol. 9, Part II. (Alternate source: "Beiträge zur Symbolik des Selbst," in Jung and Marie-Louise von Franz, *AION, Untersuchungen zur Symbolgeschichte,* Zurich, 1951.)

82 ——. "On Psychic Energy." In: *Collected Works,** Vol. 8. (Alternate source: "On Psychical Energy," in *Contributions to Analytical Psychology,* translated by H. G. and Cary F. Baynes, London and New York, 1928.)

83 ——. "Paracelsus as a Spiritual Phenomenon." In: *Collected Works,** Vol. 13. (Alternate source: "Paracelsus als geistige Erscheinung," in *Paracelsica,* Zurich, 1942.)

84 ——. *Psychological Types. Collected Works,** Vol. 6. (Alternate source: *Psychological Types,* translated by H. G. Baynes, London and New York, 4th edition, 1946.)

85 ——. *Psychology and Alchemy. Collected Works,** Vol. 12. New York and London, 1953.

86 ——. *Psychology and Religion.* In: *Collected Works,** Vol. 11. (Alternate source: *Psychology and Religion,* The Terry Lectures, New Haven and London, 1938.)

87 ——. *Psychology of the Unconscious.* Translated by Beatrice Hinkle. New York, 1915; London, 1919. (The German original of this work was revised and enlarged by the author and published as *Symbole der Wandlung:* see 91 (Jung).)

88 ——. "The Relations between the Ego and the Unconscious." In: *Two Essays on Analytical Psychology. Collected Works,** Vol. 7. New York and London, 1953.

* For details of the *Collected Works of C. G. Jung,* see announcement at end of this volume.

89 ——. "The Spirit Mercurius." In: *Collected Works,** Vol. 13. (Alternate source: "Der Geist Mercurius," in *Symbolik des Geistes,* Zurich, 1948.)

90 ——. "A Study in the Process of Individuation." In: *Collected Works,** Vol. 9, Part I. (Alternate source: "Zur Empirie des Individuationsprozesses," in *Gestaltungen des Unbewussten,* Zurich, 1950.)

91 ——. *Symbols of Transformation. Collected Works,** Vol. 5. (Alternate source: *Symbole der Wandlung,* Zurich, 1952. See also 87 (Jung).)

92 ——. "The Theory of Psychoanalysis." In: *Collected Works,** Vol. 4. (Alternate source: "The Theory of Psychoanalysis," *Nervous and Mental Disease Series* no. 19, New York, 1915.)

93 *Kabbala denudata seu Doctrina Hebraeorum transcendentalis et metaphysica atque theologica opus antiquissimae philosophiae barbaricae variis speciminibus refertissimum. . . .* Sulzbach, 1677.

KALLID (Prince Khalid ibn-Jazid ibn-Muawiyah). See 2 (*Artis auriferae*), vi–vii.

94 KEKULÉ VON STRADONITZ, FRIEDRICH AUGUST. *Lehrbuch der organischen Chemie.* Continued with the co-operation of Richard Anschütz and G. Schultz. Erlangen and Stuttgart, 1866–87. 4 vols.

95 KERÉNYI, KÁROLY. *Der göttliche Arzt; Studien über Asklepios und seine Kultstätte.* Basel, 1948.

96 KHUNRATH, HEINRICH CONRAD. *Amphitheatrum sapientiae aeternae solius verae, Christiano-kabalisticum, divino-magicum . . . Tertriunum, Catholicon.* Hanau, 1604.

97 ——. *Von hylealischen, das ist, pri-materialischen catholischen, oder algemeinem natürlichen Chaos.* Magdeburg, 1597.

98 KIRCHER, ATHANASIUS. *Oedipus Aegyptiacus.* Rome, 1652–54. 3 vols.

99 KLINZ, ALBERT. Ἱερὸς γάμος : *Quaestiones selectae ad sacras nuptias Graecorum religionis et poeseos pertinentes.* Halle, 1933.

* For details of the *Collected Works of C. G. Jung,* see announcement at end of this volume.

100 KOCH, JOSEF (ed.). "Cusanus-Texte," *Sitzungsberichte der Heidelberger Akademie der Wissenschaften, Philosophisch-historische Klasse,* 1936/37, Abh. 2.

101 KOHUT, ALEXANDER. "Die talmudisch-midraschische Adamssage in ihrer Rückbeziehung auf die persische Yima- und Meshia-sage," *Zeitschrift der Deutschen morgenländischen Gesellschaft* (Leipzig), XXV (1871), 59–94.

102 KRANEFELDT, W. M. "Komplex und Mythos." In: C. G. Jung and others. *Seelenprobleme der Gegenwart.* 4th edition. Zurich, 1950.

103 KRATES. "The Book of Krates." See **28** (Berthelot), III, pp. 44–75.

104 KRÖNLEIN, J. H. "Amalrich von Bena und David von Dinant," *Theologische Studien und Kritiken* (Hamburg), I (1874), 271ff.

LAMBSPRINGK. See **4** (*Musaeum hermeticum*), iii.

105 LAVAUD, M. B. *Vie profonde de Nicolas de Flue.* Fribourg, 1942.

106 LAYARD, JOHN. "The Incest Taboo and the Virgin Archetype," *Eranos-Jahrbuch 1944* (Zurich), XII (1945), 253ff.

107 ———. *Stone Men of Malekula: Vao.* London, 1942.

108 LEISEGANG, HANS. *Der heilige Geist.* Leipzig, 1919. Vol. I (no more published).

109 LÉVY-BRUHL, LUCIEN. *How Natives Think.* Translated by Lilian A. Clare [from *Les Fonctions mentales dans les sociétés inférieures*]. London, 1926.

110 LYDUS, JOANNES (Johannes Laurentius). *De mensibus.* Edited by Richard Wünsch. Leipzig, 1898.

LULLY, RAYMOND. See **3** (*Bibliotheca chemica curiosa*), ii.

111 MCDOUGALL, WILLIAM. "The Revival of Emotional Memories and Its Therapeutic Value," *British Journal of Psychology* (London), *Medical Section,* I (1920–21), 23–29.

112 MAIER, MICHAEL. *De circulo physico quadrato.* Oppenheim, 1616.

113 ———. *Secretioris naturae secretorum scrutinium chymicum.* Frankfort, 1687.

114 ———. *Symbola aureae mensae duodecim nationum.* Frankfort, 1617.

336

MANGET, JEAN JACQUES. See 3 (*Bibliotheca chemica curiosa*).

MARIA PROPHETISSA. See 2 (*Artis auriferae*), v.

115 MEIER, C. A. "Moderne Physik—Moderne Psychologie." In: *Die kulturelle Bedeutung der komplexen Psychologie*. Berlin, 1935. (Pp. 349–62.)

116 ———. "Spontanmanifestationen des kollektiven Unbewussten," *Zentralblatt für Psychotherapie* (Leipzig), XI (1939) , 284–303.

MELCHIOR, NICHOLAS, OF HERMANNSTADT (Cibinensis) (Nicolaus Melchior Szebeni). See 5 (*Theatrum chemicum*), x.

MENNENS, GUILIELMUS. See 5 (*Theatrum chemicum*), xiv.

MERLINUS. See 2 (*Artis auriferae*), ix.

117 MIGNE, JACQUES PAUL (ed.). *Patrologiae cursus completus.*
[*P.L.*] Latin Series. Paris, 1844–80. 221 vols.
[*P.G.*] Greek Series. Paris, 1857–66. 166 vols.
(These works are referred to in the text as "Migne, *P.L.*" and "Migne, *P.G.*" respectively. References are to columns, not to pages.)

MORIENUS ROMANUS. See 2 (*Artis auriferae*), xii.

118 MURRAY, HENRY ALEXANDER (ed.). *Explorations in Personality.* New York and London, 1938.

119 *MUTUS LIBER in quo tamen tota philosophia hermetica, figuris hieroglyphicis depingitur.* . . . La Rochelle, 1677. See also 3 (*Bibliotheca chemica curiosa*), iii.

120 MYLIUS, JOHANN DANIEL. *Philosophia reformata*. Frankfort, 1622.

121 NICHOLAS [KHRYPFFS] OF CUSA (Nicolaus Cusanus). *De conjecturis novissimorum temporum*. In: *Opera*. Basel, 1565.

122 ———. *De docta ignorantia*. In: Ibid.

123 NICOLAI, CHRISTOPH FRIEDRICH. *Versuch über die Beschuldigungen, welche dem Tempelherrenorden gemacht wurden.* Berlin and Stettin, 1782.

NORTON, THOMAS, OF BRISTOLL. See 6 (*Theatrum chemicum Britannicum*), i.

124 NOTKER (Balbulus). *Hymnus in die Pentecostes*. See 117 (Migne, *P.L.*), vol. 131, cols. 1012–13.

125 OLYMPIODORUS. See "Commentaire sur le livre 'Sur l'action' de Zosime, et sur les dires d'Hermès et des philosophes" in 29

(Berthelot), II, iv (Textes: pp. 69–106; Traductions: pp. 75–115).

126 ORIGEN. *Homiliae in Leviticum.* See 117 (Migne, *P.G.*), vol. 12, cols. 405–574.

127 ———. *Homiliae in Librum Regnorum.* See 117 (Migne, *P.G.*), vol. 12, cols. 995–1028.

128 PARACELSUS. *Labyrinthus medicorum errantium D. Theophrasti Paracelsi.* Noribergae [Nuremberg], 1553.

129 ———. *De ente Dei.* [Details unavailable.—EDITORS.]

130 PAULINUS OF AQUILEIA. *Liber exhortationis ad Henricum Foro-juliensem.* See 117 (Migne, *P.L.*), vol. 99, col. 253.

  PENOTUS, BERNARDUS GEORGIUS (Bernardus á Portu). See 5 (*Theatrum chemicum*), vii.

131 PESTALOZZI, JOHANN HEINRICH. *Ideen.* (*Pestalozzis Werk,* edited by Martin Hürlimann, II.) Zurich, 1927.

  PHILALETHES. See 4 (*Musaeum hermeticum*), iv–v.

132 PLATO. *Timaeus.* For translation, see:

133 ———. *The Timaeus and the Critias or Atlanticus.* Translated by Thomas Taylor. (Bollingen Series, III.) New York, 1944.

  PLATO, pseud. See 5 (*Theatrum chemicum*), xiii.

134 PORDAGE, JOHN. "Philosophisches Send-Schreiben vom Stein der Weissheit." See 148 (Roth-Scholz), I, pp. 557–97.

135 ———. *Sophia: das ist die holdseelige ewige Jungfrau der gottlichen Weisheit.* . . . Amsterdam, 1699.

136 PREISENDANZ, KARL (ed.) *Papyri Graeci Magicae: die griechischen Zauberpapyri.* Leipzig and Berlin, 1928–31. 2 vols.

137 PROCLUS DIADOCHUS. *In Platonis Timaeum Commentaria.* Edited by Ernst Diehl. Leipzig, 1903–1906. 3 vols. For translation, see:

138 [———.] *The Commentaries of Proclus on the Timaeus of Plato.* Translated by Thomas Taylor. London, 1820.

139 RABANUS MAURUS. *Allegoriae in universam sacram scripturam.* See 117 (Migne, *P.L.*), vol. 112, col. 907.

140 RAHNER, HUGO. " 'Mysterium lunae': ein Beitrag zur Kirchentheologie der Väterzeit," *Zeitschrift für katholische Theologie* (Würzburg), LXIII (1939), 311–49, 428–42; LXIV (1940), 61–80, 121–31.

141 RASMUSSEN, KNUD. *Die Gabe des Adlers.* Frankfort, 1937.

142 REITZENSTEIN, RICHARD, and SCHAEDER, HANS HEINRICH. *Studien zum antiken Synkretismus aus Iran und Griechenland,* (Studien der Bibliothek Warburg, VII.) Leipzig, 1926.

143 RIPLEY, GEORGE. *Omnia opera chemica.* Kassel, 1649.

144 *ROSARIUM PHILOSOPHORUM. Secunda pars alchemiae de lapide philosophico vero modo praeparando, continens exactam eius scientiae progressionem. Cum figuris rei perfectionem ostendentibus.* Francofurti [Frankfort], 1550. See also 2 (*Artis auriferae*), **xiii.**

145 ROSENCREUTZ, CHRISTIAN (Johann Valentin Andreae). *Chymische Hochzeit . . . Anno 1459.* Reprinted from a Strasbourg 1616 edition. Edited by Ferdinand Maack. Berlin, 1913. For translation, see:

146 ——. *The Hermetick Romance; or, The Chymical Wedding.* Translated by E. Foxcroft. London, 1690.

147 ——. *Turbo, sive Moleste et frustra per cuncta divagans ingenium.* Helicon, 1616.

148 ROTH-SCHOLZ, FRIEDRICH. *Deutsches Theatrum chemicum.* Nuremberg, 1728–32. 3 vols.

149 RUSKA, JULIUS FERDINAND. *Tabula Smaragdina: ein Beitrag zur Geschichte der hermetischen Literatur.* Heidelberg, 1926.

150 ——. *Turba Philosophorum: ein Beitrag zur Geschichte der Alchemie.* (Quellen und Studien der Geschichte der Naturwissenschaften und der Medizin, I.) Berlin, 1911.

151 SILBERER, HERBERT. *Problems of Mysticism and Its Symbolism.* Translated [from *Probleme der Mystik und ihre Symbolik*] by Smith Ely Jelliffe. New York, 1917.

152 SPENCER, SIR BALDWIN, and GILLEN, FRANCIS JAMES. *The Northern Tribes of Central Australia.* London and New York, 1904.

153 STAPLETON, HENRY ERNEST, and HUSSAIN, H. HIDAYAT (eds.). *Three Arabic Treatises on Alchemy,* by Muhammad bin Umail. (Asiatic Society of Bengal: Memoirs, XII, 1.) Calcutta, 1933.

154 STÖCKLI, ALBAN. *Die Visionen des seligen Bruder Klaus.* Einsiedeln, 1933.

155 STOLCIUS DE STOLCENBERG, DANIEL. *Viridarium chymicum figuris cupro incisis adornatum et poeticis picturis illustratum.* . . . Frankfort, 1624.

156 "Tabula smaragdina" ("The Emerald Table of Hermes Trismegistus"). See 149 (Ruska).

Tractatus aureus. See 1 (*Ars chemica*), i.

157 *Turba philosophorum.* See 150 (Ruska).

UMAIL, MUHAMMAD BIN (Zadith Senior; Zadith bin Hamuel). See 153 (Stapleton and Hussain) and 164 (Zadith).

158 VANSTEENBERGHE, EDMOND. *Le Cardinal Nicolas de Cues.* Paris, 1920.

VENTURA, LAURENTIUS. See 5 (*Theatrum chemicum*), ix.

159 WAITE, ARTHUR EDWARD (trans.). *The Hermetic Museum Restored and Enlarged.* London, 1893. 2 vols. A translation of 4 (*Musaeum hermeticum*).

160 ———. *The Real History of the Rosicrucians.* London, 1887.

161 ———. *The Secret Tradition in Alchemy: Its Development and Records.* London, 1926.

162 [WEI PO-YANG.] "An Ancient Chinese Treatise on Alchemy Entitled Ts'an T'ung Ch'i, Written by Wei Po-yang about 142 A.D.," translated by Lu-ch'iang Wu, *Isis* (Bruges), XVIII:53 (Oct., 1932), 210–89.

163 WINTHUIS, JOSEF. *Das Zweigeschlechterwesen.* Leipzig, 1928.

ZACHARIAS, DIONYSUS. See 5 (*Theatrum chemicum*), v.

164 ZADITH SENIOR (Zadith ben Hamuel). *De chemia Senioris antiquissimi philosophi libellus.* . . . Strasbourg, 1566. See also 153 (Stapleton and Hussain).

165 ZOSIMOS. See "Sur les substances qui servent de support et sur les quatre corps métalliques" in 29 (Berthelot), III, xii (Textes: pp. 148–53; Traductions: pp. 150–54).

166 ———. See "Sur la vertu–Leçon I" in 29 (Berthelot), III, i (Textes: pp. 107–13; Traductions: pp. 117–21).

167 ———. See "Sur la vertu et l'interpretation" in 29 (Berthelot), III, vi (Textes: pp. 118–38; Traductions: pp. 127–39).

———. (Zosimus). See 2 (*Artis auriferae*), iv.

INDEX

INDEX

Bold type is used for references to items of the bibliography.

A

343

dream(s) *(cont.)*:
tients, 150; replacing collective
controls, 11; series, 12, 13; —, interpretation of, 150; sexual interpretation, 134; symbolical knowledge in treatment of, 27; -theory,
42; varying concepts of, 139; *see
also* fantasy(-ies); image
droits de l'homme, 291
dropsy, in *Aenigma Merlini,* 263
dualism, implied, of Paracelsists, 244
duality, of alchemical end-product,
199; *see also* dual *s.v.* motifs; numbers
Dubois, Paul, 21; "rational psychic
orthopedics," 3
Du Cange, Charles du Fresne, Sieur,
40, 271*n*
dyad, feminine, 208; *see also* two *s.v.*
numbers

E

ecclesia mater, 97; *see also* Church(es)
ecstasy, religious, archetypes in, 290
education, 55, 65*ff,* 68, 69; Adlerian,
111; and self-education, 73; social,
Adler and, 67; educational method, 4
ego, 49, 102, 112, 173, 194, 233, 244*n,*
259, 264, 289; *vs.* anima, 226; and
centring process, 51; complex as
shadow-government of, 87; and
conscious mind, 50; -consciousness,
195, 265; dissolution of, 290; and
God's will, 194; isolation within,
100; lesion of, 263; "objective,"
199; -personality, 262; —, differentiation of, and *mundificatio,*
292; relation to unconscious, 290*ff;*
and self, 264; and shadow, 198,
238*f;* space/time and, 291; + unconscious-psyche, 90; union with
unconscious, 264
Egypt, ancient, incest in, 218, 229
Einstein, Alfred, 65

Elbo Interfector, 272*n*
elements: bound together in the
stone, 310; chemical, transmutability of, 168; decomposition of,
265; the four, 203, 211, 265; —,
masculine and feminine manifestations of, 212; —, warring, 303; partial union of, 238; traumatic, 23;
world made of four, 310
elixir: as integration of unconscious
contents, 209; synonyms of, 209;
vitae, 299, 310
Ellis, Havelock, 37
elucidation, 55, 60, 63*ff,* 68; in Adlerian method, 67; limits of, in psychotherapy, 66
emotions, repressed, 58
emperor and empress, 301; *see also*
king and queen
enantiodromia, 96, 279
endogamous tendency, 228, 231, 232;
in recent times, 232
energy: instinctive, and symbolical
activity, 250; loss of, 180; psychic,
179*n,* 228; of unconscious contents,
180
environment, 85
equilibrium: of ego and non-ego,
195; of psyche, 153
Eros, cult of, 174
E.S.P., *see* extra-sensory perception
essence(s), 276; three, of tincture, 299
ethical sense, 147
ethics, standards of, 278
Europe: neo-paganism and anti-
Christianity in, 196; and patriarchal order, 104; plight of, 94;
European possessed by a devil, 191
Euthicia, 294*n*
Eve, 174; and anima, 301; tree growing from her head, 300
evil: good and, 192; principle, 191;
problem of, 313
exogamy, 231*f;* and class marriage,
228; and culture, 228; and endogamy, 228, 231, 233

J

CASES IN SUMMARY *(in order of presentation, numbered for reference):*

[1] Man, who experienced a dream series showing the water-motif 26 times, followed by the motif of the "unknown woman" 51 times, and other themes. Case illustrates the continuity of unconscious themes and the method of evaluating them statistically.—12*ff*

[2] "Normal" man, whose initial dream criticised his interest in occult subjects.—44*ff*

[3] Prominent man, peasant's son, who showed symptoms resembling mountain sickness. Archetypal dreams indicated the need

N

39; *see also* psychoneuroses; transference; trauma

New Guinea, 226

Nicholas [Khrypffs] of Cusa, **121–22**, 210, 274, 307*n*, 317, 318

Nicholas of Flüe (Brother Klaus), 183*n*, 204*n*

Nicolai, C. F., **123**, 312*n*

Nietzsche, Friedrich, 54

night sea journey, 244

nigredo, 182&*n*, 197, 258*n*, 259, 269, 271, 279; *see also* black; dark *s.v.* motifs

nixie, 320*n*

Noah, 263*n*

non-ego, psychic, 261, 265; source of alchemical projections, 288

non-identification, 260; *see also* identification

normality, 70

Norton, Thomas, of Bristoll, **6,i,** 285*n*, 307*n*

"nothing but," 46, 173

Notker Balbulus, **124**, 199*n*

nous, 245; identified with *prima materia*, 314*n*

NUMBERS, 207*f*, 212, 236*n*, 304*ff*; even and uneven, 207*n*; feminine, 207; masculine, 207

one, 304*n*; born of the two, 292; ocean as monad, 206*n*

two, 207, 304*n*; dream of two beds, 144; feminine dyad, 208, mystic union of the, 306; one born of the, 292

three, 183*n*, 204*f*, 207, 236, 312; *see also* triad; trinity

four, 208, 211, 212, 223, 304*n*, 312; corners, 223; dolls, 223; elements, 203, 211, 212, 265, 303, 310; four-letter name, 285*n*; *see also quaternio*/quaternity

five, 183*n*, 184, 211, 212; *see also quinta essentia*

six, 236&*n*

seven, 204

ten, 304&*n*, 306*n*; *see also* denarius

numen: of goddess, and anima, 229; transference of, 230

nuptiae chymicae, 197*f*

O

"obfuscation of the light," 198

"obscurity," subjective nature of, 145

occultism, 44

ocean, *see* sea

Oceanus, 306*n*

Old Testament, 121

Olympiodorus, 210*n*

one, *see s.v.* numbers

one-sidedness, 33

opposites, 182, 189, 236, 303, 314; coincidence of, 291, 302, 317; describe the unknowable, 307; fusion of, 290; pairs of, 199, 250, 281; —, alchymical, 222*n*; problem of, in psychotherapy, 77; synthesis of, 165*n*; unintegrated, 281; union of, 185, 211, 250, 256, 264, 279, 280, 315, 318; united by hermaphroditic being, 243; EXAMPLES: chaos/blackness, 185; ego/anima, 226; evil/good, 64; matter/psyche, 289; shadow/ego, 198; shadow/light, 64; Sol/Luna, 200, 211; *see also* antinomies

opus, 200, 203, 212, 235, 250, 258*n*, 261, 272, 278, 294, 295, 301, 311, 319, 320*n*; *contra naturam*, 261; demands of the, 235; end of, paradoxical, 311; *magnum*, 234; man's and woman's, concerned with anima and animus, 300; as period of gestation, 251; a process of individuation, 311; *psychologicum*, aim of, 262; as rose or wheel, 260

Origen, **126–27**, 196, 197

original man, *see* Anthropos

Oxford Group movement, 16

P

painting: by patients, 47*f; see also* drawings; picture(s)

pair(s): alchemical, 296, 297, 320*n;* of angels, 320*n;* royal, 284; *see also* antinomies; opposites

Paphnutia, 294

Paracelsus, 128–29, 17, 111, 200; "firmament" of, 310; motto of, 103; on "theorizing," 100

Paradise, Man of, 299

paradox, Christian: of unconscious, 34; of unimpaired virginity, 309

paranoia, induced, 172*n*

parapsychology, 124; parapsychic levitation, 266

parent(s): archetype, 96; disposition of, as cause of neurosis, 130

participation mystique, 182*n,* 251, 293

pater patrum, Pope as, 97

patient(s): of alchemists, 200; and catharsis, 62; "normal," 44; older and younger, differences in handling, 38; paintings and drawings by, 47*f,* 200*f; see also* cases *s.v.* Jung, C. G.

patria potestas, 109

patriarchal order, 97, 98, 103; in European civilization, 99, 104

Paul, St., *see* Saul

Paulinus of Aquileia, 130, 313*n*

peacock, see *cauda pavonis* (i.e., peacock's tail)

Peirithous, 61

pelican, 313

penis, *see* phallus

Penotus, Bernardus Georgius (Bernardus á Portu), 5,vii, 269*n*

peril of the soul, 212

Persephone, 300

persona, of doctor, 176

personality, 262; of analyst, 8, 74, 88; dissociation of, 173, 228; doctor's, importance in therapy, 88; —, moral differentiation of, 18; in-

tegration of, 20; new centre of the, 102; re-education and regeneration of, 27; schizoid, 120; synthesis of, 199, 233; united, 199

persuasion, method of, 3, 111

Pestalozzi, J. H., 131, 106*n,* 108*n,* 322

Petrarch, 214

peyotl, in primitive rites, 290*n*

phallus, contrasted with penis, 157

phantoms, terminological, 317

Pharaohs, incestuous marriages of, 218; *see also* 229

Philalethes, 4,iv–v, 284*n,* 307*n*

philosophy: and instinct, 81; of life, 41, 77, 99; and psyche, 79; and psychotherapy, 79; and religion, 79*f*

phobia, 253

physician(s): medieval, 82; wounded, Greek myth of, 116

physics: and psychology, 65, 259*n;* and psychotherapy, 4

physiology, and psyche, 77

physis, 216, 245, 246, 270

picture(s): primitive symbolism in, 50, 200*f;* symbolical, 49*ff*

planets, seven, 204

Plato, 132–33, 311*n*

Plato (pseud.), 5,xiii, 271*n*

pleasure: infantile, 36; principle, 19, 66, 113

pneumatikos, 263

Poiret, Pierre, 315*n*

poisoning, as symbol, 263

Poliphile, see Songe de Poliphile, Le

politics: political creed and mythology, 16; political movements, 6, 322; psychotherapy as instrument of, 104; *see also* State

Pope: as *pater patrum,* 97; transference of imagos to, 99

Pordage, John, 134–35, 294*n,* 295&*n,* 300

possession, 87, 179

power: craving for, 66; urge to, 113; *see also* will to power; power-

drive(s), 4, 19; power fictions, 19
practica, 261, 277
"Practica Mariae," 2,v, 250*n*
pregnancy, psychological, 253, 254
Preisendanz, Karl, 136, 167*n*
prejudice, subjective, of Freud and
  Adler, 114, 118
priest, predecessor of doctor, 116
prima materia, 187, 189, 212&*n*, 218,
  244, 250; comparison with God,
  314&*n*; equated with anima and
  animus, 301
primitive cultures, ceremonies in,
  97
primitive man, 120, 123; and importance of conscious mind, 181
primitive mind, universal perceptions of, 13
Primordial Man, *see* Anthropos
principles, moral, 65
process: autonomous, 11; "the," 209
Proclus, Diadochus, 137, 304*n*
prognosis, 86, 158; and diagnosis, 86;
  given by dream, 143, 144
projection(s), 116, 170, 177, 178, 187;
  alchemical, 229; compulsion of,
  105; its descent into matter, 230;
  dissolution by reduction, 136; inductive effect of, 176; infantile, in
  marriages, 219; influence on carrier, 289*n*; integration of, 262; integration through, 187; in modern
  days, 230; object of, 289; of parental imagos, 96, 101; reduction
  to their origin, 135; in transference, 63, 136*f*, 172; — to doctor,
  170; withdrawal of, 96, 100, 218;
  —, into hero, 209
Protestants/Protestantism, 16, 97, 99,
  100*f*, 193
psychasthenic, 58
psyche, 38, 90; ambiguity of, 40;
  ancestral, 34; and body, 190; childhood, 98*ff*; collective, 35, 37; and
  consciousness, 89, 90; dissociation
  of, 131; as ego-consciousness and
  unconscious, 90; as *ens per se*, 89;

as epiphenomenon, 89; evolutionary stratification of, 160; instrument in reorganizing civilized
  community, 322; living pattern of,
  322; as microcosm, 91; natural
  science of the, 317; patriarchal organization of the, 99; pre-conscious structure of, 96*n;* primary
  splitting of, 226; a self-regulating
  system, 153; totality of, 138; as
  unique phenomenon, 17; a whole,
  95; in youth and age, 39; *see also*
  archetype(s); instinct(s)
psychoanalysis, 3, 24, 25, 31, 53, 88,
  95, 111; and catharsis, 59; and confessional, 55; as medical psychology, 54; *see also* analysis
psychologie à compartiments, 279
psychology(-ies): empirical, 76, 92;
  experimental, 76, 89; feminine,
  294, 301; medical nature of, 31;
  multiplicity of, 53; personalistic,
  95, 185*ff;* primitive, 45; *see also*
  analytical psychology; psychoanalysis
psychoneuroses: as states of possession, 87; two main groups, 7; *see
  also* neuroses
psychosis(-es), 181; latent, 15, 186,
  265; as states of possession, 87;
  totalitarian, 231
psychotherapist: authority of, 5, 18;
  position of, in analysis, 72; and
  psychic infections, 19; self-criticism by, 115; therapeutic demand
  of, 72; *see also* analyst; doctor
psychotherapy: aims of, 81, 83; *ex
  cathedra*, 116; as instrument of
  politics, 104; intellectual foundations, 76; meaning of, 111; pre-
  analytical, 177; relation to medicine, 84; as science, 95; scientific
  basis of, 104; and the State, 107;
  subject of, 89; task of, 78; "treatment of the soul," 94; ultimate
  questions of, 234; *see also* meth-
  od(s); therapy; treatment

T

The Collected Works of C. G. Jung

THE COLLECTED WORKS OF
C. G. JUNG

The publication of the first complete collected edition, in English, of the works of C. G. Jung has been undertaken by Routledge and Kegan Paul, Ltd., in England and by the Bollingen Foundation, Inc., through Pantheon Books, Inc., in the United States. The edition contains revised versions of works previously published, such as *The Psychology of the Unconscious*, now entitled *Symbols of Transformation;* works originally written in English, such as *Psychology and Religion;* works not previously translated, such as the *Mysterium Coniunctionis;* and, in general, new translations of the major body of Professor Jung's writings. The author has supervised the textual revision, which in some cases is extensive. Sir Herbert Read, Dr. Michael Fordham, and Dr. Gerhard Adler compose the Editorial Committee; the translator is R. F. C. Hull.

Every volume of the Collected Works contains material that either has not previously been published in English or is being newly published in revised form. In addition to the *Mysterium Coniunctionis,* the following volumes will in large part be new to English readers: *Psychiatric Studies; Archetypes and the Collective Unconscious; Alchemical Studies; The Spirit in Man, Art, and Literature;* and *The Practice of Psychotherapy.*

The volumes are not necessarily being published in consecutive order, but, generally speaking, new works of which translations are lacking are being given precedence. The price of volumes varies according to size; they are sold separately, and may also be ordered as a set. In the following pages the volumes of the Collected Works are listed together with their contents, as now arranged. Each volume will also contain an index and, in most cases, a bibliography; the final volume will contain a complete bibliography of Professor Jung's writings and a general index of the entire edition. Subsequent works of the author's will be added in due course.

1. PSYCHIATRIC STUDIES

2. EXPERIMENTAL RESEARCHES (BOUND IN TWO PARTS)

(continued)

372

* Published 1953.
† Originally announced as *On Psychic Energy*.   (continued)

373

376

* Published 1954.